NABOKOV'S *ADA*

Also by Brian Boyd

Vladimir Nabokov: The Russian Years
Vladimir Nabokov: The American Years
Nabokov's Pale Fire: *The Magic of Artistic Discovery*
Presents of the Past: Literature in English Before 1900

Edited by Brian Boyd:

Nabokov: Novels and Memoirs, 1941-1951:
    The Real Life of Sebastian Knight
    Bend Sinister
    Speak, Memory
Nabokov: Novels 1955-1962:
    Lolita
    Lolita: A Screenplay
    Pnin
    Pale Fire
Nabokov: Novels 1969-1974:
    Ada
    Transparent Things
    Look at the Harlequins!
Nabokov's Butterflies: Unpublished and Uncollected Writings (with Robert
    Michael Pyle)

Brian Boyd

NABOKOV'S *ADA*:

The Place of Consciousness

Second Edition

Cravereditions

Cybereditions Corporation
Christchurch, New Zealand
www.cybereditions.com
cybereditions@cybereditions.com

Cybereditions welcomes comments from readers.
In particular we wish to be informed of any misprints
or errors in our books, so that we may correct them.

ISBN 1-877275-30-1

*The first edition of this book was published by
Ardis Publishers in 1985*

Printed in the United States of America

...to try to express one's position in regard to the universe embraced by consciousness, is an immemorial urge.
Nabokov, *Speak, Memory*

...the main favor I ask of the serious critic is sufficient perceptiveness to understand that whatever term or trope I use, my purpose is not to be facetiously flashy or grotesquely obscure but to express what I feel and think with the utmost truthfulness and perception.
Nabokov, *Strong Opinions*

Contents

Abbreviations

All works by Vladimir Nabokov unless otherwise stated.

Ada	*Ada or Ardor: A Family Chronicle.* New York: McGraw-Hill, 1969, and London: Weidenfeld and Nicolson, 1969, 589 pp.
BS	*Bend Sinister.* 1947; New York: Time, Inc., 1964.
Darkbloom	"Notes to *Ada* by Vivian Darkbloom," in *Ada or Ardor: A Family Chronicle,* Harmondsworth, Middlesex: Penguin, 1970.
Gift	*The Gift.* Trans. Michael Scammell with Vladimir Nabokov. New York: Putnam's, 1963.
Lolita	*Lolita.* 1955; New York: Putnam's, 1958.
LATH	*Look at the Harlequins!* New York: McGraw-Hill, 1974
Mason	Bobbie Ann Mason. *Nabokov's Garden: A Guide to* Ada. Ann Arbor, Mich.: Ardis, 1974.
NG	*Nikolai Gogol.* Norfolk, Conn.: New Directions, 1944.
PF	*Pale Fire.* New York: Putnam's, 1962.
PP	*Poems and Problems.* New York: McGraw-Hill, 1970.
Proffer	Carl R. Proffer. "*Ada* as Wonderland: A Glossary of Allusions to Russian Literature." In *A Book of Things about Vladimir Nabokov,* ed. Carl R. Proffer. Ann Arbor, Mich.: Ardis, 1974.
RB	*A Russian Beauty and Other Stories.* New York: McGraw-Hill, 1973.
RLSK	*The Real Life of Sebastian Knight.* Norfolk, Conn.: New Directions, 1941.
SM	*Speak, Memory: An Autobiography Revisited.* New York: Putnam's, 1966.
SO	*Strong Opinions.* New York: McGraw-Hill, 1973.
TD	*Tyrants Destroyed and Other Stories.* New York: McGraw-Hill, 1975.
TT	*Transparent Things.* New York: McGraw-Hill, 1972.
VNAY	Brian Boyd. *Vladimir Nabokov: The American Years.* Princeton University Press, 1991.
VNRY	Brian Boyd. *Vladimir Nabokov: The Russian Years.* Princeton University Press, 1990.

A Note on *Ada* Editions

For a detailed account of the sources, genesis, composition and publication of *Ada*, see *VNRY* and especially *VNAY*, 487–535. For the bare outlines of the novel's composition, see the start of Chapter 17 below.

Ada or Ardor: A Family Chronicle was first published in May 1969 by McGraw-Hill in New York, in an edition of 589 pages, and was reprinted four times in hardback. The first English edition, set from the same plates, was published by Weidenfeld and Nicolson in October 1969, but introduced some textual changes, such as the correct "descried from marble steps" (instead of "described from marble steps") in the last sentence of the novel, and the incorrect correction "she was pregnant" (instead of "he was pregnant") in the last sentence of Part 1, and printed Van's closing blurb as dust-jacket copy. A 1969 McGraw-Hill book club edition reset the text in 626 pages, introducing many careless new errors.

Since *Ada* was being rushed into print in an Italian translation in November 1969, Nabokov had marked in the margins of his own copy of the McGraw-Hill first edition phrases that he thought could cause translators to trip. In 1970 in the Commonwealth outside Britain, and in 1971 in Britain itself, he polished these glosses for publication in the first English paperback edition (Harmondsworth: Penguin), entitling them "'Notes to *Ada*' by Vivian Darkbloom." Confronted with a gaudily "trendy" cover design for the first American paperback edition (Greenwich, Conn.: Fawcett, 1970), Nabokov offered Penguin his own colored-pencil drawing of the orchid *Cattleya labiata*, which became the basis for the Penguin front cover, while the rear cover printed most of Van's blurb. The "Notes to *Ada*" were reprinted in the US for the first time, and were themselves annotated, by J.E. Rivers and William Walker, in J.E. Rivers and Charles Nicol, ed., *Nabokov's Fifth Arc* (Austin: University of Texas Press, 1982).

In 1973 and 1974 Nabokov and his wife, Véra, worked briefly with German translators Uwe Friesel and Marianne Therstappen, who translated the novel as *Ada oder, Das Verlangen* (Reinbek bei Hamburg: Rowohlt, 1974). He then spent six months in 1974–1975 correcting the translation of *Ada, ou l'Ardeur*, begun by Gilles Chahine and taken over by Jean-Bertrand Blandenier (Paris: Fayard, 1975), altering allusions and puns as he saw the need and opportunity.

For the Vintage paperback reissue of Nabokov's main works, his son, Dmitri, with the help of Brian Boyd and others, produced a substantially corrected text of *Ada* (New York, 1990), the first US edition to incorporate "Notes to *Ada*." Brian Boyd and the editorial staff of the Library of America made further textual emendations, added a Note on the Texts and a list of textual variants, incorporated "Notes to *Ada*," and added more annotations, in volume 3 of the Library of America edition of Nabokov's English-language fiction and memoirs, *Novels 1969-1974: Ada or Ardor: A Family Chronicle, Transparent Things, Look at the Harlequins!* (New York, 1996).

Preface to the First Edition

Vladimir Nabokov (1899–1977) is so radically original and so true to his originality that it is difficult at first to see how seriously and profoundly he explores the nature, position and responsibilities of human consciousness. It is easy, though, to see at once how much attention he pays to surfaces – and to conclude, because we cannot immediately discern what lies behind them, that surfaces of scene and style are all Nabokov is interested in.

The aim of this book is to make readers appreciate that if Nabokov's real strategies and subjects necessitate indirection, they certainly invite us to find significant new directions out. Once his thought and his techniques are properly apprehended Nabokov seems at his best as exciting and subtle and humanly challenging as Shakespeare, Tolstoy or Joyce.

Nabokov's works have fired wider and wider enthusiasm ever since the 1920s. By the late 1960s, a decade after *Lolita* shot its author from regional appreciation to fame, the translation of his Russian novels, the publication of *Pale Fire* and the revamping of his memoirs all confirmed the versatility and inventiveness of his talent. But *Ada*, written between 1965 and 1968 and published in 1969, has dampened the excitement of many good critics and readers. After causing an initial sensation, *Ada* seemed to reveal flaws – artistic self-indulgence leading to moral self-indulgence, failures of distance and control – that some readers began to fear had always been inherent in Nabokov's writing.

I would suggest that far from exhibiting any failure of control, *Ada* is not only one of the most morally stringent of novels but is perhaps the most rigorously planned; and that if *Ada* encourages us to reappraise the works that preceded it, it should be to admit not that we were seeing too much in the earlier works, but that we were not seeing nearly enough.

Part One of this book examines Nabokov's style and strategies in general terms, terms related to the philosophical issues raised in Part Two. The examples, however, all come from *Ada*, for it is here that Nabokov's methods are at their most complex, most in need of explanation, and most misunderstood – and, too, some of the exegeses here are necessary preparation for the arguments that follow in Parts Three and Four.

Part Two (published in a slightly different form in *Southern Review*,

Adelaide, November 1981) analyzes and synthesizes Nabokov's philosophy, his concern with the position of consciousness in the universe, his questioning of the nature of space, time, mind and whatever might be beyond human consciousness. Unlike Part One, it draws on scores of Nabokov's works, not only on all the novels and major stories and prose pieces, but also on youthful plays, unpublished lectures, obscure reviews.

Parts Three and Four offer a new account of *Ada*, Nabokov's most ambitious work. Reviewers who could see no structure in the book assumed its author must have sacrificed architectonic considerations for local pleasures. In fact, every local quirk is essential to the novel beauty of the whole, as crowded as a Bosch triptych but with all the grace of a Hokusai nature study. Every flurry and twist proves to form part of a demanding critique of the moral responsibilities of consciousness and a mysterious, lucid and satisfying exploration of time, consciousness and beyond.

Auckland
August 1980

An earlier version of this book was written in 1977–78 as a dissertation submitted in the University of Toronto in 1979. It was thoroughly trimmed in 1980, but subsequent tinkering, various publishing delays and the pressure of my research for a biography of Nabokov have staved off publication until now.

I would like to thank, for their indefatigability and enterprise, the Reference Department and especially the interlibrary loan staff of the Robarts Library at the University of Toronto; and for support and encouragement and for invaluable comments on matters of fact and style in one version or another of my manuscript, Patricia Bruckmann, Simon Karlinsky, Véra Nabokov, and the late Carl Proffer.

Preface to the Second Edition

After years of requests from those wishing to find *Nabokov's* Ada: *The Place of Consciousness* (Ann Arbor: Ardis, 1985), I am delighted to be able to republish an expanded version, especially in an accessible electronic form, and especially after the publication of its companion piece, *Nabokov's* Pale Fire: *The Magic of Artistic Discovery* (Princeton: Princeton University Press, 1999).

I am particularly delighted because I realized that those who knew the book only by its title had no chance to see that it is in some senses an introduction to Nabokov as a whole: to the shape of his thought (especially his epistemology and his metaphysics), in Part Two; to the relation between his thought and his style, in Part One; and then, through the one detailed example of *Ada*, to his ethics, in Part Three, and his metaphysics, in Part Four. Part Two was the first comprehensive overview of Nabokov's metaphysics, and unlike some more recent treatments has not exaggerated the role of the beyond. It has been a foundation for all my subsequent work on Nabokov.

I developed the study of the relationship between Nabokov's thought and his style in Parts One and Two, here, in the Introduction of *VNRY* and its Chapter 13, "Nabokov the Writer," while some aspects of Part Four, themselves unexpected to me even after years of working on *Ada*, even more unexpectedly found an analogue many years later in *Nabokov's* Pale Fire.

There are many who love Nabokov who have not warmed to *Ada*. Joyce described the "Ithaca" chapter of *Ulysses* as the "ugly duckling" of the novel, and it often does end up growing in readers' minds, after initial distaste, into the chapter whose beauty they admire most. *Ada* appeals to some from the first, as does "Ithaca," but like "Ithaca," if for different reasons, it also has become gradually a favorite for many, yet while already regarded as one of Nabokov's key works, with *The Gift*, *Speak, Memory*, *Lolita* and *Pale Fire*, it has still to win the place I think it deserves in the hearts and minds of many of his readers. For those who have not reread *Ada* since an initially unfavorable response, I would invite them to read Chapter 17 below before reading *Nabokov's* Ada or rereading *Ada* itself. For those with other interests in Nabokov at present, it may be more useful to proceed directly to Part Two.

Nabokov remembers *Invitation to a Beheading* with particular esteem because he wrote it in what he later recalled as a fortnight of inspiration. I think of *Nabokov's* Ada, like *Nabokov's* Pale Fire, with especial affection, because they were both generated in bursts of discovery so intense they would repeatedly interrupt me even when I tried to eat or sleep. The first break-through, the pattern of Nabokov's metaphysics, came, after much reading and thinking, one night in April 1977. The second, the patterns and purpose of *Ada* itself, lasted for the month of August 1978, almost twenty years before a similar rush of ideas on *Pale Fire* in January 1998.

Nabokov's Ada: *The Place of Consciousness* was at first planned either as a volume of annotations (which Carl Proffer naturally wanted to name *Keys to* Ada) or as a shortened version of my University of Toronto dissertation, *Nabokov and* Ada (1979). Since I had begun research that would lead to the biography even before completing the dissertation, I chose the latter and simpler option.

Years later, in 1993, after publishing not only *Nabokov's* Ada but also *VNRY* and *VNAY* and augmenting the biography for its French and Russian editions, I was rearranging my study, putting away my Nabokov files to make room for new projects, when all the *Ada* index cards I had accumulated in the course of my PhD seemed to demand a better fate than to collect dust and silverfish. In the spring of 1993 I therefore began to publish a series of "Annotations to *Ada*," a chapter of the novel at a time, in *The Nabokovian*, in order to make Nabokov's richest novel accessible, to stop readers from being deterred by what eluded them, to spare anyone else the hard labor of annotating all of *Ada*, and yet to invite those with a nugget or lode I had never seen to cash in what they had found and keep prospecting.

I look forward to the day when not only will the "Annotations" be complete but my commentary will be hypertext to Nabokov's text, with readers able to access notes that only a rereader or a re-rereader should see, only after they have answered questions that prove they have already explored *Ada* on their own. Nabokov himself, uneasy enough about electricity to have it comically banned on Antiterra, would surely be enchanted to sample an electronic version of *Ada* that allowed a rereader to see at once the Stabian flower-girl of the first chapter or a pop-up copy of *The Babes in the Wood* in the last, or perhaps even to hear at the click of a button "the song of a Tuscan Firecrest or a Sitka Kinglet."

When the possibility of republishing *Nabokov's* Ada arose, I was encouraged to update it as I chose, to revise or expand. I knew that if I began to revise the text of the first edition, it would involve complex decisions that might lead to new discoveries and would require time that the pressure of other projects simply would not allow. In order not to defer the second edition for years, therefore, I decided to add to, rather than revise, the existing book.

Apart from a few corrected typos and three new notes, Parts One to Four of *Nabokov's* Ada remain virtually as written in 1977–80. The addendum, "Part 5: Epilogue and Introduction," is an oddity, like Part 5 of *Ada* itself, a coda, an introduction, a compendium: "Part Five is not meant as an epilogue; it is the true introduction of my ninety-seven percent true, and three percent likely, *Ada or Ardor, a family chronicle.*"

Since writing *Nabokov's* Ada I have written several introductions to the novel, for the biography, for a reference guide, for a special Nabokov issue of a journal, and for the latest Penguin Classics reprint of *Ada*. In these introductions I have tried hard to do more than merely repeat myself, and to take notice of the different audiences, although readers reading these pieces directly after reading Parts 1 through 4 of *Nabokov's* Ada will notice repetitions.

Chapter 14, "*Ada* through the Attic," originally the *Ada* chapter from *VNAY* (1991), focusses particularly on the first chapter of the novel, and assumes an audience that may never have read it at all.

Chapter 15, "The Art and the Ardor of *Ada*," was written for the journal *Europe* (1995). Less an introduction to the novel than the other chapters in Part 5, it addresses a French readership by its concentration on the second chapter of *Ada*, so steeped in homage to Proust's *A la Recherche du temps perdu*.

Chapter 16, "*Ada*, or Amplitude," was commissioned for the *Garland Companion to Vladimir Nabokov* (1995). Following the brief for the volume, I begin by looking at *Ada*'s reception, then consider obstacles the novel poses to the success many fervent readers think it deserves, before focussing on *Ada*'s multifaceted fullness.

Chapter 17, "*Ada*'s Allure," written for Penguin Classics (2000), leads up to Ardis the Second's picnic ride, a kind of antiphonal response to Van's first—but strangely doubled—ride to Ardis manor that I describe and explain in the Introduction and Conclusion of *Nabokov's* Ada. After writing this latest introduction, I also discovered that the contrast I make between the ratio of effort and reward in *Ada* and in *Ulysses* echoes an argument I had already adopted in the original Introduction to the dissertation, but had quite forgotten over twenty years later. I would not claim that, like Part 5 of *Ada* itself, this new concluding chapter is the "true introduction" to the novel, but it is the best introduction I have written to *Ada*.

In the biography, while doing all I could to orient the reader through a clear chronological structure and the dates and Nabokov's age in the running heads, I also went to some trouble to make the Indexes serve not only those who read the volumes through but also those who merely dipped into them to read about a single Nabokov work, an aspect of his thought, his relations with another writer, or whatever. In *Nabokov's* Pale Fire, by contrast, I offered a deliberately reticent index, because the whole structure of the book depended on taking the reader through a first-reading response, then a rereading, and then an expert re-rereading. Wanting to make it quite impossible for readers to find solutions before they have time to realize the problems the novel poses, I restricted the Index to names and a very few themes that would spill no secrets.

In *Nabokov's* Ada, partly because it was written as a dissertation and partly because it was first prepared for publication while I was already preoccupied with the next phase of my Nabokov research, there was no index at all, an omission readers and author have both had cause to regret, and as author I can at last rectify.

Here I assume from the first a reader who has reread *Ada* and wants more; only in Part Five do I sometimes write partly for those who have never, or have only once, read *Ada*. The new Indexes can therefore afford to be much less coy than the Index in *Nabokov's* Pale Fire. To make the book as useful as possible for those interested in *Ada*, especially as I return again and again to some key passages both within the original book and in the added chapters, I offer an Index to Passages in *Ada*, while I have devised the General Index to be of help not only to readers of *Ada* but also to those interested in Nabokov's thought and art, his relationship to his world and his readers, throughout his work.

Auckland
January 2001

PART ONE

NABOKOV AND THE READER

1. Introduction

Two surface features of Nabokov's style are commonly considered the essence of the distinctly Nabokovian: the acuity of visual detail and the insistent phonic play. The first reflects Nabokov's passion for independence, the second his delight in pattern, and as I shall show in Part Two, independence and pattern are the two poles of the axis around which Nabokov's metaphysics and epistemology revolve. In his limpidly precise details Nabokov concentrates on the distinguishing particularity, the unique combination, on the independence of the thing, on the sharply specific moment of observation. In the joyful bump of his sound play – "the dangling end of tangled bangles" (187)[1] or "senescent nonsense, says science!" (354) – he creates an extraordinarily patterned prose.[2] But I would like to suggest that independence and pattern work in far deeper ways, that they are much more fundamental in making Nabokov's prose the wonderfully individual instrument it is.

It has been appreciated too that Nabokov's style is unique not only on the surface of the prose but at a more profound level of the reading experience – unique, that is, in the challenge that exists between author and reader and in the rewards awaiting the reader who can meet the challenges the author prepares.[3] This process of challenge and reward or of resistance and solution draws each reader into the problem of determining the position of consciousness in the universe, a problem which forms the core and mantle of Nabokov's philosophical world.

The nature and the rich purposefulness of Nabokov's style and strategies cannot be understood unless readers recognize – as few yet have – the full extent of challenge and reward within his works and unless these two inverse forces are seen as Nabokov's means of investigating the nature of consciousness. Even his depiction of the external world brings these forces into operation, the "challenge" here expressing Nabokov's belief that the world resists the mind so thoroughly because it is so real, because it exists so resolutely outside the mind, the "reward" recreating his experience of the inexhaustible joy of the mind's contact with the world.

Nabokov always considers both the limitations and the possibilities of consciousness. He finds particularly frustrating the fact that human consciousness is imprisoned within time and seizes with excitement and relief on the fact that memory should have the power to escape the shackles of the present and reach out into the past. He deplores the deceptions and bias that result from the confinement of the individual personality but values the liberating power of the imagination, the tenderness and the sympathetic engagement with others that it can achieve. Perhaps most intriguing of all for Nabokov are the possibility of human consciousness's breaking through its limitations to higher states of truth, and the possibility of there being conscious design in the universe somehow, somewhere, accessible to us. Challenge and reward function in Nabokov's work in ways that reflect all of these facets of the problem of consciousness, and for this reason they are present at every level of the reading experience.

But let us for the moment concentrate upon style.

At each moment in reading any work we try to apprehend the presence and purpose of the author's choice behind each movement of the text. We try also to be aware of the relationship between the part of the text immediately before our attention and other parts of the work being read. In Nabokov's novels the relationships of part to part and reader to author are peculiar in four different ways. Each of these peculiar kinds of relationships may be seen on its own or in conjunction with others; each may manifest itself in the minutest level of the prose or in the largest features of the whole work; it is their combination that makes the process of reading Nabokov so unusual, so unpredictable, challenging and delightful.

The peculiar relationship of part to part has two opposite faces. The obverse is the sheer independence of part from part. This is evident in the very choice of material, in the cheekily deliberate "irrelevance" of the elements of a story. Even more devious and radical is Nabokov's subversion of the usual power of sequentiality to regulate the relationship of part to successive part and to control the options of the writer and the operations of the reader. It is difficult to describe the absence of inert continuity in Nabokov's novels, the rare freedom from the over-ready suggestiveness of consecutive order that he grants to each minute particle of the fiction, but perhaps it could be put thus: one creative choice does not lead on to or even limit the next; even within a sentence there may be complete changes of subject or setting, sudden switchings of every kind, from vast significance to microscopic detail, from third person to first, from compassion to indifference; the direction, speed, tone, voice, time, setting, characters, status or thought of any chapter, sentence or part of a sentence may have any or no relation to what has gone before and what will follow. Each moment in the reading process seems curiously independent of every other moment.

The reverse of this independence of narrative elements is the patterned and pointed recurrence of parts. Nabokovian recurrence occurs in complex, delicate and elusive ways. It may be of a small verbal element or a major structural feature, a tiny detail of character or a resonant thematic chord.

The relationship between reader and text or author also has two opposite aspects. The obverse might be most broadly termed "resistance," the author's arranging that the reader will be unable to detect the nature or purpose of the author's choice. On the local level resistance may appear as an external allusion or an internal cross-reference that we cannot trace. It may occur anywhere as the illusion of excess or defect, of, for instance, a formless over-profusion of subjects or of a too ruthlessly concentrated form (*Ada* has been criticized for both). It may appear, too, on the level of moral evaluation: Nabokov's indifference to his human subjects or his too close identification with some of them, his ruthlessness in judging his characters or his deplorable indulgence.

The reverse of resistance we shall call "solution." Nabokov likes to talk of reading as if it were like solving a chess problem: "It should be understood that competition in chess problems is not really between White and Black but between the composer and the hypothetical solver (just as in a first-rate work of fiction the real clash is not between the characters but between the author and the reader)" (*SM* 290).[4] Reading *Nabokov's* novels at least provides special solutions, and the solving of the myriad little problems he sets the reader has a powerful inductive effect. The thrill of finding an allusion, of locating the precise source of a teasing echo, of suddenly catching an obscure pun or seeing what should have been an obvious joke makes the reader alert, curious, eager to find new puzzles to solve. When the new and richest solutions are reached they may offer us an unexpected insight into the essence of a novel's structure or the surprise of being forced to recognize our own errors of moral perception.

Let us turn to *Ada* now to see the reading process in motion.

The last paragraph of *Ada's* Pt.1 Ch.25 ends Van Veen's 1884 summer vacation ("Ardis the First") at his uncle's country manor, where Van and his sister Ada have become intensely impassioned, lyrically lucky lovers. It is September, and fourteen-year-old Van must return to school. He does not know when he will see Ada again. They will meet next, in fact, for an hour in December that year, for another hour in July 1886, for a proper reunion when Van returns to Ardis in 1888 ("Ardis the Second"). But the radiance of their falling in love will not be repeated, though their passion remains just as intense: the meeting in December 1884 is dampened by jealousy, by company, by sullen suspicion; the July 1886 encounter is a mere spasm of feverish fornication; the full reunion in 1888 is rent by betrayal and jealous rage. With this to come, with the joy of their early companionship about to end, Van and Ada at their first farewell are indeed at a major turning point in their lives.

Bouteillan, the butler, is to drive Van in the family car from the family manor to the local railway station. But Van takes the wheel, stops en route at Forest Fork, leaves Bouteillan to wait, and plunges into the undergrowth

– where he and Ada have a last tryst, a last caress. Van asks Ada if she will be faithful to him. She replies: "my love, my Van, I'm physical, horribly physical, I don't know, I'm frank, *qu'y puis-je?* Oh dear, don't ask me, there's a girl in my school who is in love with me...." Van cuts in: "The girls don't matter ... it's the fellows I'll kill" (158). After one last embrace, he tears himself away:

> Stumbling on melons, fiercely beheading the tall arrogant fennels with his riding crop, Van returned to the Forest Fork. Morio, his favorite black horse, stood waiting for him, held by young Moore. He thanked the groom with a handful of stellas and galloped off, his gloves wet with tears. (159)

With this paragraph Ardis the First and the rapturous summer of 1884 are ended. But keep a finger on Our Paragraph.

For the casual reader the paragraph above proves attractive at once in its flamboyantly romantic culmination to the bright idyll of Ardis the First, in the fierce passion of young Van, and in the sheer color of the lines, in "melons," "fiercely beheading," in horse and groom, "a handful of stellas," "gloves wet with tears." But the more watchful reader notices details that cry out for explanation.

Our most urgent question is "What has happened to Bouteillan and the family car?" There is a very literal absence of inert continuity here – indeed, of any continuity. Horse and attendant groom have appeared as if by spontaneous generation or – though Van seems too unsurprised for this to be a real possibility – by some fantastic metamorphosis of the family's car and butler.

Three months earlier, on his first coming to Ardis Park, Van has to travel from the local railway station to the manor, and in "a miniature of the imagination, he had seen a saddled horse prepared for him" (34). But there is nothing prepared, and he takes "a hackney coach" which chance makes available. As he is driven to Ardis, the coach becomes in turn "the old calèche...the sensitive runabout...the old clockwork taxi." When he reaches Ardis Hall a "servant in waiting took his horse" (34–35). We are warned not to expect passive continuity.[5]

This episode can serve as a paradigm of the absence of inert continuity in Nabokov's prose. Just as his hero traverses the distance from A to B not by continuing to move through the intervening space in the coach in which he began but by suddenly reappearing at B on horseback, so Nabokov's sentences often provide the illusion of continuous motion in a single direction where there have really been radical breaks, sudden shifts, silent transformations.

The real cheek of the change from coach to saddlehorse is not so much in the fact of the transformation as in the pretense of bland persistence. In the same way Nabokov's sentences violate natural continuity but with a straight-face bluff that they have been guided by ordinary momentum. The imposture is even more bewitching than the more overt breaks of a Sterne or a Barthelme. And looking back from a hundred and twenty pages later, from the *end* of Van's stay at Ardis, from September 1884 and another metamorphic trip between manor and station, we recognize an enchanting recurrence, a daringly original but neat and subtle framing of Van's idyll with Ada.

To return to Van's departure, to the final paragraph of Ardis the First: just who are the horse and groom? The language suggests that the reader should know "his favorite black horse" and "young Moore." But this suggestion of ordinary fictional continuity is a mere feint of resistance: it prompts us to believe we have merely forgotten their earlier appearance. We strain to recall them in vain, for this is their only occurrence in the novel. The solution lies in a different direction: they are nothing but local figments of Van's narrative, a silent disclosure of the fact that he sees himself in romantic terms. The young groom, the black horse and Van galloping off provide a much more fitting atmosphere for the fierceness of passionate separation than a family car and an old bald butler. The romantic scene is a delight – and a warning not to trust Van's posturing, his self-projection, his *autobiographie romancée*.

The word "stellas" is a demonstration in miniature of the four different motions of the reading process. It is the simplest kind of resistance, an unknown word. But it is also an instance of the absence of inertia: not bound by common standards of appropriateness, Nabokov delights in placing an obscure word in a line of rushing narrative, in interrupting our forward motion with Van by making us scurry aside to a dictionary – though neither OED nor Webster's Third has the word. For the reader quickly satisfied a "stella" has a pleasant romantic ring (star, girl's name) – there is a Stella in Nabokov's play *Smert'* (1923), a Stella Fantasia in *Lolita*. It has the same apt romanticism for a reader who wants to know more, but what does it mean?

"Stellas" occurs in the second to last line of Pt.1 Ch.25. In the *second* line of the chapter is the word "asters."[6] An amusing recurrence[7] – but not perhaps the clue it might seem to be. The illusion of simple recurrence is as much an instance of resistance as the obscurity of "stella" itself. In fact, the solution – like that of a chess problem Nabokov describes in *Speak, Memory* – has a very "simple key move" (*SM* 292) (after the "pleasant experience of the rounda-bout route" [*SM* 291]): Webster's Second defines a stella as "An experimental four-dollar gold piece struck by the United States in 1879–80." Nabokov's historical precision is teasingly ludicrous.

After working out the reason for the sudden appearance of horse and groom, after finding the meaning of "stella," perhaps we would next seek to explain the names Van has given his invented horse and groom. There is a simple, immediately-offered solution for the Morio-Moore sound play.

But this solution itself acts as a kind of resistance by appearing (a common Nabokovian ploy) to obviate the need for further examination – which will reveal that young Moore is in fact an anagram of Romeo,[8] and with this Shake-spearean hint black Morio points towards Othello, the blackamoor Iago calls "a Barbary horse" (*Othello* I.i.112).

This pair of simple but oblique allusions encapsulates the whole of Part 1 of *Ada*. Van, the allusions hint, leaves the young Romeo behind and charges off on a black steed reminiscent of Othello: "Ardis the First" is comparable in the freshness and lyric radiance of its young love only to *Romeo and Juliet*, while the chapters between "Ardis the First"and "Ardis the Second" and that second idyll itself are marked by the ever-deepening shadow of potentially violent jealousy, hinted at for the very first time in Van's words to Ada just before their last embrace of 1884 and Van's tear-blinded departure.

Each new meeting of Van and Ada is a vital part of the pattern of their ardor. After this last embrace in 1884 they next see each other near Ada's school, Brownhill College. Ada is accompanied by Cordula de Prey, whom Van suspects of being the lesbian lover Ada had hinted at. Despite his having said "The girls don't matter" he is rabidly jealous of Cordula. At the time of their meeting it has been teeming with rain; Ada has on an oilcloth hat but dares not take it off, for she has had her hair cropped mannishly short to ease the throb of her recent migraines and "she did not want him to see her in the role of a *mori*bund *Romeo*" (169; my italics). Echoes as subtle and thematically precise as this recollection of "Morio...Moore" will be found throughout *Ada*.

Allusion certainly forms part of Nabokovian resistance, but not as forbid-ding a part as might be expected: clues are usually given to the source of the allusions, which are in any case to writers Nabokov wants to encourage us to read or reread, writers of the stature of Shakespeare and Tolstoy, Flaubert, Chekhov, Proust and Joyce. The difficulty in the majority of Nabokov's allu-sions lies not in discovering their source but in discovering their part in the patterns of hidden recurrence and in the elusive structuring of the novels. Resistance is real in Nabokov's novels, but it arises chiefly from the difficulties of mastering internal relationships.

Nabokov parodies resistance itself in his account of Van and Ada's 1884 farewell:

> Van plunged into the dense undergrowth. He wore a silk shirt, a velvet jacket, black breeches, riding boots with star spurs – and this attire was hardly con-venient for making *klv zdB AoyvBno wkh gwzxm dqg kzwAAqvo* a *gwttp vq wjfbm* Ada in a natural bower of aspens; *xliC mujzikml*, after which.... (157)

The sudden lapse into code is inexplicable, though it seems to promise something too racy to print except in cipher. In fact, though, the following chapter describes the code Van and Ada adopt for their correspondence – encoding is necessary to keep their incestuous love a secret from parents, prying maids and schoolfriends – and we can decode the passages above as the brazenly innocuous "making *his way through the brush and crossing* a *brook to reach* Ada" and "*they embraced.*"

The lines surrounding the encoded passage – the first to refer to the riding gear Van is now wearing despite the fact that he began in the family car – point towards two more key allusions in the paragraph we have been scrutinizing: "Stumbling on melons, fiercely beheading the tall arrogant fennels with his riding crop..."(159) The first phrase has been quietly lifted from Andrew Marvell's "The Garden" (pub. 1681):

> The Nectaren, and curious Peach,
> Into my hands themselves do reach;
> Stumbling on Melons, as I pass,
> Insnar'd with Flow'rs, I fall on grass.
>
> (ll. 37–40)

The second phrase alludes to another plant in a second famous lyric. Van's "fiercely beheading the tall arrogant fennels with his riding crop" echoes ll. 18–19 of Rimbaud's "Mémoire" (written 1872, pub. 1895): "l'ombrelle aux doigts; foulant l'ombelle; trop fière pour elle" (fennel is an *ombelle*, a member of the family *Umbelliferae*).[9]

How can we be expected to spot these allusions, and why are they here?

The passionate farewell of our lovers in 1884 takes place at Forest Fork. It is this spot (mentioned only these two times) that is the locale for Van and Ada's next meeting after the Brownhill fiasco, just before 8 A.M.. on July 25, 1886. This later tryst is a recurrence staged by the characters, no mere verbal recall but a deliberate reliving of their last previous embraces.

It is at this meeting that Van and Ada change the code for their correspondence. Between 1884 and 1886 they had used a simple alphabetic code, but "In the second period of separation, beginning in 1886" – after the reunion at Forest Fork – "the code was radically altered" (161), becoming now a numerical cipher geared to the lines and letters of "The Garden" and "Mémoire," which both children know by heart (the two poems had been discussed together by Van and Ada in Pt. 1 Ch. 10).

But why is the code foreshadowed in the account of Van's departure from Ada at Forest Fork? Because as Van stumbles along, flailing wildly at the undergrowth, he is in vehement despair at the possibility of Ada's unfaithfulness – "it's the fellows I'll kill if they come near you" (158–59) – and it is during the new, post-1886 phase of the coded correspondence that Ada's

letters become less frequent and Van's jealousy more inflamed. He is right to
be hurt, for Ada now writes so seldom precisely because she is entangled in
affairs with Philip Rack and Percy de Prey. Through the pairing of the Marvell and Rimbaud allusions in our paragraph, then, Nabokov anticipates the
breakdown of Van and Ada's correspondence and so prepares for the jealousy
theme that becomes dominant in Ardis the Second.

The interval between Ardis the First and Ardis the Second (1884–1888,
Pt. 1 Chs. 26–30) seems chaotic and confused and acridly unpleasant after
the unity and harmony and ambrosial joy of the Ardis the First section. Since
Van and Ada have lost their paradise, this change of structure and tone is
essential, yet it still seems excessive. The excess is a powerful example of
resistance: Nabokov thwarts the expectations he has set up; the distasteful-
ness and brokenness of the interim chapters seem greater than he would have
wished to design; all feels rather sickening and uncontrolled. But the subtle
recurrences of the last paragraph of Ch. 25 show how firmly under control
this chaos is: already Van and Ada's first, unsuccessful reunion at Brownhill,
their successful but brief tryst at Forest Fork and the letters that span their
separation and adumbrate the jealousy that will lour over their proper reunion are contained in the Morio-Moore allusions and the Marvell-Rimbaud
echoes.

On a first reading the exhilarating lyricism of Ardis the First, intensified
and specially validated by the fact that the lovers are seen to be still together
eighty years later, tends to tide us over the lapses and separations: confident
of seeing the characters reunited, we are eager to see the reunion take place,
and the separation seems hardly noticed. But on a rereading the sense of
disharmony, even of Nabokov's apparent inability to control structure and
tone, becomes disquieting. It takes a long time to discover, through details
like those of our paragraph, that every part of the apparent lapse is meticulously designed, and to reach at last the solution that Nabokov has not merely
described the failure to control happiness and promise, but has made the
reader experience this loss of control through sharing in his own unostenta-
tious, apparently undeliberate and unrecognized failure – which is ultimately
only an apparent failure.

If the subtler functions of our paragraph have a key role in enabling us to
understand Nabokov's structural strategies, still another quiet significance is
essential in helping us appreciate his moral evaluation of his characters. The
explosive tumult of Van's emotions is romantically thrilling in his "fiercely
beheading the tall arrogant fennels with his riding crop," but the riding crop
will make a transmuted appearance in less attractive form. Its role as weapon
and emotional outlet at the end of Van's first Ardis stay is matched by the
"silver-knobbed cane" (298) at the end of his second idyll at Ardis. This time,
Van is fleeing the manor and especially Ada, who has betrayed him with Percy

de Prey and Philip Rack, whom he plans to maim or destroy: "you could... thrash him with a strong cane – must not forget to choose one in the vestibule closet before leaving forever, forever" (294). But he leaves his cane behind at the railway station and has to buy "his second walking stick...a rude, stout article with a convenient grip and an alpenstockish point capable of gouging out translucent bulging eyes" (305). He is wounded in an irrelevant duel and cannot find the walking stick, "so the hospital supplied him with the Third Cane" (312). The cane's sinister portentousness seems about to be unleashed in action, but Van's weapon suddenly proves needless, for Rack, poisoned by his wife, has only days to live and Percy de Prey has already been shot in the Crimean War.

When Van and Ada are reunited in Manhattan late in 1892, Ada has with her an album of incriminating photographs: brother and sister in amorous poses, as recorded in 1884 by Ardis kitchen boy, "photofiend" (205) and black-mailer Kim Beauharnais. (Sample shot: "Another interesting plant, Marvel's Melon, imitating the backside of an occupied lad, could be made out on the floral horizon of a third photo" [405].) When Demon in February 1893 forces his too-loving children to part, Van, smarting from another separation, rushes off to unleash his anger in a manner rather less attractive than that of the 1884 riding crop or even the Three Canes of 1888. Just as the 1888 canes are a more serious form of the 1884 riding crop, so the 1893 implement makes explicit the romantic violence implicit in the "alpenstockish" second cane. For this time Van uses an alpenstock "to release a brute's fury" (445) – to blind blackmailer Kim.

To readers like John Updike and Joyce Carol Oates,[10] Nabokov seems to be unaware of the repulsive side of Van's self-congratulatory romanticism. In fact, though, Nabokov assesses uncannily well Van's arrogant selfishness, the privilege he claims for his passion. Nabokov does not forget for a moment the implications of Van's self-willed ardor; he deftly incorporates criticism by such hardly noticeable means as making the wild bitterness of the riding-crop scene contain already an anticipation of Van's ugliest deed. To the careless reader he appears simply to sanction the real charms of Van's flair; in fact he entices us to succumb to these charms and then encourages us to recognize our mistake.

Our paragraph, then, begins in fiery romanticism and in an apparent absence of relationship to anything else – the miraculous and comic dis-appearance of butler and car, the spontaneously generated groom and horse. But the emphatic independence of narrative continuity gradually discloses a wealth of intricate recurrence: the metamorphic run from station to manor at the beginning of Ardis the First is balanced by the transformation on the return trip; the jealousy theme, the next meetings at Brownhill and at Forest Fork and in Ardis the Second, and Van's Byronic rages at the end of his next sojourns with Ada are all already present, lurking like genies awaiting release. The resistance set up by external and internal allusions too only gradually gives way to solutions, to the appreciation of the masterly control behind the apparent lapse in the 1884–1888 separation, to the evidence of a tireless criticism of the romanticism that at first seems so attractive.

2. Independence and Pattern

Independence and the Absence of Inertia

The immediate allure of Nabokov's narrative style lies in its capacity to make each moment of reading seem so unrestricted by every other moment. What creates this rare freedom is the vibrant independence of each of the elements of the fiction and the unprecedented ability of the prose to move from one strikingly independent element to another in any way at all, with any degree of rapidity or retardation, lucidity or elusiveness, elegance, clumsiness or sheer preposterousness. Nabokov's narrative does not, like a smooth-flowing treacle, move steadily on by the pressure of its own sweet consistency. It can develop by breaks, sudden shifts, "spontaneous" creation.

Let us consider first the independence of the parts.

The objects and events and characters in Nabokov's fiction may be pointedly unrelated to the rest of the work – like the young groom Moore and the saddlehorse Morio, without antecedent or consequence:

> The poor fellow died that night in his sleep, leaving the entire incident suspended in midair within a nimbus of bright irrelevancy. (470)

> A dead and dry hummingbird moth lay on the window ledge of the lavatory. Thank goodness, symbols did not exist either in dreams or in the life in between. (510)

Nabokov particularly values the autonomy, the separate vitality of what he creates, an object or an instant or a character suddenly there and itself, with no purpose whatever in the development of a story or in the assignation of its meaning. In a sense, this is a special kind of realism, a challenge to the principle of artistic selection. Reality is not chosen, it is infinitely detailed, each part of it has its own life whether it affects us or not, and in the same way a flash of light, a gesture, a character is allowed into a Nabokov novel even if it has no part in the protagonists' lives. But simultaneously there is an anti-realistic effect: because something is without antecedent, with no place in the novel's scheme of things, with no need to be there, we are made very

conscious of the fresh choice of the artist that has fetched this something or
has created it in a new burst of individual fancy.

It is this special combination that Nabokov so enjoys in Gogol's creation of
cheekily centrifugal life: on the one hand, a challenge to artistic selectivity as
if on behalf of multiplex and undesigning reality and on the other a revelling
in the creative powers the artist's magic wand can unleash. Nabokov writes
with infectious fascination about the "torrent of 'irrelevant' details" (*NG*
148) in Gogol's work, the "spontaneous generation" (*NG* 83) or "'secondary'
dream characters [who] pop out at every turn of the play (or novel, or story) to
flaunt for a second their life-like existence" (*NG* 42): "Note how the newborn
Anonymous Vlassovich manages to grow up and live a whole life in the space
of a second" (*NG* 47).

Like Gogol, Nabokov can create a character charged with his own quiddity
and standing out from the work like a shock of electrified hair. In the following instance Nabokov goes even further, permitting the reader to watch the
spontaneous generation not only of a character but of a whole region:

> Dorothy Vinelander retired to a subarctic monastery town (Ilemna, now Nov-
> ostabia) where eventually she married a Mr. Brod or Bred, tender and passion-
> ate, dark and handsome, who traveled in eucharistials and other sacramental
> objects through the Severniya Territorii and who subsequently was to direct,
> and may still be directing half a century later, archeological reconstructions at
> Goreloe (the "Lyaskan Herculanum"); what treasures he dug up in matrimony
> is another question. (532)

"Mr. Brod or Bred" comes into existence, marriage and two careers in half a
sentence, to disappear from the novel at once on a cadence of flippant uncon-
cern, having flaunted the colorfulness of his improbability.

Not content to create only a momentary character, Nabokov establishes in
the same swift-moving half-sentence a momentary landscape, a whole regional
history and geography. In the rest of the novel northern North America, particularly Canada and Alaska (on Antiterra "Canady," to avoid a superfluous
"ada," and "Lyaska," from the Russian "Alyaska"), merges mysteriously with
our Russia. But in four lines of sudden detail – "a subarctic monastery town,"
a traveler "in eucharistials and other sacramental objects" – the frozen zones
spring to life as The Devout North, seething with the Russian Orthodox
faith, only to disappear as thoroughly as Mr. Brod or Bred. A context now
exists, though, for two other facts in the novel: Varvara, the fourth of Chekhov's *Four Sisters*, as the play is known on Antiterra, comes in "Act One from
her remote nunnery, Tsitsikar Convent" (429), and Marina, who plays the
part of Varvara, is later found in "Tsitsikar – flirting there with the Bishop
of Belokonsk" (437). It is an enchanting enrichment of the novel's landscape

– enchanting and utterly zany.

The same half-sentence also gives birth to a geological as well as a religious history. Mr. Brod or Bred married Dorothy Vinelander in "Ilemna, now Novostabia": Nabokov fuses Lake Il'men, near Novgorod, with Iliamna, the largest lake in Alaska and also the name of the local volcano. Since the ancient Roman town of Stabiae was destroyed by Vesuvius in A.D. 79, along with Pompeii and Herculaneum, the phrase "Ilemna, now Novostabia" implies that the volcano Ilemna has recently erupted, causing its town (perhaps still devastated) to be renamed. Presumably, however, it was a much earlier eruption which caused Goreloe to be "burnt" or "scorched" (its meaning in Russian), if the "reconstructions" Mr. Brod or Bred is directing are "archeological." If, indeed, the eruptions are real: Ilemna is foreshadowed in a "pet nightmare" Dorothy Vinelander has years before she goes near Lyaska, in the throes of which she sees "the eruption of a dream volcano" (514). She thrusts a report of the nightmare before Van, a distinguished oneirologist. Van finds Dorothy Vinelander obnoxious in general and resents in particular her foisting her dream upon him. Perhaps, as narrator, he invents her colorful fate, her marrying "a Mr. Brod or Bred, tender and passionate, dark and handsome," in order to heap disaster on her; perhaps not.

But it is not only the fantastic that Nabokov shows as spontaneous generation and encircles with a "nimbus of bright irrelevancy." Details of visual description, too, flaunt their independence. Nabokov is celebrated for the precision of his visual details, yet it is not the precision alone that imparts that special tang to his descriptions but rather the sense of the crisp autonomy of the thing described. This autonomy comes of course partly from the unique combination of details that individualizes the thing, but it also stems from the delicate implication that the description is "irrelevant," that it is chosen purely for itself and not for any function it has in the novel, and from the way in which the suddenness and enchantment of the description can stress the creative power of the novelist's invention.

The first contribution to the thing's "resplendent independence" (*SO* 226) is the vividness of Nabokov's details. His observation is meticulous, his combination of details unique, so that one moment is forever distinguished from all others:

> a tortoiseshell comb in her chestnut hair caught the amber light; the French window was open, and she was holding one hand, starred with a tiny aquamarine, rather high on the jamb as she looked at a sparrow that was hopping up the paved path toward the bit of baby-toed biscuit she had thrown to him. (48)

But there is also a keen sense in Nabokov's descriptions that the thing need not have been described, or at least that such detail was not necessary.

The "rather high on the jamb," the "starred with a tiny aquamarine" and the superb "baby-toed" in the sentence above are there for the position, light and shape of the things themselves rather than for any necessary part they play in action or characterization. It is this sense of the unnecessary that provokes William Gass to call Nabokov's descriptions "fussily decorative, like insistent blossoms on a swatch of chintz."[1] Gass does not recognize the intentional presence of the "nimbus of bright irrelevancy" that grants the thing described an independent right to exist: "only when there is this little gap left open for the inexplicable and unexpected to pop in or out," Nabokov writes, "only then can our mind find harmony and logic in the general laws it perceives."[2] In the following lines we feel it natural (in terms of novelistic convention) for Van to describe so tenderly the girl about to become his lover, but the description of the tablecloth and the honey-smeared butter are especially attractive because there is so little *need* to describe them:

> Her hair was well brushed that day and sheened darkly in contrast with the lusterless pallor of her neck and arms. She wore the striped tee shirt which in his lone fantasies he especially liked to peel off her twisting torso. The oilcloth was divided into blue and white squares. A smear of honey stained what remained of the butter in its cool crock. (75)

The magic of such description lies not only in the precision but also in the suggestion of irrelevance emphasized by the dislocation in the sudden move from Ada to tablecloth. These things are simply there, independent of any design of the author except his desire to put them there for themselves. (Nabokov, the scene as a whole shows, feels no necessity to create a convincingly solid realistic backdrop for his action and certainly would abhor any "symbolic" reading of the details.) Robbe-Grillet advocates this purity of the object: "Que ce soit d'abord par *leur présence* que les objets et les gestes s'imposent...gestes et objets seront *là* avant d'être *quelque chose.*"[3] As in life, things are bright, opaque, merely there, independent of other things and of any special import, any human "'significations' (psychologiques, sociales, fonctionelles)" (Robbe-Grillet, p. 20). By the "bright irrelevancy" of his details Nabokov, like Robbe-Grillet, produces a reality truer (because it catches us – as things in life do – by the sudden *presence* of things) than that of "realism," though unlike Robbe-Grillet Nabokov avoids the programmatic, achieves economy and leaves a shiver of wonder in a thing's autonomy from human purpose.

Nabokov's visual descriptions are not only vividly detailed and "unnecessary" but also hint at the power of artistic creativity. A second ago nothing, and now a magical image: "they crouched on the brink of one of the brook's crystal shelves, where, before falling, it stopped to have its picture taken and take pictures itself" (267). Because Nabokov does not require the steady accompaniment of a fictional setting, because the details appear in a flash without antecedent or context or function except their own vividness, each description seems a miracle of creativity and stands out as if caught by the oblique morning sun.

But even more remarkable than Nabokov's choice of the people and things of his fictive worlds is his narrative mobility, the variety of the ways in which he links together the most heterogeneous material – that special openness of narrative possibility that I have termed the absence of inert continuity.

There is nothing in Nabokov's work of automatic or even probable consecution. It is as if there is a gap after each word or each slightest motion of the prose, and in that brief shadow of a pause time for an astonishingly free exercise of creative choice: not just a search for the next word, but a questioning whether continuity should persist or whether instead a new detail or a new character might be abruptly invented, whether the tone should be drastically changed, whether the speed should be altered, the time shifted, a joke made, a new subject picked up, a fresh scene entered. Each choice not only may not lead on to the next, it may not even limit it. Even if one choice does lead on to another, in the chink between the two can still be inserted something utterly different.

In the process of composition Nabokov literally does insert new material in between two parts of a sequence: "I don't write consecutively from the beginning to the next chapter and so on to the end. I just fill in the gaps of the picture" (*SO* 16); "I do not begin my novel at the beginning. I do not reach chapter three before I reach chapter four, I do not go dutifully from one page to the next, in consecutive order; no, I pick out a bit here and a bit there, till I have filled all the gaps on paper. This is why I like writing my stories and novels on index cards, numbering them later when the whole set is complete." (*SO* 32) This provides a good image for the circumvention of the linear: anything may be composed on its own separate card and then inserted into what becomes a more or less natural sequence. But of course the constant possibility of redirection in Nabokov's works is not explained or accounted for by his methods of composition: he could have composed on index cards and still have written like Proust.

Since any part of one of Nabokov's narratives may have any or no relation to what has gone before and what will follow, continuity may be as thoroughly violated as when Bouteillan and the family car suddenly disappear and are replaced by groom and horse. Yet if he does refuse to keep within ordinary continuity Nabokov usually does not let the narrative declare itself to be disruptive or digressive. He more often prefers to stock it with the disruptive, the digressive, the fantastic and unnecessary while imparting to it a rapid motion that provides the illusion of a harmonious whole – just as the voyages from station to Ardis or Ardis to station provide the reader used to the lull of continuity with a deceptive calm, the illusion of unbroken advance. Nabokov can change his direction and speed at every step while he appears to be moving evenly forward.

Sometimes, of course, Nabokov flouts the force of narrative momentum as directly as Swift or Sterne. He may use a form that seems opposed to narrative flow – notes and index in *Pale Fire*, a philosopher's treatise, the labels from a herbarium or a parodic blurb in *Ada* – or, on the local level, he may wreak havoc upon the flow of the sentence. The following lines are the close of Ardis the Second: this time the Russian coachman Trofim Fartukov is driving Van from Ardis to the railway station, and this time there is no last embrace with Ada, for Van is fleeing from her and her unfaithfulness:

> "*Barin, a barin,*" said Trofim, turning his blond-bearded face to his passenger.
> "*Da?*"
> "*Dazhe skvoz' kozhaniy fartuk ne stal-bï ya trogat' etu frantsuzskuyu devku.*"
> *Bárin:* master. *Dázhe skvoz' kózhaniy fártuk:* even through a leathern apron. *Ne stal-bï ya trógat:* I would not think of touching. *Étu:* this (that). *Frantsúzskuyu:* French (adj., accus.). *Dévku:* wench. *Úzhas, otcháyanie:* horror, despair. *Zhálost':* pity. *Kóncheno, zagázheno, rastérzano:* finished, fouled, torn to shreds. (300)

(The *frantsuzskaya devka* in question, by the way, is the maid Blanche, whom Trofim soon marries.) The accurate but stubbornly pedestrian glosses – "this (that)," "French (adj., accus.)" – and the need to stop and start all the time are crazily inappropriate to narrative motion, and it is especially outrageous that the outburst of anguish in the last lines should retain the impersonality and indifference of the glossator's forms while suddenly taking up the story again.

More often, however, Nabokov preserves continuity but within it exercises his freedom to make the invigorating shifts that are one of the first and most enduring charms of his work for any reader. Just before the scene above we see Van, reeling from the news of Ada's unfaithfulness, adopt a mechanical patter of activity to keep his despair at bay while he prepares to leave Ardis forever:

> Good morning, and good-bye, little bedroom. Van shaved, Van pared his toenails, Van dressed with exquisite care: gray socks, silk shirt, gray tie, dark-gray suit newly pressed – shoes, ah yes, shoes, mustn't forget shoes, and without bothering to sort out the rest of his belongings, crammed a score of twenty-dollar gold coins into a chamois purse, distributed handkerchief, checkbook, passport, what else? nothing else, over his rigid person and pinned a note to the pillow asking to have his things packed and forwarded to his father's address. Son killed by avalanche, no hat found, contraceptives donated to Old Guides' Home. (295)

The first sentence wears a mask of sentimentality through whose eyeholes narrator, character and reader peer fondly together at the little bedroom. The mask is abruptly torn off, the intimacy discarded, when tone and point of view switch to the impersonal, the cold, in the insistently externalized "Van shaved, Van pared his toe-nails, Van dressed." The insistence is relaxing into ordinary third-person narration when the sentence dips quickly into Van's consciousness ("shoes, ah yes, shoes, mustn't forget shoes"): Van is trying to make trivial objects and activities fill his mind and thus leave no room for pain. The sentence withdraws again into authorial reporting and darts once more into Van and out again while it carries on the rushed methodicalness: "what else? nothing else, over his rigid person." The changes in point of view convey exactly the state of mind of this "dead man going through the motions of an imagined dreamer" (295). But the next sentence, while preserving Van's brittleness and his sense that he might as well be dead, makes a purely absurd leap into a clipped telegraphic style and a wildly projected scene since it is June and he is in almost semitropical Ardis when he envisages death by avalanche. The lines erupt into life with their attractively ridiculous detail ("contraceptives donated") despite the tone of anguish that should prevail.

We should note that though such rapid shifts in point of view as those in the passage above are indeed different from the methods of the "realistic" novel, their purpose is not, as a cliché in the making tries to suggest, to distance reader and story: "point of view is used by Nabokov to keep the reader from becoming too emotionally involved," Herbert Golden writes, echoing Alfred Appel's remark that Nabokov parodies "the reader's complete, self-indulgent identification with a character, which in its mindlessness limits consciousness."[4] Appel's point is well made, but if Nabokov often distances the reader he also often creates a rare immediacy, and it is because the reader is in uncommonly close contact with Nabokov's first-person narrators that the moral evaluation of his characters is often so testing.

It is not only by means of recognizable self-consciousness, not only by such sudden shifts as "good-bye, little bedroom. Van shaved...what else? nothing else, over his rigid person" or Humbert's famous "You can always count on a murderer for a fancy prose style" that Nabokov breaks from the web of habit clinging to continuity. Even where there is no overt manipulation of point of view and no apparent challenge to sequentiality Nabokov's esteem for the fullest possible exercise of consciousness affects his style. Because time is the medium in which the human mind operates and because consciousness becomes most fully itself when it owes nothing to habit and the promptings of ready continuity, when it perceives the openness of its choice and acts to take advantage of this freedom, Nabokov's style is marked not only by self-conscious reflections upon itself but by its openness at every instant to all possibilities. What really characterizes Nabokov's prose is not so much its self-consciousness as its astonishing exercise of free choice, its ability to ignore what sequence might prompt even when the narrative may seem vigorously linear.

By nimble transition and subordination, by asides and extravagant qualifications, Nabokov can introduce wildly disparate and centrifugal material and different manners as well as different matter into a sentence to which he has imparted a brisk forward impulse. He can stay within a scene and still flit out of it, divert from his subject, disrupt his tone, introduce "extraneous" humor and, while doing all this, maintain reckless speed. Consider this sentence:

> As an actress, she had none of the breath-taking quality that makes the skill of mimicry seem, at least while the show lasts, worth even more than the price of such footlights as insomnia, fancy, arrogant art; yet on that particular night, with soft snow falling beyond the plush and the paint, *la Durmanska* (who paid the great Scott, her impresario, seven thousand gold dollars a week for publicity alone, plus a bonny bonus for every engagement) had been from the start of the trashy ephemeron (an American play based by some pretentious hack on a famous Russian romance) so dreamy, so lovely, so stirring, that Demon (not *quite* a gentleman in amorous matters) made a bet with his orchestra-seat neighbor, Prince N., bribed a series of green-room attendants, and then, in a *cabinet reculé* (as a French writer of an earlier century might have mysteriously called that little room in which the broken trumpet and poodle hoops of a forgotten clown, besides many dusty pots of colored grease, happened to be stored) proceeded to possess her between two scenes (Chapter Three and Four of the martyred novel). (10–11)

To recognize just how absurdly swift this sentence is, we must keep in mind that it is virtually introducing Marina and Demon: neither has been in front of us in a real "scene" before. Even the fact that Marina is an actress has to be introduced, but in three words this is slily assumed to be known and a general assessment of her talent is under way. The sentence then moves from the general to a particular performance, during which the temporary potency of Marina's personal charms arouses in Demon the desire to make her his mistress – which he has done before the first act[5] and the sentence end. The narrative speed is phenomenal, yet within this speed there is anything but simple sequence. After the opening few words, the beginning of a character assessment, comes a half-digressive comment on the merits of drama, the first broaching of a topic that will recur throughout the novel. It is followed, as the sentence switches to a particular evening, by a depiction of setting, in which in ten words Nabokov not only localizes the action at a theatre, but provides a dream-like view of both the auditorium and the night outside, and uses tactile values ("soft," "plush") to dream-transport the reader to both the within and the within and without: a masterpiece of sudden evocation. Having established the enchantment, Nabokov digresses in a series of impish jokes that ignore the general mood: "great Scott," "bonny bonus" and the implausible "seven thousand gold dollars [not paper money but a groaning sackful] a week [$364,000 a year] for publicity alone [in 1868]." When the parenthesis finishes, the sentence briefly returns to its plot function ("had been from the start of the trashy ephemeron") but is already off on another tone-shattering digression: the angry dismissal in "trashy ephemeron" and "pretentious hack" ignores the romantic mood even more brazenly than the comedy of "great Scott" and "bonny bonus" and initiates another recurrent theme, that of "adaptation" (the adaptation of a work of art to another medium, as of *Eugene Onegin* from verse novel to opera or play, or of novel into film, of painting into fiction). After easily returning to the "so dreamy, so lovely" mood, Nabokov disrupts it again with a comic allusion: since the romance is *Eugene Onegin*, in which Prince N. is the husband of Tatiana, the role Marina is playing, "Demon is betting the man whom he will enhorn" (Proffer 254). A dash through the theatre's backstage is halted as Nabokov quite "unnecessarily" calls up "a French writer of an earlier century" – Jean-Jacques Rousseau (1712–1778), in his *Julie, ou La Nouvelle Héloïse* (1761), Pt. II, Letter XXVI: "Je fus surpris, en revenant à moi, de me trouver dans un cabinet reculé, entre les bras d'une de ces creatures"[6] (a whore) – then shifts direction again to describe the new setting with exquisite evocativeness and precision ("dusty pots of colored grease") and the superb but again "inappropriate" and "extraneous" pathos of the broken gear of "a forgotten clown." As soon as Nabokov informs us that Demon "proceeded to possess her" (by which time the deed is finished with: subsequent sentences do not pursue the subject) an explanatory comment dips in again to the digressive theme of adaptation, and in "martyred" there is a last irruption of inappropriate tonal energy.

After one choice has been made, the next remains quite unrestrained by the first; it may or may not develop what went before. Like "the great Scott" above, each choice may be without antecedent, a new freak of fancy that owes nothing to the developing situation. Here as elsewhere, to be sure, most of Nabokov's choices make at least some contribution to the surrounding scene. Yet many contain matter of no relevance whatsoever to situational development: the sudden burst of "cabinet reculé" and its attendant elaboration furthers nothing in the scene (though Saint-Preux's impossible innocence in Rousseau is amusingly unlike Demon's cynic calculation). The "broken trumpets and poodle hoops" and "dusty pots of colored grease" relate in no way to Marina and Demon, though they *are* unique, unforeseeable, as immediate as hallucination.

As remarkable as the darting irrelevance in this sentence is the way it ceaselessly changes its purpose. Though looking back we can see its primary function is one of plot (the beginning of the Demon-Marina affair), it begins with exposition (Marina is an actress), changes into character assessment (her ability as an actress), becomes digressive (the merits of the theatre) only to start setting a scene – at which point the changes in direction only become more rapid. These swift and multiple transitions of function are not at all accidental. Nabokov has said that "in the study of transition a clear perception of matter and manner leads to an appreciation of one of the most important elements of a story in verse or prose,"[7] and he has read other writers with keen attention to their transitions: neither Pushkin "nor any novelist of his time," he declares, "had mastered the art of transition that Flaubert was to discover three decades later" (*EO* III, 18).

Such changes in function as those in the Marina-Demon sentence are exactly what Nabokov defines as transition:

> If we replace the notions story, character, landscape, recollection, and didactic digression by the letters S, C, L, R, and D, then we can define all types of transition as more or less distinctly expressed switchings from S to C, from C to S, from S to L, from S to R, from S to D, from C to D, and so forth, in all possible combinations and successions, with inner or outer doors and natural or artificial bridges providing passages from one theme to another. (*EO* 1, 19)

Nabokov finds it fascinating to expand the potential of transition: to extend the "combinations and successions" beyond what has seemed possible to other writers, to speed up or slow down the rate of change, to combine transitional movements with continuing forward motion or to isolate them, to make them smooth or awkward. Slow, isolated, awkward, the following paragraph, a single transition but parodically bumpy about its business, is the very opposite of the multiple glide in the Marina-Demon sentence:

> The modest narrator has to remind the reader of all this, because in April (my favorite month), 1869 (by no means a mirabilic year), on St. George's Day (according to Mlle Larivière's maudlin memoirs) Demon Veen married Aqua Veen – out of spite and pity, a not unusual blend. (19)

If this sentence is not allowed to build up any continuity despite its single transition, another may show continuity run mad, "combinations and successions" with a lunatic energy – as if a sprinter were suddenly to repeat his sprint, then to do it again and instead of falling down exhausted set off on a double steeplechase. Demon has challenged to a duel his rival for Marina's love, Baron d'Onsky ("Skonky"):

The challenge was accepted; two native seconds were chosen; the Baron plumped for swords; and after a certain amount of good blood (Polish and Irish – a kind of American "Gory Mary" in barroom parlance) had bespattered two hairy torsoes, the white-washed terrace, the flight of steps leading backward to the walled garden in an amusing Douglas d'Artagnan arrangement, the apron of a quite accidental milkmaid, and the shirtsleeves of both seconds, charming Monsieur de Pastrouil and Colonel St. Alin, a scoundrel, the latter gentleman separated the panting combatants, and Skonky died, not "of his wounds" (as it was viciously rumored) but of a gangrenous afterthought on the part of the least of them, possibly self-inflicted, a sting in the groin, which caused circulatory trouble, notwithstanding quite a few surgical interventions during two or three years of protracted stays at the Aardvark Hospital in Boston – a city where, incidentally, he married in 1869 our friend the Bohemian lady, now keeper of Glass Biota at the local museum. (14–15)

With its rapid rushes, its comic asides, its flurries of spontaneous generation and absurd identification, the sentence will neither stop nor keep on its tracks. This is not mere caprice, but consciousness brilliantly able to demonstrate its freedom within time: as Nabokov has written, "This capacity to wonder at trifles no matter the imminent peril, these asides of the spirit, these footnotes in the volume of life are the highest forms of consciousness."[8]

That claim might seem overstated, but consider one last example. Van, who usually writes about himself in the third person, records the uneasiness brewing in his fourteen-year-old self in the nights he spent sleeping outside at Ardis in the summer of 1884:

> His nights in the hammock (where that other poor youth had cursed his blood cough and sunk back into dreams of prowling black spumas and a crash of symbols in an orchal orchestra – as suggested to him by career physicians) were now haunted not so much by the agony of his desire for Ada, as by that meaningless space overhead, underhead, everywhere, the demon counterpart of divine time, tingling about him and through him, as it was to retingle – with a little more meaning fortunately – in the last nights of a life, which I do not regret, my love. (73–74)

After a brief aside on the nights his uncle, "that other poor youth," spent at Ardis in 1861, Van returns to 1884, to an intimate and poetic recapitulation of the metaphysical qualms of his own boyhood, then adroitly, suddenly – "as it was to retingle" – the sentence glides from third-person, reported 1884 to 1967, to a mellow and moving address from dying Van to his dying love. In these drastic switches of time, tone, scene and subject – from Van's tender sympathy for his uncle to a lashing of satiric scorn at Freudian "career physicians," from young desire and the ache of metaphysical anxiety to a nonagenarian's and lover's quietly proud serenity – Nabokov's style seems to have found new ways to manifest the free range of the human mind and the varied richness of its experience.

Pattern and Recurrence

At the same time as Nabokov maximizes the independence of each part, he can also make the relationship between part and part more elaborately patterned than in the work of any other novelist.

Odd though it may at first seem, the independence of the parts in Nabokov's works makes possible their intricate relatedness. Where most fiction aims at solidity, Nabokov's novels are a gas: the independence of choice makes each moment of his novels like a molecule on the move, free from its neighbors but precisely for that reason able to collide with a vast number of other molecules. While it might seem at first that the lack of ordinary fictional solidity in Nabokov's work results in a shortage of matter, there proves to be an extraordinary amount of matter here that reaches out to cover more and more space in an expanding universe.

Of the various kinds of highly patterned relationships in Nabokov's writing, the most obvious – so obvious that it is often taken as the quintessence of his style – appears within a single attention span, often as a striking play of letters or sounds: "back to the ardors and arbors! Eros *qui prend son essor!* Arts that our marblery harbours: Eros, the rose and the sore." (367) Nabokov delights in suddenly making or seeing things stand in a new relation to one another, but even pattern as marked as this never becomes *pure* pattern. The relationships Nabokov sets up are between real discrete objects and meanings and his love of independence never allows him to forget this (it is precisely for this reason he finds symbols objectionable: because in them the uniqueness and individuality of words and things are denied). What is so ornately patterned that we could swear it must have been invented for the pattern alone turns out to be absurdly apt. Not only does Van's "Eros, the rose and the sore" reflect the pain as well as the joy of his days of love at Ardis, but the phrase also comes to mean even more in the novel's underlying moral evaluations than Van would wish. Similarly, in another frequent form of local patterning – the playful parallelism of "The early afternoon sun found new places to brighten and old places to toast" (81) – what looks like dainty design is accurate and precise observation.

But though patterns like these catch our attention immediately, they are only the glossy skin on the fruit. We still have to find the real flavor inside, in patterns that cannot be perceived at once, in a whole system of interlocking systems of recurrence.

Each of Nabokov's novels is a complicated arrangement of recurrent elements all separated from one another in reading time but to be connected in the reader's memory and imagination. Why construct a novel like this, rather than simply out of the development of events? There are two essential reasons. The first: to show how consciousness works in its world. If perception refines itself by full attention to particularities, by seeing the isolated thing or moment in itself, not in a fuzzy haze of generalization, it also depends on noting the relationship between one thing or one moment and another. On the one hand consciousness is free within time and can turn its attention anywhere and move within or withdraw its attention from its immediate environment, but on the other hand it does exist within space and time, and hence its store of perception and memory accumulates slowly, in piecemeal fashion. Nabokov takes these facts into account as he constructs his novels, so that they are apprehended in the same way as the mind apprehends its world. Reading one of Nabokov's works allows us to become aware of the process of gradually distinguishing and relating things in more and more detail: we experience an ever-deepening knowledge of reality, a succession of mingled pleasures and vexations, in which attention meets with obstacles, distractions, the illusion of insignificance, but can suddenly discover a connection hitherto unseen. That flash of excitement makes up for any frustration at the elusiveness of a world too rich and real to master.

The mind fully engaged with its world participates in a continual process of discovering new relationships in part merely because the world's elements are so numerous and independent that they allow for so many interconnections on so many levels – a fact particularly reflected in Nabokov's verbal leitmotivs. Of the patterns in his novels which are submerged in time and so not visible within a single attention span, the leitmotivs are probably the first to be noticed. But even these are patterns we can trace only slowly.

Let's take a simple example. Van, looking at a photograph of a dance at Ardis, remarks to Ada:

> "Ah, drunken Ben Wright trying to rape Blanche in the mews – she has quite a big part in this farrago."
>
> "He's doing nothing of the sort. You see quite well they are dancing. It's like the Beast and the Belle at the ball where Cinderella loses her garter and the Prince his beautiful codpiece of glass." (401)

The "Beast and the Belle" here is one example of the minor leitmotiv, "the Beauty and the Beast." It might not be spotted immediately, on a first reading, because of its distance in reading time from other instances of the motif, because of the constant variations in form (the other occurrances are: beastly but beautiful [180], only one beau, only one beast [190], the beau and the beast [276], The Beau and the Butterfly [425], so that you may interrupt her beauty sleep, lucky beast [437], Bellabestia [438], of beauties and beasts [464], bullies and beasts [582]), and because the phrase forms part of other patterns on the same and different levels. The phrase and the leitmotiv, for instance, form part of the widespread fairy-tale motif, which itself becomes an essential constituent of the atmosphere of the Ardis sections of the novel. But "the Beast and the Belle at the ball" also merges into the cliché "the belle of the ball." Nabokov is interested in showing how our attention can be distracted, how in a case like this we may at first note the variation on the familiar phrase and not the leitmotiv, or vice versa; the mind has to cope with many different kinds of relationships at once. The "Belle at the ball" in turn leads on naturally to the Cinderella leitmotiv, itself another part of the fairy-tale motif. But the Cinderella leitmotiv serves also as an attribute of character. Here, as often, Blanche, the hard-done-by servant girl, one of three sisters, is naturally associated with Cinderella; yet the Cinderella motif is also associated, in tragic counterpoint, with Van's half-sister Lucette (who, like Blanche, is unrequitedly in love with Van). And when Cinderella loses her garter here, not her glass slipper, it becomes an element of quite a different sort of pattern, a specific echo of an earlier scene where a lost garter becomes a clue to Ada's unfaithfulness to Van: "and once in a small alder thicket, duplicated in black by the blue stream, they found a garter which was certainly hers, she could not deny it, but which Van was positive she had never worn on her stockingless summer trips to the magic islet" (218).

Because the patterned relationships move in so many directions it is difficult for us to track them down at once, though we are aware of elusive connections awaiting discovery. It is even more difficult to discern the *significance* of patterns moving in so many directions, on so many levels – until the discovery of insistent new relationships forces us to even more energetic attempts to understand.

Not only does consciousness confront a world of complex interconnections; it also operates in time. The patterns and relationships the mind perceives are not perceived instantaneously but by gradual accumulation which can, however, lead to sudden spurts of understanding which the slow process of accumulation had not seemed to promise. Nabokov's novels, in the same way, set up a process of continual discovery, in which a character or an event, even a whole ethical or metaphysical system, may suddenly emerge with unanticipated clarity as we discover more and more relationships – and even then surprise us with an unexpected "more."

In real life few things are resolved for us at once. Details about, say, a person or a city we are coming to know are registered at different moments in time and pieced together by memory, to make a gradually more definite picture.

We are not, as Pinter often implies, completely lost on being introduced to something new; but on the other hand a first general impression will hardly be a fair summary and will need to be altered as new facts come to light. The way new details and new relationships appear for possible processing by the mind is most unlikely to be in the neatly convenient order of logical exposition: much more probably, it will be a combination of chance event and mental readiness. In his novels, therefore, Nabokov frequently withholds generalizing information, offering details a few at a time and in ways that at first might seem unrelated, so that we do not know in advance the pattern that is being filled out. Joyce, too, withholds summary information, but whereas Joyce's motive is a scrupulous truth to the reality of the situation (what gaps would there be, how much would be taken for granted, in Bloom's thought here?), Nabokov is more concerned with the reader – with making the mental operations of the reader akin to those of a person trying to appreciate his world.[9]

If things are perceived and understood not by instantaneous summary but by our accumulating details and apprehending their relationships, this process is often complicated by our merely looking elsewhere at the wrong moment or by our slowness to take into account what does not seem likely to form part of any significant pattern. Nabokov considers such factors carefully; he drops hints that seem flamboyantly discrete, as if they are ready to vouch for their being too accidental and ephemeral to be taken into account; or he deliberately waylays our attentiveness, encouraging us *not* to see the point of a particular connection.

Because the process of understanding is not that of swallowing at a gulp a predigested porridge of facts, Nabokov presents information often piece by piece, often implying a detail will not recur, often distracting our attention. He makes no attempt to provide the immediate illusion of fictional solidity in his settings, his characters, his plots: these are not distributed neatly packaged, they are not *given* to the reader. Nabokov releases, only a few at a time, details that seem too slight or too frivolous to be more than colorful passing fancies, but *if* we connect this deceptively offhand information we find substance and complexity everywhere in the plot, in characterization, even in the inanimate physical setting. Unlike Faulkner, Nabokov does not veto the possibility of understanding: rather, he infuses it with the challenge of discovery. As we suddenly perceive one apparently casual detail has recurred, and then another, we begin to discover dense matter in what had seemed mere flimsiness: without warning, newly perceived relationships pinpoint new galaxies of meaning.

We will see this later, in terms of *Ada*'s surprising richnesses of character or in the moral or metaphysical structures of the book. But for now, let us consider something manageable. Take the case of Dan Veen, a middle-range character, dull, talentless, unimaginative. Though he is depicted in terms of details that seem fantastic, disposable, and certainly not composed to create a fictionally rounded character, his depth of character can be discovered if we pay close heed to every detail and note what recurs. Nabokov lets fall what appears in context a trifling remark, but when a similarly skittish observation reappears much later we see that the offhand is a tenderly selected revelation:

> He had revisited only a few times since his boyhood another estate he had, up north on Lake Kitezh, near Luga, comprising, and practically consisting of, that large, oddly rectangular though quite natural body of water which a perch he had once clocked took half an hour to cross diagonally. (5)

The disclosure is bizarrely out of place, amusingly capricious in itself and because it is so uncalled for: this is the only detail we have of Dan's whole youth. But when Van first meets his uncle in 1884 Dan "informed Van that it was going to rain in a few minutes 'because it had started to rain at Ladore,' and the rain, he said, 'took about half-an-hour to reach Ardis.' Van thought this was a quip and chuckled politely but Uncle Dan looked perplexed again." (67) Poor moony Dan obviously has his watch out often: he takes to timing things, it seems, in a pathetic attempt to inject some interest into his life, and he obtusely assumes that a perch or rain will move at constant speeds. Absurdly enough, he is proved right about the rain.

Dan, whose nickname is Red Veen, figures infrequently in Ada, despite being Van's uncle, Ada's putative father and the master of Ardis. For during the times when Van might meet him (when Van is staying on his uncle's estate in the summers of 1884 and 1888) Dan prefers not to visit Ardis. Why? The nickname gives the clue: his red pigmentation (very understated despite the nickname) makes country life in the summer sun uncomfortable for him, and hence "he spent only a few carefully shaded summer weekends at Ardis, his magnificent manor near Ladore" (5). His redness is transmitted to his daughter Lucette, in whom it is a mark of her sensitivity, her vulnerability, her being easily burnt (as she is by her half-siblings). Dan's helplessness is another trait he shares with his daughter, and the stark blackness of Ada's hair must be a painful reminder that his presumptive daughter is really the child of Demon or "Dark" Veen. But to return to Dan's "carefully shaded summer weekends":

> Marina remained for almost a minute wordlessly stretching across the table her husband's straw hat in his direction; finally he shook his head, glared at the sun that glared back and retired with his cup and the *Toulouse Enquirer* to a rustic seat on the other side of the lawn under an immense elm. (89)

Nabokov says no more: it is up to the reader to recall why Dan and the sun are such enemtes.

That newspaper should be noted. After tea on the first day Van sees him at Ardis "Uncle Dan retired to his study, pulling a folded newspaper out of an inner pocket" (68). Nabokov says nothing of Dan's dependence on newspapers, but later we watch Dan "with a slight cough put on his spectacles, but no morning paper had come – and he took them off again" (125). By now we may recognize Dan's newspaper-reading habit as a sign of his sorry unimaginativeness: without his paper he has nothing to fill his vacuity. But this delicate psychological touch also provides colorful comedy:

> He wore suitable clothes for a suitably hot day in the country – namely, a candy-striped suit over a mauve flannel shirt and piqué waistcoat, with a blue-and-red club tie and a safety-goldpinned very high soft collar (all his trim stripes and colors were a little displaced, though, in the process of comic strip printing, because it was a Sunday). (124)

Dan has become one of the characters in the color comic strips of the paper he is restlessly awaiting – which, indeed, comes late "because of the voluminous Sunday supplements" (128) and the colored cartoons! Four years and one hundred and fifty pages later the joke quietly returns when we see "Uncle Dan, very dapper in cherry-striped blazer and variety-comic straw hat" (273).

Other facets of Dan's character are composed through equally precise patterns of recurrence: his reckless driving, for instance, or his inability to appear on time for an appointment. If we stay alert, we can spot the traits meeting secretly: Dan's bad driving, his missing appointments and his newspaper-reading come together in "Uncle Dan calmly reading a newspaper in his little red motorcar, hopelessly stuck in black mud on the Ladore road" (400).

A more significant but still muted trait is his helplessness in love. When Marina rejects his marriage proposal in 1871, "to air his feelings" he sets off "in a counter-Fogg direction on a triple trip around the globe" (5) (this is two years before Verne's novel is published in *our* world). During the trip he films his seedy doings, and when in 1881 his empty marriage with Marina is openly breaking up he again finds a palliative in the combination of travel and photography: "a semi-divorced Dan went to some place in equatorial Africa to photograph tigers (which he was surprised not to see)" (151). His attempts to find sexual satisfaction are meek, shabby and mournful. There are squalid hints of pederasty in 1871. In 1876, while Marina is in hospital giving birth to Lucette, he makes "an unexpected (and rather halfhearted, really – let us be fair) pass" (131) at the governess Mlle Larivière, "a bosomy woman of great and repulsive beauty" (77). He tries a furtive fumble with Lucette: "Papa wore one like that on his hateful pink paw. He belonged to the silent-explorer type. Once he took me to a girls' hockey match and I had to warn him I'd yell for help if he didn't call off the search." (466) His final sordid "satisfaction" is in "Bess (which is 'fiend' in Russian), Dan's buxom but otherwise disgusting nurse, whom he preferred to all others and had taken to Ardis because she managed to extract orally a few last drops of 'play-zero' (as the old whore called it) out of his poor body" (435).

In contrast to Van's adulation of his father is the lively disgust Uncle Dan evokes in his nephew:

> He had just finished his first buttered toast, with a dab of ye-old Orange Mar-
> malade and was making turkey sounds as he rinsed his dentures orally with a
> mouthful of coffee prior to swallowing it and the flavorous flotsam. Being, as I
> had reason to believe, plucky, I could make myself suffer a direct view of the
> man's pink face with its (rotating) red "tashy," but I was not obliged (mused Van,
> in 1922...) to stand his chinless profile with its curly red sideburn. (124–25)

Van's scornful depiction of his uncle and the persistent contrast of his attitudes to Demon and to Dan are at one level two of many entertaining minor themes in *Ada*; at another, they prove to be a key to the novel's moral code.

Dan is only a middle-range character. He is, emphatically, dull. He is never presented more than a very little at a time, so that we do not easily see a picture of the whole man. But if we notice the interlocking details and the recurrent patterns we see the careful consistency of his traits, his comic value and the variety of comic effects he produces, the fascinating disgust he elicits in Van, the range of his ruefulness. There is keen pleasure in apprehending his character without the help of authorial summaries or commentaries or even, as it seems, without the solid presence of the character. Nabokov seems to let fall a detail too quirky to recur (clocking a perch, say), an action too unimpor-
tant or accidental to matter (sitting under an elm), but if we remember the apparent oncer, the incidental action, and connect it with other elements of the same pattern, we realize the coherence of character, the engrossing and sorry life Nabokov has created in quiet drabness.

So far we have considered the first function of recurrence in Nabokov's novels: to suggest the difficulties and delights facing consciousness as it builds up an understanding of its very concrete world. Besides this general epistemologi-
cal function, though, recurrence in Nabokov's work usually serves a second function, as a means to specific artistic effects dependent on delay. Nabokov often controls the gradualness of the apprehension of meaning so tightly as to conceal something crucial at a particular stage of reading (or even rereading)

and yet allow for its disclosure later.

If there are good reasons for doing so Nabokov will render it difficult to make out just what lies before us – Van's blinding, for instance, of the black-mailer Kim Beauharnais.

Since it is essential to Nabokov's purposes that Van – "the charming villain of my book" (*SO* 143) – at least *seems* unusually attractive, the blinding inci-dent must not create too pronounced an effect, particularly on a first reading. This complaint Ada lodges is therefore the most explicit reference to Van's action: "'But, you know, there's one thing I regret,' she added: 'Your use of an alpenstock to release a brute's fury – not yours, not my Van's. I should never have told you about the Ladore policeman. You should never have taken him into your confidence, never connived with him to burn those files – and most of Kalugano's pine forest.'" (445–46). Ada does not even name Kim or the consequence of Van's fury, though Van in his reply does make clear that Kim is the victim, and that he now is blind. But the emphasis is merely on the fact that Van has somehow unleashed his rage, and if we are to see exactly what happens to Kim, we must connect Ada's remark with an earlier passage. In these earlier lines we can see all too horribly what happens to Kim, but not that it is Van who is the attacker: "...Kim who would have bothered Ada again had he not been carried out of his cottage with one eye hanging on a red thread and the other drowned in its blood" (441). This disclosure cannot be made less reprehensible by any special pleading, yet it is defused because our attention has been distracted: this is a hurried digres-sion within a digression that occurs at a moment of high (attention-absorb-ing) dramatic tension. We should note, too, that the first quotation also involves a strategic distraction of attention: who is the Ladore policeman? When did Ada tell Van about him?

We can answer these two questions by summing up the Kim Beauharnais subplot. In 1884 Kim, the kitchen boy at Ardis, photographs the furtive love-making of Van and Ada, who are known to be first cousins and suspected by at least some of the Ardis staff of being half-siblings. Since Kim's addiction to photography persists, he is able to record Ada with her successive lovers, Dr. Krolik, Philip Rack, Percy de Prey, and by June-July 1888, Van again. By 1892 Kim realizes that Van will not oblige by updating the portfolio and when Ada revisits Ardis he shows her the album; she pays him a thousand dollars. In November 1892, having torn out the post-1884 photographs, Ada brings the album with her when she rejoins Van in Manhattan. After she tells Van that she has paid Kim off her exasperated brother points out the obvious: Kim will still have the negatives and they will still be at his mercy. When Van tries to find out the whereabouts of former Ardis staff members who might know Kim's exact address, Ada evades his questions. But while they are looking at the photographs together, Van asks:

Isn't that wheezy Jones in the second row? I always liked the old fellow."
"No," answered Ada, "that's Price. Jones came four years later. He is now a
prominent policeman in Lower Ladore....(407)

Van then contacts Jones, gets him to locate Kim, who is living in a cottage in
Kalugano's pine forest, and brings him along to help burn Kim's files while
Van makes sure Kim will never photograph anything again. He later pays
Jones off by placing him and his family in a penthouse apartment he owns
in Manhattan.

Ada's "I should never have told you about the Ladore policeman," then,
is a reference that we can identify precisely. But we must reconstruct the
events from details often dropped casually, recurrent references to a single
sequence that do not readily disclose either their own interconnections or
Van's calculating savagery.

We should also note that disguised recurrence allows us not only to construct a course of events but also to appreciate another level of dramatic
tension behind the apparent one. While Van and Ada are looking through
Kim's album, Van declares, "I will have to destroy him" (403), but this seems
more an immediate venting of anger than a literal statement of intent. They
examine more of the photographs:

Ada was represented by her two hands rearranging her hair while her Adam
stood over her, a frond or inflorescence veiling his thigh with the deliberate
casualness of an Old Master's device to keep Eden chaste.

In an equally casual tone of voice Van said: "Darling, you smoke too much,
my belly is covered with your ashes. I suppose Bouteillan knows Professor
Beauharnais's exact address in the Athens of Graphic Arts."

"You shall not slaughter him," said Ada. "He is subnormal, he is, perhaps,
blackmailerish, but in his sordidity there is an *istoshniy ston* ("visceral moan")
of crippled art... (406)

Though Van's "equally casual tone" has the *"deliberate* casualness" of an Old
Master, and though Ada recognizes Van's intentions are not to be taken too
casually, it is only when we appreciate how Van does locate and dispose of
Kim that we realize exactly how he is scheming here. When Ada happens to
mention Jones's present position, Van is even more calculating:

"He is now a prominent policeman in Lower Ladore. Well, that's all."

Nonchalantly, Van went back to the willows and said:

"Every shot in the book has been snapped in 1884, except this one. I never
rowed you down Ladore River in early spring." (407)

Van is accusing Ada of unfaithfulness. We take the "nonchalantly," then, as ironic, but it is much more heavily ironic when we recognize that in the second after Ada has let slip how he can get in touch with Jones Van has already formulated his plan of attack against Kim Beauharnais and yet has the presence of mind to launch a second attack, against Ada herself.

Like many of the narrative strands in *Ada*, Van's plotting to dispose of Kim is not presented at once or even identified when the details are disclosed. It is the reader's task to appreciate the real drama beneath the ostensibly casual exchange, to recognize the development, complexity and tension built up through the recurrence of an unstated subject, through interconnections between apparently throwaway remarks. Behind the lyric concentration and charm Van has tried to emphasize in presenting his romantic story the attentive reader can discover a dense dramatic tangle in which Van and Ada are far from being the only characters to matter and in which they play roles far less attractive than they think.

The interlocking references that establish Van has blinded Kim Beauharnais are fairly simple to find, like most of the recurrent details of *Ada's* plot. But these patterns fuse with more oblique ones, so that for instance the alpenstock with which Van blinds Kim is foreshadowed in the three canes at the end of Ardis the Second and in the riding crop with which the distraught Van lashed at the fennels at the end of Ardis the First. As this sort of recurrence accumulates – as, for example, Van's blinding Kim becomes associated not only with the riding crop and canes but also with Van and Ada's treatment of Lucette – it suddenly opens up moral and metaphysical issues as fundamental to the novel as they were unexpected. No longer offering us any resistance, recurrence has by this stage begun to yield up solution after solution.

3. Resistance and Solution

In reading Nabokov we will be struck at different points either by the way one authorial choice stands out from its context, remaining so unexplained by its immediate situation that it prompts us to wonder why the choice was made at all (independence, here, leads to resistance), or by the way one choice seems to relate to a more remote context, in a pattern we can't quite resolve (in this case, recurrence poses the challenge). In the first case, we enjoy the flash of local vitality which flutters by the wayside with satisfying color even if it cannot be netted. In the second, we smile inwardly at the pleasure of even an imprecise recognition. In both cases the sense of resistance probably remains faint: we would like to know but need not worry too much why this phrase juts out so boldly or that one recalls something we cannot quite place. We are both excited and mildly bemused by the attractive mobility (but why did Nabokov make that move?) and the pleasing orchestration (but where did we hear that melody before, and was it in the same key?): we are offered an immediate reward, and at the same time warned that some further reward has slipped by.

We know the sorts of rewards we are missing because we have already encountered many of the simpler puzzles that can be solved almost at once, without resistance. "Wipex" tissues provoke an immediate chortle; it takes only a moment longer to see in the randy King Victor a remodeled Queen Victoria or to make out in the *Village Eyebrow* both the *Village Voice* and the *New Yorker.* And while *"The Puffer* by Mr. Dukes" (343) might hold out longer – the book is Bellow's *Herzog,* "Herzog" being German for "duke" – the answer can still come in a flash. These are only limited, local pleasures, of course. But even early on a first reading we are invited to solve problems much more resonant within the developing fiction. When we first read the difficult pages of the attic scene in *Ada's* first chapter, we are at a loss to see how Van can deduce his true parentage from that obscurely-labeled flower album he and Ada have found. But not many pages later, the *"lieu de naissance* plainly marked X"* (25) and *"c'est bien le cas de le dire"* (26) should send us back to *"c'est bien le cas de le dire….Ex en Valais, Switzerland...my lieu de naissance"* (8). By the time we have read *Ada* as far as the second *"c'est bien le cas de le dire"* we have been given all the plot information we need to decipher the events coyly recorded in the album and to appreciate the bizarre circumstances of Van's birth. Nabokov has given us the chance to solve the album problem ourselves – and the excitement and sense of accomplishment we gain from finding the first solution to that forbiddingly resistant exposition becomes a fierce incentive to further curiosity.[1] After such rewards we start to hanker for similar satisfactions everywhere: successful solutions only make us more conscious of and more eager to overcome whatever resistance lies in our way.

Both our anticipation of new discoveries and our recognition that much has eluded us invite us back for another reading. Now that we know the shape of the whole, will we be able to find reasons for the peculiarities of some of the parts? Now that we are aware of patterns just becoming visible as we finished reading, can we watch for them from the start? But a rereading of one of Nabokov's novels alerts us to as many new freakish choices or elusive connections as it allows us to resolve: by increasing both the rewards and the challenges, it only makes more pressing the invitation to return for still another rereading.

As we reread, any problem that remains unsolved becomes more and more acute: either because we appreciate all the intricacies of its local context better, and see even more clearly than before that the context offers no reason at all for this particular choice; or because we can now see even more insistent relationships between this and other parts of the novel and feel how urgently these accumulating relationships are in need of explanation. Despite and even because of our new discoveries resistance is rising.

Even when we do find a solution that really resolves an important part of our understanding of the novel, it will not continue to be enough. Because everything is so intricately interrelated, there may be unsolved minor riddles associated with the major one we have solved which are not quite peripheral enough to reassure us that our solution is fixed and final. Or even if this is not the case, we will simply become ready to question more deeply after the flush of discovery has faded. The peculiarity of Van's setting off with suitcases and car and continuing the journey with riding crop and horse becomes explicable as an echo of the earlier metamorphic journey. We enjoy such a discovery for its own sake, and for the artistry and humor of the link: but then new resistance arises as we recognize that what we have discovered may not be quite adequate to explain such a strange choice and that perhaps we should probe further. *Why* did Nabokov go to the trouble of constructing such a weird double journey? And a new solution is required, the search for which leads us into new cycles of immediate reward, delayed challenge, deeper reward....

Let us examine a single passage for the questions it provokes and for the recurrent patterns it encourages us to trace.

This early scene, in Pt.1 Ch.10, shows Van and Ada rapidly becoming friends and their beginning to exclude others as their rapport deepens. Marina, Van has noticed, turns any conversational opportunity into a lecture on the theater. To keep her at bay, he unleashes Ada and her botanical skill:

Van: "That yellow thingum" (pointing at a floweret prettily depicted on an

Eckercrown plate) " – is it a buttercup?"

Ada: "No. That yellow flower is the common Marsh Marigold, *Caltha palustris*. In this country, peasants miscall it 'Cowslip,' though of course the true Cowslip, *Primula veris*, is a different plant altogether."

"I see," said Van.

"Yes, indeed," began Marina, "when I was playing Ophelia, the fact that I had once collected flowers – "

"Helped, no doubt," said Ada. "Now the Russian word for marsh marigold is *Kuroslep* (which muzhiks in Tartary misapply, poor slaves, to the buttercup) or else *Kaluzhnitsa*, as used quite properly in Kaluga, U.S.A."

"Ah," said Van.

"As in the case of many flowers," Ada went on, with a mad scholar's quiet smile, "the unfortunate French name of our plant, *souci d'eau*, has been traduced or shall we say transfigured – "

"Flowers into bloomers," punned Van Veen.

"*Je vous en prie, mes enfants!*" put in Marina, who had been following the conversation with difficulty and now, through a secondary misunderstanding, thought the reference was to the undergarment.

....

"...But, to go back to our poor flower. The forged *louis d'or* in that collection of fouled French is the transformation of *souci d'eau* (our marsh marigold) into the asinine 'care of the water' – although he had at his disposal dozens of synonyms, such as mollyblob, marybud, maybubble, and many other nicknames associated with fertility feasts, whatever those are." (63–65)

The avalanche of Ada's information bears all before it, like a Rabelaisian catalogue or a Sternean monomania – with, of course, the extra element of a Nabokovian passion for precision and, as we shall see, a peculiar mixture of the crafty and the compassionate.

The drama of the whole conversation is pleasantly perverse. Why, we wonder, should Van think *this* preferable to Marina's lecturing on the theater? But then Marina speaks. When the conversation is hitched to her hobbyhorse for a mere second ("when I was playing Ophelia, the fact that I had once collected flowers – ") it seems about to plunge into an abyss of tedium, and her leading the conversation suddenly seems a doom to be resolutely avoided. In finishing Marina's sentence, Ada brutally cuts her mother off, but the brutality lies in Ada's getting right the horrible inanity Marina would have used: where else could such a lame interruption hobble? Even Van's slight role is amusing: at first reduced to a vacant "I see" and an even emptier "ah," he suddenly darts in with an apt pun that makes Marina reveal how far out of her depth she is.

The whole of Ada's disquisition is on the name of a single plant. She provides the correct English common name, the scientific name, an ambiguous local name (it is quite true that in the United States "cowslip" is used for the marsh marigold), then two Russian variants, one with a misapplication. With the introduction of the French name she changes tack towards the subject of translation.

The mistranslation she pours scorn upon is Wallace Fowlie's 1946 version of a poem already glanced at, Rimbaud's "Mémoire."[2] Ada calls "the transformation of *souci d'eau* (our marsh marigold) into the asinine 'care of the water'" the "forged *louis d'or* in that collection of fouled French." Her image means simply that this misreading is the richest fake. But it is more than an image: it points to a second unfaithfulness in translation. Rimbaud has:

> Plus pure qu'un louis, jaune et chaude paupière
> Le souci d'eau
> (Purer than a louis, a yellow and warm eyelid:
> the marsh marigold).[3]

Fowlie in 1946 had translated it thus:

> More golden than a louis, pure and warm eyelid,
> The care of the water.

Not only did he botch "le souci d'eau," but he also took away "pure" from "louis": hence the "forged" *louis d'or.*

Ada's conversational wit is impossibly lush here. But underneath it, unknown to her, shimmer two more Nabokovian jokes.

The *"d'or*...transformation...marigold...asinine" subliminally flashes out the title of the Latin novel, the *Metamorphoses* or *The Golden Ass*, of Lucius Apuleius (fl. 2nd century AD). In that novel, of course, Lucius is transformed into an ass – and what it takes to make him whole again is to eat a rose. A flower in Fowlie's translation, too, will turn the asinine transformation back to the original.

Though Ada's "marybud" is another name for the marigold, "mollyblob" and "maybubble" are inventions, produced by fission from the genuine "mayblob" (marsh marigold). Why does Nabokov invent "mollyblob" and "maybubble" here? The answer is not easy, but it is precise: the suggestion of popping in "maybubble" combines with "mollyblob" to point unmistakably to Molly Bloom's famous musing on the blob of a ruptured hymen: "and they always want to see a stain on the bed to know youre a virgin for them. . . theyre such fools too you could be a widow or divorced 40 times over a daub of red ink would do or blackberry juice no thats too purply."[4] By means of this allusion Nabokov strengthens the comic charge he made against Fowlie by way of *The Golden Ass:* Fowlie's mistranslation of the word for marsh marigold has "deflowered" the poem.

Why does Nabokov go to such trouble to align the loss of "souci d'eau" in a translation with the flower that brings on a transformation in Apuleius and the verbal play via Joyce on loss of virginity as "deflowering"?

The main reason for this peculiar emphasis is that it anticipates Lucette's death. Lucette commits suicide after she fails to entice Van to deflower her, and she is brought to such an extreme – as we will discuss more fully later – because her whole emotional development has been twisted by her being sexually "initiated" far too young, in watching Van and Ada constantly making love. The tragic irony of Lucette's fate is that she loses her innocence at too early an age (when she sees Van and Ada in action, when Ada leads her into tactile temptations) but remains a virgin and cannot get Van to take the virginity she so desperately offers.

Nabokov takes great care to bring Lucette into the discussion of the Rimbaud mistranslation – and significantly, at the very moment it is stressed that she is excluded from the discussion because she is *too young* to be up at this hour:

> "our learned governess...drew my attention...to some really gorgeous bloomers, as you call them, Van, in a Mr. Fowlie's *soi-disant*, literal version...of *Mémoire*, a poem by Rimbaud....Incidentally, she will come down after tucking in Lucette, our darling copperhead who by now should be in her green nightgown – "
>
> "*Angel moy,*" pleaded Marina, "I'm sure Van cannot be interested in Lucette's nightdress!"
>
> " – the nuance of willows, and counting the little sheep on her *ciel de lit* which Fowlie turns into 'the *sky's bed*' instead of 'bed ceiler.' But, to go back to our poor flower. The forged *louis d'or* in that collection of fouled French is the transformation of *souci d'eau* (our marsh marigold) into the asinine 'care of the water' – although he had at his disposal dozens of synonyms, such as mollyblob, marybud, maybubble....(64–65)

Ada's remarks closely identify Lucette with the Rimbaud text: she directly associates Lucette's green nightdress, "the nuance of willows," with the lines "Les robes vertes et déteintes des fillettes font les saules," and she goes on to picture Lucette in "her *ciel de lit* which Fowlie turns into 'the *sky's bed*.'" Nabokov has painstakingly embedded Lucette in the discussion of Rimbaud's poem and Fowlie's mistranslation so that the "deflowering" in the translation can foreshadow her doom.

The importance of the deflowering motif established through the linking of Lucette and the "deflowered" translation is stressed in a later chapter, Pt. 1 Ch. 20, where the subject appears to be *Ada's* loss of virginity. In the preceding chapter Van and Ada almost make love, "but impatient young passion...did not survive the first few blind thrusts; it burst at the lip of the orchid" (121). The action of Pt. 1 Ch. 20 takes place the next morning, when the youngsters *do* manage to consummate their love.

Flowers pervade the chapter. Van sits in the dining room "full of bright yellow flowers" (124), waiting anxiously for Ada to come down for breakfast: "Suddenly Van heard her lovely dark voice on the staircase saying in an upward direction, *'Je l'ai vu dans une des corbeilles de la bibliothèque'* – presumably in reference to some geranium or violet or slipper orchid." (125) In fact the reference is to a slipper Cinderella-like Blanche lost the night before, but here the atmosphere of the chapter metamorphoses the lost slipper into a lost flower.

After Ada has breakfasted, Van waylays her on the landing, and they agree to meet as soon as they can – in an hour's time – in the Baguenaudier Bower, (Those "yellow flowers" in the dining room have come from the bower; "baguenaudier" is the French for the bladder-senna flower.) There, after retreating deeper into the larchwood, Van and Ada make love, as we can see from the photos Kim takes of the event (pp. 405–06), though the present chapter ends with Van and Ada being coyly evasive on the subject of Ada's defloration:

> Neither could establish in retrospect, nor, indeed, persisted in trying to do so, how, when and where he actually "deflowered" her – a vulgarism Ada in wonderland had happened to find glossed in *Phrody's Encyclopedia* as: "to break a virgin's vaginal membrane by manly or mechanical means.".…Was it that night on the lap robe? Or that day in the larchwood? Or later...? We do not know and do not care.
>
> (You kissed and nibbled, and poked, and prodded, and worried me there so much and so often that my virginity was lost in the shuffle: but I do recall definitely that by midsummer the machine which our forefathers called "sex" was working as smoothly as later, in 1888, etc., darling. Marginal note in red ink.) (129)

But how are the earlier *souci d'eau* "deflowering" and Lucette involved in this chapter? There are three quite exact links.

Ada's "Marginal note in red ink" on the subject of loss of virginity very precisely recalls the Molly Bloom observation alluded to via Ada's equivalents for the French *souci d'eau*, "maybubble" and "mollyblob": "and they always want to see a stain on the bed to know youre a virgin for them...a daub of red ink would do." (*Ulysses* 769)

The earlier "deflowering" had been mentioned after Mlle Larivière had brought a mistranslation to Ada's attention. Here, in Pt. 1, Ch. 20, Ada cannot go off with Van immediately after breakfast because she has a French-English translation of her own to finish for Mlle Larivière. When she shows Van her draft translation, he pours scorn on her effort:

> She had to finish a translation for Mlle Larivière. She showed him her draft. François Coppée? Yes.
>
> > Their fall is gentle. The woodchopper
> > Can tell, before they reach the mud,
> > The oak tree by its leaf of copper,
> > The maple by its leaf of blood.
>
> "*Leur chute est lente,*" said Van, "*on peut les suivre du regard en reconnaissant* – that paraphrastic touch of chopper' and 'mud' is, of course, pure Lowden (minor poet and translator, 1815–1895). Betraying the first half of the stanza to save the second is rather like that Russian nobleman who chucked his coachman to the wolves, and then fell out of his sleigh."
>
> "I think you are very cruel and stupid," said Ada. "This is not meant to be a work of art or a brilliant parody. It is the ransom exacted by a demented governess from a poor overworked schoolgirl. Wait for me in the Baguenaudier Bower." (127–28)

Van's comment points out the absurdity that Ada's glib version whisks us past: the "woodchopper" in her lines implies the fall of whole trees, not the mere autumnal leaves of the original (Coppée's "Matin d'Octobre"). Just one of her rhyme-words thus makes nonsense not only of "Their fall is gentle" but of the whole stanza, whose hushed mood is devastated by the unintended crashing of great trunks. One translation robbed of its flower, a second stripped of its leaves.

Just before Ada shows Van her draft mistranslation, "guileless Lucette" trots into the dining room "with a child's pink, stiff-bagged butterfly net in her little fist, like an oriflamme" (127). The "oriflamme" links Lucette again to Rimbaud's poem and to Joan of Arc, "La Pucelle": "des oriflammes sous les murs dont quelque pucelle eut la defense" ("Mémoire," 11.34). The aptness of Lucette's being identified with Joan of Arc, virgin (*pucelle*) and martyr, becomes clearer much later. When sixteen-year-old Lucette stays with Van and Ada in Manhattan, Ada orchestrates a *débauche à trois*; when Ada will not let Lucette go and brings Van's hand over to caress her Lucette lies back "on the outer half of Ada's pillow in a martyr's pudibund swoon" (418) before escaping, distraught. When twenty-five-year-old Lucette meets Van in Paris a few days before her death, she invites him back to her room:

> "I'll stretch out upon the divan like a martyr, remember'?"

"Are you still half-a-martyr – I mean half-a-virgin?" inquired Van.
"A quarter," answered Lucette. "Oh, try me, Van!" (464)

The Rimbaudian "oriflamme," the loss of leaves in a French-English
translation for Mlle Larivière and the Molly Bloomian note in "red ink" all
serve to recall the *souci d'eau* and the tragic irony focussed upon that peculiar
"deflowering." Just when Van treats his deflowering Ada as a triumph,
Nabokov emphatically demurs: the blind selfishness of Van and Ada's ardor,
he insists, will make a martyr of the little girl entangled in their love.

The irony of Lucette's "deflowering," established so precisely yet so
obscurely in the *souci d'eau* passage, pervades the whole novel. But when
Nabokov drew on Apuleius and Joyce to define the implications of deflowering," why did he resort to such obscurity? The obliqueness of the allusions is
Nabokov's way of making absolutely clear that Lucette's being horribly
implicit whenever Rimbaud's "Mémoire" is mentioned is part of *his* design,
not Van's. Van, an expert literary craftsman who has worked on writing *Ada*
for ten years, and who can thus be considered responsible for many of its
subtler effects, does evoke "Mémoire" intentionally, as a means of adding to
his celebration of his magical memories with Ada; but Nabokov's buried
purpose in introducing the Rimbaud poem is always quite different.

Nabokov also wants to ensure that the irony is not immediately accessible,
so that we are encouraged at first not to consider Lucette, to view her as Van
and Ada do, as a rather irritating little pest who gets in the way of their extraordinary love. When we find Nabokov's ironies and see the extent of *his* concern
for Lucette, we are forced to admit how readily we were beguiled into insensitivity – when events themselves should have made us take thought for Lucette
– merely because we were looking from Van and Ada's point of view.

In the closing paragraphs of Ardis the First –

> Stumbling on melons, fiercely beheading the tall arrogant fennels with his
> riding crop, Van returned to the Forest Fork. Morio, his favorite black horse,
> stood waiting for him, held by young Moore. He thanked the groom with a
> handful of stellas and galloped off, his gloves wet with tears. (159)

– Van uses the paired Marvell and Rimbaud allusions to anticipate the breakdown of his coded correspondence (see above, p. 26). But for Nabokov the
allusion performs very different functions.

The more important of these I had noticed some years ago, but let's begin
with the one that I discovered only in the process of rewriting. It demonstrates
perfectly how Nabokov's moral strategy works: he encourages us to fail to make
a necessary judgement, then by the controlled irony of his recurrent patterns

makes us suddenly aware how readily we could make a moral blunder.

I knew from an early stage that the conjunction of Marvell and Rimbaud in this paragraph anticipated the code outlined in the following chapter and hence the breakdown in the correspondence as Ada's attention is consumed by other lovers. That, it seemed, sufficed for the conjunction of "Mémoire" and "The Garden." Now I also knew that these two poems had appeared together only once before, where, after Ada's denouncing the loss of *souci d'eau* from the English version of "Mémoire," Van posits "The Garden"'s being botched into French. But I had always accepted that this was just natural, without special significance: it was Nabokov's economical way of showing that Van and Ada knew the two poems and knew that the other knew them, and certainly the two poems' appearing together seems very right – just the way things happened – in the scene where it occurs.

But just as I was revising the lines on the final paragraph of Ardis the First I asked myself *why* does the "Stumbling on melons, fiercely beheading the tall arrogant fennels" group these poems together again, when they haven't been paired since that dinner-table conversation with Van, Ada and Marina? Is there some special connection between the two occurrences? (We should always ask such questions, of course, but there are thousands of other questions to ask in *Ada*, and we have only so much energy.)

As so often happens, once the question was formulated an answer sprang up quickly – and as so often happens, it proved to be a reprimand for my insensitivity of judgement.

The "Mémoire"–"The Garden" allusions at the end of Ardis the First are there to foreshadow the coded correspondence designed to keep others out of Van and Ada's love affair. In the dinner-table scene where Van and Ada talk of translation, the two youngsters are not yet lovers, but their highly ornate allusiveness in referring to Rimbaud and Marvell rudely excludes Marina from the conversation. Despite Van's arguments on Ada's behalf, Ada – with Van's support – behaves abominably to her mother, prattling away so Marina cannot lead the conversation, talking in too complicated a manner to allow her a chance to participate or follow. Marina's tediousness, the persuasiveness of Van's arguments, the sheer intelligence of the two children, and the fact that we see the story from their point of view – all of these encourage us *not* to see the insensitivity to Marina. The later coupling of "Mémoire" and "The Garden," by focussing on Van and Ada's exclusiveness (the code) makes us realize the callous exclusiveness in the scene where these two poems were paired before. The shock of realizing how easily we can condone insensitivity (when we are not especially warned – as we usually are warned in literature, in ways we cannot be in life) has a salutary forcefulness. Now I may be especially insensitive not to have disapproved of Van and Ada's behavior towards Marina in that supper scene, though I think that given Nabokov's careful manipulation of the scene many would have responded in the same way; but there would be very few indeed who would read *Ada* without being lulled into *any* such moral lapses, and those few obviously do not need Nabokov's sudden correctives. For the rest of us, though, Nabokov's fiction can prove to be a healthy lesson – and it makes us keep on learning, usually about lapses far more serious than mere conversational rudeness.

The closing paragraph of Ardis the First, for instance, also anticipates the way Lucette is driven to her death. Van's "fiercely beheading the tall arrogant fennels with his riding crop," as we have already seen, prefigures the alpenstock with which he will blind Kim Beauharnais after another bitter parting from Ada. But the riding crop and alpenstock return just hours before Lucette's death, on the ship where the "hysterical virgin" (484) is trying to get Van to sleep with her. They look at a glass case: "The presence of a riding crop and a pickax puzzled Van" (486). The unlikely appearance of the riding crop in mid-Atlantic is one means by which Nabokov aligns the brutality with which Van treats Kim Beauharnais with the fatal lack of concern he shows towards Lucette, in allowing her to be initiated too early, in not seeing how all-consuming is her desire to lose her virginity to him.

With this in mind we can see that in Van's beheading the fennels with his riding crop – already an allusion to "Mémoire" – *his* chopping off the herb's flowery head brings back the "deflowered" in the *souci d'eau* mistranslation, and at the same time recalls the "woodchopper" in the other mistranslation which accompanies Ada's defloration. In case we miss the point Nabokov provides, as he often does, another means of discovering it: the "asters" at the beginning of this last chapter of Ardis the First are matched by the "stellas" at the end, but the second cluster of "stars" is no longer of flowers.[5]

On a first reading this final paragraph of Ardis the First depicts in the most colorful terms Van's distraught grief at leaving Ada, and the quite unwarranted fears fueled by his jealous disposition. By means of Van's own sly artistry, though – by the paired Rimbaud and Marvell echoes – the lines also foreshadow that when he returns to Ardis Van will have ample grounds for the bitterest jealousy. But Nabokov also suggests that Van's real cause for regret at Ardis is the way his self-centeredness, which he portrays as romantic intensity – when the family car becomes a black steed – leads to his brutal indifference to those who interfere with his love for Ada, including not only Kim Beauharnais but also Lucette. Nabokov also makes it clear to us that if we have accepted Van and Ada's own evaluation that the intensity of their passion is all, we should realize how far we have fallen short of any true imaginative sensitivity to the needs of others.

Nabokov has made Lucette the center of all of *Ada's* major motifs and structural interconnections. This fact and its consequences are difficult to discover, because Van is so self-aware in telling his story and sees the torridness of his and Ada's love as its own resounding vindication. Though he regrets his half-sister's death he fails to see the extent of his and Ada's responsibility for the tragedy or how their treatment of her merely highlights the shortcomings of all their conduct. It is difficult to discover Lucette's importance, too, because it is essential to Nabokov's purposes that at first we should not fully recognize what Van and Ada are doing to Lucette, and that we are made to appreciate how easy it is to overlook the responsibilities that arise from the fact that people's lives are so interrelated.

The epistemological point of Nabokovian strategy, that the complex relationship of things guarantees the world is a constant challenge to apprehend, merges into the moral points that Nabokov makes by way of Lucette. Douglas Fowler could not be further from the truth when he asserts that "the private systems of correspondence" in Nabokov's novels are "annotated red herrings."[6] In all of Nabokov's novels the patterns and puzzles are anything but caprice and decoration: they are a consequence of Nabokov's original examination of the problems consciousness faces in apprehending and acting in its complicated world.

Yet because Nabokov is bold enough to withhold, during the earliest stages of our reading, much of the structural harmony, the moral force or the metaphysical scope of his novels, it is understandable that a reader could suspect the novels to be deficient in organisation or implication. If Nabokov's method of delaying the unfolding of his meanings involves the danger of suggesting that there is nothing but attractive surface or at best the shallow complexities of elaborate patterns and circumscribed puzzles, why does he persist in and even extend his methods as his career continues? Why does he work by challenge and reward?

The first answer is simple economy. As in the paragraph ending Ardis the First, multiple solutions can allow an incomparable concision, offering in a few lines a multi-faceted insight into details of character, points of psychology or moral evaluation, into the subtle graces of a novel's structure. Nabokov's hiding things for the reader to find, it will become increasingly apparent, is not the idle amusement of someone with nothing to say but the very means by which Nabokov enables himself to say perhaps more than any other novelist has ever done.

No less important is his determination that his works will be apprehended in the same way he apprehends his world. Nabokov enjoys deeply the bright immediacies of the world, but he always craves the excitement of discovering what remains unknown just behind the apparent – and what remains behind *that*, and so on, and so on. Resistance and solution recreate the possibility of this excitement: behind the immediate attractiveness of Nabokov's prose lurk intimations of hidden but extricable meaning, incentives to read on and read again, drawing us back time after time to the novel until we can see how the process of concealment and discovery puts into kinetic form the philosophical (epistemological, moral, metaphysical) problem of consciousness, which for

Nabokov is "the greatest mystery of all" (*BS* 168).

Nabokov makes the relationship between reader and text an image and an enactment of the tussle between the individual mind and the world. Reality is elusive, Nabokov feels, not because it is not there but because there is so much there and because, since human understanding is limited by the very conditions of its being, the tireless effort of all the powers of one's consciousness is required if one is to see life as freshly and as sharply as possible. By overcoming the deadening assumption that we know enough about life to cope, by overcoming habit or lack of curiosity or attentiveness, by striving to extend the limits of our knowledge, Nabokov suggests, we can discover the bounty of life: "Pour qui sait regarder, la vie quotidienne est...pleine de révélations et de jouissances."[7]

Nabokov encourages us to exercise and feel the thrill of exercising all our faculties, to delight in pitting our minds against the world. The process of rereading is essential here: it intensifies our sense of what we do not know, discourages us from accepting *anything* without curiosity, and poses new challenges that make possible the rewards of discovery. Consider, for instance, "mollyblob, marybud, maybubble." On a first reading the attractive euphony may be enough, but curiosity will soon prompt the good reader to reach for a dictionary: we find that "maybud" is a genuine synonym for "marigold" and that the other two are invented derivatives of the genuine "mayblob." The mixture of obscure fact and plausible fictitiousness is amusing. But after continual rereadings even the smallest details come to seem insufficiently explained by their immediate environment and provoke our curiosity further – why have these invented words taken *these* particular forms? – until they render their secret in a flash of surprised recognition (Molly Bloom!). Even now new rereadings may be needed to goad our imaginations (mine took several months to budge) if we are to see how apt the "de-flowering" in Molly's remark on maidenheads is to the loss of "marsh marigold" in translation. Then, suddenly, we can see how Lucette's fate is implicated – and, as this insight expands, how her presence seems to pervade everything that matters most in the novel.

Nabokov designs resistance and solution especially to provide the unutterable exhilaration of discovery. Only by making his clues as oblique and deceptive as he does, only by confronting us with real resistance that imagination and curiosity must overcome can he ensure that we know we have made our own way to the excitement prepared for us. As lepidopterologist and artist, as chess problemist and thinker, Nabokov knows that there is no substitute for experiencing for oneself the shock and the joy of discovery.

If in its perpetual encounter with the world around it the human mind can be repeatedly frustrated by the limitations of its knowledge, the frustrations are far more than matched by the triumphs of discovery, by the riches that observation, curiosity, memory and imagination can unearth. But there are other kinds of discoveries to be made in Nabokov's works and about our relationship to our world that are much less triumphant. Nabokov cherishes the tenderness, the sensitivity, the imaginative sympathy possible to human consciousness, but he also recognizes the moral limitations we can impose on ourselves through not endeavoring to compensate for the bias of personality and the force of self-interest, through not being ready to imagine the feelings of others. He compels us to discover these limitations of moral imagination in ourselves and makes the shock of discovery here different indeed from an abstract knowledge of "other people's" faults. For us to feel this shock it is valuable if at first we do respond according to bias, interest, unimaginative inconsiderateness, and that only upon rereading, perhaps only after numerous rereadings, do we find the acute moral judgments that Nabokov has woven into the fabric of the novel and that we ourselves have not been able to see. As we shall find in Part Three of this book the ethical implications Nabokov can engender through his strategies of resistance are an essential component of his work and the solutions can be chastening indeed, proof that the normal laziness of our imaginative sympathy may well make us capable of injuring others, that we can be all too ready to limit the moral capacity of our consciousness.

If Nabokov is fascinated by the limits of human consciousness, he is also fascinated by the possibility of there being something beyond these limits, something outside human time and the blindness of human self-interest.

In "ordinary" life we may seem to feel, at rare peaks of consciousness, a strange promise of significance behind the visible world, an intimation of transcendental sense pressing through the fabric of space and time. In reading Nabokov too we can find strangely similar apprehensions of limitless promise. Solutions are not isolated but can give rise to other solutions with unforeseeable alacrity until the expectation that the whole work is about to disclose its secret significance, the mystery underlying its world, seems to tingle in every word. In *The Real Life of Sebastian Knight* V. writes of his half-brother's last novel:

> I sometimes feel when I turn the pages of Sebastian's masterpiece that the "absolute solution" is there, somewhere, concealed in some passage I have read too hastily, or that it is intertwined with other words whose familiar guise deceived me. I don't know any other book that gives one this special sensation, and perhaps this was the author's special intention. (*RLSK* 180)

Like Sebastian Knight, Nabokov is fascinated by the possibility of sudden vistas of new truth, of a solution to all that has seemed riddling and inexplicable.

At their profoundest level, resistance and solution serve a double purpose in Nabokov's work. The first is the charged accumulation of meaning which builds until we are hurled into a new dimension of understanding by a shock perhaps resembling that which human consciousness might feel in passing from its time-bound mortal condition to a state beyond time in which it could trace the pattern of its world. The second purpose is to offer the reader a uniquely generous opportunity to discover the ever-deeper presence of creative choice in the novel's world and through the thrill of such discovery to partake as fully as possible of the thrill of creation. It may be that Nabokov even hints that the second purpose is "somehow, somewhere, connected" (*Lolita* 316–17) to the first.

But perhaps we can understand all this better if we look directly at Nabokov's philosophy.

PART TWO

NABOKOV AND THE WORLD

4. Space, Time and Consciousness

The driving force in all of Nabokov's work is the "immemorial urge" "to try to express one's position in regard to the universe embraced by consciousness" (*SM* 218). For Nabokov human consciousness exists far above other known orders of being but far below what consciousness might imaginably attain to, and hence he proposes these divisions: "Time without consciousness – lower animal world; time with consciousness – man; consciousness without time – some still higher state" (*SO* 30). This ascending scale of being, essential to his vision of things, he describes most explicitly in *Speak, Memory*:

> every dimension presupposes a medium within which it can act, and if, in the spiral unwinding of things, space warps into something akin to time, and time, in us turn, warps into something akin to thought, then, surely, another dimension follows – a special Space maybe, not the old one, we trust, unless spirals become vicious circles again. (301)

The structure of Nabokov's whole metaphysics retains this helical design: its initial coil is the world of space, the second, the world of time, the third the world of human, time-bound consciousness, and the next, if there is another stage, a consciousness beyond time.

But before examining each of these twists of the spiral, we must take into account two essential qualities of Nabokov's mental make-up. The first is his "innate passion for independence,"[1] a passion easily visible in his literary attitudes, in the practice of his art, in his science, his philosophy, his politics. The second is his equally marked love for pattern, whether in literature (in the surface ornateness of his prose, for instance), in his own life (his patterning the past in *Speak, Memory*) or in nature (the complexities of mimicry). "Independence" and "pattern" complement and oppose each other throughout each of Nabokov's divisions of the conditions of being. They form the two strands of his spiral, which thus becomes, like some freak DNA molecule, a conical double helix. We shall examine Nabokov's inquiry into the forms independence and pattern take or might take within each of the twists of his spiral.

Space

First the world of space, "Furnished Space, *l'espace meublé* (known to us only as furnished and full even if its contents be 'absence of substance'...)" (*Ada* 504). When considering the furniture of space, Nabokov has an unmatched sense of the utter individuality of each thing, the wonder of its distinctness, and the narrator of *Pnin* seems to speak for him when he notes: "one of the main characteristics of life is discreteness."[2]

For Nabokov the world of furnished space is to be seen, enjoyed and understood in terms of live details: "Only myopia condones the blurry generalizations of ignorance. In high art and pure science detail is everything" (*SO* 168). Things exist in specificity; it is the accumulation of details that reveals the independence of one thing from another and from the mind.

Nabokov finds the reality of the external world elusive, but not at all because he doubts its existence outside the mind.[3] That, he considers, is everywhere testified to by the sharpness of phenomena: "Doubting Tom should have worn spectacles" (*SO* 79). What makes reality so elusive is that it is infinitely richer than any single person's knowledge of it, or even the sum of science's specifications. The world is so real that it always exceeds our knowledge of its reality; the details of anything in nature – seen "under the microscope of reality (which is the only reality)" (*Ada* 221) – prove more myriad than we expect:

> Reality is a very subjective affair. I can only define it as a kind of gradual accumulation of information; and as specialization. If we take a lily, for instance, or any other kind of natural object, a lily is more real to a naturalist than it is to an ordinary person. But it is still more real to a botanist. And yet another stage of reality is reached with that botanist who is a specialist in lilies. You can get nearer and nearer, so to speak, to reality; but you never get near enough because reality is an infinite succession of steps, levels of perception, false bottoms, and hence unquenchable, unattainable. (*SO* 10–11)[4]

Reality is elusive not because it is doubtful whether it exists outside the mind, but because it exists out there so resolutely, so far beyond human modes of perception and explanation in its endlessly detailed complexity, so real even in its minutest parts. As Richard Wilbur writes in "Thyme Flowering Among Rocks," the unimaginable inexhaustibleness of detail shockingly confirms the reality of a thing. He comes upon an out-of-the-way thyme flower, full of fantastic detail though the plant's absence would never have been felt and its presence might never have been noticed:

> Crouching down, peering
> Into perplexed recesses,
> You find a clearing
>
> Occupied by sun
> Where, along prone, rachitic
> Branches, one by one,

Pale stems arise,
One branch, in ending,
Lifts a little and begets
A straight-ascending

Spike, whorled with fine blue
Or purple trumpets, banked in
The leaf-axils. You

Are lost now in dense
Fact, fact which one might have thought
Hidden from the sense,
Blinking at detail
Peppery as this fragrance,
Lost to proper scale....

....

It makes the craned head
Spin. Unfathomed thyme! The world's
A dream, Basho said,

Not because that dream's
A falsehood, but because it's
Truer than it seems.[5]

In confirming the reality of the thing, detail also confirms the thing's independence of the mind: "strangely enough," Nabokov says, the split between ego and non-ego "is intensified the stronger the reality of the world is stressed."[6]

Detail not only vouches for the existence of things independent of the mind; it also insists that things are independent of one another: "the unique feature defeats the would-be lumper."[7] It is only the laziness and limitedness of human perception that makes us fail to see the differences between things, the live specificity of the phenomenon.

For Nabokov only the perception of a thing's uniqueness is worthwhile. Unless this is grasped, reality has no tang. To grasp it requires the full alertness of the conscious mind, fresh observation, an accumulation of detail, a refusal to sacrifice the discreteness of a thing. The generalization, the abstraction, the symbol, the tarnish of habit all take away the bright particularity of the world. Dreyer in *King, Queen, Knave* misses the recurrent stab of wonder at the directness of things:

Luckily for Franz, his observant uncle's interest in any object, animated or not, whose distinctive features he had immediately grasped, or thought he had grasped, gloated over and filed away, would wane with its every subsequent reappearance. The bright perception became the habitual abstraction. Natures like his spend enough energy in tackling with all the weapons and vessels of the mind the enforced impressions of existence to be grateful for the neutral film of familiarity that soon forms between the newness and its consumer. It was too boring to think that the object might change of its own accord and assume unforeseen characteristics. That would mean having to enjoy it again, and he was no longer young.[8]

While the independence of phenomena in the world of Space is perceived through the alert isolation of detail, the patterns they form involve combination rather than isolation. But though independence and pattern are opposite, they are also complementary. Pattern is most intriguing for Nabokov when its perception requires uncommon attention to individual details, the details of light and shade, say, or of butterfly speciation and distribution. Victor, likely to become an unusually gifted painter, can discern or create elaborate patterns in the colors or shapes of shade because he does not accept the generalized notion of shadow and thus is able to see each shadow's unique hue:

> at six, Victor already distinguished what so many adults never learn to see – the colors of shadows, the difference in tint between the shadow of an orange and that of a plum or of an avocado pear. (*Pnin* 90)

Similarly Nabokov's examinations of details of organic structure that enable him to differentiate butterflies also enable him to see surprising correlations:

> Views may differ in regard to the hierarchic element in the classification I adopt, but no one has questioned so far the fact of the structural relationship and phylogenetic circumstances I mean it to reflect. The whole interest of *Hemiargus* is that it is allied to *Lycaeides* etc., while bearing a striking superficial resemblance to an African group with which it does not have the slightest structural affinity. ("On Some Inaccuracies in Klots' *Field Guide*," *SO* 320)

For Nabokov the most fascinatingly complex and provocative example of pattern in the spatial world is natural mimicry in plants and animals. He finds the subject "a game of intricate enchantment and deception" (*SM* 125) – a double deception indeed, for the first is practised on the predator or pollinator, the second is reserved for the human investigator who by detailed observation recognizes the full complexity of the pattern and who must wonder at its being so deliberately designed, as it seems, for man's eyes. Nabokov writes:

The mysteries of mimicry had a special attraction for me. Its phenomena showed an artistic perfection usually associated with man-wrought things. Consider the imitation of oozing poison by bubblelike macules on a wing (complete with pseudo-refraction).... "Natural selection," in the Darwinian sense, could not explain the miraculous coincidence of imitative aspect and imitative behavior, nor could one appeal to the theory of "the struggle for life" when a protective device was carried to a point of mimetic subtlety, exuberance, and luxury far in excess of a predator's power of appreciation. (*SM* 124–25)

In *The Gift* Fyodor Godunov-Cherdyntsev's father, a lepidopterist, tells Fyodor "about the incredible artistic wit of mimetic disguise, which...seemed to have been invented by some waggish artist precisely for the intelligent eyes of man" (122).

It is less the sheer esthetic pleasure of complex design than the inexplicability of the pattern that tantalizes Nabokov: the ornate and excessive elaborateness seems to rule out both chance and necessity. Strangest of all is the eerie impression that the full measure of the pattern seems to have been hidden specially for eventual discovery by man – a hint that foreshadows the other kinds of pattern Nabokov investigates in the higher arcs of his spiral of being.

Time

Time, Nabokov insists, is quite distinct from space. The hero of *Look at the Harlequins!* is subject to numerous mild insanities, the greatest of which is not being able to "tell the difference between time and space"[9]: no sane man could fail to distinguish them, Vadim's creator implies. Van Veen declares:

We reject without qualms the artificial concept of space-tainted, space-parasited time, the space-time of relativist literature. Anyone, if he likes, may maintain that Space is the outside of Time, or the body of Time, or that Space is suffused with Time and vice versa, or that in some peculiar way Space is merely the waste product of Time, even its corpse, or that in the long, infinitely long, run Time *is* Space: that sort of gossip may be pleasing, especially when we are young.... (*Ada* 541)

Since time is a dimension of being much more difficult to comprehend than space, Nabokov's interests in independence and pattern accordingly become more complex: here, his zeal for independence leads him to deny the existence of the future while his curiosity about pattern leads him to examine the workings of fate.

Nabokov defends the independence of events in time by denying the future: "the future does not exist" (*SO* 184); "the basic element of the future...is complete non-existence" (*BS* 43). The idea that there is a future "somewhere ahead" to which we will arrive in time is false, he points out: "the future has no such reality (as the pictured past and the perceived present possess); the future is but a figure of speech, a specter of thought (*TT* 1).[10]

The idea of the future is an extrapolation from succession in the past: "At best, the 'future' is the idea of a hypothetical present based on our experience of succession, on our faith in logic and habit" (*Ada* 560). We hypothesize, not too unreasonably, that the succession of moments we have noted as a feature of experience in the past will continue – though Nabokov shows that even this is far from inevitable (*Ada* 536). But "at worst we perform trivial tricks" (*Ada* 560): we extrapolate from the succession of definite *states* in the past to an assumption of such definite states in "the future."

Every moment "is an infinity of branching possibilities" (*Ada* 561), and if the state that is now the present is later than an earlier moment that had been "present," that does not make this Now the future of that earlier "Present." What lay ahead of the earlier Present was not this Now and an infinity of equally precise intervening and succeeding states, but infinite openness, an endless succession of moments (again hypothesizing "on our experience of succession, on our faith in logic and habit"), *each* of which is an infinity of possibilities. That each Present after the first marked one took such-and-such a precise shape does not mean that such a shape was necessary, it merely happened to *be*.

We can call a given state (say, what happened on January 15, 1870) a "future" of a past moment (say, January 1, 1870) only because it is itself *past*. At January 1, we could postulate, "based on our experience of succession," a certain time lapse, say two weeks. But for the inhabitants of January 1 no *state* January 15 exists, no being, only an infinite set of possibilities. The *state* January 15 that matched the postulated time January 15 can be seen to have been "the" so-called "future" of January 1 only by virtue of its *having been*, of its being past – which still does not mean that on January 1 the way January 15 actually turned out was somehow "realer" than other possibilities.

To rephrase the argument: the basic flaw in the idea of the future is that it is assumed to contain *events*, not possibilities.[11] Somehow events are considered to exist before they become. Why does this false notion arise? Simply by analogy with earlier-than and later-than relationships in the past: "Some time after Mrs. Brown became pregnant, she gave birth to Eberthella. Therefore Eberthella's birth was in the future at the time of Mrs. Brown's conceiving." But one cannot project the "future" back into the past in this way: Eberthella's birth at the time of Mrs. Brown's conceiving was no realer (though, perhaps, more likely) than the possibilities of Mrs. Brown's death before delivery or of the fetus's aborting. At the time of Mrs. Brown's conceiving, "Eberthella's birth" is "later," but it is a possibility, not an event; now, *after* Eberthella's birth, one can say that the birth is later than the conception (as one cannot now say, for example, that the fetus aborted), but that is totally different. An earlier-than/later-than relationship between *events* – between possibilities that have "become" – is quite unlike a relationship between any present moment and later *possibilities*.

If, then, the future can be said to exist, it is only a continuity hypothesized on the basis of "our experience of succession, on our faith in logic and habit," and it consists not of "future events," which do not exist, but of possibilities compounded instantaneously – and what sort of consistency does that leave the future?

That the future is open does not imply that all possibilities are equally likely to become events. It is a question of detail: the set of possibilities at each moment is infinite less because anything may happen (our world of "logic and habit" is unlikely to become a tadpole) than because the world is infinitely detailed. It seems likely that there will be a sunset tomorrow, but will I see it? Will I be facing it with a view unobstructed by whatever my surroundings will be and by whatever the weather will be? How will the sun strike what cloud-formations? What will I be thinking then? Van Veen writes for Nabokov:

> nor do I believe that the future is transformed into a third panel of Time, even if we do anticipate something or other – a turn of the familiar road or the picturesque rise of two steep hills, one with a castle, the other with a church, for the more lucid the forevision the less prophetic it is apt to be.

Suddenly emphasizing that chance is the infinite product of the interacting of infinite details, the passage continues:

> Had that rascal behind me decided to risk it just now he would have collided head-on with the truck that came from beyond the bend, and I and the view might have been eclipsed in the multiple smash. (*Ada* 550)

The infinite details in this scene include all Van Veen's past life, which alone explains why he is driving at this time in this direction; the details of his day; the invention of the internal combustion engine; the power of Van's new car; the exact configuration of the road (the engineer's choice and the road authority's plans as well as topographical features); the impatience and the whole character and history of the driver behind Van; the business designs of the enterprise despatching the truck, and so on. The loose interactions of trillions of details suddenly coincide to raise the unforeseen possibility of the crash; further subtle combinations of chance happen to make this possibility (really, this group of possibilities) *not* the actual event of the present, then past, moment.

In *Transparent Things*, one of two Nabokov novels principally about the future (the other is *King, Queen, Knave*, in which the arrangements of a murder are an exercise – easily foiled by life – in foreseeing the future), the superhuman narrators, who can see any level of matter or time past, cannot see "the future" any more than the human characters can. They observe that a person's destiny is not

> a chain of predeterminate links: some "future" events may be likelier than others, O.K., but all are chimeric, and every cause-and-effect sequence is always a hit-and-miss affair, even if the lunette has actually closed around your neck, and the cretinous crowd holds its breath. (92)[12]

Nabokov's dismissal of the future is not only philosophically sound, essential in his view to the very nature of Time, but also a satisfaction of his passion for independence, for the freedom of human action and thought. Otherwise we are left with "the miserable idea of determinism, the prison regulation of cause and effect. We know from real life that however obediently we may follow the paths of causation, some queer and beautiful force, which we call free will from want of a better expression, allows or at least appears to allow us to escape again and again from the laws of cause and effect."[13] Van Veen speaks for his creator when he says that the future is

> At every moment…an infinity of branching possibilities. A determinate scheme would abolish the very notion of time….The unknown, the not yet experienced and the unexpected, all the glorious "x" intersections, are the inherent parts of human life. The determinate scheme by stripping the sunrise of its surprise would erase all sunrays – (*Ada* 560–61)

Nabokov's exclusion of the future coexists in his novels with something apparently quite incompatible with his strenuous insistence on freedom: the intrusive designs of fate, that patterner of human lives. Readers have objected to the intrusiveness of Nabokov's Fate, but in fact Nabokov examines the subject from every angle with scientific precision and tentativeness, not a novelist's irresponsible self-assertion.

He treats fate exactly as a maker of fine patterns, a master craftsman: "Let me pick out several fatidic points, cleverly disguised at the time, within the embroidery of our seven winters." (*LATH* 57) But the phrase "cleverly disguised at the time" reveals the essential qualification on fate's craft: it is visible only in retrospection. Nabokov writes:

As with so many phenomena of time, recurrent combinations are perceptible as such only when they cannot affect us any more – when they are imprisoned so to speak in the past, which *is* the past just because it is disinfected. (*BS* 43)

The lurking presence of Quilty and his part in Humbert Humbert's fate are obvious to the reader of *Lolita* – but only since Humbert, because he is looking back on his past, can make it clear to the reader:

> I now warn the reader not to mock me and my mental daze. It is easy for him and me to decipher now a past destiny; but a destiny in the making is, believe me, not one of those honest mystery stories where all you have to do is to keep an eye on the clues. In my youth I once read a French detective tale where the clues were actually in italics; but that is not McFate's way – (212–13)

What may be the patterns of fate can be clumsy, subtle, or inexplicable: the heavy hand of calamity; a delicate flexibility that may be chance or design; the baffling presence of coincidence or foreshadowing.

At its simplest, fate may be mere calamity, forming its stark patterns either through consequences or through causes. When on the very eve of Humbert's arrival in Ramsdale lightning burns down the McCoo house,[14] where Humbert expects to board, the causality seems, in human terms, no pattern but only stupendous chance, the insurance agent's "act of God." But in later retrospection it can be placed in the significant pattern of Humbert's nymphetolepsy, for because of the emergency he is offered a room by Charlotte Haze, Lolita's mother. In a subsequent accident, Charlotte's being killed by a car, it is the elaborate causes that form the suggestive pattern of fate. There is a mixture of pure chance (the coincidence in space and time of dog, car, and tear-blinded Charlotte) and of pure but totally undesigning causality (the discovered diary, the letters it calls forth that must at once be posted across the street, the tears):

> I had palpated the very flesh of fate – and its padded shoulder. A brilliant and monstrous mutation had suddenly taken place, and here was the instrument. Within the intricacies of the pattern (hurrying housewife, slippery pavement, a pest of a dog, steep grade, big car, baboon at its wheel), I could dimly distinguish my own vile contribution. Had I not been such a fool – or such an intuitive genius – to preserve that journal, fluids produced by vindictive anger and hot shame would not have blinded Charlotte in her dash to the mailbox. But even had they blinded her, still nothing might have happened, had not precise fate, that synchronizing phantom, mixed within its alembic the car and the dog and the sun and the shade and the wet and the weak and the strong and the stone. (*Lolita* 105)

The two major accidents together form a pattern of bizarre coincidence which seems to suggest fate is controlling all to bring Humbert and Lolita together. But this leaves out the constant meshing of chance and free will: had not Humbert been tempted by the thought of lodging with Ginny McCoo, he would never have come to Ramsdale; had not Charlotte been tempted (*Screenplay* 28) by the thought of "a professor of French poetry" (*Screenplay* 23) she may not have offered to take in the McCoo's stranded lodger; had not Humbert by chance spotted Lolita, he would not have stayed at 342 Lawn Street; had not Charlotte, overripe for love, forced Humbert to choose marriage or departure, the nymphetolept would not have married her and thus ensured his access to Lolita after Charlotte's death; had Humbert's cruelty not appeared in the diary, had Charlotte's possessive curiosity not led her to it, and so on, and so on. When lightning installs Humbert in Lolita's house, when Lolita's mother is eliminated by a car, fate's axe falls as if only in fulfillment of Humbert's dreams. Yet even this dreamlike grossness of fate would have meant nothing in Humbert's life without free will and chance.

"Fate" may work by the gross intervention of accidents in life. But, Nabokov suggests, it may also be operating busily in ways less discernible and more flexible than we have ever suspected. Its method might be to combine chance and causality with such delicacy and flexibility, such reluctance to appear overtly, that only a faint hint of persistence could alert one to the possibility of fate's having an end in mind. It might prepare for its designed end a subtle plan delicately combining chance and apparently unrelated threads of causality, and if "a minute mistake (the shadow of a flaw, the stopped hole of an unwatched possibility, a caprice of free will) spoils the necessitarian's pleasure" (*RLSK* 97), it might then work out new plans of equal delicacy until its purpose is fulfilled. At an ominous moment in *Ada* Demon's suddenly swerving to avoid an acquaintance "advancing toward him…along his side of the street" foils an elaborate little plan, but "precisely in regard to such a contingency, Fate had prepared an alternate continuation" (433–34).

If we were to look back on and examine minutely a major change in our lives, it might be possible to discern a pattern in what had seemed an aimless meshing of chance and slack, seemingly discrete strands of causality. Knowing the significance of the outcome might enable us to discern the pattern of persistence in the seemingly random antecedents of the event. In *The Gift* unrelated scenes and lines of plot prove to have been near-meetings of Fyodor Godunov-Cherdyntsev and Zina Mertz; when they finally meet it is an apparently incidental by-product of other lines of development in Fyodor's life. It is only after their love has blossomed that Fyodor (and with his help the reader) discovers how fate seems repeatedly to have striven to bring himself and Zina together. Is it simply his new sense of the sweet inevitability of his love for Zina that leads Fyodor to see the pattern of Fate's successive attempts to unite them? Or is it rather that his love prompts him to examine the past with the tenderer care needed to distinguish "the development and repetition of the secret themes of an evident fate"?[15] Is the design Fyodor discerns only a reflection of his wishes or, as the novel suggests, has he glimpsed fate, has he had a special insight into the flexible patterns of purpose in time?

The structural basis of *Success*, the second novel of Nabokov's Sebastian Knight, is surprisingly like that of *The Gift*. When the past is examined to see how two lovers were first brought together, the circumstances of their meeting are seen to be a combination of chance, routine, irrelevant lines of causality:[16]

> The meeting is or seems accidental: both happen to use the same car belonging to an amiable stranger on a day the buses went on strike.... The author's task is to discover the exact way in which two lines of life were made to come into contact, – the whole book indeed being but a glorious gamble on causalities or, if you prefer, the probing of the aetiological secret of aleatory occurrences.... Working backwards the author finds out why the strike was fixed to take place that particular day and a certain politician's life-long predilection for the number nine is found to be at the root of the business.... Another false scent is the stranger's car... (*RLSK* 96)

To find exactly why man and girl come to stand side by side on the curb it is necessary to trace the life of each back a little way, and it is discovered that

> there have been at least two occasions in these two peoples' [sic] lives when unknowingly to one another they all but met. In each case fate seemed to have prepared such a meeting with the utmost care; touching up now this possibility now that one;...leaving nothing to chance. (97)

But unforeseen chance or free will *do* jam these elaborate traps. Yet

> fate is much too persevering to be put off by failure. And when finally success is achieved it is reached by such delicate machinations that not the merest click is audible when at last the two are brought together. (98)

Nabokov raises the possibility that, could the past be scrutinized finely enough – with a novelist's power or the endless curiosity of a gifted lover – a pattern of fate might emerge: fate with infinite care combining possibilities and, if foiled, preparing "an alternate continuation" (*Ada* 434). The successful continuation might, indeed, prove to be that in which fate's plan of attack had been most oblique. From one angle it seems a mixture of pure chance, routine, and the casual crossing of causal lines; from another, the triumph of and key to another of destiny's designs. Because so subtle a fate would allow freedom, the possibility of failure, it would be hard to discern, yet the very persistence of its efforts after early failures would form the pattern disclosing the secret intent.[16]

The most disturbing kinds of fatidic pattern in time are those (abundant in Nabokov's novels) of temporal coincidence and of apparent foreshadowing, of portents and prophecies. Even these, though, do not break the "no future" rule. They can be considered prophetic only after the event: "the innocent incident will turn out to possess, if jotted down and looked up later, the kind of precognitive flavor..." (*Ada* 361).

In *Transparent Things* even the considerably more than human consciousnesses of the ghostly narrators do not see any future, but they do recognize two types of what appear to be prophetic signs: images of falling and of fire. Aware of the plans of an arsonist, they link the two groups of signs and expect that Hugh Person will die trying to jump from his hotel room to escape the fire. They are wrong: the fire kills him too quickly. The fire motif is confirmed to have been prophetic only in retrospect,[17] but it seems to have been created by a patterner, someone who *can* create the future he wants. We have to leave the confines of the book's world to see who this is: Nabokov. Or, to interpret the metaphor, such mighty control of fate and future *could* exist, but only infinitely beyond even the enormously expanded human consciousnesses of *Transparent Things*, only in the hands of a creator in a realm of being forever beyond their access.

At this level pattern in time, perhaps the pattern of a foreknowing fate, is eerie, and invigoratingly unfathomable. A fatidic "number, a dream, a coincidence," Nabokov says, "can affect me obsessively – though not in the sense of absurd fears but as fabulous (and on the whole rather bracing) scientific enigmas incapable of being stated, let alone solved" (*SO* 177). Perhaps we can only say, with Van, that "portents and prophecies" make us feel we are "catching sight of the lining of time" (*Ada* 227).

Consciousness

After space and time comes the third arc in Nabokov's spiral of being, the richest we know: consciousness in time, or "time with consciousness – man" (*SO* 30). For Nabokov "consciousness is the only real thing in the world and the greatest mystery of all" (*BS* 168).

Human consciousness, Nabokov insists, is intimately bound up with time, a medium "quite different from the spatial world, which not only man but apes and butterflies can perceive" (*SM* 21–22). Having dismissed the future, he finds the present and the past left for human consciousness. Indeed, human consciousness is absolutely distinguished from the animal, Nabokov considers, by its special relationship to both present and past. Our consciousness, by being reflexive, "conscious not only of matter but also of its own self" (*Lolita* 262), has a unique involved detachment from the present:

Being aware of being aware of being....if I not only know that I am but also
know that I know it, then I belong to the human species. All the rest follows
– the glory of thought, poetry, a vision of the universe. In that respect, the gap
between ape and man is immeasurably greater than the one between amoeba
and ape. (*SO* 142)

Human consciousness has a special relationship to the past, too, in the capacity
of memory. Completing the remark above, Nabokov declared that the "difference between an ape's memory and human memory is the difference between
an ampersand and the British Museum library."

Nabokov's rage for freedom makes him feel that we are cruelly confined, by
the very nature of our consciousness, to the present moment. Yet at the same
time *within* the present our reflexive consciousness is wonderfully free to share
in all that sense, emotion and thought can offer. Through memory, moreover,
we are further liberated, able to range beyond the present moment at least in
imagination, and when memory is working at its highest so as to be able to
pattern the past Nabokov feels that we can taste the flavor of a consciousness
no longer bound by time.

Nabokov repeatedly stresses that human consciousness is inseparable from
the time in which it dwells, the mobile present of perception. "I can imagine
anything," Van insists (*Ada* 478), yet the mind is quite strictly finite: it operates
only within the present. At no time in one's life can one think to oneself (and
be right): "This is not Now."[18] As Van says, "This nowness is the only reality
we know; it follows the colored nothingness of the no-longer and precedes
the absolute nothingness of the future. Thus, in a quite literal sense, we may
say that conscious human life lasts always only one moment." (549–50)

Because human self-awareness dwells only in the present, the human "sense
of Time is a sense of continuous becoming" (*Ada* 559), a *perpetual* sense of
present being from which self-consciousness cannot advance or retire, coupled with a recognition of the absence of all other moments in which one has
known just this intense feel of presentness, the feeling that *this* is the moment
of my being. Fyodor Godunov-Cherdyntsev suggests the paradox that this
present one cannot stay within but can never step out of is merely an illusion
that is built into the structure of the human mind:

> Our mistaken feeling of time as a kind of growth is a consequence of our finite-
> ness which, being always on the level of the present, implies its constant rise
> between the watery abyss of the past and the aerial abyss of the future. (*Gift*
> 354)

Nabokov strongly suspects that the human sense of becoming and of time
is illusory, for it accentuates the utter difference between all one's past experience and one's self-awareness in the present:

Certain mind pictures have become so adulterated by the concept of "time" that we have come to believe in the actual existence of a permanently moving bright fissure (the point of perception) between our retrospective eternity which we cannot recall and the prospective one which we cannot know. (*BS* 155)

The dwelling of human consciousness within the absurd present is an inescapable confinement: "the prison of time is spherical and without exits." (*SM* 20) This is the greatest of all barriers to the freedom Nabokov longs for. He rages at "the walls of time separating me and my bruised fists from the free world of timelessness" (*SM* 20). The mind is confined in the present and away from the past, from events that have been, from "immobile time" (*LATH* 168). By the nature of human consciousness we are locked away from the vivid being, the rich self-awareness of even the personal past we have lived through.

Nabokov's passion for independence, for untrammeled enjoyment, makes him see the position of consciousness in time as one of humiliating limitation. Yet his exasperation at this limitation comes not from any feeling of the paltriness of the gifts of consciousness, but from a sense of their fantastic richness: he bemoans "the utter degradation, ridicule, and horror of having developed an infinity of sensation and thought within a finite existence" (*SM* 297). Depicting his simultaneous recognition in infancy of selfhood and time, Nabokov writes:

I felt myself plunged abruptly into a radiant and mobile medium that was none other than the pure element of time. One shared it – just as excited bathers share shining seawater – with creatures that were not oneself but that were joined to one by time's common flow, an environment quite different from the spatial world. (*SM* 21)

If our confinement to time is ridiculous, we have an exhilarating freedom of consciousness *within* time, the opportunity to savor all the riches of perception, emotion and thought.

Perhaps no writer has cared as much as Nabokov for the rapture of the senses, the precision of perception, the glory of consciousness in its apprehension of the things of the world. At one moment he is scientific sensualist and poetic pendant: "the little Vaporer fellow [the caterpillar of the Persian Vaporer, a tussock moth], its black coat enlivened all along the back with pointed tufts, red, blue, yellow, of unequal length, like those of a fancy toothbrush treated with certified colors" (*Ada* 55). At another, he wafts the reader back to the curiosity and sweet terror of childhood in a masterpiece of empathetic recreation, using touch, smell, sight and sound to place us wholly within the thudding boy who

> had the fantastic pleasure of creeping through that pitch-dark tunnel, where I lingered a little to listen to the singing in my ears – that lonesome vibration so familiar to small boys in dusty hiding places – and then, in a burst of delicious panic, on rapidly thudding hands and knees I would reach the tunnel's far end, push its cushion away, and be welcomed by a mesh of sunshine on the parquet under the canework of a Viennese chair and two gamesome flies settling by turns. (*SM* 23)

Because Nabokov is interested in the non-human, some poor readers have concluded he is not interested in the human, in human emotions. But it is just because of the inexplicable magnitude of emotion that Nabokov feels he needs to know the place of human life in the cosmos:

> Whenever I start thinking of my love for a person, I am in the habit of immediately drawing radii from my love – from my heart, from the tender nucleus of a personal matter – to monstrously remote points of the universe. Something impels me to measure the consciousness of my love against such unimaginable and incalculable things as...the dreadful pitfalls of eternity, the unknowledgeable beyond the unknown, the helplessness, the cold, the sickening involutions and interpenetrations of space and time.... I must know where I stand, where you and my son stand. (*SM* 296–97)

The quick flicking from feeling to feeling in the short stories, a giant wave of tenderness in *Speak, Memory*, quiet married love and helpless loneliness in *Pale Fire*, unjust misery in *Bend Sinister* or "Signs and Symbols," the wry pathos of a Pnin, the happiness of young Van and Ada, the intricacies of twisted passion, cruelty and real and tender love in Humbert Humbert – these are some of the fascinatingly rich and strange possibilities of emotive consciousness. If Nabokov treats emotion in bizarre, unsettling ways it is because he knows how bizarre and unsettling this tumult of feeling is in "obscenely brief" lives on a "pinpoint planet" (*Ada* 314, 220).

"I trust that my reader...will agree with me that there is nothing more splendid than lone thought" (*Ada* 540). The rapid range, the teasing energy, the metaphoric and metaphysical tumble of Nabokov's works celebrate the munificence of thought even when they show thought unable to keep up with itself:

> Now let us have this quite clear, what is more important to solve: the "outer" problem (space, time, matter, the unknown without) or the "inner" one (life,

thought, love, the unknown within) or again their point of contact (death)? For we agree, do we not, that problems as problems do exist even if the world be something made of nothing within nothing made of something. Or is "outer" and "inner" an illusion too, so that a great mountain may be said to stand a thousand dreams high and hope and terror can be as easily charted as the capes and bays they helped to name? (*BS* 154–55)

Even as Nabokov finds the brief present of awareness cruelly limiting in comparison with the freedom he can imagine, he also appreciates the vast range of the mind's maneuvers *within* the present of consciousness: "I love and revere the present."[19] The narrating voice in any of Nabokov's novels may act as an unnoticed lens, passively observing a scene it feigns not to have created or, caught by a sudden sparkle, it might move in, a magnifying glass now, on a cluster of details. It may then start to take stock of itself perceiving, let slip it is actually creating, wrench itself awkwardly out of the consciousness it has been transparently following or glide unnoticed into another. Or it may withdraw while the scene goes on, and remember or create something quite different, or address itself or anyone else, or watch itself remembering or creating or "[b]eing aware of being aware of being" (*SO* 142). What better way of letting the reader share in the capacity of the mind to delight in the world or itself, to stay within its physical situation or withdraw into the space behind sensation?

Though human consciousness operates only within the present, it has access to the past, through memory operating within the present of consciousness: "I also know that you, and, probably, I, were born, but that does not *prove* we went through the chronal phase called the Past: my Present, my brief span of consciousness, tells me I did" (*Ada* 535). Yet on the other hand the present "is but memory in the making" (*Ada* 559), what we perceive is "a form of memory, even at the moment of its perception" (*Ada* 221). Thus to the extent that our present perception of a particular scene is alert and precise, our chance of being able to recall it accurately in memory is increased and our capacity to transcend the confinement of a later present is enhanced.

Individuals expand the dimensions of their existence not only by being able to recall a particular scene from the past but also by being able to discern the continuity in their memories. For Nabokov, indeed, the very definition of personal identity is the retention of specific memories and the apprehension of their continuity: "'To be' means to know one 'has been'" (*Ada* 559). If personal identity is defined thus, the responsibilities of memory are enormous, the "shaping and strengthening of that *backbone of consciousness*, which is the Time of the strong" (*Ada* 559). The order and exactness of one's memories form the measure of the very degree of one's existence in a way, a horrifying thought:

> Oh, he remembers his old enemies, of course, and two or three books he has read, and how the man thrashed him for falling off a woodpile and crushing to death a couple of chicks: that is, a certain crude mechanism of memory does function in him, but, if the gods were to propose that he synthesize himself out of his memories, with the condition that the synthesized image be rewarded wish immortality, the result would be a dim embryo, an infant born prematurely, a blind and deaf dwarf, in no sense capable of immortality. ("Tyrants Destroyed," *TD* 24)

If the past is accessible to the human mind only through traces available to present consciousness, this does not mean that only the present exists, that the past *ceases to exist*. The inaccessibility of the past seems tantamount to its being in a sense unreal, but it is no way comparable with the inaccessibility of the future. In the future, events do not exist, only possibilities; nothing has come into being. In the past, events *have* come into being, and their inaccessibility to our consciousness is a reflection not on the status of these events but on our consciousness. The master, clutching a pencil with an abraded eraser, sits in his armchair; outside, beyond the balcony, a coot scoots. The moment is real, and it is not less real because in a year's time it is accessible, if at all, only in a mental trace. The past exists all around, Nabokov suggests, but outside our consciousness: "had our organs and orgitrons not been asymmetrical, our view of Time might have been amphitheatric and altogether grand, like ragged night and jagged mountains around a small, twinkling, satisfied hamlet" (*Ada* 539). Or again, "everything is the present situated like a radiance outside our blindness" (*Gift* 354). Thus the past is fully accessible to the ghostly narrators of *Transparent Things*, human consciousnesses that have passed through death. It is not directly accessible to mortal man, but to know through the indirections of memory that we inhabit the past can be to recognize that we share the "deathless reality"[20] – perceivable and perhaps even perceived by some more-than-human consciousness – of a past event.

Nabokov writes: "I witness with pleasure the supreme achievement of memory, which is the masterly use it makes of innate harmonies when gathering to its fold the suspended and wandering tonalities of the past." (*SM* 170) He likes to treat mortal memory, "individual recollection, and its expression in words" (*SM* 24), as the forerunner of a consciousness to which the past is directly accessible and which can endlessly reinvestigate it to discover new harmonies and designs. Such a form of consciousness would satisfy Nabokov's passion for pattern even as it satisfied his love for unhindered freedom.

In his autobiography Nabokov tells of a general, a friend of the family, who in 1904 shows four-year-old Vladimir a disappointing little match trick. In 1919 a man in peasant attire who asks Nabokov's father for a light turns out to be the general in disguise. "What pleases me is the evolution of the match theme.... The following of such thematic designs through one's life should be, I think, the true purpose of autobiography." (*SM* 27) The discovery of pattern of this type not only affords an immediate esthetic thrill but seems to Nabokov to prefigure the powers of an immortal consciousness for whom time did not exist and who could bring to light endless pattern in an always available past. Such arranging of pattern in events, Nabokov feels, is the supreme negation of time and the restrictions it places on consciousness: "I confess I do not believe in time. I like to fold my magic carpet, after use, in such a way as to superimpose one part of the pattern upon another." (*SM* 139) Cincinnatus C., in *Invitation to a Beheading*, uses exactly the same image for the timeless patterning of time. "Not here," he writes, not in *this* world, but

> *there* time takes shape according to one's pleasure, like a figured rug whose folds can be gathered in such a way that two designs will meet – and the rug is once again smoothed out, and you live on, or else superimpose the next image on the last, endlessly, endlessly, with the leisurely concentration of a woman selecting a belt to go with her dress....[21]

Nabokov delights in the freedoms of human consciousness, the unending abundance of the materials with which it can work. But his passionate desire for independence makes him see human consciousness as a very confining state compared with the greater freedoms he can imagine – the freedom, above all, to escape the trap of the present and to enjoy endlessly the riches of time available under such a dispensation. Memory always allows a partial release from ruthless enslavement to the moment, but it is only when memory satisfies his passion for pattern that Nabokov feels he is near to savoring the full freedom of timelessness, consciousness without the degradation of loss.

5. Beyond Consciousness

Nabokov proposes that "if, in the spiral unwinding of things, space warps into something akin to time, and time, in its turn, warps into something akin to thought, then, surely, another dimension follows – a special Space maybe, not the old one, we trust, unless spirals become vicious circles again" (*SM* 301). The new dimension is only a proposition, but it is true that if we want to know the position of human consciousness in the universe we must take into account the possibility of states beyond consciousness. Is human consciousness final in the universe, or is it an arc of a continuing spiral of being? May it even *itself* become, after death, the next arc? Not to know the answers to these questions, Nabokov thinks, is tantamount to gaping dumbfoundedly at life's "complete unreality," at "the marvel of consciousness – that sudden window swinging open on a sunlit landscape amidst the night of non-being."[1]

Nothing could be more surprising than suddenly to discover that the night of non-being was in fact unglimpsed day. But such surprise is essential to Nabokov's thought: the possibility of a sudden shift in understanding that the persistence of human consciousness beyond death would entail, the possibility of a drastically non-human way of seeing the universe that would be open to some higher forms of consciousness. With the unimaginable change in vantage from the human to the non-human, from the mortal to the timeless, everything might be fantastically different. Everything that has seemed to us solid might start to flap in the cosmic breeze, everything that has seemed opaque might become translucent or incandescent, every value we have might be instantly readjusted. The novelist R., whose ghost "actually" writes *Transparent Things*, records on his deathbed that "the favors of death knowledge are infinitely more precious than those of love" (82). "Death knowledge" seems all-deciding indeed after a passage such as this:

> This is the moment when a wave of light suddenly floods the book.... We feel that we are on the brink of some absolute truth, dazzling in its splendour and at the same time almost homely in its perfect simplicity. By an incredible feat of suggestive wording, the author makes us believe that he knows the truth about death and that he is going to tell it. In a moment or two, at the end of this sentence, in the middle of the next, or perhaps a little further still, we shall learn something that will change all our concepts.... "The hardest knot is but a meandering string; tough to the fingernails, but really a matter of lazy and

graceful loopings. The eye undoes it, while clumsy fingers bleed. He (the dying man) was that knot, and he would be untied at once, if he could manage to see and follow the thread. And not only himself, everything would be unravelled – everything that he might imagine in our childish terms of space and time, both being riddles invented by man *as* riddles, and thus coming back to us: the boomerangs of nonsense...."

...And the word, the meaning which appeared is astounding in its simplicity: the greatest surprise being perhaps that in the course of one's earthly existence, with one's brain encompassed by an iron ring; by the close-fitting dream of one's own personality – one had not made by chance that simple mental jerk, which would have set free imprisoned thought.... (*RLSK* 178–79)

What fascinates Nabokov is not the possibility of some specific revelation – he would think anything we could imagine almost certain to be wrong (and too dull) *because* imaginable – but the shock of the intensity and completeness of the change from "imprisoned" human thought.

Imprisoned indeed: man's knowledge of the universe he inhabits, Nabokov feels, is harshly confined. We can perceive our own and previous twists of the spiral of being – space, time, consciousness – but even these remain beyond our comprehension: "We shall never know the origin of life, or the meaning of life, or the nature of space and time, or the nature of nature, or the nature of thought" (*SO* 45). We do not know why the visible universe exists, what are the conditions of its existing, or what role chance and design have in the whole. Fyodor states the case with delightful dismissiveness: "The absurdity at which searching thought arrives is only a natural, generic sign of its belonging to man, and striving to obtain an answer is the same as demanding of chicken broth that it began [*sic*] to cluck." (*Gift* 354) Human reasoning is inevitably circular: "human thoughts, admirably coordinated though they may be, cannot escape the confines of their private circle of hell" (*KQK* 255). Adam Falter, who has become quite non-human after having had the essence of things revealed to him, tells his interlocutor: "Logical reasoning may be a most convenient means of mental communication for covering short distances, but the curvature of the earth, alas, is reflected even in logic...logical development inexorably becomes an envelopment."[2]

We cannot reason outside the circle set by the limits of our being or know what sort of consciousness could "enjoy other varieties of being and dreaming, beyond man's notion of Time" (*Ada* 536) or how human life might appear to a consciousness outside the bounds of human thought. But that we know nothing of what lies outside our circular cell need not mean that there is nothing there. There may be nothing beyond, but it is just as possible that our utter ignorance of states transcending our own is merely another instance of our confinement. Nabokov considers there is no need for the possibility of other states of being to depend on notions humanity's limited thought can form.

Surely, Nabokov asks, it is imperative for us to know what we cannot know: whether other states of being exist. If there are states of being beyond the restrictions of human consciousness and beyond human apprehension, do we participate in them after death? Though he knows we cannot answer this, his passion for the fullest freedom makes him imagine what a "yes" to this question might mean. If remote states of being exist, do they affect our world? Here Nabokov's love of pattern comes into play, and he throws all his scientific curiosity and his artistic inventiveness into exploring how the pattern of our lives might be undecipherable evidence of the participation of the beyond. But while he is a prolific producer of possible, often enticing, sometimes disconcerting, answers to these humanly unanswerable questions, he never disregards the limits of the knowable.

Let us consider the first of these questions, whether there is human participation in a freer state of consciousness, "the free world of timelessness" (*SM* 20) outside our confinement to the conscious present and to mortality. Nabokov sees human consciousness as a circular prison, a vicious circle, but he sees the possibility of going beyond it: "The spiral is a spiritualized circle. In the spiral form, the circle, uncoiled, unwound, has ceased to be vicious; it has been set free." (*SM* 275) A peep past the brain's iron ring might come in the momentary insight of ecstasy, and a final breaking free in death – "not the crude anguish of physical death but the incomparable pangs of the mysterious mental maneuver needed to pass from one state of being to another" (*TT* 104). And if a state beyond death cannot be examined by the reason, it can be explored by the imagination.

Perhaps at special moments the mind can see beyond itself, perhaps "the hereafter stands slightly ajar in the dark" (*LATH* 26). Nabokov writes of "shadows linking our state of existence to those other states we dimly apprehend in our rare moments of irrational perception" (*NG* 145). One should not be misled by the "dimly" and the "irrational" here: Nabokov is no infatuate of mystic fog, and his "irrational perception" is not less than rational, but superrational, lucidity and beyond. A possible hint of something larger than human consciousness is likely to come only when consciousness is already working at its alertest, when mystery is met by acuteness: "It is certainly not then – not in dreams – but when one is wide awake, at moments of robust joy and achievement, on the highest terrace of consciousness, that mortality has a chance to peer beyond its own limits". (*SM* 50)

When perception, emotion or thought are pulsing through one's being in a surge of ecstasy, love or inspiration the spirit can find "loopholes, translucences in the world's finest texture...and stealthily into the eternal pass through" ("How I love You," *PP* 81)[3] Nabokov admits that such an intimation of something beyond mortality's limits and beyond ordinary apprehension cannot be clear, yet its intensity carries inexplicable conviction: "although nothing much can be seen through the mist, there is somehow the blissful feeling that one is looking in the right direction" (SM 50).

But whatever irrational and intense yet very subjective perception suggests, death remains an unpromising blank to our reason. Falter in "Ultima Thule" says:

> For look what happens in the case of the poor little human mind. Either it has no way to express what awaits you – I mean, us – after death...or, on the contrary, death *can* be imagined, and then one's reason naturally adopts not the notion of eternal life, an unknown entity, incongruent with anything terrestrial, but precisely that which seems more probable – the familiar darkness of stupor. (*RB* 177)

Nabokov sees both alternatives clearly. Death may be mere nullity, "blank and black, an everlasting nonlastingness" (*Ada* 585), or it may be something outside human time, and hence "an unknown entity, incongruent with anything terrestrial": "Death...is perhaps a surprise, perhaps nothing."[4]

If death is the mere blank of non-existence, Van Veen muses, "what courage man must have had to go through that commonplace again and again and not give up the rigmarole of accumulating again and again the riches of consciousness that will be snatched away!" (*Ada* 585) But with the help of two of his favorite writers, Pierre Delalande (1768–1849) and Fyodor Godunov-Cherdyntsev, both his own inventions, Nabokov suggests how it might be that we could see nothing of a real something beyond death. If we cannot see past death, perhaps it is simply because life reflects only life, and death is a step outside life:

> I know that death in itself is in no way connected with the topography of the hereafter, for a door is merely the exit from the house and not a part of its surroundings, like a tree or a hill. One has to get out somehow, "but I refuse to see in a door more than a hole, and carpenter's job" (*Delalande, Discours sur les ombres*, p. 45).... The other world surrounds us always and is not at all at the end of some pilgrimage. In our earthly house, windows are replaced by mirrors; the door, until a given time, is closed; but air comes in through the cracks. (*Gift* 321–22)

In an exceptional spiritual state, in a rare systole of the soul, we may feel our utter ignorance of the existence of something beyond consciousness to be just slightly relieved. Air does come in through the cracks, Nabokov suggests, "penetrating our being with the beyond's fresh breath" (*SO* 227), but we remain locked within the house of life, we cannot see out; the mirrors reflect ourselves and our surroundings, we have no access to the outside. Nabokov seethes at being under house arrest for life and sneaks outside in imagination. Cincinnatus C., sentenced to death, mutters to his executioner:

> "You speak of escape.... I think, I surmise, that there is someone else too who is concerned with it..."
> He sighed and paused.
> "This is curious," said M'sieur Pierre. "what are these hopes, and who is this savior?"
> "Imagination," replied Cincinnatus. (*Invitation to a Beheading*, 114)

Imagination is for Nabokov the only means to the complete otherness that a persistence of consciousness beyond death would entail. But the imagination he has in mind is not one spurred by faith and disregarding the criticism of reason. He explicitly mocks such feebleness:

> There exists an old rule – so old and trite that I blush to mention it. Let me twist it into a jingle – to stylize the staleness:
>
> > The I of the book
> > Cannot die in the book.
>
> I am speaking of serious novels, naturally. In so-called *Planchette-Fiction* the unruffled narrator, after describing his own dissolution, can continue thus: "I found myself standing on a staircase of onyx before a great gate of gold in a crowd of other bald-headed angels...."
> Cartoon stuff, folklore rubbish, hilarious atavistic respect for precious minerals! (*LATH* 239)

Reason tells us that mortal life provides no means to conceiving "eternal life...a moist 'yes' would suggest that you accept the existence of an international heaven which your reason cannot fail to doubt." ("Ultima Thule," *RB* 177–78) Nabokov, who admits that "in my metaphysics, I am a confirmed non-unionist and have no use for organized tours through anthropomorphic paradises" (*SM* 297), points out the absurdities of such sentimental Floridas of the hereafter. There is, for example, the problem of the relationship between the ever-changing mortal condition and the eternal one. What state of the mortal entity could be eternalized?

> How can a man who trusts in his reason admit, for instance, that someone who is dead drunk and dies while sound asleep from a chance external cause – thus losing by chance what he no longer really possessed – again acquires the ability

to reason and feel thanks to the mere extension, consolidation and perfection
of his unfortunate condition? ("Ultima Thule," *RB* 177)

Or as John Shade puts it,

> What moment in the gradual decay
> Does resurrection choose? What year? What day?
> (*PF* 40, ll.209–10)

Then there is the problem of mortal interpersonal relationships:

> timelessness is bound to disarrange
> Schedules of sentiment, we give advice
> To widower. He has been married twice:
> He meets his wives; both loved, both loving, both
> Jealous of one another...
> ....
> How to begin? which first to kiss?
> (*PF* 54, ll.568–81)

Van Veen, translating Shade's lines, stops to ponder both relational problems:

> One is free to imagine any type of hereafter, of course: the generalized paradise
> promised by Oriental prophets and poets, or an individual combination; but
> the work of fancy is handicapped – to a quite hopeless extent – by a logical
> ban: you cannot bring your friends along – or your enemies for that matter
> – to the party. The transportation of all our remembered relationships into an
> Elysian life inevitably turns it into a second-rate continuation of our marvelous
> mortality. Only a Chinaman or a retarded child can imagine being met, in that
> Next-Installment World, to the accompaniment of all sorts of tail-wagging and
> groveling of welcome, by the mosquito executed eighty years ago upon one's
> bare leg, which has been amputated since then and now, in the wake of the
> gesticulating mosquito, comes back, stomp, stomp, stomp, here I am, stick
> me on. (*Ada* 586)

But just because it can detect the absurdity of merely eternalizing human
life, reason suggests that the imagination should discard its anthropomorphic
confines and give itself free reign. Even the imagination's wildest flights would
be unlikely to be as rich and strange as a consciousness beyond ours:

> It isn't that we dream too wild a dream;
> The trouble is we do not make it seem
> Sufficiently unlikely; for the most
> We can think up is a domestic ghost. (*PF* 41, ll.227–301)

John Shade captures perfectly the challenge and the excitement:

> Yet, *if* prior to life we had
> Been able to imagine life, what mad,
> Impossible, unutterably weird,
> Wonderful nonsense it might have appeared!
> (*PF* 40–41, ll.217–20)

Or, as he says in conversation: "Life is a great surprise. I do not see why death should not be an even greater one." (*PF* 225)

Nabokov's imagination is at its most fertile in inventing these "greater surprises". Since we know nothing of the nature of electricity, John Shade says, why not suppose that "the gentle dead...In tungsten filaments abide":

> And maybe Shakespeare floods a whole
> Town with innumerable lights,
> And Shelley's incandescent soul
> Lures the pale moths of starless nights.
> (*PF* 192)

In a rather less charming vein Humbert tells Quilty just before killing him that "The hereafter for all we know may be an eternal state of excruciating insanity" (*Lolita* 299). Even stranger than the straightforwardly-offered metaphysical possibilities and the easy variety of metaphor are the bizarre manipulations of structure and point of view: the rather fluid identities, all ghosts of dead characters in the novel, and somehow concentrated in R., who write *Transparent Things* (and submit it to a mortal publisher?), or the two dead girls in "The Vane Sisters" who influence the narrator (unbeknownst to him) to think about the possibilities of other forms of consciousness (he remains unconvinced) and actually dictate the story's last paragraph to him without his being able to discern their participation. Perhaps even more bizarre is the case of "Ultima Thule." Sineusov, the narrator, is writing a letter (the story itself) to his wife, who has died, six months pregnant, of tuberculosis of the throat. Sineusov realizes how futile his letter is, yet still tells his inaccessible wife of the strange case of Adam Falter, his quondam tutor, who has become utterly non-human after having had the essence of things revealed to him (this is all quite convincing within the story). Sineusov seems not to realize that Falter's sudden change is an eerie transmutation of the child his own dead wife was to have borne, and the sign he had so fervently hoped for from that dead woman.

Scrupulously avoiding the logical absurdity of eternalizing the necessarily finite condition of human consciousness, Nabokov satisfies his desire for freedom by imagining the various limitations of the mind transcended in

death. Death could offer us a completely new relation to time: freedom from
our being pegged to the present, freedom of access to the whole of the past.
The spectral narrators of *Transparent Things* can enjoy direct participation in
whatever has happened, so that a plain pencil, drab enough in the world of
space, becomes a fantastic character for them in the pageant of time:

> Going back a number of seasons (not as far, though, as Shakespeare's birth year
> when pencil lead was discovered) and then picking up the thing's story again
> in the now direction, we see graphite, ground very fine, being mixed with moist
> clay by young girls and old men.... It is now being cut into the lengths required
> for these particular pencils (we glimpse the cutter, old Elias Borrowdale, and
> are about to mouse up his forearm on a side trip of inspection but we stop...).
> (7)

Death could free the senses from the "straightjacket of the flesh,"[5] from
the sense-limits of the human body: "the liberation of the soul from the
eye-sockets of the flesh and our transformation into one complete and free
eye, which can simultaneously see in all directions" (*Gift* 322). The ghosts of
Transparent Things can see through matter, discerning "A mess of sprouts and
mashed potatoes...performing hand-over-fist evolutions in Person's entrails"
(101). But death might change our apprehension of the material world in
more drastic fashion. Nabokov reveres the senses and is justly famous for his
love of the visual, but he asks

> is visibility really as dominant as that in all imaginable knowledge of Nature?
> Though I personally would be perfectly satisfied to spend the whole of eternity
> gazing at a blue hill or a butterfly, I would feel the poorer if I accepted the
> idea of there not existing still more vivid means of knowing butterflies and
> hills.[6]

Delalande, therefore, suggests death might bring "a supersensory insight into
the world" (*Gift* 322).

Nabokov recognizes personality – "personality consisting mainly of the
shadows of its own prison bars" (*PF* 227) – as another of the great limitations
on human consciousness. He writes of V. Sirin, his pseudonymous self, that
his "best works are those in which he condemns his people to the solitary
confinement of their souls.'" In death "the close-fitting dream of one's own
personality" (*RLSK* 179) might be transcended: "The hereafter may be the full
ability of consciously living in any chosen soul, in any number of souls, all of
them unconscious of their interchangeable burden." (*RLSK* 204–05)

Finally, perhaps, the incapacity of man's sense-bound, time-bound, reasoning and mortal consciousness to understand existence, to solve the riddle of

being, may also be overcome. For transparent things "there are no mysteries now" (22). Or as Fyodor puts it: "you will understand when you are big"
(*Gift* 354).

Nabokov's passion for unlimited freedom sharpens his sense of the limits of
human knowledge and the very conditions of human existence: he *must* find
out what he knows it is impossible to know, whether human consciousness
warps into something else beyond death. His reason tells him that the medium
of his existence is "time with consciousness" and suggests that consciousness
altered in death would become "consciousness without time – some still
higher state" (*SO* 30); but it also tells him that an eternalization of anything
resembling his mortal life is logically impossible. Something drastically *other*
than human life, perhaps, is possible, and imagination may be the shadow of
this otherness. Feeling "locked up" "in this hive" of space and time (*PF* 40),
Nabokov revels in the power of imagination to range beyond the hive of space
and time, beyond the closed house of life, to schedule its own celebrations
"for Independence Day in Hades" (*PF* 226).

If Nabokov's longing for the utmost freedom sends him off to explore the
possibility of human consciousness transcending death, his fascination with
pattern prompts him to ponder how deeply design might be ingrained in
things, and whether the elusive presence of design might indicate the possible participation of higher forms of consciousness in the ordinary world of
our experience.

The dizziness of moments of rare exhilaration always seems importunate:
what is it here that's causing such happiness? All that I see appears more vivid
than anything that merely occupies space and time. Behind the bright imper-
viousness of the world, animation seems to lurk, almost as if it were signaling
to me through the very opacity of matter:

> Where shall I put all these gifts with which the summer morning rewards me –
> and only me? Save them up for future books? Use them immediately for a
> practical handbook: *How to Be Happy?* Or getting deeper, to the bottom of things:
> understand what is concealed behind all this, behind the play, the sparkle, the
> thick, green grease-paint of the foliage? For there really is something, there is
> something! And one wants to offer thanks but there is no one to thank. The list
> of donations already made: 10,000 days – from Person Unknown. (*Gift* 340)

"From Person Unknown": it is no small part of the ecstasy that it seems to
derive from a source – a quite undefinable source – outside me:

> And the highest enjoyment of timelessness – in a landscape selected at random
> – is when I stand among rare butterflies and their food plants. This is ecstasy,
> and behind the ecstasy is something else, which is hard to explain. It is like a

momentary vacuum into which rushes all that I love. A sense of oneness with sun and stone. A thrill of gratitude to whom it may concern – to the contrapuntal genius of human fate or to tender ghosts humoring a lucky mortal. (*SM* 139)

Like us all, Nabokov is fascinated by the momentary pressure of ecstasy, the urgent hints of something behind the visible, "behind the play, the sparkle, the thick green grease-paint." He associates this with the shock of discovering inexplicable design, for in both cases there is the same gasp of surprise at the intimation of an undefinable source. But in a manner very much his own he goes on to probe this inkling of design, questioning what it might mean to discern a pattern that seems greater than accident, blind necessity or natural law could account for – a pattern invented, perhaps, like natural mimicry, "by some waggish artist precisely for the intelligent eyes of man" (*Gift* 122).

Nabokov records how ecstasy and the inkling of design can fuse in a "chance" event that seems so well patterned it is hard not to assign it to a patterner. Fyodor watches five nuns, each stooping in turn to pluck a flower. The whole is like a ballet: "it all looked so much like a staged scene – and how much skill there was in everything, what an infinity of grace and art, what a director lurked behind the pines, how well everything was calculated" (*Gift* 356). In his own person Nabokov expresses the same amazement at the designedness of life: "l'esprit divin semble maintenant mieux installé dans le monde…quel est cet artiste qui en passant change tout à coup la vie en un petit chef-d'oeuvre…. J'ai vu des comédies dirigées par quelque génie invisible…."[8] Nabokov's attribution of the patterned scenes to a director behind the pines, to *quelque génie invisible*, is of course only sportive, a playful celebration of the sheer variety of the world, of the fact that some of its innumerable casual combinations chance to seem planned.

But when he considers not a single event but the patterns formed through a whole life Nabokov conveys a real sense that there might well be planning somewhere, if we only knew how to distinguish such plans. In his own autobiography he seeks for the "razvitie i povtorenie taynïh tem v yavnoy sud'be,"[9] "the development and repetition of the secret themes of an evident fate." Fyodor in *The Gift* models his whole novel on what he calls the "ingenious" patterns and deceptions that "fate" or "destiny" has woven into his own life (375–76). In *Pale Fire* John Shade reveals that the "topsy-turvical coincidence" of his life is "Not flimsy nonsense, but a web of sense" (63, ll.809, 810), that he has

> A feeling of fantastically planned.
> Richly rhymed life.
> (68, ll.969–70)

It is surely no coincidence that the two characters in Nabokov's fiction who feel most acutely the richness and mystery of the patterning of their lives are the two characters closest to their maker in talent and temper and artistic independence.

It is quite possible that there are states of consciousness other than the human and that even the very pattern of the world bears witness to this, if we knew how to read the signs correctly. In Sebastian Knight's *The Doubtful Asphodel* it is imagined that in death a man finds the answer to all things

> written all over the world he had known: it was like a traveller realising that the wild country he surveys is not an accidental assembly of natural phenomena, but the page in a book where these mountains and forests, and fields, and rivers are disposed in such a way as to form a coherent sentence....the meaning of all things shone through their shapes....(*RLSK* 178–79)

Imagining yet another afterlife, Nabokov asks:

> who can care
> for a world of omnipotent vision,
> if nothing is monogrammed there?
> ("Oculus," *PP* 101)

Yet if other states of consciousness are somehow present and their designs are somehow manifest in the world of space and time, neither their presence nor their patterns are accessible to us.

Many characters in Nabokov's fiction imagine, for instance, that the dead may be hovering over them, trying to communicate with them through the things of space and time:

> Martin...tried to comprehend his father's death and to catch a wisp of posthumous tenderness in the dark of the room. He...even made certain experiments: if, right now, a board in the floor creaks or there is a knock of some kind, that means he hears me and responds.[11]

After his mother's death, "Van tortured himself with thoughts of insufficient filial affection....He looked around, making wild amends, willing her spirit to give him an equivocal, and indeed all-deciding, sign of continued being behind the veil of time, beyond the flesh of space. But no response came, not a petal fell on his bench, not a gnat touched his hand." (*Ada* 452) The story "Ultima Thule" is a letter written by Sineusov to his dead wife. He knows just how pitiful his position is: "Are you able to hear me? That's from a banal questionnaire, which ghosts do not answer." (*RB* 150) But "[j]ust in case," he says, "I am keeping all the windows and doors of life wide open, even though

I sense that you will not condescend to the time-honored ways of apparitions." (182) He notes that "never once since you died have you appeared in
my dreams. Perhaps the authorities intercept you, or you yourself avoid such
prison visits with me." (151) Nabokov will not permit any "unequivocal, and
indeed all-deciding sign," communication even with a form of consciousness
still only one stage removed from the human and where a strong "personal"
motive is involved.

Similarly he rules out the possibility of the unequivocal human decipher-
ment of a consciously designed pattern in the visible universe. In a delirium
Timofey Pnin tries desperately to determine the exact recurrences of the
pattern on his wallpaper:

> It stood to reason that if the evil designer – the destroyer of minds, the friend
> of fever – had concealed the key of the pattern with such monstrous care, that
> key must be as precious as life itself and, when found, would regain for Timofey
> Pnin his everyday health, his everyday world.... (*Pnin* 23)

It is only in delirium that one could think that the visible world does have a
pattern that might be humanly graspable. Or in outright madness, as in "Signs
and Symbols," where the "incurably deranged"[12] son imagines

> that everything happening around him is a veiled reference to his personality
> and existence.... Clouds in the staring sky transmit to one another, by means of
> slow signs, incredibly detailed information regarding him.... Pebbles or stains
> or sun flecks form patterns representing in some awful way messages which
> he must intercept. Everything is a cipher and of everything he is the theme.
> (*Nabokov's Dozen* 69)

From within the confines of human nature we cannot know whether other
states of consciousness are present or if their designs are somehow hidden
in our world. But, proposes Nabokov, we can imagine we are looking from
the other side, from beyond the human. He envisages more-than-human
consciousnesses delighting in a world in which they can discern or create
endless new patterns, in which they participate by means of subtle and complex designs.

Sensing that his life is "fantastically planned," John Shade feels that he can
understand the way things are arranged only by arranging things himself:

> I feel I understand
> Existence, or at least a minute part
> Of my existence, only through my art.
> In terms of combinational delight;
> And if my private universe scans right

So does the verse of galaxies divine....
(*PF* 68–69, ll.970–75)

He suspects that there is point and pattern to existence beyond his knowledge. In coming to know the thrills of "combinational delight," he surmises, he can sample the sort of pleasure higher natures than ours might have in watching over our sphere of existence. By imaginatively imitating the role of attendant spirit, fate or god, he savors the special pleasures of design, and perhaps discerns the hidden justification of the game of life:

> It sufficed that I in life could find
> Some kind of link-and-bobolink, some kind
> Of correlated pattern in the game,
> Plexed artistry, and something of the same
> Pleasure in it as they who played it found.
> It did not matter who they were. No sound,
> No furtive light came from their involute
> Abode, but there they were, aloof and mute,
> Playing a game of worlds....
> (*PF* 63, ll.811–19)

Shade's "it did not matter who they were" echoes Nabokov's own "to whom it may concern" and Fyodor's "from Person Unknown." If some higher force were shaping our lives, we could not expect to understand its nature, but in imaginatively usurping its functions we might at least see why such a shaping of life would have point and pleasure.

The simplest kind of combinational delight, the nearest to the human, might be that made possible when consciousness by shuffling off mortality would gain unlimited access to the past whose designs could be sought out and brought into focus – as they are, for instance, by the spectral narrators of *Transparent Things*, who fold each of Hugh Persons's earlier trips to Switzerland within the ongoing time of the present one. No longer confined to the imperfectly preserved traces of a personal past, they can revisit another's history. Just for the fun of the pattern, too, they even fold into one of these earlier trips, during which Hugh engages a prostitute, a distant part of the past, the trip to Switzerland of "a minor Dostoevski" (*SO* 195) who happens to have briefly inhabited the same room as Hugh and whore.

It would be rather more difficult for post-mortal consciousness to participate in or leave its pattern upon the present. *Transparent Things* opens thus: "Here's the person I want. Hullo person! Doesn't hear me."(1) The spectral narrator is trying to catch Hugh Person's attention but fails. Nabokov will not allow such direct, much too human communication to succeed: "Direct interference in a person's life does not enter our scope of activity." (*TT* 92)

But a much more oblique kind of participation, an unrecognized communication," a silent patterning, may be possible. Cynthia Vane, in "The Vane Sisters," has evolved a "theory of intervenient auras": "Fundamentally there was nothing particularly new about her private creed since it presupposed a fairly conventional hereafter, a silent solarium of immortal souls (spliced with mortal antecedents) whose main recreation consisted of periodical hoverings over the dear quick." (*TD* 227) After her sister Sybil commits suicide, Cynthia, whose "ridiculous fondness for spiritualism" (231) the narrator openly scorns, thinks she can detect in her life the intermittent influence of Sybil's spirit. The narrator has lost touch with Cynthia for some years when, owing to an unlikely chain of circumstances, he happens to hear of her death. The chain begins thus: while the narrator is out strolling one day, his attention is caught by the eerily beautiful shadows of icicle drips. They deflect him from his normal path as he pursues them from eave to eave, street to street, for several hours:

> finally the sequence of observed and observant things brought me, at my usual eating time, to a street so distant from my usual eating place that I decided to try a restaurant which stood on the fringe of the town. (220)

He is just leaving when the red tinge (from a neon light) in the shadow of a parking meter makes him dawdle: he anticipates more visual treats, perhaps a blue shadow from blue neon lights. At this moment another person whom he has not seen in years (and who is merely passing through the town) chances upon him and tells him of Cynthia's death. The news perturbs him. That night, he feels apprehensive in the dark, but decides "to fight Cynthia. I reviewed in thought the modern era of apparitions...." (236). He cannot get to sleep until dawn, when he has "a dream that somehow was full of Cynthia" (237). Yet he finds the dream disappointing. Brave in daylight, he would like to be able to discern Cynthia clearly in the dream. But, he concludes,

> I could isolate, consciously, little. Everything seemed blurred, yellow-clouded, yielding nothing tangible. Her inept acrostics, maudlin evasions, theopathies – every recollection formed ripples of mysterious meaning. Everything seemed yellowly blurred, illusive, lost. (238)

The initial letters of this paragraph form an acrostic message: "ICICLES BY CYNTHIA. METER FROM ME, SYBIL."

Cynthia's theory of "intervenient auras," then, has been verified, yet the narrator, in providing the proof, remains unaware of it. Dead Cynthia and Sybil have led the narrator to meet the person who can tell him of Cynthia's death; they have shaped his dream but kept it elusive; and they have been rigorous muses in dictating their signature into the story's final paragraph. They have imposed their pattern upon the narrator's life, they have laid claim to the pattern as theirs in another pattern to which the narrator does not have the key – and which, moreover, is his very expression of his failure to grasp their participation. The Vane sisters have respected the narrator's independence, his characteristic visual curiosity, at the same time, paradoxically, as they have imposed their undeviating design on his life.

Nabokov is willing to suppose that human life may be shaped by forms of consciousness far beyond his "transparent things" or the inhabitants of Cynthia Vane's "conventional hereafter" – far beyond anything like human time and with insight into and even control over the future.

He stresses that from the human point of view the patterns of "fate" can be seen only in retrospect and that it is impossible to attribute such patterns to conscious etiology. A single accident may make the casual appear ominously patterned: in "Spring in Fialta," Nina dies when her car crashes into a circus truck, and suddenly the strangely insistent circus posters previously noticed become awesomely fatidic. Or the very "failure" of fate to impose immediate control on events may seem to form part of fate's pattern, of "the feigned naïveté so typical of Fate, when meaning business" (*SM* 229), as in *The Gift* and in Sebastian Knight's *Success*.

But pattern in events may be so distinct that it suggests the deliberate, fore-planned artificing of human lives, even if this artifice employs chance and free will and the particulars of personality as its tools. In *The Defense* Luzhin "goes mad when chess combinations pervade the actual pattern of his existence."[13] Nabokov acts as Grandmaster Fate:

> I greatly enjoyed taking advantage of this or that image and scene to introduce a fatal pattern into Luzhin's life and to endow the description of...a sequence of humdrum events, with the semblance...of a regular chess attack demolishing the innermost elements of the poor fellow's sanity.[14]

So tightly controlled a patterning of events (which we may not notice fully in life amongst the welter of evanescent details) obviously presupposes a capacity to arrange future events. Such a capacity in turn presupposes a consciousness enormously superior to our own. In *Transparent Things* the phantomic narrators have a much more than human ability to *recognize* time's patterns, but as they begin recording the events with which the book opens, even they do not know what the events which close it will be. They do not create fatidic design, though they can highlight the pattern of the past. They write:

> Perhaps if the future existed, concretely and individually, as something that could be discerned by a better brain, the past would not be so seductive: its demands would be balanced by those of the future. Persons might then strad-

dle the middle stretch of the seesaw when considering this or that object. It might be fun. (1)

But behind *Transparent Things* there *is* a "better brain" that discerns the future. This force, far beyond even the more-than-human consciousnesses of the narrators, knows, even invents, the future; it patterns the deadly fires and falls and even the feints of fate. Nabokov has fictionally usurped the role of a foreknowing providence.

John Shade does the same, but acting within the real details of his own past. He senses the unfathomable design of the "contrapuntal theme" in his own life and feels it may be the key to his life, a source of mysterious satisfaction to higher beings. He has no idea of the beings that might have such control over events:

> No furtive light came from their involute
> Abode, but there they were, aloof and mute.
> Playing a game of worlds, promoting pawns
> To ivory unicorns and ebon fauns....
> (*PF* 63, ll.817–20)

Nevertheless, he resolves to imitate these powers:

> Coordinating these
> Events and objects with remote events
> And vanished objects. Making ornaments
> Of accidents and possibilities.
> (*PF* 63, ll.826–29)

Thus in Canto Two Shade heavy-handedly orchestrates a dreadful night from the past. Knowing the elapsed events, he presents them now as if he were designing them all in advance, as if he were Fate itself composing the elaborate counterpoint of events. The whole calamity seems to have been meticulously foreplanned purely for the plangent ironies of the counterpoint in which Shade juxtaposes his uncomely daughter's last night (blind date, humiliation, suicide by drowning) and the tense banality of her parents' watching television to fill the time until Hazel's never-eventuating return:

> Oh, switch it off! And as life snapped we saw
> A pinhead light dwindle and die in black
> Infinity.

> *Out of his lakeside shack*
> *A watchman, Father Time, all gray and bent,*
> *Emerged with his uneasy dog and went*
> *Along the reedy bank. He came too late.*
> (*PF* 50, ll.472–77)

Fate seems to have fore-arranged all this for the very purpose of the poignancy and tenderness of the loss.[15]

Nabokov, like Shade, deliberately and pointedly impersonates fate. Like Shade he realizes that any power which could pattern human lives would have to be far beyond the human, beyond the fathoming of reason. But, he feels, the imagination might be able to imitate this power and create a "correlated pattern in the game," thereby, perhaps, sharing "something of the same pleasure in [the patterned game of life] as those who played it found." Nabokov's acting as fate is not merely the normal privilege of a novelist to invent his events: in those novels where pattern in human lives is a major concern, his role is deliberately and specifically intrusive. Nor is his handling of fate a mere disclosure of the controlling hand of the novelist, a revelation or celebration of the novelist's powers. On the contrary, he precisely alters the usual powers of the novelist to demonstrate how design in human lives might work.[16]

By manipulating the power of fate, Nabokov suggests the possibility of design in human affairs without suggesting more about a putative designer than that his participation in the world of our events would be totally out of the realm of our being, as a novelist is "out of" his invented world, forever beyond his characters, and that the rules governing his participation would bear no relationship to the rules of human conduct, of our "real, or at least responsible, life" (*Ada* 97).

The ethical irresponsibility of the architects of fate is a key hypothesis in Nabokov's examination of the possible patterning of human life. Nabokov of course does not deny the ethical responsibility of human conduct[17] or that there are moral responsibilities in an artist's work.[18] But he does suggest that if there were "architects of fate," their obligation to the human lives they pattern might be the same (none at all) as the obligation of a human artist to the characters he has invented. An artist of fate might employ the responsibility of his characters. He might create his own ends as different from the ends of human actions as a writer's choices in inventing his narrative differ from his characters' choices in enacting the narrative. Thus the point of *Laughter in the Dark* is the contrast between the elaborate artistry of fate (the key element of whose pattern is the blinding of Albinus Kretschmar) and the revoltingly evil "artistry" of Axel Rex, who toys with blind Kretschmar's mistress, money, faith and sanity. The purpose of the cruelty in fate's pattern is to elicit an aghast tenderness for Kretschmar, an inconsiderate and unattractive fool, and to elicit horror at the vileness of the talented Rex. It has nothing whatever in common with the purpose of the nauseating designs Rex weaves around his live prey.

Nabokov remains always aware that with some sudden shift in viewpoint – say, from the level of the characters to that of the reader, or from the human to the non-human, from the mortal to the immortal – everything may change, every value and significance may be reassessed in a flash. Though in "real, or at least responsible, life" human responsibility and human emotions matter, must matter, more than anything, perhaps they do not really count in a more ultimate view: "But perhaps what matters is not at all human sufferings and joys, but the play of shadows and light on a living body, the harmony of tri-fles..."[19] Sineusov addresses his dead wife:

> My angel, oh my angel, perhaps our whole earthly existence is now but a pun to you, or a grotesque rhyme. something like "dental" and "transcendental" (remember?) and the true meaning of reality, of that piercing term, purged of all our strange, dreamy, masquerade interpretations, now sounds so pure and sweet that you, angel, find it amusing that we could have taken the dream seriously. ("Ultima Thule," *RB* 153–54)

Or, as Sebastian Knight sketches it, after death

> "many ideas and events which had seemed of the utmost importance dwindled not to insignificance, for nothing could be insignificant now, but to the same size which other ideas and events, once denied any importance, now attained." Thus, such shining giants of our brain as science, art or religion fell out of the familiar scheme of their classification, and joining hands, were mixed and joy-fully levelled. (*RLSK* 179)

But surely even with a radical change of perspective the notion of there being a pattern of human lives is rather repugnant? The narrator in "The Vane Sisters" asks: "And what about God? Did or did not people who would resent any omnipotent dictator on earth look forward to one in heaven?" (*TD* 228)

But when John Shade recognizes pattern worked into his own life he finds "something of the same pleasure in it as they who played it found," and Nabokov, too, is more delighted than appalled.

If our lives were patterned by a consciousness far greater than ours, it need mean no diminution of the mortal value of our lives. We feel ourselves free to choose, we are responsible, the future does not exist for us or even (as the narrators in *Transparent Things* show) for any imaginable extension of human consciousness. If our lives are patterned by a force beyond ourselves, that force would seem to create its patterns, as a good novelist does, through individual human freedom.

The patterning of one's life not only need not diminish its human value, its value visible from within mortality, but it might also reveal a resplendent worth to the more than mortal gaze. Nabokov conceives how wonderful it might be to see one's life from above, to glimpse suddenly the complex design of the whole. In *Pale Fire* Kinbote quotes and Nabokov gleefully appropriates as an apt and serendipitous expression of his own thoughts a passage from the *Letters of Franklin Lane*. Lane imagines what satisfaction it would be, in "that other land," for one to

> "take, like reins from between his fingers, the long ribbon of man's life and trace it through the mystifying maze of all the wonderful adventure....The crooked made straight. The Daedalian plan simplified by a look from above – smeared out as is were by the splotch of some master thumb that made the whole involuted, boggling thing one beautiful straight line." (*PF* 261)[20]

It would be relief and bliss, Nabokov anticipates, to find that even the muddle and pain of one's life had had a value and a pattern for some transcendent imagination, a purpose and harmony necessarily hidden at the human level. In *Bend Sinister* it is bungling ineptitude, apparently anything but design, that increases Krug's torture beyond unbearableness, and it is an "infinite relief" (210) when "in a sudden moonburst of madness" he "understands that he is in good hands" (*BS* xiv), that his destiny is being controlled by a being far beyond himself, that the misery of his fate is designed *with* an intense tenderness to show "the torture an intense tenderness is subjected to" (*BS* x). Compare this with Nabokov's remark in the Foreword to *The Eye*:

> The forces of imagination which, in the long run, are the forces of good remain steadfastly on Smurov's side, and the very bitterness of tortured love proves so be as intoxicating and bracing as would be its most ecstatic requital.[21]

Shade, too, feels the tender interest of the forces of imagination in his life, a sense of pattern even behind the anguish of his own loss, and from that "something of the same pleasure in it as those who played it found." For, to twist Nabokov's most famous line from its context, it might not be horrifying, it might even afford a strange bliss, to think that we are "somehow, somewhere, connected with other states of being where art (curiosity, tenderness, kindness, ecstasy) is the norm" (*Lolita* 316–17).

Perhaps, Nabokov suggests, every fragment of a person's life might be part of a pattern wrought from above, necessarily unknowable in mortal life. The jarring vicissitudes of mortality might all prove part of an infinite tenderness operating in some quite non-human way. Even its allotment of pain, wantonly cruel in human terms, might be a necessary part of the pattern of tenderness.

Whereas the son in "Signs and Symbols" is mad to see reference to his own plight in everything that surrounds him, the reader is coaxed into seeing almost every detail of the story as being part of a pattern, an adumbration of the loss that is coming to the boy's helpless and tortured parents. The story ends with three phone calls to the parents: the first two are wrong numbers, the third has not yet been answered when the story ends. If the reader accepts the story's details as signs and symbols, the final phone call must be about to inform the parents that their deranged son has at last succeeded in committing suicide. Yet it remains quite possible that this phone call could prove to be irrelevant, another wrong number, and that what one has seen as "signs" are without signification.[22]

The son is mad to see everything as signs and symbols; the reader might be wrong, too, to take the story's details as part of a pattern of adumbration. Yet there is a difference: whereas the son is inside his world and without knowledge of its creator, the reader is outside the story's world and views it from a position similar to that of its maker. And from this position the story would lose the special pointedness of its details if one did not accept the significance of the pattern. But in accepting that significance the reader is decreeing that the third phone call must convey news of the boy's death. To round out the pattern means to inflict insufferable loss on the story's characters.

On the other hand if the pattern does involve an unbearably poignant loss, it also reveals with what compassionate care the creator of the pattern has infused each trifle of his created world. The pain of the story's world is real, but it is far from being pointless or allotted in a spirit of cruelty; nothing could be gentler or more loving than this elaborate patterning of miseries. In this bizarre irony it is the anguish which completes the pattern and proves the all-suffusing compassion. What is from within the story a pointless accumulation of grief is from outside its created world an exaltation of tenderness and love.

If beyond human consciousness there existed some conscious power to pattern human life it is likely that it would merge at some point (as it does in "Signs and Symbols") with the power to create life. As Emerson (with whom Nabokov has much in common) expresses it: "the foresight that awaits / Is the same Genius that creates" (Motto to "Fate," 1860).

Nabokov's investigation of states beyond the human by imaginatively acting as if from the beyond culminates in his playing the role of a creator. Again he assumes the role not merely passively, in the way every writer of fiction can be said to create his own world, nor as an empty gesture of fashionable self-consciousness or facile self-display. His deliberate enactment of the role of a creator beyond the created world becomes a serious imaginative exploration of the possibility of a designing consciousness in the universe. It might be quite explicit, as in *Bend Sinister,* into which intrudes, as Nabokov describes it, "an anthropomorphic deity impersonated by me" (*BS* xiv). It might remain implicit but still be carefully delineated. In *Transparent Things* the more-than-mortal consciousnesses of the narrators are distinguished from the mortal consciousnesses of the characters but also from the creator whose immanence these illumined souls can discern –

> We recognize its presence in the log as we recognized the log in the tree and the tree in the forest and the forest in the world that Jack built. We recognize that presence by something that is perfectly clear to us but nameless.... (7–8)

– and whose patterns they can highlight but not create. In almost all of Nabokov's works a chief function of the various stratagems of involution is to intimate the presence or the design of the inventor behind the invented world. The author's presence might be glimpsed directly through "a sudden thinning of the texture, a rubbed spot in the bright fabric, allowing the nether life to glimmer through,"[23] or it might be recognized in a scrambled or parodied appearance of the Nabokov whom we, being outside the work's world, can easily know, but who is forever beyond the characters. *Look at the Harlequins!*'s Vadim Vadimovich does not know his missing wand, his invisible lath, is Nabokov's butterfly net:

> what form of mysterious pursuit caused me to get my feet wet like a child, to pant up a talus, to stare every dandelion in the face, to start at every colored mote passing just beyond my field of vision? What was the dream sensation of having come empty-handed – without what? A gun? A wand? (155–56)

The author's design, too, the characters cannot fully discern – though the more artistic characters, like Humbert, Fyodor or Shade do see much of the "correlated pattern in the game" (*PF* 63) – and though we as readers are privileged to be looking from above the invented world we too must strive to discover the hidden and ever-increasing richness of the pattern, the complete pervasion of the creation by arcane design.

The presence and pattern of a creator at once outside his creation yet allowing his presence within it to be suspected or glimpsed are vitally important in Nabokov's work. But it is not the only part of his "creation" that matters. The elements of the created world are not there as blank tiles to be arranged in an abstract mosaic or to spell out the tile-maker's name but are valued for their variety and the fullness with which their separate existence has been realized. This applies not only at the level of characters – the freshness and individuality of a Luzhin, a Humbert, a Pnin, a Kinbote – but in every facet of the imagined world. It is particularly noticeable in visual terms: the lavish – to some, infuriatingly lavish – disbursement of sharp visual detail, quite pointedly unnecessary in its precision to a story's events and moods:

> The forest road remained reasonably smooth if you kept to its middle run (still sticky and dark after a rainy dawn) between the sky-blue ruts, speckled with the reflections of the same birch leaves whose shadows sped over the taut nacrine silk of Mlle Larivière's open sunshade....(*Ada* 78)

The use of unnecessary detail is not a shoddy lack of economy: these details – especially the "sky-blue rut" filled with the recent rain, reflecting the cleared sky, mirroring the leaves overhanging the forest road – exist in "resplendent independence" (*SO* 226). They *mean* nothing; what matters is their mere being there, with all the unexpected sharpness of reality.

The independence of the created objects as much as the patterns lurking within the creation are part of Nabokov's complete image of a creator. Kinbote, one of the few Christians in Nabokov's work, is sure "that somehow Mind is involved as a main factor in the making of the universe," and adds that

> In trying to find the right name for that Universal Mind, or First Cause, or the Absolute, or Nature, I submit that the Name of God has priority. (*PF* 227)

Nabokov too thinks that Mind is a main factor in the universe: he has declared that "Philosophically, I am an indivisibile monist" (*SO* 85), by which he means that there is "a oneness of basic reality" (*SO* 124), that mind and matter are one. But unlike Kinbote he thinks the concept of a God of little use. As Falter says in "Ultima Thule":

> By the very act of your mentioning a given concept you placed your own self in the position of an enigma.... And if it seems to you that from this answer you can draw the least conclusion about the uselessness or necessity of God, it is just because you are looking in the wrong place and in the wrong way. Wasn't it you, though, that promised not to follow logical patterns of thought? (*RB* 175)

Nabokov does not think that human concepts or logic or language are adequate. Asked "do you believe in God?" he replied:

> To be quite candid – and what I am going to say now is something I never said before, and I hope it provokes a salutary little chill – I know more than I can express in words, and the little I can express would not have been expressed, had I not known more. (*SO* 45)

To express his sense of the possible role of mind in the universe Nabokov employs not the doomed directness and humanness of rational concepts but the indirection and sense-shifting of the imagination. Specially honing the possibilities of the dynamics of fiction, he builds up something of an image of a creating consciousness, of the way Mind might operate "in the making of the universe."

Suppose one were to usurp in imagination the role of a creating force, what might one choose? Nabokov suggests that such a force might operate by granting full independence and individuation to what it creates and yet at the same time work to reintegrate and repattern the endlessly differentiating. Its highest achievement might be to allow each independent created consciousness its own chance of participating, through the thrill of discovery, in the miracle and glory of its *own* acts of creation. In a world possibly called into being by the self-limitation of a creative force, it could be the endlessness of that self-limitation that lies behind the endless detail of nature. In that case, the exhilarating shock of discovering ever-deeper levels of differentiation might be a reward planted for human effort to earn. Perhaps in the same way the surprise of discovering hidden design could be a reward for the attention, memory and imagination needed to discern all "the invisible links between things" (*LATH* 40). The sudden discovery of a deeper level of differentiation, of a further plane of pattern, might be as close as possible to the thrill and triumph of originally creating such independence and design. According to Nabokov it was Shaxpere or Shagspere or "William X, cunningly composed of two left arms and a mask...who said (not for the first time) that the glory of God is to hide a thing, and the glory of man is to find it" (*BS* 94).

Nabokov's own imaginative enactment of the role of a creative force which prizes the autonomy its patterns give and which allows life to become freer and more conscious of its freedom, more capable of discerning independence and design and thus of sharing in the thrill of creativity, is both generous and invigorating.[24] But Nabokov knows that though his literary speculations about possible transmutations of consciousness may not be incompatible with the way things are, there is no way for mortal man to know. Summarizing with keen approval Frederick Woodbridge's major assumption in *An Essay on Nature*, Nabokov declares that "man being within nature, there cannot be any independent explanation of what we do and of the world in which we do it."[25] Yet because he knows how limited and frail human explanations are, he delights in imagining the sudden shift that will topple all our notions and disclose a reality just not comprehensible to human consciousness.

Probing through the actual and the possible, he discovers both a wealth of sensation and thought in the here and now and exhilarating possibilities of transcendent bliss, transcendent sense. As he says, "To be a good visionary you must be a good observer. The better you see the earth the finer your perception of heaven will be."[26] But actual and potential bliss is undercut in Nabokov by the most disturbing unease. Everything is so fragile, being surrounded by our finiteness, our mortality and ignorance. Everything might disintegrate "at one furtive touch – words, conventions of everyday life, systems, persons" ("Ultima Thule," *RB* 154). What we are within is infinitely rich, but we soon cease to be within it. And what are we within? We could see only from outside. Can we ever see from outside?

PART THREE

ADA: THE RESPONSIBILITIES
OF
CONSCIOUSNESS

6. Introduction

Every major novel invents a new game, and the reader who masters its rules, which are nothing less than the sum of the book's words, can then return to play again and again, with deepening satisfaction at outcomes that persist in being different each time. In charting the basic operations involved in reading Nabokov and in mapping his metaphysics we have discovered enough to know that his novels constitute a new *genre* of games, quite distinct from Joyce's orienteering or Tolstoy's stalking after truth or James's constrained charades: something like board games where the pieces are arrayed in time rather than space. But to understand the general principle of positioning counters on a board requires much less attention, imagination and thought than to comprehend in detail the rules of a particular form, chess or backgammon or Go, and the art of playing it well. Following the moves of Nabokov's most compendious and inexhaustible game, *Ada*, takes great effort, but the rewards are magnificent.

In Parts Three and Four of this book, things begin with deceptive ease as I summarise aspects of *Ada*'s plot to establish sequence, motivation and even plain narrative fact. If critics have scrambled these matters, so presumably can readers with less time to devote to *Ada*. But I have another reason for beginning this way.

Ada actively invites its readers to compare the book with Bosch's *Garden of Earthly Delights*. In Bosch's masterpiece two wings depicting Eden and Hell flank the central panel of teeming copulators; when the wings are folded shut, their outer sides disclose a picture of the earth in a crystal ball, seen by God. *Ada* works in a similar fashion. It begins with Ardis, which Van presents as first a paradise and then also (while still paradisal) a hell of jealousy; after the expulsion from their youthful Eden Ada and Van move out into a larger world tinted from time to time by a gleam of ether or brimstone. But unknown to Van, the book can be shut up and its whole world looked at from outside, through eyes not his own, and in a completely new light. That light is, in a word, Lucette, who allows us to see the infernal in Van and Ada that they themselves cannot see (and this will be the subject of Part Three), and the celestial in and around them (the subject of Part Four) to which they remain equally blind. These utterly unexpected views from outside transform the book's world entirely. But just as in Nabokov's definition of a good visionary, the perception of the heaven and hell that *Ada*'s world discloses from outside Van's vision depends on our seeing that world very well indeed. We have to be sure that we have completely understood the larger configurations depicted on the exposed panels before we burrow through the wood, detail by minute detail, to the other side.

The surprising worlds that can be discovered in *Ada* reveal themselves slowly to the careful rereader through the piecemeal accumulation of obscure but exact relationships between details that have no apparent connection to someone early in the reading process or even (despite his deliberateness as a writer) to Van himself. It should be understood especially by those readers who cannot recall every whisper in *Ada* that items whose secret association I point out and try to explain are not steady parts of the fictional environment whose repetition could be explained on that basis – as a mullioned door, say, might recur in Hardy, or a tavern sign in Fielding. Elements of these patterns tend to be freaky where they occur – and when the same elements reappear quite transformed and in a totally new setting, some explanation needs to be sought. Two boatloads of Cornish fishermen off Land's End fit naturally into their world, but a Cornish fisherman, a Latvian dolls'-dressmaker and a sick gaucho – all strangers to one another – in a boat in Falmouth Bay and the same trio, still ostensibly strangers, in a railway carriage between Madras and Bombay would invite us at least to account for the coincidence.

The explanations I have been driven to are often difficult, and require us to follow almost simultaneously patterns branching out in several directions, metamorphosing, interlacing, twisting back on themselves. They are also radical, but in all that follows I have tried and rejected other explanations for these elusive echoes: the natural recurrence of parts of a stable fictional world; chance; unconscious prompting by Nabokov's memory; his love of pattern for its own sake; or more specific artistic reasons other than those I suggest. There is simply not room to set out the degree to which each connection exceeds what could be accounted for by chance or conventional authorial design, or to run through the rejected possibilities. But in the Appendix to Part Four, in order to contrast my own methods with those of another critic who also offers radical interpretations for *Ada* and other Nabokov works (but of things that do not need explaining and without weighing far more probable and quite sufficient explanations) I do work through a few examples in this way. Anyone reading Parts Three and Four who becomes so alarmed by proliferating detail and pattern as to balk at my methods might want to check there.

7. Lucette

For most readers *Ada* seems at once a jubilant experience – because its two central characters tingle with such intellectual, emotional and physical vitality and because the love that develops between them with such speed and force eventually proves more durable than even young ardor could expect. All this we glean immediately, and – like the book's color and sheer fun – can be taken as read. But some scrupulous readers have suspected that beneath the bright stream of the book there are undercurrents or murk of which Nabokov remains unaware. There are those who feel that since he has endowed his central characters with so much intelligence and lively self-awareness and that since Van depicts his and Ada's love as a resounding triumph, Nabokov therefore cannot sense what might seem distasteful in the two Veens; others feel that he has been so won over by the enchantment of young passion that he fails to provide the book with more artistic shape than the unity the love affair already contributes. Both reactions remain uncommon, though: the great majority of readers perceive only the radiance that Van intends.

The fact is, however, that Nabokov *has* planted something beneath that glittering stream and in composing the book has paid as much attention to the undercurrents as to the surface. He bestows on Van and Ada the intellects of genius and a limitless capacity for passion because he believes in the enormous scope of human possibility, but for him that belief cannot get rid of its shadow: the enormity of human limitation. Van and Ada are not only the exhilarating exemplars of joyful youth and joyful age that most readers take them to be; they are also a study in the moral blindness that can accompany even the most exceptional intelligence and love.

Throughout this and the next three chapters, I will focus exclusively on Nabokov's moral evaluation of Van and Ada. I do not want to suggest for a moment that Nabokov wrote *Ada* primarily to expound an ethical system, but the evidence shows that he expended extraordinary artistic energy in documenting via Lucette the demonic side of Van and Ada in a way that the ordinary reader cannot even suspect. Nabokov is not a solemn moralist, but his efforts in *Ada* prove beyond all doubt that he was a serious and scrupulous one. A common view of his novels holds that he treats a few characters, creatures of unusual intelligence, often artistically gifted and trilingual or nearly so – surrogates for himself, in other words – as favorites, and lavishes attention on them while ignoring or heaping contempt upon almost everyone else. Van and

Ada seem Nabokov's obvious favorites in *Ada*, but far from cocooning them in his indulgence at the expense of other characters, Nabokov throughout the novel criticizes severely their lack of concern for those they dismiss as immaterial to their own needs and wants. When Lucette, Greg Erminin, Kim Beauharnais, Dan or Andrey Vinelander is ignored or despised or made to suffer by Van, Nabokov defends each of them – whether charming or dull or positively unsavory – against the characters on whom he has visibly showered every advantage.

Lucette the Pest

On a first reading of *Ada* we regard Lucette, throughout the first, Ardis, half of the book, as a pest, an impish little child who intrudes upon Van and Ada's extraordinary love and thwarts our own eagerness to see them enjoy the bliss they describe so transcendently.

Because Van and Ada do not become lovers until well into Van's first summer sojourn at Ardis ("Ardis the First," 1884) the Lucette theme is announced only two chapters before school resumes. During the five days in August when a sprained back keeps Mlle Larivière in bed,

> the second upstairs maid, French, whose moods and looks did not match the sweet temper and limpid grace of Blanche, was supposed to look after Lucette, and Lucette did her best to avoid the lazy servant's surveillance in favor of her cousin's and sister's company. The ominous words: "Well, if Master Van lets you come," or "Yes, I'm sure Miss Ada won't mind your mushroom-picking with her," became something of a knell in regard to love's freedom. (142)

Van and Ada have to devise various stratagems to keep Lucette away from their lovemaking; tying her up to a tree, as if she were "a fairy-tale damsel in distress" (143), making her soak a full fifteen minutes in the bath, goading her into going off to learn a poem by heart.

In Ardis the Second (summer 1888) the Lucette theme is announced at once when her drumming on the door interrupts Van's very first embrace with Ada. As the theme persists, we become quite impatient with the little girl, especially since the subtle echoes of Ardis the First encourage us to appreciate Van's and Ada's reunion as a reversal of time, a triumph almost of a metaphysical order. We become eager to witness the passionate siblings retrieve time past through the ardor and tenderness of the lovemaking Lucette continually threatens to interrupt:

> Whenever not supervised by her schizophrenic governess, whenever not being read to, or walked, or put to bed, Lucette was now a pest.... Lucette...seemed to lurk behind every screen, to peep out of every mirror. (211)

Lucette, the shadow, followed them from lawn to loft, from gatehouse to stable, from a modern shower booth near the pool to the ancient bathroom upstairs. Lucette-in-the-Box came out of a trunk. Lucette desired they take her for walks. (213)

Constantly "playing her part of the clinging, affectionately fussy lassy" (204–05), Lucette seems a nosy, charming but very ordinary child who has no right to mar the rare and exalted love Van and Ada share.

Van does not see Lucette from 1888 until November 1892, when she arrives with a letter from Ada warning that should Van refuse to take her back she will agree to marry an unnamed Arizonian with whom she admits she has almost nothing in common. In the fall of 1891 Lucette herself has sent Van "a rambling, indecent, crazy, almost savage declaration of love in a ten-page letter" (366), and when she now brings Ada's plea the girl Van "had hardly known...before – except as an embered embryo"(367) turns out to be a rousingly beautiful young woman who can expertly imitate all Ada's "*shtuchki* (little stunts)" (386) – but still to no avail.

Van does not see Lucette again in 1892 except for the day of Ada's return – when she knocks perfunctorily on the door and walks straight in to glimpse Van and Ada in mid-convulsion – and except for a night out at the Ursus restaurant that slides into a three-way debauch (the three Veen children in bed together) the next morning. After 1892 another nine years pass before Van has more than a passing glimpse of Lucette. When he meets her in a Parisian bar in 1901 he finds her still desperately in love with him, eager for him to come up to her suite and begin at a physical level a relationship that she wants to become a much richer bond. When Lucette discovers Van will shortly be travelling back to America on the liner *Admiral Tobakoff*, she calls up to arrange a cabin, and determines to seduce Van or die:

Long ago she had made up her mind that by forcing the man whom she absurdly but irrevocably loved to have intercourse with her, even once, she would, somehow, with the help of some prodigious act of nature, transform a brief tactile event into an eternal spiritual tie; but she also knew that if it did not happen on the first night of their voyage, their relationship would slip back into the exhausting, hopeless, hopelessly familiar pattern of banter and counterbanter, with the erotic edge taken for granted, but kept as raw as ever. (485)

Her plan fails, and since she cannot bear knowing she can never have the only man she loves, she takes her own life.

The chapter set on board the *Tobakoff* is the most dramatically charged in the novel. When Van spots Lucette's name on the passenger list, he searches her out; they lunch together; they spend the afternoon by the swimming pool on deck, where Van as he lies sunbathing only manages "to fan, with every shiver and heave of the ship, the fire of evil temptation" (482) and Lucette fearfully suspects a grotesque bikinied blonde to be one of Van's "gruesome girls" (483) (she is not). They dine and drink together, Lucette still imploring Van to visit her cabin. To take the tension out of the situation, he steers Lucette in to watch a pre-release film, *Don Juan's Last Fling*. Lucette brushes his "cheek with her lips in the dark, she took his hand, she kissed his knuckles, and he suddenly thought: after all, why not? Tonight? Tonight."

> He enjoyed her impatience, the fool permitted himself to be stirred by it, the cretin whispered, prolonging the free, new, apricot fire of anticipation:
> "If you're a good girl we'll have drinks in my sitting room at midnight." (488)

The film turns out to include Ada in her biggest role yet and Van sees all her moves as "a perfect compendium of her 1884 and 1888 and 1892 looks" (489). When three old ladies walk out of the movie in disgust, the Robinsons, "old bores of the family" (475), shuffle over from beyond the vacant seats and plump down

> next to Lucette, who turned to them with her last, last, last free gift of staunch courtesy that was stronger than failure and death. They were craning already across her, with radiant wrinkles and twittery fingers toward Van when he pounced upon their intrusion to murmur a humorous bad-sailor excuse and leave the cinema hall to its dark lurching. (490)

Shocked out of his mood by Ada's appearing on screen, Van retires to his room, masturbating twice to get "rid of the prurient pressure" (490) the alluring and adoring Lucette has built up all day. When after the film Lucette phones Van's cabin, asking can she come over now, Van replies that he is not alone. Lucette accepts that he must be with the predatory blonde and takes an overdose of "Quietus" pills (seasickness tablets that double as sleeping pills) before jumping from the ship. Van's one attempt at sexual restraint has ended in disaster.

Rediscovering Lucette

If on a first reading we tend to be irritated by little Lucette, we ought to be appalled when we reread the novel with her death already in mind. We should be able to see plainly Van and Ada's indifference to their sister, their lack of sensitivity to her needs and her frailty, their deliberate playing on her affection. We should also recognize the failure of our own moral vision and acknowledge how easily we succumbed to Van and Ada's partiality of interest, becoming so caught up in their eagerness to be alone together that we became impatient with Lucette and only wished her out of the way.

We *should* feel all this, for we know Lucette is doomed to die. But in fact most readers seem not to respond in this way.[1] We wince at the precise and poignant anticipations of Lucette's death that Van has clearly highlighted out of his own real remorse. We nod in agreement when Van and Ada accept some measure of responsibility for her fate, though we may be inclined to interpret this as an index of their sensitivity rather than their guilt. Even though we know Lucette will die, even though Van and Ada's inconsiderateness is not hidden, we still tend to regard Lucette as merely a poignant corollary to the splendor of Van and Ada's love.

Certainly we squirm at the grim exactness with which the stratagems Van and Ada had used to curb their little sister during Ardis the First anticipate her death:

> Ada sat reading on a...bank, wistfully glancing from time to time at an inviting clump of evergreens (that had frequently sheltered our lovers) and at brown-torsoed, barefooted Van, in turned-up dungarees, who was searching for his wristwatch that he thought he had dropped among the forget-me-nots (but which Ada, he forgot, was wearing). Lucette had abandoned her skipping rope to squat on the brink of the brook and float a fetus-sized rubber doll. Every now and then she squeezed out of it a fascinating squirt of water through a little hole that Ada had had the bad taste to perforate for her in the slippery orange-red toy. With the sudden impatience of inanimate things, the doll managed to get swept away by the current. Van shed his pants under a willow and retrieved the fugitive. Ada, after considering the situation for a moment, shut her book and said to Lucette, whom usually it was not hard to enchant, that she, Ada, felt she was quickly turning into a dragon, that she scales had begun to turn green, that now she *was* a dragon and that Lucette must be tied to a tree with the skipping rope so that Van might save her just in time. For some reason, Lucette balked at the notion but physical strength prevailed. Van and Ada left the angry captive firmly attached to a willow trunk, and, "prancing" to feign swift escape and pursuit, disappeared for a few precious minutes in the dark grove of conifers. Writhing Lucette had somehow torn off one of the red knobbed grips of the rope and seemed to have almost disentangled herself when dragon and knight, prancing, returned. (142–143)

While the doll ghoulishly foreshadows Lucette's drowning, the whole scene links up with her fate even on the level of simple causality. As Ada later finds out, Lucette had in fact witnessed Van and Ada copulating before running back to tie herself up as well as she could, so that she "seemed to have almost disentangled herself when dragon and knight, prancing, returned" (143). Van recalls this scene as he imagines her death: "She did not see her whole life flash before her as we all were afraid she might have done; the red rubber of a favorite doll remained safely decomposed among the myosotes of an unanalyzable brook" (494). "Myosotes" are the "forget-me-nots" of the earlier brook: Van acknowledges here that he must never forget Lucette and how wretchedly he and Ada have treated her. Van's deliberate evocation of the brookside scene at the moment of Lucette's death is one reason – we shall soon see another – that it is wrong for Bobbie Ann Mason to declare that Van tries "to rationalize away his guilt" (Mason 13).

The second of Ada and Van's stratagems is to keep Lucette soaking in the bathtub while they make love around the corner of the L-shaped bathroom:

> The liquid prison was now ready and an alarm clock given a full quarter of an hour to live.
>
> ....
>
> "I'm Van," said Lucette, standing in the tub with the mulberry soap between her legs and protruding her shiny tummy.
>
> ....
>
> "And remember," said Ada, "don't you dare get out of this nice warm water until the bell rings or you'll die, because that's what Krolik said. I'll be back to lather you, but don't call me; we have to count the linen and sort out Van's hankies."
>
> ...barely had they finished their violent and uncomfortable exertions in that hidden nook, with an empty medicine bottle idiotically beating time on a shelf, when Lucette was already calling resonantly from the tub.... (144–45)

When Ada tells Van that she has made Lucette confess that she had untied and retied herself that day by the brook, Van exclaims: "Good Lord...that explains the angle of the soap!" (152). The humor we catch on a first reading is eclipsed on a rereading by the ghastly irony of the "liquid prison." That Van has chosen these words deliberately out of remorse is indicated by his recollecting the medicine bottle "idiotically beating time on a shelf" after he tries to analyze Lucette's state of mind in the chapter that culminates in her death: "He understood her condition or at least believed, in despair, that he *had* understood it, retrospectively, by the time no remedy except Dr. Henry's oil of Atlantic prose could be found in the medicine chest of the past with its banging door and toppling tootbrush."(485)

In Ardis the First Lucette is trapped by Van and Ada's ardor – trapped, in fact, into watching them make love, though this is of course not what they intend. In Ardis the Second, Lucette finds herself entangled – quite literally – in Van and Ada's amours.

Ada always tends to view sex as intense but harmless physical pleasure and eagerly initiates Lucette into muddled intimacies for which the child is not ready. When in Pt. 1 Ch. 32 Lucette follows Ada who is in turn following Van away from the pool, the three youngsters stop underneath a sealyham cedar, where the imitative imp ends coiled on the ground with her big sister and brother. Van tells her she is as cold "as two halves of a canned peach":

> "Why two? Why?"
> "Yes, why," growled Ada with a shiver of pleasure, and, leaning over, kissed him on the mouth. He struggled to rise. The two girls were now kissing him alternately, then kissing each other, then getting busy upon him again – Ada in perilous silence, Lucette with soft squeals of delight.... Ada, her silky mane sweeping over his nipples and navel, seemed to enjoy doing everything to jolt my present pencil and make, in that ridiculously remote past, her innocent little sister notice and register what Van could not control. The crushed flower [a helleborine Ada has picked; Van is wearing only swim trunks] was now being merrily crammed under the rubber belt of his black trunks by twenty tickly fingers. (205)

It is in much the same spirit as that which prompts her to make "her innocent little sister notice and register what Van could not control" that Ada brings forth a much more dangerous stratagem than any devised four years earlier:

> Ada thought up a plan that was not simple, was not clever, and moreover worked the wrong way. Perhaps she did it on purpose. (Strike out, strike please, Van.) The idea was to have Van fool Lucette by petting her in Ada's presence, while kissing Ada at the same time, and by caressing Lucette when Ada was away in the woods ("in the woods," "botanizing"). This, Ada affirmed, would achieve two ends – assuage the pubescent child's jealousy and act as an alibi in case she caught them in the middle of a more ambiguous romp. (213)

The quotation marks around "in the woods" and "botanizing" should indicate to the good rereader that Ada has devised this strategy at least partly to keep Van busy while she is away meeting Percy de Prey.

Unlike Ada, Van tries to take care not to arouse sexual excitement in Lucette before she is ready to handle it. Nevertheless he abuses his little sister by taking advantage of her doting on him, and knows the power of the tiniest gesture, the least caress. On one occasion Lucette proves even more recalcitrant than usual:

> "The simplest answer," said Lucette, "is that you two *can* tell me exactly why you want to get rid of me."

"Perhaps the simplest answer," continued Ada, "is for you, Van, to give her a vigorous, resounding spanking."

"I dare you!" cried Lucette, and veered invitingly.

Very gently Van stroked the silky top of her head and kissed her behind the ear; and, bursting into a hideous storm of sobs, Lucette rushed out of the room. Ada locked the door after her. (229)

Insatiable Ada has Van stroke Lucette so that she can go off and make love with Percy; Van, more modestly, chooses to caress his little sister only to be free for another torrid spasm with Ada.

After Ardis Lucette next appears in Van's quarters at Kingston, in 1892. By now the warping of her emotional growth has become manifest. As she tells Van, her sexual initiation progressed one risky stage further when Ada took her in hand: "She taught me practices I had never imagined.... We interweaved like serpents and sobbed like pumas. We were Mongolian tumblers, monograms, anagrams, adalucindas." (375) This began in 1890; now, two years later, her agitation still shows as she puns "in an Ophelian frenzy on the feminine glans" (394). She reminds Van of a game of Russian Scrabble they played in which the six letters she has left spell the Russian for "clitoris," though at eight the word means nothing to her:

"Mind you, I was eight and had not studied anatomy, but was doing my poor little best to keep up with two *Wunderkinder*. You examined and fingered my groove and quickly redistributed the haphazard sequence which made, say, LIKROT or ROTIKL and...when you had completed the rearrangement, you and [Ada] came simultaneously, *si je puis le mettre comme ça* (Canady French), came falling on the black carpet in a paroxysm of incomprehensible merriment; so finally I quietly composed ROTIK ("little mouth") and was left with my own cheap initial. I hope I've thoroughly got you mixed up, Van, because *la plus laide fille au monde peut donner beaucoup plus qu'elle n'a*, and now let us say adieu, yours ever.

"Whilst the machine is to him," murmured Van.

"Hamlet," said Lucette. (379)

A host of *Hamlet* allusions in this chapter confirm Lucette's role as Ophelia: painfully obsessed with the idea of her virginity, she will carry her obsession to a watery grave.

For despite the fact that she has been made aware of sex too early, despite her confused childhood impulse to imitate the passion and prowess of her hyperactive siblings, despite the fact that Ada has so rawly awakened her sexual needs, Lucette is determined to remain a virgin – until Van will have her. The strain tells:

"Oh, to be sure, it was not easy! In parked automobiles and at rowdy parties, thrusts had to he parried, advances fought off! And only last winter...there was a youngster of fourteen...an awfully precocious but terribly shy and neurotic young violinist.... Well, for almost three months, every blessed afternoon, I had him touch me, and I reciprocated, and after that I could sleep at last without pills, but otherwise I haven't once kissed male epithelia in all my...life" (371)

Since Van will not answer the letter Ada sends by even the most expensive of special couriers, loyal Lucette has come to Kingston with a letter from her sister. She knows the letter will probably lead to Van and Ada's reunion, but her staunch kindness requires her to bring it. Desperately agitated by her need for sexual solace and her love for Van, Lucette cannot help long-ing – her loyalty to her sister not withstanding – for the "decisive embrace" (369). But it does not come, and she turns away, "her fragile shoulders shak-ing unbearably" (369). Van recognizes the compulsiveness of her passion, but he knows it would jeopardize Ada's love forever if he "tasted [Lucette's] wound and its grip" (485). Yet he cannot resist the momentary gratification of stoking her desire:

He thrust his hands into the warm vulvas of her mole-soft sleeves and held her for a moment on the inside by her thin bare elbows, looking down with meditative desire at her painted lips.
"*Un baiser, un seul!*" she pleaded.
"You promise not to open your mouth? not to melt? not to flutter and flick?" (386–87)

Deciding after all not to kiss her, he tries to console her by declaring his admiration for her is painfully strong. When she cries: "I want Van...not intangible admiration," he responds: "Intangible? You goose. You may gauge it, you may brush it once very lightly, with the knuckles of your gloved hand. I said knuckles. I said once. That will do." (387)

A few days later Van, Ada and Lucette are together for the last time. Here, in Manhattan, Lucette's initiation and entanglement edge one step closer to disaster.

The thoughtlessness Van showed towards Lucette at Ardis and his habit of exploiting her devotion recur with particular acuteness. While Ada is briefly absent from the restaurant table, Van unthinkingly pets poor Lucette: "He went back to whatever he was eating, and cruelly stroked Lucette's apricot-bloomed forearm" (411). Later that night, when the three have returned to Van's apartment, Van decides "to kill two finches with one fircone" (414), to gratify Lucette while he obtains from her the name of the man who almost became Ada's fiancé – and whom Van would like to eliminate in a duel. Lucette suspects Van's designs and will not divulge the name, but he offers a bribe he knows she will be unable to resist:

> "Please, little vixen! I'll reward you with a very special kiss" [on the armpit]... for a few synchronized heartbeats [Van] fitted his working mouth to the hot, humid, perilous hollow.
> She sat down with a bump on a chair, pressing one hand to her brow.
> "Turn off the footlights," said Van. "I want the name of that fellow."
> "Vinelander," she answered. (415)

The night ends with Van manipulating Lucette's affection more blatantly and for a more sinister purpose than ever before; the next morning begins with Ada's forcing Lucette into an entanglement more dangerous than any in their past. Van wakes, as usual, before Ada. He takes a shower and returns to the bedroom naked and "in full pride, only to find a tousled and sulky Lucette, still in her willow green nightie" (417), sitting on the bed. As Lucette tries to leave, Ada holds her back, plucks off her nightie, and proceeds to orchestrate the debauch, leading Van's hand over to stroke poor Lucette's "firebird" (418). Ada's attentions to Van bring him to orgasm, which releases the pressure on Lucette, who escapes, writes a note – "Would go mad if remained one more night" (421) – and rushes off with her bags.

When Van next sees Lucette in Paris, nine years later, less than a week before she dies, her love and her determination to be loved by Van are unchanged. He is all her life: as she pokes at a trout on her plate she tells him that under all she enjoys "there is absolutely nothing, except, of course, your image, and that adds only depth and a trout's agonies to the emptiness" (464). A few minutes earlier, she has invited Van to her room – "I'll stretch out upon the divan like a martyr, remember?...Oh, try me, Van!" (464) – alluding to her reaction when Ada plucked her nightdress off at the beginning of the *débauche*: "Involuntarily Lucette bent her head and frail spine; then she lay back on the outer half of Ada's pillow in a martyr's pudibund swoon." (418) In fact she has been a martyr to Van and Ada's love ever since they first made her stand tied to a tree while they pranced off to their enjoyment.

Yet while Van and Ada's inconsiderateness to Lucette should have become evident to us at least by the time of the *débauche à trois*, it is not at all as obvious as the selectivity and emphases of this summary might suggest. True, we already know what Lucette's fate will be; we have even seen it starkly foreshadowed in the stratagems Van and Ada use to keep her at bay; and Van and Ada's irresponsibility and inconsiderateness ought to be visible in all they do. Being aware of Lucette's fate, we should sense that despite Van's glorying in the opulence of his style in, say, the *débauche* scene, what really matters is the sordidness of his conduct.

But though we *should* see this, we – most readers – tend to be mesmerized by the brilliance of Van's style, by his and Ada's intelligence, by the intensity and durability and the sheer specialness of their love. Lucette's tragedy seems to add a deeper strain to the tune of their happiness, but one that only swells the exaltation; the triumph of their love must be quite unassailable, we suppose, if it can incorporate even the tragedy of the child who stumbles across their path.

It proves chasteningly difficult for most of us to discover how wrong such an assessment is, to wean ourselves from Van and Ada's position and see how blinded they – and we – have been by the claims of their intelligence, their love, their uniqueness. Though Nabokov presents Van and Ada's irresponsibility in terms of both action and effect, we are distracted completely by the dazzle and tease of their style and the power of their thoughts and feelings. For most of us, real insight into the implications of Van and Ada's conduct and our own less-than-wary moral sensitivity will come only when we find how Nabokov's tender care for Lucette makes her presence ripple through every part of the novel.

It takes some sudden discovery – the *souci d'eau*, for example – to propel us to a new understanding of Lucette's place in the novel. Once we appreciate (to keep with this example) how powerfully Nabokov means to imply, whenever he invokes Rimbaud's "Mémoire", the irony that Lucette is initiated too early and for that reason becomes tragically fixed on the idea of Van's deflowering her,[2] the whole book changes.

Lucette watches Van and Ada make love for the first time that day they tie her up to a willow tree – but too hastily, so she can escape and find out what they are up to. In Chapter 3 we saw how Nabokov brings Lucette into the *souci d'eau* discussion, even though she is not physically present, by linking Rimbaud's "les robes vertes...des fillettes font les saules" with Lucette's "green nightgown...the nuance of willows" (64). In the scene of Lucette's being tied up we find not only the Rimbaudian willow but also Ada sitting reading on the bank of a brook (142) – which echoes the "Mémoire" line, "des enfants lisant dans la verdure fleurie" (of another brookside bank). In Pt.1 Ch.20, the defloration chapter, Lucette's "child's...stiff-bagged butterfly net...like an oriflamme"(127) associates her with the Joan of Arc, virgin and martyr, who appears amidst oriflammes in the first stanza of "Mémoire," and throughout *Ada*, she will be linked with burnings at the stake, with persecution, with torture, with all the ravages of human cruelty. When we appreciate that "Mémoire" and its Joan of Arc are quietly implied in Lucette's being tied up to the tree, we can see how decidedly Nabokov reproves Van and Ada for their disregard of Lucette in this scene. For the pleasure of satisfying a momentary urge, they are ready to sacrifice her happiness. They do not scruple about trapping her – and trap her all the more permanently because she soon wriggles free of her skipping rope. The inventiveness of Ada's dragon-and-knight pretext for tying Lucette up seems charming at first blush; now it only raises the question why someone with Ada's imagination refuses to envisage someone else's feelings.

But we have not finished with the Rimbaud in this scene. When Lucette's doll is swept away, Van is "searching for his wristwatch that he thought he dropped among the forget-me-nots (but which Ada, he forgot, was wearing)" (142–43). These words are recalled in the last sentence of the novel: "Not the least adornment of the chronicle is the delicacy of pictorial detail: a latticed gallery; a painted ceiling; a pretty plaything stranded among the forget-me-nots of a brook...." (589) There is a pleasant irony in the wristwatch being a "plaything," in this novel so seriously concerned with the nature of time – but the watch was not after all stranded among the forget-me-nots. What *does* get stranded there is the doll which Lucette again lets drown – as Van recalls when he describes her death. Through this association the "plaything" alludes to Lucette's death, but in recalling both the brookside scene and the line "Jouet de cet oeil d'eau morne" from "Mémoire," the word also points to the tragically early initiation that began Lucette's journey to suicide.

The last sentence in the novel connects with *souci d'eau*; so does the first. Ada's *souci d'eau* harangue at the dinner table focusses on a mistranslation; and in opening the chapter where this scene takes place, Van characterizes Ada's table talk, which might be about the "'monologue intérieur' borrowed from old Leo [Tolstoy] – or some ludicrous blunder in the current column of...a vulgar demimondaine who thought that Lyovin went about Moscow in a *nagol'nïy tulup*,'a muzhik's sheepskin coat...'" (61). The Tolstoy references here and the blunder Ada denounces confirm that the *souci d'eau* mistranslation in another of Ada's dinner table talks should be seen as essential to understanding the Tolstoy mistranslation with which *Ada* begins: "All happy families are more or less dissimilar; all unhappy ones are more or less alike." (3)

In inverting *Anna Karenin's* opening sentence, Van tries to claim that unlike Tolstoy's novel *Ada* is no tragedy but the happy story of a unique family. But as Ada's denunciation of the *souci d'eau* mistranslation suggests, the original meaning should be restored: "All happy families are alike, each unhappy family is unhappy in its own way." For while Van is justified in claiming that the Veens, like the Karenins, are unique, the contrast he implies between the two – that he and Ada are supremely happy in their love as the Karenins are not – is eclipsed by the central fact that both families include a heroine who takes her own life. Despite Van's claims, *Ada* is a tragedy: the tragedy of Lucette's part in what Van wants to think the happiest of families.

Incest

Lucette, we should now be able to see, is the real reason for the prominence given to incest in *Ada*. Incest here functions not as it has generally been conceived, as an emblem of solipsism or self-love[3] – Nabokov detests such symbols – but rather to stress the intimate interconnections between people's lives, interconnections which impose on human life all the obligations of moral responsibility.

When Van uses the phrase "real, or at least responsible, life" (97) he expresses Nabokov's position exactly: uncertainty about the "reality" of human life, certainty about the demands of responsibility within the human. We do not know whether life as seen through human consciousness is a very big part of the possibilities of existence, but we *do* know that within the limits of our existence, each of our lives is inevitably connected with other lives for which we are responsible in proportion to the intimacy of our contact with them. Van and Ada see their incest as a more or less amusing confirmation of their remarkable similarity and of the degree to which they are each a sufficient world unto the other. But because their love takes place within a family, because there is a little girl around who sees what an eight-year-old is not ready to see, because their connections with Lucette are so intricate, their passion cannot be seen as something which can exclude relations with the surrounding world. It is this, of course, that makes incest so danger-ous and damaging: not that there is something inherently sacred about the relationship of brother and sister, father and daughter, mother and son, but that incest takes place within a network of already intimate relations that it can only cruelly disrupt. Incest in *Ada*, as we shall see more clearly soon, is a specific instance of the tax of responsibility, a tax enacted on human life by consciousness in return for the privileges and delights consciousness can derive from the intimate interconnections of life.[4]

Through such things as the playful and prominent Chateaubriand allusions[5] and an apparent acceptance of the modern standard of sexual freedom without responsibility, *Ada* encourages a sophisticated, unserious approach to incest. But this is only another feint to make the reader first acquiesce in a dismissal of responsibility and then see how wrong the acquiescence has been. That this is the real role of the incest in *Ada* is confirmed by the fact that Chateaubriand is present not, as reviewers and critics have assumed, to mark the relationship between Van and Ada but to mark the presence and entanglement of Lucette in that relationship. The first Chateaubriand allusion in *Ada* occurs at the first (1884) picnic: "Lucette, one fist on her hip, sang a St. Malô fisher-song" (81). (Chateaubriand was born in St. Malô and celebrated his kinship with the sea.) The association of Chateaubriand with Lucette should remind us that Lucette is also called Lucile, after Chateaubriand's dearest sister, who served as the basis for the Amélie of *René* and who is believed to have committed suicide.[6] A few minutes afterward at the picnic,

> Ada asked her governess for pencils and paper. Lying on his stomach, leaning his cheek on his hand, Van looked at his love's inclined neck as she played anagrams with Grace, who had innocently suggested "insect."
> "Scient," said Ada. writing it down.
> "Oh no!" objected Grace.
> "Oh yes! I'm sure it exists. He is a great scient. Dr. Entsic was scient in insects." Grace meditated, tapping her puckered brow with the eraser end of the pencil, and came up with:
> "Nicest!"
> "Incest," said Ada instantly.
> "I give up," said Grace. "We need a dictionary to check your little inventions."
> But the glow of the afternoon had entered its most oppressive phase, and the first bad mosquito of the season was resonantly slain on Ada's shin by alert Lucette. (85)

The connection between insects and incest is very firmly established; and that mosquito is identified later as *Culex chateaubriandi* Brown (105), Chateaubriand's mosquito:

> During the last week of July, there emerged, with diabolical regularity, the female of Chateaubriand's mosquito. Chateaubriand (Charles), who had not been the first to be bitten by it...but the first to bottle the offender...was not related to the great poet and memoirist born between Paris and Tagne (as he'd better, said Ada, who liked crossing orchids).
>
> > *Mon enfant, ma soeur;*
> > *Songe à l'épaisseur*
> > *Du grand chêne à Tagne;*
> > *Songe à la montagne,*
> > *Songe à la douceur –*
>
> – of scraping with one's claws or nails the spots visited by that fluffy-footed insect characterized by an insatiable and reckless appetite for Ada's and Ardelia's, Lucette's and Lucile's (multiplied by the itch) blood. (106)

Note not only Lucette's appearing as Lucile, and the suggestion of the confusion of Ada's and Lucette's blood (in the spirit of Donne's "The Flea": "And in this flea, our two bloods mingled be"), but also the particularly precise confusion in "Ardelia." The name plays upon Ada's full name, Adelaida, but recalls too Van's first arrival at Ardis, when he sees Lucette and decides "she must be 'Ardelia,' the eldest of the two little cousins he was supposed to get acquainted with" (36). "Ardelia" derives from "ardelio," busybody (Webster's Second lists the former as "Fem. proper name" and the latter in its small print at the foot of the page)[7] – which at first is all we think Lucette to be. Note too that the poem is supposed to be by the unrelated namesake of Charles Chateaubriand, though it is chiefly an adaptation of Baudelaire's "L'Invitation au voyage." In Pt. 3 Ch. 3, where Van tells Lucette he is sailing across the Atlantic and where Lucette manages to get herself on the same boat in the hope that she might be able to entice him to her cabin, Van notes, among other paperbacks on a revolving stand, the multiply ironic *Invitation to a Climax* (459).

The purest of the Chateaubriand allusions reworks the romance in *Les Aventures du Dernier Abencérage*, which has nothing to do with incest but will become fatally associated with the night of Lucette's death. Much earlier in the novel, Van plays some fine variations on Chateaubriand's lines:

> *Oh! qui me rendra mon Aline*
> *Et le grand chêne et ma colline?*
> ....
> *Oh! qui me rendra, mon Adèle,*
> *Et ma montagne et l'hirondelle?*
>
> *Oh! qui me rendra ma Lucile,*
> *La Dore et l'hirondelle agile?* (138–39)

Note the punctuation here: only before the name obviously formed from Ada's, Adèle, is there a comma: only in this case is the girl apostrophized. In the other two cases "mon Aline" and "ma Lucile" are included in the things the speaker wants to be given back. If "Aline" is a play on Chateaubriand's "Hélène," it is also the exact name of his sister-in-law, who like Lucette came to a tragic end (she was guillotined in 1794); Lucette is explicitly related to Aline in the remark: "She was, cette Lucette, like the girl in *Ah, cette Line*" (152). Moreover, Nabokov takes the trouble in his Darkbloom notes to point out that Lucile in Van's poem is "the name of Chateaubriand's actual sister" (Darkbloom 467), the suicide.

Chateaubriand appears also as the implicit "source" of Mlle Larivière's *Les Enfants Maudits*,[8] the name René having been borrowed from *René*, Hélène from the romance in *Les Aventures du Dernier Abencérage*. But *Les Enfants Maudits* has no intrinsic content, only a plot composed of a ludicrous ad hoc relation to the events of the surrounding narrative. The only "accursed" one among the three Veen children is Lucette; and the only time Chateaubriand's name (disguised) is associated with *Les Enfants Maudits* is that dangerous moment when Ada and little Lucette are both tumbling over Van:

> The two girls were now kissing him alternatively, then kissing each other, then getting busy upon him again – Ada in perilous silence, Lucette with soft squeals of delight. I do not remember what *Les Enfants Maudits* did or said in Monparnasse's novelette – they lived in Bryant's château, I think, and it began with bats flying one by one out of a turret's *oeil-de-boeuf* into the sunset, but *these* children (whom the novelettist did not really know – a delicious point) might also have been filmed rather entertainingly had snoopy Kim, the kitchen photo-fiend, possessed the necessary apparatus.... Ada ...seemed to enjoy doing everything to...make...her innocent little sister notice and register what Van could not control. (205)

On the return voyage from the second (1888) Ardis picnic, while Lucette sits on Van's knee, becoming blended in his mind with the Ada who sat on his knee on the voyage back from the 1884 picnic, the present Ada reads "her vellum-bound little volume, *Ombres et couleurs*, an 1820 edition of Chateaubriand's short stories" (280).

The Chateaubriand allusions, then, occur where Lucette is also present, and especially where there is a confusion between her and Ada that reflects her long entanglement in Van and Ada's lives.

8. Inseparable Fates

Lucette's fate can be traced through two intricately entangled patterns which pervade the whole of *Ada* – and which would be unavoidably difficult to pursue even if Nabokov's only point were that the designs of fate can take a long time to discern through the welter of haphazard detail. But he has something much more specific in mind. The fact that there are such ubiquitous interlacings in the lives of the Veen children stresses that Van and Ada's relationship *always* affects Lucette's fate, and that as a consequence their responsibility for her must be very considerable indeed, no matter how much they want to see their love as something special and apart from the rest of the their world.

After not having encountered Lucette since 1893, Van meets her again in Paris in 1901. On hearing she is in town, he searches her out at her hotel; not finding her there he crosses the rue des Jeunes Martyres to Ovenman's tavern. As he heads for the bar, having surrendered his coat but "kept his black fedora and stick-slim umbrella as he had seen his father do in that sort of bawdy, albeit smart, place which decent women did not frequent" (460), Van notices Lucette sitting there alone. Before approaching her, he ogles her intently, and now, as narrator, describes her in exceptionally caressive detail. She is all in black, wearing a picture hat, drinking alone. Van's description seems strangely insistent:

> For a minute he stood behind her, sideways to remembrance and reader (as she, too, was in regard to us and the bar), the crook of his silk-swathed cane lifted in profile.... We know, we love that high cheekbone (with an atom of powder puff sticking to the hot pink skin), and the forward upsweep of black lashes and the painted feline eyes – all this in profile, we softly repeat. (460)

He concludes the meticulous rhapsody thus:

> Her Irish profile sweetened by a touch of Russian softness, which adds a look of mysterious expectancy and wistful surprise to her beauty, must be seen, I hope, by the friends and admirers of my memories, as a natural masterpiece incomparably finer and younger than the portrait of the similarly postured lousy jade with her Parisian *gueule de guenon* on the vile poster painted by that wreck of an artist for Ovenman. (461)

That "wreck of an artist" is Toulouse-Lautrec, and the "vile poster" is his famous "Divan Japonais" (1892–1893), painted for Fournier (Ovenman), the proprietor of the cabaret Le Divan Japonais, 75, rue des Martyrs.[1] Lucette's attire and posture – and Van's too – are exactly homologous with the scene depicted in Toulouse-Lautrec's poster, though Van's attention to the finest detail, the most delicate glints of light, stands in marked contrast to Toulouse-Lautrec's bold but flat coloring and his vigorous but crude handling of line.

But there is a peculiar insistence in Van's description of Lucette at the bar that even the presence behind the scene of the Toulouse-Lautrec poster seems insufficient to account for. There is, too, a special engagement with the reader, an overt challenge to imagine the details correctly and with precision. We should note, particularly, that Van stands *behind* Lucette but *sideways* "to remembrance and reader": though Van sees Lucette from behind, his memory projects the recorded scene so that both figures appear in profile – as we, too, imagine them as we read.

Indeed, there is a good reason for Van's (and Nabokov's) exceptional insistence in this scene. For what the scene describes, in fact, is *not* the Tou-louse-Lautrec poster, but an advertisement for Barton and Guestier wines that appeared in the *New Yorker* in the 1960s[2] and that places two models in the position of Toulouse-Lautrec's models (Jane Avril and Edouard Dujardin), with the original poster on the wall behind them. (See photograph opposite.) Lucette gets served by bartender Ed Barton, whose name nicely conflates Toulouse-Lautrec's lettering ("Ed Fournier directeur") and the "Barton & Guestier" of the advertisement.

Nabokov slyly confuses the boundaries between life and art with this advertisement that is at once an *objet* both *trouvé* and already very much *com-posé* before he makes it more elaborate still. The advertisement which he has appropriated shows the differences between the subtlety and variety of light and line in life and the much less interesting reductionism of Toulouse-Lau-trec's kind of art. By being so much less spontaneous, so much more contrived than Toulouse-Lautrec, too, Nabokov comes closer to lifelikeness as he describes Lucette (even as he is imitating an advertisement) and closer to understanding the deceptions of the real, that the real "deceives" us by not being *less* but by being *more* real, more detailed, than we are prepared to notice. Van and Lucette's scene is, within the world of the book, "real" life imitating art (or life imitating life – what is realer, more part of the furniture of the everyday, than an advertisement? – imitating art), though of course we know it is Nabokov's art imitating life imitating either life or art. But this comic relationship between life and picture will shortly be played in another key.

Let us move on now to the climax of Lucette's drama, four days after she has met Van at Ovenman's bar. She sails on the *Tobakoff* with Van in the hope that she can make this a sort of honeymoon voyage. She has spent most of the day with him, at lunch, by the pool, over dinner and champagne, and her looks, her love, her insistence are tempting him more than he wants:

the wines you loved in Paris!

They come to you from France, with love. For these are
wines of the best growths and the best years from Barton & Guestier
——backed by more than two hundred
years of wine authority. Ask for B&G——wherever
fine wines are sold or served,
the finest wines of France

B&G

Browne-Vintners Co., New York, N.Y., Sole Dist. for the U.S.A.

Advertisement for Barton & Guestier wines,
New Yorker, 23 March 1963 and later issues

He cast around for a straw of Procrustean procrastination.

"Please," said Lucette. "I'm tired of walking around, I'm frail, I'm feverish, I hate storms, let's all go to bed!"

"Hey, look!" he cried, pointing to a poster. "They're showing something called *Don Juan's Last Fling*. It's prerelease and for adults only. Topical *Tobakoff!*" (487)

Within the cinena however, Van's resistance is at last worn down as Lucette brushes his cheek with her lips, takes his hand, kisses his knuckles:

the fool permitted himself to be stirred by it, the cretin whispered, prolonging the free, new apricot fire of anticipation.

"If you're a good girl we'll have drinks in my sitting room at midnight." (488)

At this point the main feature starts. The chief ingredient of *Don Juan's Last Fling* is the Don Juan legend, as retold by Pushkin in his verse play *Kamenniÿ gost'* (*The Stone Guest*, written 1826–1830, pub. 1839), and its main plot is the revenge of the "stone guest," Donna Anna's dead – and about-to-be-"cuckolded" – husband. But in the film the "Stone Cuckold" (490), as Van calls him, does not return in person. His revenge is accomplished by unmanning Don Juan, which he does through the agency of "Dolores, a dancing girl (lifted from Osberg's novella, as was to be proved in the ensuing lawsuit)" (488). But Dolores is none other than Lolita (given her full name, and in her Carmen role), and "Osberg" is the Borges to whom critics have often suggested Nabokov should be compared.[3] As if this distortion of literary history were not enough, "cadaverous Don Juan" is ridiculously blended with Don Quixote and "paunchy Leporello on his donkey" with Sancho Panza. But perhaps we had better see the film itself, at least as far as Van sees it:

On the way to the remote castle where the difficult lady, widowed by his sword, has finally promised him a long night of love in her chaste and chilly chamber, the aging libertine nurses his potency by spurning the advances of a succession of robust belles. A *gitana* predicts to the gloomy cavalier that before reaching the castle he will have succumbed to the wiles of her sister, Dolores, a dancing girl.... She also predicted something to Van, for even before Dolores came out of the circus tent to water Juan's horse, Van knew who she would be.

....

Lucette recognized Ada three or four seconds later, but then clutched his wrist:

"Oh, how awful! It was bound to happen. That's she! Let's go, please, let's go. You must not see her *debasing* herself. She's terribly made up, every gesture is childish and wrong –"

"Just another minute." said Van.

Terrible? Wrong? She was absolutely perfect, and strange, and poignantly familiar....

....

The Don rides past three windmills, whirling black against an ominous sunset, and saves her from the miller who accuses her of stealing a fistful of flour and tears her thin dress. Wheezy but still game. Juan carries her across a brook (her bare toe acrobatically tickling his face) and sets her down, top up, on the turf of an olive grove. Now they stand facing each other. She fingers voluptuously the jeweled pommel of his sword, she rubs her firm girl belly against his embroidered tights, and all at once the grimace of a premature spasm writhes across the poor Don's expressive face. He angrily disentangles himself and staggers back to his steed. (488–89)

This "premature spasm" is in fact the Stone Cuckold's revenge, for it renders Don Juan impotent when he arrives at Donna Anna's castle. But Van does not appreciate this twist of the plot, because the sudden appearance of Ada on screen – wholly unexpected, of course, even though she has long been pursuing an acting career – has quite jolted him out of the mood of anticipation Lucette had at last succeeded in creating, and at this point he rushes out of the cinema hall. In his bathroom he masturbates twice to make sure that Lucette's attractiveness and persistence will not tempt him again.

There is a surprising and absurd comic significance in the fact that Van rushes out at this moment and thus fails to realize "that what seemed an incidental embrace constituted the Stone Cuckold's revenge" (490). When in 1888 Van asks Ada when she first "guessed that her shy young 'cousin'...was physically excited in her presence" (110) she cannot recall, for in 1884 she had known little about "mammalian maleness" and "had still been rather hazy about the way human beings mated" (111). The closest she had come to "sexual contact" was with an elderly gentleman, a distinguished painter, who – note the "picture" pattern here too – drew his diminutive nudes invariably from behind" (111). Indeed, he has a penchant for little girls' bottoms, Ada's in particular. Ada recalls that "Every time...Pig Pigment [her version of "Paul J. Gigment"'s name] came, she cowered when hearing him trudge and snort and pant upstairs, ever nearer like the Marmoreal Guest, that immemorial ghost, seeking her, crying for her in a thin, querulous voice not in keeping with marble" (111). The "Marmoreal Guest, that immemorial ghost" is a punning reference to Pushkin's *The Stone Guest* (cf. also Proffer 258): while *gost'* is the Russian for "guest," Pushkin's "Stone Guest" is the marble *ghost* who gains his revenge by coming as a guest to frighten Don Juan to death.

If "Pig Pigment" is the first male to come into some sort of "sexual contact" with Ada, Van is the second. Just as the old painter who draws his nudes "invariably from behind" enjoys girls' bottoms, so Van too finds a special thrill in being behind Ada. When he is perched behind her for their first slight touch, not many minutes after their first meeting at Ardis, the moment is at once associated with orgasmic release:

> "You can catch a glint of it from here too," said Ada, turning her head and, *pollice verso*, introducing the view to Van who put his cup down, wiped his mouth with a tiny embroidered napkin, and stuffing it into his trouser pocket, went up to the dark-haired, pale-armed girl. As he bent toward her…she moved her head to make him move his to the required angle and her hair touched his neck. In his first dreams of her this re-enacted contact, so light, so brief, invariably proved to be beyond the dreamer's endurance and like a lifted sword signaled fire and violent release. (39)

The "children's first bodily contact" (86) occurs during the first picnic, when Ada's bottom settles down on Van's lap:

> With his entire being, the boiling and brimming lad relished her weight as he felt it responding to every bump of the road by softly parting in two and crushing beneath it the core of the longing which he knew he had to control lest a possible seep perplex her innocence. He would have yielded and melted in animal laxity had not the girl's governess saved the situation by addressing him. (87)

Their first full sexual experience occurs on the night of the Burning Barn, when Van, sitting with Ada in the "picture window" (116) of the library, begins by moulding Ada's buttocks:

> he continued to fondle the flow of her hair, and to massage and rumple her nightdress, not daring yet to go under and up, daring, however, to mold her nates until, with a little hiss, she sat down on his hand and her heels, as the burning castle of cards collapsed. She turned to him and the next moment he was kissing her bare shoulder, and pushing against her like that soldier behind in the queue.
> First time I hear about him. I thought old Mr. Nymphobottomus had been my only predecessor. (117)

(Mr. Nymphobottomus is a nonce name for Gigment.) Not long after the Burning Barn, but when Van and Ada are already becoming expert in the erotic arts, they decide to adopt a rear-entry approach for their lovemaking after Van reads an absurd report that suggests certain bizarre "contraceptive" advantages of such an amatory position. Delicate or not-so-delicate details tend to confirm that this position is regularly adopted. Early in Ardis the Second Van notes that all he "saw there of his new Ada were her ivorine thighs and haunches" (212). He records another scene later that summer: "As they crouched on the brink of one of the brook's crystal shelves...Van, at the last throb, saw the reflection of Ada's gaze in the water flash a warning" (267). Four years later, in Manhattan:

> she strained across the low tub to turn on both taps, and then bent over to insert the bronze chained plug: it got sucked in by itself, however, while he steadied her lovely lyre and next moment was at the suede-soft root.... (392)

Since Van adopts "Pig Pigment"'s approach to Ada from behind and since he has her so often this way, it is comically apt that Gigment, Ada's first "sexual partner," should be described as the cuckolded Marmoreal Guest. In *Don Juan's Last Fling* we can see him as the Stone Cuckold to Ada's Donna Anna and Van's Don Juan: just as the "premature spasm writhes across the poor Don's expressive face" – and this is "the Stone Cuckold's revenge" – Van gets up to leave, and thus is deprived of the end and promised climax of the film.

But of course Ada is most obviously the Dolores of the film, and to this Dolores, Lucette is Donna Anna, for it is she who is waiting for her Juan, looking forward to "a long night of love" (488). Lucette's hopes are spoiled by Ada's appearance in the role of Dolores:

> By some stroke of art, by some enchantment of chance, the few brief scenes she was given formed a perfect compendium of her 1884 and 1888 and 1892 looks.
>
> The *gitanilla* bends her head over the live table of Leporello's servile back to trace on a scrap of parchment a rough map of the way to the castle. Her neck shows white through her long black hair separated by the motion of her shoulder. It is no longer another man's Dolores, but a little girl twisting an aquarelle brush in the paint of Van's blood, and Donna Anna's castle is now a bog flower. (489)

It is this vision of Ada that is too much for Van and forces him to leave the movie to get

> rid of the prurient pressure as he had done the last time seventeen years ago. And how sad, how significant that the picture projected upon the screen of his paroxysm...was not the recent and pertinent image of Lucette, but the indelible vision of a bent bare neck and a divided flow of black hair and a purple-tipped paint brush. (490)

The Don's premature spasm in response to Dolores, unmanning him for Donna Anna, is an exact parallel to Van's own spasm in response to an image of Ada which will unman him for Lucette.

The scene in which Ada appears recalls for Van a picture of Ada in the past that he projects "upon the screen of his paroxysm." Let us look at this earlier picture, which forms another key link in the "behind" chain and which at the time, too, Van had carried off and masturbated over. In the hot afternoons of July 1884 Ada often sits in the music room copying flowers from a botanical atlas or painting new species and variants she subtly invents. Van repeatedly steals up behind her to peer "down her sleek *ensellure* as far as her coccyx and inhale the warmth of her entire body. His heart thumping, one miserable hand deep in his trouser pocket...he bent over her, as she bent over her work." (99–100) When he can no longer bear the throbbing excitement he slinks away to his room to "grasp a towel, uncover himself, and call forth the image he had just left behind, an image still as safe and bright as a hand-cupped flame – carried into the dark, only to be got rid of there with savage zeal" (100). The vision of Ada painting on those bright afternoons is one that Van retains with special joy, one that four years later he would like Ada again to imitate: "One of these days I will ask you for a repeat performance. You will sit as you did four years ago, at the same table, in the same light, drawing the same flower, and I shall go through the same scene with such joy, such pride, such – I don't know – gratitude!" (264) The most detailed of these magical afternoons is the last:

> One afternoon he came up behind her in the music room more noiselessly than ever before because he happened to be barefooted – and, turning her head, little Ada shut her eyes and pressed her lips to his in a fresh-rose kiss that entranced and baffled Van.
>
> "Now run along," she said, "quick, quick, I'm busy," and as he lagged like an idiot, she anointed his flushed forehead with her paintbrush in the semblance of an ancient Estotian "sign of the cross." "I have to finish this," she added, pointing with her violet-purple-soaked thin brush at a blend of *Ophrys scolopax* and *Ophrys veenae*, "and in a minute we must dress up because Marina wants Kim to take our picture – holding hands and grinning" (grinning, and then turning back to her hideous flower). (101)

Ophrys orchids have flowers that resemble insects; male insects "attempt to copulate with the flowers, which resemble females of their own species. During this process, pollen sacs become attached to the insect's body and are transferred to the next flower visited."[4] Nabokov makes this process, known as pseudo-copulation, artfully parallel Van's own pseudo-copulation before his evoked image of Ada. Just as Van's later masturbation, on the night of

Lucette's death, before a picture of Ada projected onto "the screen of his paroxysm" (a picture of Ada painting on those very afternoons in the music room) strangely mimics the paroxysm in *Don Juan's Last Fling*, so in these earlier scenes themselves Van's actions before his mental picture of Ada curiously mimic the literal picture Ada paints.

That first "fresh-rose kiss" from Ada at the end of the flower-painting scenes initiates the next stage of their love affair, their kissing phase. In recounting this phase Van eulogizes whatever of Ada he is allowed to kiss, her face and neck and hands. Note here the white neck showing through separations of black hair that Van will see again in Ada as Dolores:

> He learned her face. Nose, check, chin – all possessed such a softness of outline (associated retrospectively with...picture hats, and...courtesans...) that a mawkish admirer might well have imagined the pale plume of a reed...shaping her profile, while a more childish and sensual digit would have liked, and did like, to palpate that nose, cheek, chin. Remembrance, like Rembrandt, is dark but festive. Remembered ones dress up for the occasion and sit still. Memory is a photo-studio de luxe on an infinite Fifth Power Avenue. The fillet of black velvet binding her hair that day (the day of the mental picture) brought out its sheen at the silk of the temple and along the chalk of the parting. It hung lank and long over the neck, its flow disjoined by the shoulder; so that the mat white of her neck through the black bronze stream showed in triangular elegancy. (103–104)

We should note too the mingling of different kinds of "picture," the "mental picture" and Van's images of memory as a painter or a photo-studio de luxe. Indeed, though Van makes no indication of the fact – and though we do not find out until three hundred pages later – the mental picture corresponds exactly to an actual photograph taken just after that fresh-rose kiss, immediately after which the children had gone to change for their formal photographs. Because their poses in this photograph mimic their repeated respective poses on the previous afternoons, Van and Ada know even as it is taken that the photograph will have a secret significance for them:

> Another photograph was taken in the same circumstances but for some reason had been rejected by capricious Marina: at a tripod table, Ada sat reading, her half-clenched hand covering the lower part of the page. A very rare, radiant, seemingly uncalled-for smile shone on her practically Moorish lips. Her hair flowed partly across her collarbone and partly down her back. Van stood inclining his head above her and looked, unseeing, at the opened book. In full, deliberate consciousness, at the moment of the hooded click, he bunched the recent past with the imminent future and thought to himself that this would

remain an objective perception of the real present and that he must remember the flavor, the flash, the flesh of the present (as he, indeed, remembered it half a dozen years later – and now, in the second half of the next century). (402)

A future recollection such as this is always a rare and magic moment for Nabokov, an escape from the order of time and the ordinary process of memory's casual accumulation.[5] For Van such magic here can only add to the blissful fact that this memory has and will have so special a place in the whole history of his love for Ada.

When all this accumulation of exceptionally vivid and treasured memories – each one part of the pattern of pictures and behinds – reappears in Ada's Dolores role, it is no wonder that the past should break on and overwhelm the sexual tension Lucette has managed to build up in the present or that Ada as Dolores should so thoroughly unman Van, Don Juan to poor Lucette's desperate Donna Anna.

But the plot of the movie continues to thicken. In a new sense, Lucette is Dolores to her own Donna Anna, while Ada becomes the *gitana*, Dolores's sister: "A *gitana* predicts to the gloomy cavalier that before reaching the castle he will have succumbed to the wiles of her sister, Dolores" (488). After Lucette flies from the *débauche à trois*, Van pens a note apologizing to her. On scanning the letter, Ada complains to Van:

> "I call this pompous, puritanical rot....Why *should* we apollo for her having experienced a delicious *spazmochka*? I love her and would never allow you to harm her. It's curious – you know, something in the tone of your note makes me really jealous for the first time in my...life...Van, Van, somewhere, some day, after a sunbath or dance, you will sleep with her, Van!" (421)

In the letter itself, Van had written: "We are even sorrier to have inveigled our Esmeralda and mermaid in a naughty prank" (421). Van calls her "Esmeralda" because the name of Esmeralda, the gipsy dancing girl in Victor Hugo's *Notre-Dame de Paris* (1831), comes from the Spanish for "emerald," the color Lucette usually wears; but unwittingly Van's letter and Ada's prophesy establish that Lucette, like Ada herself, is Dolores, the gipsy dancing girl of *Don Juan's Last Fling*. The identification is twice confirmed. When Lucette meets Van at Ovenman's four days before they see *Don Juan's Last Fling*, she says to him (referring to "Osberg"'s novel): "I'm like Dolores – when she says she's 'only a picture painted on air'" (464), and in the pose of Jane Avril in the Toulouse-Lautrec poster, our virgin in Paris occupies the role of Toulouse-Lautrec's cabaret star. Lucette, who wears a "short evening frock" (484) on her fateful last night with Van, is also specifically linked with a dancing girl, "a Crimean cabaret dancer in a very short scintillating frock" (185), who had been Van's partner years earlier when he played Mascodagama: "Fragile, red-haired 'Rita'...bore an odd resemblance to Lucette as she was to look ten years later" (185).

Lucette is Dolores to her own Donna Anna: she is present in *Don Juan's Last Fling* in Ada's evocation of Ada's own past, because *her* own past is so inextricable from her sister's. If Ada as Dolores evokes herself painting orchids and that acute memory of the mental picture that becomes also a photograph, she also evokes Lucette. Let us look once more at the passage quoted on p. 137, where Van describes Ada's features in the kissing chapter, features remembered particularly from the pose adopted for that photograph taken just after Ada kisses Van while painting her *Ophrys* orchids. Note now the stress on the profile, a stress we observed before in the scene at Oven-man's bar, and the combination of back view (the photograph of this "mental picture" shows Van *behind* Ada, though the picture is taken from the side) and profile, a combination also witnessed in the "Divan Japonais" re-enactment. That the lines quoted expressly refer to Lucette and the Divan Japonais scene is established by the echoes of the *"softness* of outline (associated retrospectively with...*picture hats,* and...*courtesans*...shaping her *profile"* in the later scene: "in that sort of bawdy...place which *decent women did not frequent*...the *picture hat...profile* sweetened by a touch of Russian *softness"* (460–61: italics added). It should be noted too that the rhapsody on Ada's features combines painting (Rembrandt), photograph and actual scene, the same combination as can be seen in the lavish description of Lucette: the Toulouse-Lautrec poster, the Barton & Guestier photograph, the scene of Lucette and Van together.

The confusion of picture and picture in the Divan Japonais scene, then, is more than a play on the relationship of life to art. This confusion and the remarkable insistence on "behind" and "profile" make clear that even when Van is hyperconscious of Lucette's identity and individuality, as he is in the bar room scene, she is still tightly entangled with Ada and with the cumulative force of Van's vividest memories. Even if we grant that Dolores is Lucette she cannot help evoking for Van his past with Ada.

Lucette at the bar with Van behind her is linked by some fatal network to Ada at her table with Van behind her. But the odd web of fate formed by this "behind" and "picture" relationship stretches right across Lucette's past, signaling her entanglement in Van and Ada's affairs. We have to begin with a rather grotesque example, but it should be no secret by now that Nabokov finds the grotesque a useful means to his ends. It disguises his patterns (who would think of looking for an artistic pattern in, say, details of sexual position or an outbreak of flatulence?) for a long time before confirming their existence (why else would he repeatedly single out such details when there is no local necessity to do so?).

On the journey back from the 1884 picnic, when "Ada's bottom" (87) is perched on Van's lap, Lucette is seated next to the coachman: "Lucette refused to give up her perch (accepting with a bland little nod the advice of her drunken boxfellow who was seen to touch her bare knees with a good-natured paw)" (86). When Ben Wright is drunk, as he is now, he is exceptionally flatulent, and Lucette complains: "I want to sit with you. *Mne tut neudobno, i ot nego nehorosho pakhnet* (I'm uncomfortable here, and he does not smell good)." (88) This is only a pointer, for what matters is the way Ben Wright and his "good-natured paw" will be recalled in the crucial second picnic ride, when *Lucette's* bottom is perched on Van's lap: "that other coachman who for several months had haunted her dreams" (280). Underneath the comedy of Ben Wright's flatulence lies an advance warning that for a vulnerable child like Lucette even the coachman's drunken leer and his hand on her knee can conjure up fears not easily dismissed.

The day after the picnic, the family gathers for high tea in the garden. Listening to the conversation of the older people around her, Lucette queries a strange word:

> "Are we Mesopotamians?" asked Lucette.
> "We are Hippopotamians,'" said Van. "Come," he added, "we have not yet ploughed today."
> A day or two before, Lucette had demanded that she be taught to hand-walk, Van gripped her by her ankles while she slowly progressed on her red little palms.... (91)

The "Hippopotamians" here pairs Van, behind little Lucette, holding her legs, with "Mr. Nymphobottomus," who would revel in Van's part in the continuing scene: "Her bright hair hung over her face, her panties showed from under the hem of her skirt, yet still she urged the ploughboy on." (92) Mlle Larivière complains about these "indecent gymnastics" which are "no good for" Lucette (92). Since she has no idea of Van and Ada's interest in each other, we tend to agree with Van that Larivière is "pathologically unobservant" (96). But Larivière, who sees more of Lucette than she does of Van and Ada, has been more observant than proud Van: she can see that he is indeed turning little Lucette's head.

More obviously part of the "behind" pattern, now, are the glimpses curious little Lucette gets of her big sister and "cousin" at Ardis the Second:

> All Van saw there of his new Ada were her ivorine thighs and haunches, and the very first time he clasped them she bade him, in the midst of his vigorous joy, to glance across her shoulder over the window ledge, which her hands were still clutching in the ebbing throbs of her own response, and note that Lucette

was approaching – skipping rope, along a path in the shrubbery.

...Lucette was rocking the glum dackel...or with various pretty contortions unhurriedly mounting the gray-looped board and swinging gently and gingerly as if never having done it yet.... She increased her momentum so cannily that Ada and her cavalier, in the pardonable blindness of ascending bliss, never once witnessed the instant when the round rosy face with all its freckles aglow swooped up and two green eyes leveled at the astounding tandem. (212–13)

Having seen the older children in action, Lucette is comically but pitiably eager to join their "games": "Lucette insisted on their playing 'leaptoad' with her – and Ada and Van exchanged dark looks" (213). Her mixture of innocence and imitativeness is both funny and a revelation of the dangerous degree to which her development depends on Van and Ada's actions and example.

At the second picnic, while "the rustic feast was being prepared" (266), Lucette hides among the burnberry bushes to watch Van and Ada in their usual position:

As they crouched on the brink of one of the brook's crystal shelves, where, before falling, it stopped to have its picture taken and take pictures itself, Van, at the last throb, saw the reflection of Ada's gaze in the water flash a warning. Something of the sort had happened somewhere before: he did not have time to identify the recollection that, nonetheless, led him to identify at once the sound of the stumble behind him.

Among the rugged rocks they found and consoled poor little Lucette.... (267)

Here the brook's stopping "to have its picture taken and take pictures itself" and Van's seeing Ada's image in the water bring the picture motif into prominence just as Lucette gets her closest view yet of Van behind Ada.

On the way back from the picnic the "behind" and "picture" motifs reach the first of two climaxes before *Don Juan's Last Fling*. Because there are too few places left in the last carriage, little Lucette seats her tight little crupper on Van's lap, her "remarkably well-filled green shorts...stained with burnberry purple" (280) – a significant trace of the stumble near her big siblings earlier that afternoon. Though it is Lucette he is holding, Van starts to project on her an image of Ada and the 1884 picnic: "Lucette's compact bottom and cool thighs seemed to sink deeper and deeper in the quicksand of the dream-like, dream-rephrased, legend-distorted past...it was that other picnic which he now relived and it was Ada's soft haunches which he now held as if she were present in duplicate, in two different color prints." (280) Van portrays the experience as a miraculous retrieval of time – but the confusion of Ada and

Lucette here, their inextricability from one another, should sound a note of caution. Van almost reaches orgasm under Lucette as he projects onto her the image of Ada; but "the little proxy's neck, glistening with sweat, was pathetic, her trustful immobility, sobering, and after all no furtive friction could compete with what awaited him in Ada's bower" (281). The situation curiously anticipates *Don Juan's Last Fling*: here, Van nearly succumbs to the sort of "premature spasm" that unmans Don Juan for Donna Anna, but he remembers the real Ada just in time; here, too, it is the projected image of Ada that leads towards orgasm, despite Lucette's being physically so much closer, just as when Van rushes out of the cinema hall, the "picture projected upon the screen of his paroxysm" will not be "the recent and pertinent image of Lucette, but the indelible vision of a bent bare neck and a divided flow of black hair and a purple-tipped paint brush" (490).

The eerie anticipation of *Don Juan Last Fling* hints that we should consider the effect of the picnic ride on Lucette. She has just seen Van make love to Ada from behind; she knows no more about sex than her own observations and hopes and fears have told her; and she has felt Van stir under her. That something about the picnic ride troubles her becomes clear three days later, when Ada is trying to teach her to draw flowers:

> obstinate Lucette kept insisting that the easiest way to draw a flower was to...trace the outline of the thing in colored inks.... Casually, lightly, [Ada] went on to explain how the organs of orchids work – but all Lucette wanted to know, after her whimsical fashion, was: could a boy bee impregnate a girl flower through something, through his gaiters or woolies or whatever he wore?
>
> "You know," said Ada in a comic nasal voice, turning to Van, "you know, that child has the dirtiest mind imaginable and now she is going to be mad at me for saying this and sob on the Larivière bosom, and complain she has been pollinated by sitting on your knee."
>
> "But I can't speak to Belle about dirty things," said Lucette quite gently and reasonably. (288–89)

Little Lucette's fears of being impregnated from behind at first seem comical; but by now we should be able to sense something more foreboding. The child does not know how to interpret what may be some special experience with the big "cousin" on whom she has doted for years: the stigma of her obsessiveness has just been pollinated.

We should note too Lucette's integration here into the retrospectively ominous repetition of her sister's flower-painting. Four years later, after Ada's rudely initiating her into sexual manipulation, Lucette, "considerably more dissolute [at sixteen] than her sister had seemed at that fatal age" (367), makes plain how well her obsession is thriving: now all she copies are "beautiful erotic pictures from an album of Forbidden Masterpieces" (376).

Lucette's peering at Van and Ada on the afternoon of the picnic is repeated in 1892 when Van takes Ada from behind as she bends over the bath: "and now their four eyes were looking again into the azure brook of Pinedale, and Lucette pushed the door open with a perfunctory knuckle knock and stopped, mesmerized by the sight of Van's hairy rear" (392–93). On the night of the restaurant outing, a week later, Ada says to Lucette: "Let's all go to bed. You have seen our huge bed, pet?" (413) – and prepares the way for the next climax of the "behind" and "picture" patterns. When they are back at the apartment, Van cruelly kisses Lucette to find out Vinelander's name. The scene flows into the last and most brutal instance of the "behind" motif as part of Van and Ada's lovemaking:

> "I want the name of that fellow."
>
> "Vinelander," she answered.
>
> He heard Ada Vinelander's voice calling…and a minute later, without the least interruption of the established tension, Van found himself, in a drunken dream, making violent love to Rose [his black maid] – no, to Ada, but in the rosacean fashion, on a kind of lowboy. She complained he hurt her....He went to bed and was about to doze off for good when she left his side. Where was she going? Pet wanted to see the album.
>
> "I'll be back in a rubby," she said (tribadic schoolgirl slang), "so keep awake. From now on by the way, it's going to be *Chère-amie-fait-morata*" – (play on the generic and specific names of the famous fly) – "until further notice."[6]
>
> "But no sapphic *vorschmacks*," mumbled Van into his pillow. (415–16)

In other words, after roughly making love to Ada from behind – presumably, in fact, this is anal intercourse, a sort of revenge on Ada as he anticipates duelling Vinelander – Van is not to use the rear-entry method again. Significantly, this last copulation from behind occurs just after Van's most calculated manipulation of Lucette's thirst for affection and just before Ada's most serious incorporation of Lucette into their lovemaking – for this scene leads straight into the *débauche à trois*.

> Lucette shrugged her shoulders and made as if to leave, but Ada's avid hand restrained her.
>
> "Pop in, pet (it all started with the little one letting wee winds go free at table, *circa* 1882)...." (418)

"Pet" (from the French for "fart") is a nickname given to Lucette, especially by Ada, throughout the book – and it should recall too Ben Wright and his "letting winds go free" (140) as he drove back from the first Ardis picnic, patting Lucette's knee in a way she was haunted by for months. For "pet" has another, sinister connotation throughout Lucette's past – "The idea was to have Van fool Lucette by petting her in Ada's presence" (213) – and reaches its apotheosis here in the scene of the debauch: "'Pet stays right here,' cried audacious Ada, and with one graceful swoop plucked her sister's nightdress off." (418) And when Van adopts the most dazzlingly rococo style in describing the scene on the bed as if it were a picture – as if the three Veen children merged into a "canvas…reproduced (in 'Forbidden Masterpieces') expertly enough to stand the scrutiny of a bordel's *vue d'oiseau*" (418) – we should know by now *not* to be dazzled, for: "Ten eager, evil, loving, long fingers belonging to two different young demons caress their helpless bed pet." (420).

The picture pattern and the whole bevy of "behinds" and "bottoms" and "pets" establish how enmeshed Lucette's life is in the lives of her siblings, how hopelessly her frailty has been entangled in Van and Ada's passion and their inconsiderate strength. As the "behind" motif suggests, they have buggered up her life.

The complex interrelationship of the patterns in Ada's and Lucette's lives, all of which come together in the interchangeability of Lucette and Ada as Dolores – Ada recalling herself, Lucette recalling herself only to recall Ada – stresses the impossibility of treating their fates as separate, as Van and Ada have tried to do, and the cruel insensitivity of Van and Ada's insistence that they matter only to each other and affect no one else. The patterns endlessly intertwining the two sisters emphasize that their contact has been too intimate for the development of one not to be affected by the other. No matter how Van and Ada's love seemed, by its intensity and concentration, to exclude the surrounding world, someone else was involved and her frailty, her needs, the reality of her feelings, should not have been ignored.

Lucette's life has been closely and as it turns out fatally bound up with the lives of Van and Ada. Because their lives have touched the younger and much more defenseless girl so often Van and Ada should have considered the effects of their behavior. Instead, they have aroused a too-early curiosity, entangled Lucette in too-early embraces, played upon her imitative but powerful passion that has not allowed the rest of her personality to develop. They have reveled quite magnificently in the infinity of their own emotion for each other – as if the privilege of an infinity of emotion for another person could exist without one's also being interconnected with other lives and without one's being responsible for each of those interconnections.

9. Lucette and Others (1)

Most of us can be kind when it suits, most of us can fail to be so when our feelings guide us onto another track. Solicitude for someone else even when it costs what we most dearly crave and most urgently need is as difficult as it is admirable, but at the climax of *Ada* Lucette instinctively manages exactly this. On the last night of her life, when she seems to have finally subdued Van's resistance to her advances, she remains politely with the Robinsons, those well-meaning but boring family friends, rather than follow Van out of the theater as she yearns to do: she sacrifices the crucial and precarious hold she has won over her brother in order not to bruise, even lightly, someone else's sensitivity. Van, on the other hand, ablaze with the image of Ada in *Don Juan's Last Fling*, keeps Lucette at bay (he pretends to have female company) when she rings him after the Robinsons have left her cabin: he refuses to derail his thoughts of Ada by attending to his younger sister's distress.

Lucette, doomed by her vulnerability and, as chance would have it, that last act of kindness, turns out to be *Ada's* moral center, even – most unexpectedly – in scenes where she plays no part. Nabokov assesses quite unblinkingly Van and Ada's behavior towards their sister, but he also examines with the same scrupulous care *all* their actions towards whomever they meet in the novel, and every shortcoming he detects he silently indicates by noting its consistency with the Veen thoughtlessness that tears Lucette apart.

Nabokov operates silently because the very challenge he has set himself is to show the moral myopia possible even in a person blessed with extreme self-awareness and a remarkable capacity for tenderness and sensitivity – when they suit. Van does recognize, too late, his and Ada's responsibility towards Lucette, but those actions of his that Nabokov surreptitiously criticizes *he* construes not as flaws but as the vivid proofs of the romantic timbre of his personality. And if Van pens the book with any purpose, it is not merely to depict Ada but to celebrate and justify his own romantic nature.

Because he maneuvers with such stealth, Nabokov can inveigle most of us into accepting *Ada* on Van's own rapturous terms, until he obliges us to notice and perhaps learn from our mistake. While *Ada* certainly celebrates the romance of life, all its energy of mind and emotion, Nabokov's version of the book – so much more farseeing than his narrator's memoir – also takes pains to point out the casual cruelties that can coexist even with the clearest thought and the finest feelings.

Lucette, Demon and Aqua

Van eulogizes his father as the personification of fiery-eyed romance. Nabokov on the other hand also sees Demon as romantic selfishness incarnate. Provided his own feelings have full sweep, Demon remains indifferent to what happens to others. To pique Marina he marries her frail twin Aqua – and then ignores her as his passion and vanity impel him on from woman to woman. Aqua, meanwhile, must jolt her way down through madness to suicide. In his refusal to heed anything but the pressure of his own impulse, Demon stands as the antithesis of Lucette and the source and model for Ada and especially the romantic egotism in Van. Throughout the novel Nabokov criticizes Van and Ada by intimating how their behavior mimics their father's more lurid ways, the basic term of both the mimicry and the criticism being that both Lucette and Aqua are driven to suicide by being so entangled in the lives of the self-absorbed Veens.

Aqua dies because she can no longer bear the possibility that the anguish of her madness might return. Though she has never been mentally sturdy, it is not until Demon starts to wreck her life that she actually requires hospitalization. After his affair with Marina erupts into a jealous row Demon suddenly marries Aqua "out of spite and pity" (19). But he soon returns to Marina, in the first of the infidelities that shatter Aqua's nerves. She has to enter a sanatorium, by which time she is pregnant – but so is Marina, who had conceived just before the row that led to Demon's marrying Aqua. When Aqua has a miscarriage at six months, the unmarried Marina substitutes her child – Van – for the dead one. Aqua's mind is overcast enough for her not to recognize quite what has happened, but the suspicion of the truth adds to her mental precariousness. Her uncertainties about Van compound the torment of Demon's infidelity with Marina and countless others so that her "disintegration [goes] down a shaft of phases, every one more racking than the last" (22). But when Van is thirteen Aqua has a brief respite of real confidence "that Van was *her, her,* Aqua's, beloved son," and being "unwilling to suffer another relapse after this blessed state of mental repose, but knowing it could not last" (27), she takes her life.

Aqua's fate foreshadows Lucette's in starker form – so stark, indeed, we tend to overlook what seems too obvious to be meaningful. Lucette dies because her fate is inextricable from her sister's; not only does Aqua die for the same reason, but in keeping with the paradigmatic nature of her case the virtual inseparability of her fate from her sister's is indicated by their being twins – called Aqua and Marina! Lucette dies partly because her sister and the man both she and her sister love are irresponsible in their amours, just as Demon and Marina, in much more brazenly melodramatic fashion, are so plainly irresponsible towards Aqua. Here again the sheer overtness of Demon's name and the fact that his black hue and his virtually winglike cape make him almost an angel of darkness, deflect us: anything so absurdly direct we erroneously suppose can only be colorful parody.

Nabokov also stresses the similarity of Aqua's and Lucette's fates by means of the deaths themselves. Aqua dies in Arizona, by poisoning herself with pills, Lucette in mid-Atlantic, by drowning: superficially there would appear to be little to connect the two suicides. But Aqua has been staying at a sanatorium called "Centaur" or "St. Taurus," Lucette spends the month before her death at "Minotaor." Aqua dies wearing "yellow slacks and a black bolero" (28); Lucette – commemorating the black divan with yellow cushions in the Ardis Library – dons "black slacks and a yellow shirt" (492) before diving from the *Tobakoff*.[1] Aqua acquires two hundred pills and gulps them down at a picnic; Lucette takes five pills to numb her quickly in the water, and as she climbs up to the deck from which she will dive, a fragment – an anecdote of a picnic – from a painter's journal she has just been reading floats into her stream of consciousness:

> Six, seven – no, more than that, about ten steps up. *Dix marches.* Leg and arms. *Dimanche. Déjeuner sur l'herbe. Tout le monde pue. Ma belle-mère avale son râtelier. Sa petite chienne,* after too much exercise, gulps twice and quietly vomits, a pink pudding onto the picnic nappe. *Après quoi* she waddles off. These steps are something. (493)

By implanting around Lucette's death these minutiae which Van does not realize echo Aqua's own end, Nabokov indicates that Van and Ada repeat a generation later Demon's more blatant cruelty in driving Aqua to suicide. Because he has aligned the two cases so closely Nabokov also enables himself to identify a local flaw in Van or Ada's behavior by a brief and apparently innocuous reference to Demon. Since Van, especially, adulates and imitates his father's flash and flair, a brief hint of Demonic style in Van will often quickly pinpoint a moral lapse we might otherwise have overlooked. We shall see this in more detail as we move from the novel's prologue – the pre-Ardis chapters which establish the relationship between Aqua and Lucette – to Ardis itself.

Injurious Desire: Ardis and its Images

Paradise Lost: Lucette and Aqua

For Van and Ada Ardis seems to be genuinely the paradise its name suggests, and in fact Van makes its Edenic qualities exuberantly explicit. While climbing Ardis's shattal tree – which he has Ada refer to as "the Tree of Knowledge ...from Eden National Park" (95) – he and pantyless Ada fall so that his "expressionless face and cropped head were between her legs and a last fruit fell with a thud" (94). Since the mishap leads to a new stage of their love, their crashing down along with the fruit seems to confirm Robert Alter's remark that the incident "clearly enacts a Happy Fall."[2] Alfred Appel, Jr., is even more enthusiastic: "theirs would instead seem to be a Fortunate Fall. Innocence still prevails....In regaining Paradise, Nabokov has miraculously succeeded in retelling a story so old that it becomes utterly new."[3] But Nabokov makes clear that the implications of the scene are very different indeed.

A few pages after the incident Van recalls that "first contact, so light, so mute, between his soft lips and her softer skin...established – high up in that dappled tree, with only that stray ardilla daintily leavesdropping" (98). The "stray ardilla [a type of squirrel] daintily leavesdropping" should send us back to a "silver-and-sable skybab squirrel" that "sat sampling a cone on the back of a bench" (94) as Van and Ada climbed their tree – but also to the fact that Mlle Larivière (who, however, is notoriously unobservant) and Lucette are "just within earshot" (94). This precise cross-reference signals that the squirrel was not alone in eavesdropping on the children's tumble. Because *Lucette* also overheard the two older children's reactions to Van's accidentally falling on Ada's naked crotch, her curiosity is now fired. The significance of the incident is underlined by the fact that when Van first sees Lucette and misremembers Ada's formal name, Adelaida, he assumes this unknown child must be "Ardelia" (busybody) – an exact homophone of "ardilla," the squirrel. The prominence given to this identification of Lucette as "busybody" and "'leavesdropping' squirrel" emphasizes that the "Edenic" scene depicts the beginning of a loss of innocence that will prove far from fortunate.

Even earlier in his first stay at Ardis, Van had caught a glimpse of Ada "washing her face and arms over an old-fashioned basin" (60):

> A fat snake of porcelain curled around the basin, and as both the reptile and [Van] stopped to watch Eve and the soft woggle of her bud-breasts in profile, a big mulberry-colored cake of soap slithered out of her hand, and her black-socked foot hooked the door shut with a bang which was more the echo of the soap's crashing against the marble board than a sign of pudic displeasure. (60)

The fall of the mulberry soap and the "bang which was more the echo of the soap's crashing" comically imitate the fruit of the Fall and nature's groaning echo of man's first disobedience:

> Forth reaching to the fruit, she plucked, she ate:
> Earth felt the wound, and nature from her seat
> Sighing through all her works gave signs of woe.
> (*Paradise Lost* IX, 781–83)

But the soap reappears on the day when Van and Ada imprison Lucette in the bath while they make love around the corner of the L-shaped room:

> "I'm Van," said Lucette, standing in the tub with the mulberry soap between her legs and protruding her shiny tummy.
>
> "You'll turn into a boy if you do that," said Ada sternly, "and that won't be very amusing." (144)

Ada tells Van later that their tying Lucette up by the bank had not worked as planned: Lucette *had* watched them make love. "Good Lord," reacts Van, "that explains the angle of the soap!" (152): Ardis may be a sexual paradise for Van and Ada, but it is a dangerous wonderland for little Lucette.

The difference between the romantic self-absorption which characterizes Van and Ada's affair at Ardis and the demanding circumspection Nabokov prefers underlies the passage that records Van's final departure from Ardis. Having just found out from Blanche of Ada's unfaithfulness, Van rides off from the Veen manor in a carriage and pair:

> They passed undulating fields of wheat speckled with the confetti of poppies and bluets....
>
> "The express does not stop at Torfyanka, does it, Trofim?"
>
> "I'll take you five versts across the bog," said Trofim, "the nearest is Volo-syanka."
>
> His vulgar Russian word for Maidenhair; a whistle stop; train probably crowded.
>
> Maidenhair. Idiot! Percy boy might have been buried by now! Maidenhair. Thus named because of the huge spreading Chinese tree at the end of the platform. Once, vaguely, confused with the Venus'-hair fern. She walked to the end of the platform in Tolstoy's novel. First exponent of the inner monologue, later exploited by the French and the Irish. *N'est vert, n'est vert, nest vert. L'arbre aux quarante écus d'or,* at least in the fall. Never, never shall I hear again her "botanical" voice fall at *biloba,* "sorry, my Latin is showing." *Ginkgo,* gingko, ink, inkog. Known also as Salisbury's adiantofolia, Ada's infolio, poor *Salisburia:* sunk; poor Stream of Consciousness, *marée noire* by now. Who wants Ardis Hall! (299–300)

By sending his narrator-hero off to the railway station in the bleakest of moods, Nabokov makes it almost inevitable that someone of Van's literary disposition and tendency to self-dramatization should express the suicidal depth of his despair by comparing his thoughts to the stream of consciousness flowing through Anna Karenin's mind (in Bk.7 Chs.29–30) as she heads towards the railway station where she will throw herself under a train.

But Nabokov suggests that Van has a much more valid reason for overwhelming regret than the loss of Ada and Ardis – namely, his and Ada's indifference to Lucette. For the lines above continually refer to Lucette's death and to the whole irony of her fate. Merely in recording his thoughts as the inner monologue of someone in a suicidal state, Van also foreshadows the one other inner monologue in *Ada*, Lucette's thoughts just before her death: "ten steps up. *Dix marches*. Legs and arms. *Dimanche. Déjeuner sur l'herbe*" And if the form of his monologue foreshadows Lucette's death, its content focusses intently on the tragic irony of the "deflowering" which brings her death about.

The "Maidenhair" with which the paragraph begins combines a hint of "maidenhood" or "maidenhead" with the name of a plant to indicate that the monologue's real subject will be Lucette's tangled virginity, as unwittingly evoked by Ada in *the souci d'eau* diatribe. Circling around and around his memories of Ada, Van follows the pattern of her explanations – she had jumped from the "marsh marigold" to its scientific name to a misnomer, and then on to Russian and French equivalents – as he retraces his way from a common name (maidenhair) to a misnomer (Venus'-hair) to a French term (*l'arbre aux quarante écus d'or*) to two scientific names (*Ginkgo biloba* and *Salisburia adiantifolia*) of the ginkgo tree. Most pointedly of all, the *écus d'or*, the golden ginkgo leaves, recall the petals of a marsh marigold *"plus pure qu'un louis,"* and especially the passage linking Lucette and the "forged *louis d'or*" (64–65).

Just as in the *souci d'eau* scene precocious Ada's self-display incorporates both botanical nomenclature and translating, so amid the jumble of Van's thoughts at the station we find not only Ada's disquisition on the maidenhair tree but also her interest in translation. She parodies mistranslation in her wild version of Lear's "Never, never, never, never, never":

> *Ce beau jardin fleurit en mai,*
> *Mais en hiver*
> *Jamais, jamais, jamais, jamais, jamais*
> *N'est vert, n'est vert, n'est vert, n'est vert,*
> *n'est vert. (92)*

As if to compensate for the loss of the flower in Fowlie's version of Rimbaud, Ada here adds flowers, when none are present in the original – although the flowers disappear again by the time we reach the line echoing Lear over the dead Cordelia. Ada happens to quote her mock translation only once, while Van is holding Lucette from *behind* as he steers her on her hands across the lawn: "she slowly progressed on her little red palms, sometimes falling with a grunt on her face or pausing to nibble a daisy" (91). The daisy-nibbling on one level jolts the scene into comic life and guarantees Lucette a charmed place in the reader's imagination; on another it adds to Nabokov's cumulative emphasis on Lucette's "deflowering" – her initiation, her attachment to Van, her entanglement with Ada.

As Van approaches the Maidenhair station, he thinks of Anna Karenin walking to her death ("She walked to the end of the platform in Tolstoy's novel") but in the next sentence recalls Ada's comment on Tolstoy – "First exponent of the inner monologue" (299–300) – for the phrase echoes the opening of Pt. 1 Ch. 10, where Van prepares for Ada's discussion of the "Mémoire" translation by describing her customary mealtime prattle: "Arch and grandiloquent, Ada would be describing a dream, a natural history wonder, a special belletristic device [such as the] '*monologue intérieur*' borrowed from old Leo...." (61)

By virtue of the "maidenhair" and the "*écus d'or,*" the themes of Ada's botanical names and "floral" translations and by this specific recollection of her mealtime volubility, the whole of Van's monologue refers back to the novel's most emphatic play upon Lucette's fatal virginity – and we can see now that its last lines also directly suggest the black tide in which she drowns: "sunk; poor Stream of Consciousness, *marée noire* by now."

But if the end of Ardis foreshadows the fate that devolves from Lucette's too early initiation, it also – even more unexpectedly – recalls *Aqua's* fate. To see why this should be we must turn back in time. Reminiscing with Van in the woods near Ardis, Ada recalls a visit she made as a little girl of four to Demon's summer home at Radugalet, "the 'other Ardis'" (149). It appears that Dan has had word from Demon that a young cocotte, a former scullery maid at Ardis, is now keeping him company. Marina suspects something of the sort is behind Dan's excursion to Radugalet and at the last minute insists to her uncomfortable husband that she and Ada are coming too:

> However, when they arrived, it became instantly clear that Demon had not expected ladies. He was on the terrace drinking gold wine (sweet whisky) with an orphan he had adopted, he said, a lovely Irish wild rose in whom Marina at once recognized an impudent scullery maid who had briefly worked at Ardis Hall, and had been ravished by an unknown gentleman – who was now well-known. In those days Uncle Dan wore a monocle in gay-dog copy of his cousin, and this he screwed in to view Rose, whom perhaps he had also been promised.... The party was a disaster. (150)

Marina, Ada remembers, stalks off in anger, but "Van had not the slightest recollection of that visit or indeed of that particular summer, because his father's life, anyway, was a rose garden all the time" (151). The "rose garden" seems gracefully sportive at first, until one recollects the strain Demon's behavior puts on Aqua's frailty, and the suicide that results; significantly, it is "in the rose garden of Ardis Manor" (29) that Van and Ada read and discuss Aqua's suicide note.

While the account of Van's departure from Ardis obliquely affirms that Lucette's death as well as Van's immediate loss is necessary to any assessment of Ardis, the passage also subtly evokes Aqua's death in order to point out the relationship between Van and Ada's conduct here and their father's at Radugalet, the "other Ardis": their common assumption that one's immediate pleasure need not be spoilt by consideration for others. In Pt. 1 Ch. 3 Aqua's suicide is compared to Anna Karenin's. After gulping down an overdose of drugs, Aqua smiles, "dreamily enjoying the thought (rather 'Kareninian' in tone) that her extinction would affect people about as deeply as the abrupt, mysterious, never explained demise of a comic strip in a Sunday paper one had been taking for years" (28).

These thoughts are "Kareninian" in tone particularly in that they reflect the mood of Anna's inner monologue, her final vision of people's not caring for one another, the penetrating cynicism she suddenly applies to the most routine actions. This in itself relates Aqua to Van's Kareninian monologue, but within the stream of Van's thoughts there runs also a definite ripple of Aqua. The greatest single shock to Aqua's mental security was delivered by the substitution of Van for her stillborn child, a melodrama recorded in that herbarium in the attic. A sample item: "Golden [ginkgo] leaf: fallen out of a book 'The Truth about Terra' which Aqua gave me before going back to her Home. 14.XII.69" (7: brackets in original). Another entry rather grue-somely commemorates the day Aqua's skiing accident kills her unborn child: "[blue-ink blot shaped accidentally like a flower, or improved felt-pen dele-tion] *Compliquaria compliquata* var. *aquamarina*. Ex. 15.1.70" (8) Ginkgo leaf, inkblot and taxonomic Latin are all recalled as Van reflects: "Never, never shall I hear again her 'botanical' voice fall at *biloba*, 'sorry, my Latin is showing.' *Ginkgo*, gingko, ink, inkog." (300)

The last scene of the Ardis sections, then, while being moving in terms of Van's loss of his paradise, also emphasizes the irresponsibility of Van and Ada at Ardis towards Lucette by comparing it with Demon's more blatant inconsiderateness towards Aqua. If the "other Ardis" at Radugalet is anything but the proverbial "rose garden" of bliss, Ardis is certainly not to be taken as the paradise it seems.

Ardis: Lucette and Blanche

Myths of Love

Ada ends with a rapturous summary of the book that focusses on the delight of the Ardis sections. Even though Van here quite consciously parodies the tone of a blurb-writer, he stands proudly by the truth of his assessment:

> Ardis Hall – the Ardors and Arbors of Ardis – this is the leitmotiv rippling
> through *Ada*, an ample and delightful chronicle, whose principal part is staged
> in a dream-bright America.... Nothing in world literature, save maybe Count
> Tolstoy's reminiscences, can vie in pure joyousness and Arcadian innocence
> with the "Ardis" part of the book. (588)

Van still rejoices in the happiness of his and Ada's special destiny at Ardis:
somehow they had seemed charmed there, privileged to reenact not only
myths of Edenic or Arcadian innocence but also – and only increasing the
paradisal joy – myths of sexual experience, of Venus, Cupid or Eros. For the
surname of the amorous young Veens obviously recalls Venus; the "arrow "
in "Ardis" (Greek *ardis*, point of an arrow) alludes to the arrow of desire in
Cupid's quiver ("Ardis. Arrowhead Manor. *Le Château de la Flèche*, Flesh Hall"
[318]); and even after he leaves Ardis in jealous despair, Van's mind still flies
back to its days of sexual bliss, "back to the ardors and arbors! Eros *qui prend
son essor!*" (367) But because little Lucette becomes tragically embroiled in
Van and Ada's love, her fate inevitably belies the apparent splendor of these
resurrected myths of sexual ardor.

Van and Ada have the most enthusiastic support in Blanche, the romantically-
inclined handmaid at Ardis, who revels in the intensity of their passion – she
has often seen them fiercely engaged as she heads off for her own nocturnal
trysts – and gossips their story abroad with such admiration that it develops
into a local legend:

> their first summer in the orchards and orchidariums of Ardis had become a
> sacred secret and creed, throughout the countryside. Romantically inclined
> handmaids...adored Van, adored Ada, adored Ardis's ardors in arbors.... Virgin
> chatelaines in marble-floored manors fondled their lone flames fanned by Van's
> romance. (409)

But though Blanche tries to exalt Van and Ada to legendary status her own
life bizarrely undermines the apparent romance of Ardis.

The Veens' surname not only hints at Venus but also, less glamorously,
means "peat" in Dutch;[4] Blanche, curiously, is "Blanche de la Tourberie"
(407) after her native village, Tourbière, the French for "peaty." Since she
romanticizes Van and Ada's fervor, since her own lovemaking so often serves
as a comic counterpoint to theirs, Blanche seems to have been positioned for
some ironic comment on the myths of Ardis.

But why? Because Blanche is also a representative of Venus – she has venereal disease – and because she seems to infect others both with her enthusiasm
for Van and Ada and with her gonorrhea. For in that parodic summary of the

"sacred secret and creed" of Ardis's romance, Blanche's lover during Ardis the
Second, "Sore, the ribald night watchman" (211), is commemorated thus:
"Nightwatchmen fought insomnia and the fire of the clap with the weapons of
Vaniada's Adventures." (409) Sore's new soreness comically ironises the terms of
Van's constant celebration of Ardis's eros, so neatly summed up in that "Ardors
and Arbors of Ardis" leitmotiv: "back to the ardors and arbors! Eros *qui prend
son essor*! Arts that our marblery harbors: Eros, the rose and the sore." (367)

On his first morning at Ardis, Van makes a pass at Blanche; she fends him
off, declaring: "*quant à moi, je suis vièrge, ou peu s'en faut* [as for me, I'm a
virgin, or almost one].... I might add that I have the whites...."(49) Blanche
here protests her virginity at the same time as she makes the first reference
to what turns out to be her VD. Though the discrepancy is at first merely
amusing, it becomes more serious when we remember the other ironies of
virginity that surround Lucette: the paradox that she genuinely has preserved
her virginity yet has also, like Blanche, sustained real damage through her
initiation into sex.

During the Night of the Burning Barn, when Van and Ada become lovers
(imperfectly, for Van ejaculates prematurely), a flurry of Cinderella images
emphasizes the exclusion of Blanche and Lucette, Van's two perpetually unre-
quited admirers. We have already seen (pp. 55–57) that the next chapter, Pt.1
Ch.20, focusses on "defloration" – ostensibly only because it records Ada's
loss of virginity, but also because both Lucette *and* Blanche are involved. Van
comes down to breakfast before Ada, and eagerly awaits her descent:

> Suddenly Van heard her lovely dark voice on the staircase saying in an upward
> direction, "*Je l'ai vu dans une des corbeilles de la bibliothèque*" – presumably in
> reference to some geranium or violet or slipper orchid....after the maid's dis-
> tant glad cry had come from the library Ada's voice added: "*Je me demande*, I
> wonder *qui l'a mis là*, who put it there." *Aussitôt après* she entered the dining
> room. (125)

What Ada has seen in one of the library's wastepaper baskets is, in fact, as the
reader knows, not "some geranium or violet or slipper orchid" but a slipper
that Cinderella-Blanche had lost on the staircase the night before (young
Bout, her newest lover, had been "devotedly kissing the veined instep of a
pretty bare foot raised and placed on a balustrade"[405]) and that Ada had
brought into the library before joining Van on the divan. Against the lyric
theme of Ada's defloration Nabokov sets not only the tragic counter-theme
of Lucette's fatal "defloration" but also the ironic theme of Blanche's merely
changing lovers, and losing only a slipper imagined to be a lost flower – a
"geranium or violet or slipper orchid" – while she herself is very safe from any
danger of being deflowered.

But in fact though Blanche's sexual experience and especially her gonorrhea seem to be merely a cynically playful qualification of the 'innocent" ardor of Ardis, they remain so only if we consider no-one but Blanche herself. For her promiscuity has ruined someone else's life: she has a child born blind.

When Ada informs Van of this grim twist of fate, he recollects that even before marrying Blanche Trofim had known she had VD, and in a flash he callously snorts: "Love is blind." (408) But he softens the offence by asking: "Will their child remain blind? I mean, did you get them a really first-rate physician?" In her reply Ada skips from the cliché Van twisted in such grisly fashion to its mythological counterpart, blindfolded Cupid: "Oh yes, hopelessly blind. But speaking of love and its myths" (408) – and from here she launches straight into that "sacred secret and creed" Blanche's gossip has made of Ardis's romance. A negative Venus, lover of an inverse Eros, mother of a "hopelessly blind" Cupid, Blanche undermines completely the myths of love she has tried to disseminate.

The ironies of Blanche's lovemaking, like the ironies surrounding Van and Ada, cease to be funny when someone else is at stake. Despite the comedy of Blanche's claim to be almost a virgin, the consequence of her promiscuity proves gruesome; despite the apparent farce of Lucette's spying on Van and Ada, it evolves into tragedy. Blanche's child is born blind; Lucette Veen will have her "light," too, put out too soon. Little Lucette keeps on peering at Van and Ada making love because they ignore her in the throes of passion, in what Van calls "the pardonable blindness of ascending bliss" (213). But Nabokov suggests that the myths of love accepted by Blanche and apparently embodied by Van and Ada can only be dangerous – if romantic intensity is allowed to justify all, if passion is allowed to blind one to the consequences one's actions can have on innocent others.

Exploitation: Dispersed Evil, Focused Guilt

When Blanche in the blindness of her sexual passion ignores the consequence her behavior might have, Van is certainly not involved: he has no part in her disease. Yet the precise conditions of his relationship with Blanche turns out to be essential to judging the moral implications of Ardis and *Ada*.

Van's seigneurial attitude towards women shows itself on his very first morning at Ardis. Rising very early "with the intention of going for a dip in the brook he had observed on the eve" (48), he comes across

> a young chambermaid whom he had glimpsed (and promised himself to investigate) on the preceding evening. She wore what his father termed with a semi-assumed leer "soubret black and frissonnet frill.".…the savage sense of opportune license moved Van so robustly that he could not resist clasping the wrist of her tight-sleeved arm. (48)

Blanche tells him that Mlle Larivière calls her "'Cendrillon' because her stockings got so easily laddered, see" (49); she notes that Van's loose attire reveals his desire; and though she resists his advance by claiming "je suis vièrge," it is only because his lust is cooled by her romantic patter – "were I to fall in love with you...it would be, for me, only grief, and infernal fire, and despair, and even death, Monsieur" (49) – that he does not try again to possess her in the day or two before he begins to fall in love with Ada.

Towards the end of Van's second stay at Ardis Blanche has determined to quit the manor after offering herself to Van: "*C'est ma dernière nuit au château...* 'Tis my last night with thee." (292) But Van, too obsessed by the likelihood of Ada's unfaithfulness, cannot respond to her invitation; wresting from her the fact that Ada has been involved with other lovers, he resolves to fly Ardis – in deadly pursuit of his rivals – as early as he can the next morning. Since Blanche is also leaving, he offers to drop her off at Tourbière – and tells "Aunt" Marina: "I'm not eloping with your maid, Marina. It's an optical illusion." (298) As he lets Blanche out, he "kissed Cendrillon's shy hand and resumed his seat in the carriage, clearing his throat and plucking at his trousers before crossing his legs." (299) On both his first morning and his last at Ardis, Van is aroused by Blanche as "Cendrillon." Why is his whole Ardis experience framed in this way?

It is from Demon that Van has learnt the exploitative and calmly presuming attitude to women he brings to Ardis and displays in his first approach to Blanche. On the one brief visit we see Demon make to his cousin's summer manor, he notices Blanche and remarks to Van:

> "A moment ago, in that gallery, I ran into a remarkably pretty soubrette.... Do you like the type, Van – the bowed little head, the bare neck, the high heels, the trot, the wiggle, you do, don't you?"
> "Well, sir – "
> (Tell him I'm the youngest Venutian? [i.e. a member of the exclusive villa Venus chain of bordellos] Does he belong, too? [In fact, Demon is on the Villa Venus Club Council.] Show the sign? Better not. Invent.)
> " – Well, I'm resting after my torrid affair, in London, with my tango-partner whom you saw me dance with when you flew over for that last show – remember?" (244)

Van *is* inventing here, to satisfy his father's expectations: though he did approach that tango partner, she had "indignantly refused, saying she adored her husband" (185). But he knows his father's attitudes to women – and that an adulterous affair will impress him.

Even more significant in suggesting the "Demonic" quality of Van's sexual attitudes are the close links between the servant girls in Demon's life and

those in Van's. We have already seen the "Irish wild rose...an impudent scullery maid who had briefly worked at Ardis Hall"(150) and whom Demon has
at Radugalet. This wench – who because Van and Ada cannot remember her
name actually becomes "Rose" (150) – indicates just how well Van follows the
parental example, for Van's rooms in his Manhattan apartment are looked after
by "Rose, the sportive Negro maid whom he shared in more ways than one
with the famous, recently decorated cryptogrammatist, Mr. Dean, a perfect
gentleman, dwelling on the floor below" (390). "Dean" here neatly combines
the beginning and end of "Demon Veen" in order to stress that Van fully
shares his father's assumption that he may treat others as a means to satisfy
his own ends.

The earlier "Rose" is a maid who has left Ardis to be with Demon. Blanche
leaves Ardis with Van – who sets her off at her "poor shack smothered in
roses" (299). Another maid who has run away from Ardis and who has
venereal disease associates Demon's exploitativeness even more strongly with
Van's. Demon writes to Marina: "Your runaway maid, by the way, has been
found by the police in a brothel here and will be shipped to you as soon as she
is sufficiently stuffed with mercury." (16) The brutal "stuffed with mercury"
here alludes to the fact that mercury was long used as a "cure" for syphilis;
the maid has been identified, obviously, because Demon has frequented yet
another brothel – as his son will, almost every second day, from the age of
fourteen.

Van's seigneurial approach to women does not prevent him from offering a
service without expectation of a sexual return – if, as when he flies from Ardis,
other matters preoccupy him. But that his attitude is habitually "Demonic"
and exploitative we can ascertain when he travels off with Blanche – as the
Cendrillon-and-arousal pattern of his first morning at Ardis recurs, as the
mere fact of Blanche's leaving her job allies her with the former Ardis maids
in Demon's life. If we now look again at Van's last voyage from Ardis, and if
we keep in mind that his inner monologue ("Maidenhair...sunk; poor Stream
of Consciousness, *marée noire* by now"), which begins just after Blanche has
been dropped off, also evokes Lucette with reference to the defloration images
in the "Mémoire" discussion, we can appreciate that Nabokov is once more
comparing Lucette's virginity-cum-initiation with Blanche's disease. For these
are the words that break in on Van's silent soliloquy:

> "*Barin, a barin*' said Trofim, turning his blond-bearded face to his passenger.
> "*Da?*"
>
> "*Dazhe skvoz' kozhaniy fartuk ne stal-bï ya trogat' etu frantsuzskuyu devku.*"
> *Bárin:* master. *Dázhe skvoz' kózhaniy fártuk:* even through a leathern apron.
> *Ne stal-bï ya trógat* I would not think of touching. *Étu:* this (that). *Frantsúzskuyu:*
> French (adj., accus.). *Dévku:* wench. (300)

The coachman Trofim's "even through a leathern apron" also pointedly echoes Lucette's confused question, "could a boy bee impregnate a girl flower *through* something, through his gaiters or woolies or whatever he wore?" (289) – a question which was provoked by her sitting on the lap of highly-aroused Van on the victoria being driven back from the picnic by Trofim.

By drawing a parallel between the gonorrhea of a girl Van expects to be able to avail himself of and the dangerous initiation of Lucette into a world of frenzied sexual energy, Nabokov seems to be insisting that the indifference shown to others in treating them as only a means to one's own sexual satisfaction resembles the cruelty of neglecting such an intimate personal responsibility as Van bears towards Lucette.

This comparison of Blanche and Lucette may seem unjustified: Van is not responsible for Blanche's disease, whereas his responsibility in Lucette's case is painfully evident. Both girls are linked, certainly – both, for instance, being Cinderellas, poor girls left out, unrequitedly in love with Van – but while the fact that Van will never make love to Lucette proves disastrous for her, Blanche's being similarly unbroached by her young Prince Charming only draws attention to the fact that Van can have no part in her disease.

But this very difference in responsibility proves essential to Nabokov's point. Venereal disease is spread not through a single person's neglect but through the actions of many who assume their right to use other people and take no thought for those they may be helping to destroy. But if an extensive evil (venereal disease, the degradation of women, the abuse of privilege) cannot be traced to a single source, nevertheless individual acts within such a contagion can and should be as fully governed by the demands of responsibility and consideration for the feelings of others as actions in which – as in Van's treatment of Lucette – a simpler sum of relationships makes the vectors of responsibility far easier to determine.

10. Lucette and Others (2)

Brownhill

On each flank of Van's early sojourns with Ada Nabokov maneuvers his willing hero into position with other sexual partners. Despite their color these encounters seem ragged and pointless after the harmony of Van's idylls at Ardis, but Nabokov calibrates the apparently random with the greatest exactitude to disclose the contradictions of Van's – and man's – moral nature.

When Van leaves Ardis in 1884 he happens to meet a dumpy girl called Cordula de Prey, who turns out to be Ada's schoolmate. Cordula tells him Ada's first letter from Ardis has gushed

> "about how sweet, clever, unusual, irresistible –"
>
> "Silly girl. When was that?"
>
> "In June, I imagine. She wrote again later, but her reply – because I was quite jealous of you – really I was! – and had fired back lots of questions – well, her reply was evasive, and practically void of Van." (164)

The "quite jealous of you" prompts Van to wonder whether Cordula might be the lesbian lover Ada had implied when farewelling Van at Forest Fork. He dismisses her suggestion that Ada is in love with him, but Cordula remains unconvinced:

> "I wonder," murmured Cordula, with such a nice nuance of pensive tone that Van could not tell whether she meant to close the subject, or leave it ajar, or open a new one.
>
> "How could I get in touch with you?" he asked. "Would you come to Riverlane? Are you a virgin?" (165)

Van treats Cordula here as crudely as if she were a whore – and in fact when he next sees her, as Ada's chaperone at Brownhill College, it strikes him "that the dumpy little Countess resembled his first whorelet" (168).

That first whorelet appears in Pt. 1 Ch. 4, the chapter immediately preceding Ardis the First, where Van depicts his amatory explorations – before finding Ada – during his first year at Riverlane, an English "public school" in Luga, Mayne. He falls abstractly in love with the daughter of Mrs. Tapirov, who runs a shop selling objets d'art, and makes very concrete love to "a fubsy pig-pink whorelet" "among crates and sacks" at the back of the corner shop run by "old deaf Mrs. Gimber" (33).

Mrs. Tapirov's daughter and the "whorelet" are paired in order to be contrasted: Van encounters both amidst shop items, both are associated with a lone older woman, one seems to be Van's "true love," the other simply a whore. The contrast of the two girls prefigures the contrast between Ada (who in her flower paintings mixes flowers real and imaginary, combining "one species with another (unrecorded but possible)" [99], just as Mrs. Tapirov's daughter "always puts a bunch of real [flowers] among the fake" [32] in the shop) and Cordula de Prey (whom Van accosts in a bookstore and who explicitly reminds him of "his first whorelet"). Both girls are the daughters of actresses, but while one is Van's true love, the other he comports himself with as if she were just a whore.

When he comes to Brownhill College to meet Ada, Van finds her with Cordula acting as the chaperone the school's strict etiquette requires. Recalling his former momentary suspicion of Cordula Van soon flares with jealousy towards the innocent girl. Months ago when Ada had hinted at a lesbian lover, Van had replied: "The girls don't matter…it's the fellows I'll kill," and even now he refuses to recognize that he can be jealous of Cordula, since the thought of her making love with Ada excites him sexually. In fact despite this titillation his suspicion and envy enrage him so that he harangues the girls with insulting allusions to Albertine's lesbian infidelities in Proust. Having found the milk bar approved by Brownhill College to be too crowded, Van, Ada, and Cordula walk on toward the railway station cafe:

> The railway station had a semi-private tearoom supervised by the station-master's wife under the school's idiotic auspices. It was empty, save for a slender lady in black velvet, wearing a beautiful black velvet picture hat, who sat with her back to them at a "tonic bar" and never once turned her head, but the thought brushed him that she was a cocotte from Toulouse. Our damp trio found a nice corner table and with sighs of banal relief undid their raincoats. He hoped Ada would discard her heavy-seas hat but she did not, because she had cut her hair because of dreadful migraines, because she did not want him to see her in the role of a moribund Romeo.
> (On fait *son grand Joyce* after doing one's *petit Proust*. In Ada's lovely hand.)
> (169)

The "moribund Romeo," as we saw in Chapter 1, echoes Van's wild jealousy without object at the end of Ardis the First. Here, Van passes on from the snide Proustian innuendoes to even more blatant taunts, until he suddenly sees he was wrong to place his suspicions on Cordula and dashes off after his train, trembling with frustration. But even as his jealousy gathers strength during this scene, he takes note of a woman he thinks he can recognize as a harlot – whom he obviously knows well if he can identify her merely from behind. The juxtaposition replays in brief the whole chapter's contrast between Van's brutal forwardness to Cordula – his treating her, in fact, as a whore – and his intense jealously of what he supposes (quite wrongly) to be a lesbian relationship between her and Ada. "On fait *son grand Joyce* after doing one's *petit Proust*" distracts us by demanding that the allusion be identified[1] – but much more important is that we resist being diverted from noting the purity of Van's hypocrisy.

Kalugano

When Van flees Ardis at the end of his second stay there, the ensuing action recalls both his agitated departure from Ardis the First and the Brownhill chapter we have just considered. Again there appears the same combination of jealousy (now even more obviously violent), readiness to treat women with brutal carnality, and hypocrisy.

From Ardis Van heads for Kalugano, intending to hunt out Philip Rack, the nearer of his two rivals (the other is Percy de Prey). He leaves one crammed train and changes into another "even more jerky and crowded" (301). He pushes through the first-class sections and spots Cordula and her mother in a full compartment. Suddenly realizing he might be able to find Percy de Prey's address from his cousin, Van enters the compartment. As the train lurches he steps on the toes of an old man who asks him, not impolitely, to take care. Quivering with hostility towards the rivals he has not yet caught, Van savagely berates the elderly passenger until Cordula's mother intervenes: "Cordula...why don't you go with this angry young demon to the tea-car? I think I'll take my thirty-nine winks now." (302)

Van and Cordula find a table "in the very roomy and rococo 'crumpeter,' as Kalugano College students used to call it in the 'Eighties and 'Nineties" (302). (Note how precisely the train's crumpeter and the school slang recombine aspects of the railway station cafe at Brownhill School.) Van declares to Cordula that she has "grown lovely and languorous. You are even lovelier now. Cordula is no longer a virgin! Tell me – do you happen to have Percy de Prey's address? I mean we all know he's invading Tartary – but where could a letter reach him?" (303) After Cordula tells him she will try to find Percy's address, Van asks about her love life, starts to caress her under the table, orders a half bottle of cognac, "having the waiter open it in his presence as Demon advised," and lets Cordula's monologue blend with the rapid landscape:

...or a romantic stream running down a cliff and reflecting her brief bright affair with Marquis Quizz Quisana.

A pine forest fizzled out and factory chimneys replaced it. The train clattered past a roundhouse, and slowed down, groaning. A hideous station darkened the day.

"Good Lord," cried Van, "that's my stop."

He put money on the table, kissed Cordula's willing lips and made for the exit. (303–04)

The sudden departure from the train's crumpeter inverts but closely re-enacts Van's sudden departure from the Brownhill cafe as he heard an incoming train and suddenly fled the intolerable strain of the situation. At the same time there is a double irony: Van makes advances to Cordula here in a carriage that recalls the scene of his being jealous of Cordula's relations with Ada four years earlier – and these advances are made to a girl from whom he has just sought the address of a rival he intends to destroy. Demon's advice on drinking etiquette has also been deftly tucked in: masquerading as a mere detail of social style, this in fact points out that Van's coarseness and hypocrisy are based on the parental model.

As Van rushes for the exit, he crashes

> into somebody who had stooped to pick up a bag: *"On n'est pas goujat à ce point,"* observed the latter: a burly military man with a reddish mustache and a staff captain's insignia.
>
> Van brushed past him, and when both had come down on the platform, glove-slapped him smartly across the face. (304)

Like Dr. Platonov, the invalid on whose foot Van had stepped, Captain Tapper has nothing to do with the real cause of Van's fury[2] yet is nevertheless the object Van seizes to vent his hostility upon. Van and the soldier exchange cards: "'Demon's son?' grunted Captain Tapper, of Wild Violet Lodge, Kalugano. 'Correct,' said Van. 'I'll put up, I guess, at the Majestic; if not, a note will be left for your second or seconds. You'll have to get me one, I can't very well ask the concierge to do it.'" (304–05) Van books in at the Majestic and sets off looking for a music store, where he might be able to find the address of piano-teacher Rack. On the way he buys his second cane, having left the previous one at the Maidenhair station. He suddenly remembers he has not left a message for Tapper's seconds, so he returns to the hotel.

By the time he gets back to the music shop, it is closed:

> He stared for a moment at the harps and the guitars and the flowers in silver vases on consoles receding in the dusk of looking-glasses, and recalled the schoolgirl whom he had longed for so keenly half a dozen years ago – Rose?

Roza? Was that her name? Would he have been happier with her than with his pale fatal sister?

He walked for a while along Main Street – one of a million Main Streets – and then, with a surge of healthy hunger, entered a passably attractive restauant. He ordered a beefsteak with roast potatoes, apple pie and claret. At the far end of the room, on one of the red stools of the burning bar, a graceful harlot in black – tight bodice, wide skirt, long black gloves, black-velvet picture hat – was sucking a golden drink through a straw. In the mirror behind the bar, amid colored glints, he caught a blurred glimpse of her russety blond beauty; he thought he might sample her later on, but when he glanced again she had gone. (307)

The pairing of Ada and Mrs. Tapirov's daughter here and the second vision of a harlot in a bar remind us of the cocotte from Toulouse in the bar at Brownhill and the association Van made between Cordula and his first whorelet. Just as then Van was hypocrite enough to treat Cordula as a whore and to be wildly jealous of her relations with Ada, so now he caresses Cordula under the dining-car table as he seeks from her the address of one rival and thinks of accosting a whore while looking out for the other rival he hopes to destroy.

At the beginning of this chapter, the chapter of the duel, Van writes:

> Aqua used to say that only a very cruel or very stupid person, or innocent infants, could be happy on Demonia, our splendid planet. Van felt that for him to survive on this terrible Antiterra, in the multicolored and evil world into which he was born, he had to destroy or at least maim for life, two men. He had to find them immediately; delay itself might impair his power of survival. (301)

It is a telling irony that in invoking Aqua to confirm the reality and the intensity of human anguish Van calls on an example of Demon's hypocrisy at its worst and points, though he cannot see it, right at the model for his own blind self-concentration. No sooner had Demon found Marina unfaithful than he pursued his rival and tried to castrate him in a duel; but almost immediately on marrying Aqua, he had begun to be unfaithful to her, ignoring the pain his infidelity might cause her frail mind. With the same perfect hypocrisy, Van races after his rivals, so full of his own grief he cannot spare a thought for anyone else's pain – the pain his violence of temper unleashes on an incidental Platonov or would unleash on an out-of-range Percy de Prey – and yet so unwilling to consider the feelings of anyone but himself that he does not think of the lasting pain the satisfaction of a momentary sexual urge might cause the woman he loves.

Paris

After his separation from Ada at the end of their Manhattan reunion in 1893 the first full scene in which Van appears takes place in Paris in 1901:

> On a bleak morning between the spring and summer of 1901, in Paris, as Van...up-swinging a furled English umbrella, strode past a particularly unattractive sidewalk café...a chubby bald man cafe stood up and hailed him.
>   Van considered for a moment those red round cheeks, that black goatee.
>   "*Ne uznayosh'* (You don't recognize me)?"
>   "Greg! Grigoriy Akimovich!" cried Van tearing off his glove.
>   "I grew a regular *vollbart* last summer. You'd never have known me then. Beer? Wonder what you do to look so boyish Van."
>   "Diet of champagne, not beer," said Professor Veen putting on his spectacles and signaling to a waiter with the crook of his 'umber.' (453)

As Van says, he has not seen Greg Erminin since 1888, since the picnic at Ardis the Second:

> "I last saw you thirteen years ago, riding a black pony – no, a black Silentium. *Bozhe moy!*"
>   "Yes – *Bozhe moy*, you can well say that. Those lovely, lovely agonies in lovely Ardis! Oh, I was *absolyutno bezumno* (madly) in love with your cousin!"
>   "You mean Miss Veen? I did not know it. How long – "
>   "Neither did she. I was terribly – "
>   "How long are you staying – "
>   " – terribly shy, because, of course, I realized that I could not compete with her numerous boy friends." (454)

Note the lightning-quick rush of Van's jealousy, the coldness of "Miss Veen? I did not know it," the speed with which Van finds an alternative continuation when Greg's next remark reveals that he has never actually been a serious rival. But that Van's rapid jealousy would have led to something else – a duel, in fact – Nabokov leaves no room to doubt.

Greg Erminin first appeared during the 1884 Ardis picnic, and presumably it was during that picnic that he first fell madly but mutely in love with Ada, for the next day he returned hoping to offer Ada a ride on his new black pony:

> "I mean, I would love lending him to you for a ride any time. For any amount of time. Will you? Besides, I have another black."
>   But she shook her head, she shook her bent head, while still twisting and twining her daisies.

"Well," he said, getting up. "I must be going. Good-bye, everybody. Good-bye, Ada. I guess it's your father under that oak, isn't it?"

"No, it's an elm," said Ada. (92)

Ada's refusal of the pony and her brusque "No, it's an elm" both reveal to the reader that she does not care at all for Greg – and indeed that since the picnic of the day before and the journey home (during which, because of the accidental shortage of seats, she had sat on Van's lap) Ada now regards herself as Van's. Greg is at once Van's rival and a proof that he has no real rivals. Hence when as they make their farewells at the end of Ardis the First Van asks Ada "will you be faithful, will you be faithful to me?...it's the fellows I'll kill if they come near you"(158–59) and then rides off on "his favorite black horse" (159), the black horse–black pony link only proves that despite the romantic fierceness of his jealousy, Van has no cause for fear, for during this first stay at Ardis he has won Ada's love forever. A "rival" like the Greg Erminin Ada dismissed is no rival at all.

But what if Van had been wrong in believing that in fact "Ada remained unaffected by Greg's devotion" (268)? The answer is contained in the furled umbrella which Van has by his side as he sits with Greg in the Parisian cafe. The umbrella and its crook recall the three canes Van acquires during his hunting down of Philip Rack at the end of Ardis the Second and the riding crop at the end of Ardis the First: had Van's swift jealousy not been dissipated at once by Greg's "Neither did she" it would indubitably have led to a duel on the first pretext that could be found.

Van and Greg part and

> A moment later, as happens so often in farces and foreign cities, Van ran into another friend. With a surge of delight he saw Cordula in a tight scarlet skirt bending with baby words of comfort over two unhappy poodlets attached to the waiting-post of a sausage shop. Van stroked her with his fingertips, and...she straightened up indignantly and turned around (indignation instantly replaced by gay recognition).... (456)

Van notes that fashions have revolved back to what they were a dozen years ago, when he last saw Cordula – so time has been recaptured, as the eager rake points out:

> "Let's not squander," he said, "the tumescence of retrieved time on the gush of small talk. I'm bursting with energy, if that's what you want to know. Now look: it may sound silly and insolent but I have an urgent request. Will you cooperate with me in cornuting your husband? It's a must!"
>
> "Really, Van!" exclaimed angry Cordula. "You go a bit far. I'm a happy wife.

My Tobachok adores me. We'd have ten children by now if I'd not been careful with him and others." (456–57)

But Van puffs down Cordula's perfunctory resistance, and they cross the street to a drab little hotel where "Their brisk nub and its repetition lasted fifteen minutes in all" (457). Cordula has to rush off to lunch, and as she goes she declares: "You're a very bad boy and I'm a very bad girl. But it was fun – even though you've been speaking to me not as you would to a lady friend but as you probably do to little whores." (458)

When Van treats Cordula purely as a whore, his crassness (of a piece with his treatment of her in Ladoga – "Are you a virgin?" – and on the Kalugano train) remains unsavory despite Cordula's compliance and enjoyment. No less unattractive is this new manifestation of his hypocrisy: he shows himself ready, even if only for a moment, to wreak vengeance upon Greg Erminin for being one of Ada's lovers but within half an hour has twice made love to Cordula, of whom he had also once been jealous.

Just before parting with Van, Greg had told him that he had heard from Tobak, Cordula's husband, that Lucette was in town, at the Alphonse Four. When Van runs into Cordula, he confirms the address, and heads for the hotel. Lucette is out, so Van crosses the street to Ovenman's:

> Upon entering, he stopped for a moment to surrender his coat: but he kept his black fedora and stick-slim umbrella as he had seen his father do in that sort of bawdy, albeit smart, place which decent women did not frequent – at least, unescorted. He…made out…the girl whose silhouette he recalled having seen now and then…ever since his pubescence, passing alone, drinking alone, like Blok's *Incognita*. It was a queer feeling – as of something replayed by mistake, part of a sentence misplaced on the proof sheet, a scene run prematurely, a repeated blemish, a wrong turn of time. (460)

It is no wonder that Van should feel this a wrong turn of time, for Lucette at the bar in black, wearing a picture hat and mimicking the Toulouse-Lautrec poster bizarrely recalls both the "cocotte from Toulouse" in the railway station cafe where Van sat, frustrated, with Ada and Cordula, and the "harlot in black," in a "black velvet picture hat," Van sees at the bar in a Kalugano restaurant shortly after leaving Cordula and her train.

Let us focus on two details of the opening lines above: a "stick-slim umbrella" that calls to mind Demon's earlier "slim umbrella" (433), and a hint of Demonic style. Demon's treatment of others as means to his own sexual ends is by now firmly associated with Van's own sexual exploitativeness, and Lucette, by means of the Brownhill cocotte and the Kalugano harlot and by virtue of the locale, "that sort of bawdy…place which decent women did not frequent," has been aligned with the whores Van so freely uses. Yet Van will *not* make love to Lucette, despite her adoration and eagerness and beauty: he exercises a restraint beyond what his father could manage – even if the restraint is tragically overdue.

Van shows self-control and considerateness towards Lucette in turning down her imploring invitations because he knows he could never love her as he does Ada, because he refuses "to wreck her life with a brief affair" (491); but these very virtues serve to point out the limitations of his moral vision. In Part 4 Van describes the past as "a constant accumulation of images...a generous chaos out of which the genius of total recall...can pick anything he pleases: ...a russet black-hatted beauty at a Parisian bar in 1901; a humid red rose among artificial ones in 1883" (545). From Nabokov's point of view, there is no "chaos" in this juxtaposition of Lucette at the bar and the real rose placed among artificial ones by Mrs. Tapirov's daughter, nor is it accidental that just before the first appearance of a black-hatted whore, Van remembers his "first whorelet" (168), or that just before the second harlot in black he thinks of "the schoolgirl whom he had longed for so keenly half a dozen years ago – Rose? Roza?" (307).

Van thinks of that girl as Rose or Roza because he recollects the real roses she puts among the imitations:

> in passing, he touched a half-opened rose and was cheated of the sterile texture his fingertips had expected when cool life kissed them with pouting lips. "My daughter...always puts a bunch of real ones among the fake pour *attraper le client.*" (32)

"On another occasion," Van records, "he saw her curled up with her school-books in an armchair – a domestic item among those for sale" (32). Lucette for Van is a real rose among the fakes, a domestic item among those for sale. Not only is she real in comparison with the art of Toulouse-Lautrec, she is real in comparison with the whores who offer a simulacrum of love; she is a domestic item, the little girl he has known too well, among the whores she is linked with in time (Brownhill, Kalugano) and space (the not quite reputable Ovenman's bar).

Van can see that Lucette is not someone with whom he can just engage in sex without considering the rest of her life: she is simply too real for him. Yet he cannot see that others, too, whom he uses merely as whores, are equally real, have lives that extend beyond his need for them and that must be affected by their contact with him. The women whom he uses may be conditioned into an indifference towards themselves akin to the indifference shown them by Van and his like. They may be degraded into accepting their being used as means, but nevertheless they too are real, and though Van is

at least better than his father in not continuing to ignore Lucette's needs as
Demon has Aqua's, though he recognizes the reality of Lucette's life, it is an
appalling failure of his imagination that he can still treat all other women
as if, almost, they had no life beyond their existence as a means to fulfilling
his "needs."

Lucette and the Rivals

In Ovenman's bar Van, still wearing his hat and carrying his stick-slim
umbrella, stands ogling Lucette with "the crook of his silk-swathed cane
lifted in profile almost up to his mouth" (460). If Van's canes are so emphatically the emblem and instrument of his violence, and if indeed this very "silk-
swathed cane" has been significantly present as Van's jealousy momentarily
flared towards Greg Erminin, is it not awkward to stress the umbrella here,
as Van looks at Lucette?

No, not at all. Indeed, the cane here is the culmination of another unexpected but necessary pattern.

The picture-hatted girls at the bar have before been associated with Van's
violent jealousy. In the Brownhill railway cafe the cocotte from Toulouse
appears just when Ada as "moribund Romeo" serves to recollect Van's whirling
riding crop in the earlier Morio-Moore passage, and it is only minutes before
he sees the "graceful harlot in black" at the bar of a Kalugano restaurant that
Van acquires "his second walking stick...with...an alpenstockish point capable
of gouging out translucent bulging eyes" (305).

Lucette too has before – many times, indeed – been associated with the
fury of Van's intended revenges upon Percy de Prey, Philip Rack, Andrey
Vinelander and others. When she visits Van at Kingston and tells him of her
having made love with Ada, he responds apparently with amusement to her
disclosure:

> "Are you horrified, Van? Do you loathe us?"
>
> "On the contrary," replied Van, bringing off a passable imitation of bawdy
> mirth. "Had I not been a heterosexual male, I would have been a Lesbian."
> (382)

But just as at Brownhill, where an imagined picture of Ada and Cordula's
"fondling each other kept pricking him with perverse gratification" (168), a
sexual titillation in envisaging Ada's involvement with another girl is not
incompatible in Van with intense jealousy. He reacts to the beginning of
Lucette's disclosure by "quivering with evil sarcasm, boiling with mysterious
rage" (378), but lets her conclude her story:

"She abandoned me....Yes, she started a rather sad little affair with Johnny, a young star from Fuerteventura...her exact *odnoletok* (coeval), practically her twin in appearance, born the same year, the same day, the same instant – " (380)

Enraged by the thought of this hitherto unknown affair, Van replies to the "twin...born...the same instant" with a controlled outburst on the impossibility of simultaneous twins: as he notes later, he is apt to relieve a pang of anger by "bombastic and arcane utterances" (530) like his remarks on Proust at Brownhill. Lucette carries on:

"I only meant...that he was a handsome Hispano-Irish boy, dark and pale, and people mistook them for twins. I did not say they were really twins. Or 'driblets'."

Driblets? Driplets? Now who pronounced it that way? Who? Who? A dripping ewes-dropper in a dream? Did the orphans live? But we must listen to Lucette.

"After a year or so she found out that an old pederast kept him and she dismissed him, and he shot himself on a beach at high tide but surfers and surgeons saved him, and now his brain is damaged; he will never be able to speak."

"One can always fall back on mutes," said Van gloomily. "He could act the speechless eunuch in 'Stambul, my bulbul' or the stable boy disguised as a kennel girl who brings a letter." (381)

This passage ripples with allusions to both of Van's earlier rivals, Philip Rack and Percy de Prey – and, simultaneously, with cross-ripples linking Lucette with each of them.

The second paragraph focusses on Rack, to whom "Driplets" points directly: at the beginning of Ardis the Second Rack has "to return to Kalugano with his Elsie, who Doc Ecksreher thought 'would present him with driplets in dry weeks'" (202). When Van after his duel with Tapper is wounded and taken to the Lakeview Hospital in Kalugano, he finds Rack there too because "a poison had seeped into his system...administered...by...his wife who...had just had a complicated miscarriage in the maternity ward. Yes, triplets – how did he guess?" (313) Just as Van does not attack Rack only because he finds him on the verge of death, so, it is implied here, he does not chase after Johnny only because *this* potential rival has been almost destroyed by his suicide attempt.

But the "dripping ewes-dropper" refers not only to Rack's wife and her triplets, but also to Lucette: the "ewes-dropper" particularly recalls "that stray ardilla daintily leavesdropping" which Nabokov equates so delicately with eavesdropping Lucette.[3]

In the fourth paragraph of the passage above Van calls up the ghost of Percy de Prey. The "stable boy disguised as a kennel girl" recalls the aftermath of the second Ardis picnic – during which Van had wrestled with Percy. The next day a messenger, a boyish-looking girl or girlish-looking boy, delivers Van a note from Percy, who offers to meet for a duel if Van wishes it. But since Van remains unaware that Percy is Ada's lover, he declines the offer, and after telling the pretty messenger this, he adds: "I would be interested to know – this could be decided in a jiffy behind that tree – what you are, stable boy or kennel girl?" (284)

The grotesque concoction "Stambul, my bulbul" points also to Percy de Prey. Since Percy will pass through "Stambul" – one version of the name "Istanbul" – en route to the Crimea, Van slily associates him, in a sort of whispered warning of Ada's unfaithfulness, with Turkey or tobacco or Turkish tobacco. On the day Ada has seen Percy off, for instance, Van and Ada stand embraced, "she playing her limp light fingers over his collarbone, and how he 'ladored,' he said, the dark aroma of her hair blending with crushed lily stalks, Turkish cigarettes and the lassitude that comes from 'lass'" (286–87). And when Van has been told by Blanche of Ada's lover, he confronts Ada with the fact:

> "But he exists, he exists," muttered Van, looking down at a rainbow web on the turf.
> "I suppose so," said the haughty child, "however, he left yesterday for some Greek or Turkish port...." (296)

"Bulbul" – which means "nightingale" – proves rather more convoluted. Percy de Prey flies from the complications of his affair with Ada to become a soldier in the second (Antiterran history!) Crimean War. After having been "shot in the thigh during a skirmish with Khazar guerillas" (319) he regains consciousness to see a smiling old Tartar trying to talk to him. The "kindly old man" picks up the pistol Percy has dropped and shoots him in the temple. Van imagines Percy's thoughts from the moment of recovering consciousness to his death:

> I'm alive – who's that? – civilian – sympathy – thirsty – daughter with pitcher – that's my darned gun – don't...*et cetera* or rather no *et cetera*....But, of course, an invaluable detail in that strip of thought would have been – perhaps, next to the pitcher pen – a glint, a shadow, a stab of Ardis. (320)

Four years later, in 1892, Van and Ada look at Kim Beauharnais's photographs of the early days of Van's stay at Ardis in 1884. Three closely-related shots include the first of Van, which shows him at fourteen,

> shirtless, in shorts, aiming a conical missile at the marble fore-image of a Crimean girl doomed to offer an everlasting draught of marble water to a dying marine from her bullet-chipped jar.

Skip Lucette skipping rope.
Ah, the famous first finch.
"No. that's a *kitayskaya punochka* (Chinese Wall Bunting). It has settled on the threshold of a basement door. The door is ajar...."(399)

The first of these three photographs records the scene where Van, newly arrived at Ardis and made by Mlle Larivière to walk hand in hand through the ornamental park with his young cousin Ada disengages himself "under the pretext of picking up a fir cone:

> He threw the cone at a woman of marble bending over a stamnos but only managed to frighten a bird that had perched on the brim of her broken jar.
> "There is nothing more banal in the world," said Ada, "than pitching stones at a hawfinch." (50)

In describing Kim's snapshot of this simple scene Van curiously embellishes it to incorporate his own imagined version of Percy's death – chiefly because it is just after he and Percy throw stones together at a signboard during the second Ardis picnic that the two young men clash in a sharp scuffle that victorious Van later narrates with vindictive relish as compensation for the duel he was cheated of by Percy's death in the Crimea. But something peculiar seems to be welling up through the text at this point. In the original scene, a bird; in Van's fanciful description of the plain photograph, a girl aiding a dying soldier in a Crimean war: who can this bring to mind but Florence Nightingale? The peculiarity does not stop here. Note the "marble fore-image," the "everlasting draught of marble water," and the "jar" or stamnos: we are suddenly directed to Keats's great odes, "To a Nightingale" and the stopped time, the marmoreal memorial of "On a Grecian Urn."

The "stable boy...who brings a letter" recalls Van's decision not to duel Percy when he did not yet recognize him as a rival; the "Stambul, my bulbul" alludes to Percy's death. The doubling of the allusions stresses the fact that only Percy's being already dead prevented Van from trying to kill him in a duel – and the position of the allusions confirms again that had not Lucette just told him that Johnny had virtually disposed of himself by his botched suicide attempt he would have hounded this new rival with the same ferocity he had hoped to turn on Percy.

The passage that weirdly associates Percy with Florence Nightingale and "To a Nightingale" leads at once to Lucette – "Skip Lucette skipping rope" (399) – and a few lines later Van refers to Lucette's scholarly identification of a peacock moth in a fresco in *Florence* (400). Lucette returns, in more significant conjunction with this recollection of the cone-throwing incident and with another of Van's rivals, a little later. Van wants to find out the name of the man (Andrey Vinelander) Ada might have married, so he can challenge him to a duel; he also knows Lucette is desperate for the least token of affection. He can accomplish two tasks at once, he thinks, if he offers to give Lucette a kiss in return for telling him the name of his new rival: he will be able "to kill two finches with one fircone" (414).

The "stable boy disguised as a kennel girl who brings a letter" in Van's arcane reaction to Lucette's account of Ada's latest lover also implicates Lucette. Like Lucette, the youth (actually a girl) whom Van remembers has striking "chestnut curls" (283)[4]; like this youth, Lucette brings Van a letter – the very occasion of her coming to Kingston and so of her reporting on her own and Johnny's involvements with Ada.

Johnny too is paired with Lucette; because his and her relationships with Ada both come to Van's attention at the same time; because he tries to commit suicide on a beach, and is picked up by the high tide before being rescued; by the insistent association of both with birds (he is John Starling, from one of the Canary Islands, and in *Four Sisters* plays the part of Skvortsov, from Russian *skvorets*, "starling"; Lucette is identified with not only the finches but also grebes, peacocks, ostriches and especially birds of paradise, and Van addresses her as both "darling firebird" and "bird of paradise" [421]). Most forcefully of all, when Lucette tells Van that Johnny is Ada's exact coeval, "her twin in appearance, born...the same instant" (380) and Van thunders against the possibility of "simultaneous twins" (381), the exchange recalls Lucette's description of her own entanglement with Ada:

> She kissed my *krestik* while I kissed hers, our heads clamped in such odd combinations that Brigitte, a little chambermaid who blundered in with her candle, thought for a moment, though naughty herself, that we were giving birth simultaneously to baby girls, your Ada bringing out *une rousse*, and no one's Lucette, *une brune*. (375)

Even Van's brief outburst on hearing of Ada's new lover links Lucette very closely with three of Van's rivals. The oblique emphasis on the fact that Van would have tried to kill Johnny, too, if his brain damage had not left him less than a man, makes clear that Lucette escapes Van's vengeance only because she happens to be a woman. But more importantly the pointed connections between Lucette and Van's intended victims indicate that behind his vengeful violence and his unthinking neglect of his frail sister there lies the same passionate self-concern.

Van's intended vengeance on his rivals is always frustrated by their seeming almost to do away with themselves. But on one occasion he *does* unleash his rage. Since he is awed by his father and has always followed his example, Van accepts the terms of Demon's edict at the end of Part Two: that his affair with

Ada must cease; that she should be safely married off to someone like Andrey Vinelander. In wild despair at being separated from Ada, he decides to revive an old plan. As soon as he had heard of the incriminating photographs Kim Beauharnais was using to blackmail Ada, Van had resolved to eliminate the threat Kim posed, but the happiness of his reunion with Ada had been more than enough to divert him. But now he can again kill two finches with one fircone: by taking an alpenstock to Kim, he removes the blackmail threat and at the same time finds the most convenient outlet for his seething jealousy.

Van's blinding of Kim ranks with Lucette's death as the gravest consequence of his egotism, and in the account of Lucette's last night Nabokov insists on the relationship between Van's indifference to his victims – both actual and potential – and his thoughtlessness towards Lucette. When Van and Lucette come out of the restaurant that fateful night on the *Tobakoff* they examine "without much interest the objects of pleasure in a display window. Lucette sneered at a gold-threaded swimsuit. The presence of a riding crop and a pickax puzzled Van." (486) A riding crop and a pickax on an ocean liner – with fields to ride in and mountains to climb many miles away – indeed make an odd combination, but we can see the connection which Nabokov wants to stress. A few minutes later Van and Lucette are watching *Don Juan's Last Fling* and its farcical indebtedness to *Don Quixote*:

> The Don rides past three windmills, whirling black against an ominous sunset, and saves her from the miller who accuses her of stealing a fistful of flour and tears her thin dress. Wheezy but still game, Juan carries her across a brook.... Now they stand facing each other. She fingers voluptuously the jeweled pommel of his sword, she rubs her firm girl belly against his embroidered tights, and all at once the grimace of a premature spasm writhes across the poor Don's expressive face. He angrily disentangles himself and staggers back to his steed. (489)

Behind the parody there lies a demanding seriousness. The phrase "The Don rides past three windmills" – three foes Don Quixote could well have attacked – commemorates Van's not attacking Philip Rack or Percy de Prey or Andrey Vinelander, despite having intended to dispose of each of them. But after having ridden past three windmills, Juan/Van engages in a real struggle. The words "whirling *black* against an ominous sunset, and saves her from the *miller* who accuses her of stealing a fistful of flour" (my italics) evoke the blackmailer, Kim, from whom Van saves Ada and whose being blinded by Van we hear of during a digression on that other blackmailer, "Black Miller" (440–41).

It is immediately after this portion of the movie – after the spasm Dolores elicits from Juan – that the sight of Ada makes Van rush out and leave Lucette to her doom. Once again Van's concentration on the intensity of his own emotions makes him suddenly abandon Lucette, just as in his rage he takes no thought for the injury he inflicts on Kim Beauharnais or the repulsive injustice of his using Kim as a substitute for Andrey Vinelander.

Adultery

One of Nabokov's crucial moral emphases in *Ada* is to stress the similarity between the inconsiderateness with which Van and Ada treat Lucette and the lack of concern they show to the victims of their adulterous affairs.

The adultery theme emerges fully only in Part 3. In Pt. 3 Ch. 1 Van records that at the time of his mother's death he could not bear the thought of facing Ada and her husband at the graveside; but later he reproaches himself for having missed a chance to begin anew with Ada. It was "a petty, timorous, and stupid deed," he declares, to decline by cable to attend the funeral mentioned in "Lucette's cable from Nice": "for, actually, who knows, the later antlers might have been set right then, with green lamps greening green growths before the hotel where the Vinelanders stayed" (451–52). Van evidently considers it an act of moral cowardice not to have rejoined Ada and cuckolded Andrey Vinelander – but despite the ubiquitous ostensible acceptance of adultery throughout *Ada*, Nabokov himself thinks differently indeed.

The second chapter of Part 3 contains Van's meetings with Greg Erminin and Cordula de Prey (now Cordula Tobak). Greg and Van are both noticeably plumper than when they last met, and Van wonders:

> "What about Grace. I can't imagine *her* getting fat?"
> "Once twins, always twins. My wife is pretty portly, too."
> "*Tak ti zhenat* (so you are married)? Didn't know it. How long?"
> "About two years."
> "To whom?"
> "Maude Sween."
> "The daughter of the poet?"
> "No, no, her mother is a Brougham."
> Might have replied "Ada Veen," had Mr. Vinelander not been a quicker suitor. I think I met a Broom somewhere. Drop the subject. Probably a dreary union: hefty, high-handed wife, he more of a bore than ever. (454)

The lines from "so you are married" to "Brougham" allude to a passage in the last chapter of *Eugene Onegin* and indeed follow the *Eugene Onegin* stanza form exactly (iambic tetrameter, the first four lines with feminine and masculine rhymes abab)[5]. Here is Nabokov's interlinear translation of Pushkin's verses:

– *"Tak tï zhenát! ne znál ya ráne!*
"So you're married! I did not know before!
Davnó lï?" – *"Ókolo dvuh lét."*
"How long?" "About two years."
 – *"Na kóm?"* – *"Na Lárinoy."* *"Tat'yáne!"*
"To whom?" "The Larin girl." "Tatiana!"
 – *"Tï éy znakóm?"* – *"Ya im soséd."*
"You to her are known?" "I'm their neighbour."
(*EO* III, 184; VIII. xviii. 1–4)

After returning from his long wanderings, Onegin is surprised to find at a
society ball that the radiant young woman who has just reminded him of the
Tatiana who had once written him a letter of fervent adoration is not only
Tatiana but also the wife of his old friend Prince N. Onegin writes her a letter
as passionate as the one she had written him years earlier. Receiving no reply,
he languishes for months until impetuously dashing one day to Prince N.'s
home to find Tatiana alone, "pale, reading some letter or another," and softly
weeping. Though she admits to caring little for her fashionable life, she tells
Onegin firmly:

"I married. You must,
I pray you, leave me;
I know: in your heart are
both pride and genuine honor.
I love you (why dissimulate?);
but to another I've been given away:
to him I shall be faithful all my life."
(*EO* 1, 307; VIII. xlvii. 8–14)

In a rare observation on character and morality in *Eugene Onegin*, Nabokov
remarks:

Tatiana, if anything, is now a much better person than the romanesque
adolescent who (in [Chapter] Three) drinks the philter of erotic longings
and, in secret, sends a love letter to a young man whom she has seen only
once. Although she may be said to have sacrificed certain impassioned ideals
of youth when yielding to the sobs of her mother, it is also obvious that her
newly acquired exquisite simplicity, her mature calm, and her uncompromising
constancy are ample compensations, morally speaking, for whatever naïveté she
has lost with the rather morbid and definitely sensuous reveries that romances
had formerly developed in her. (*EO* III, 235–36)

Nabokov takes seriously the virtues of Tatiana's faithfulness. Just after the lines uttered above, Tatiana sweeps away from the kneeling Onegin and Pushkin declares that he will now leave his hero and the reader: the poem closes. Nabokov alludes affectionately to this situation in his only other attempt to incorporate the *Eugene Onegin* stanza into prose – at the end of *The Gift* (as Julian Moynahan calls it, "that great wedding song"[6]), just after Fyodor Godunov-Cherdyntsev and Zina Mertz have committed themselves tenderly to a life together:

> Good-by, my book! Like mortal eyes, imagined ones must close some day. Onegin from his knees will rise – but his creator strolls away. And yet the ear cannot right now part with the music and allow the tale to fade; the chords of fate itself continue to vibrate; and no obstruction for the sage exists where I have put The End: the shadows of my world extend beyond the skyline of the page, blue as tomorrow's morning haze – nor does this terminate the phrase. (*Gift* 378)

In the Foreword to *The Gift*, Nabokov asks: "I wonder how far the imagination of the reader will follow the young lovers after they have been dismissed." What he wanted us to imagine and enjoy can be inferred from a remark he made while writing *Ada*: "Fyodor in *The Gift* is blessed with a faithful love."[7]

The *Eugene Onegin* allusion in Van's conversation with Greg Erminin indicates how highly Nabokov values the faithfulness of love and how greatly his attitude differs from Van's sense that he has almost a moral obligation to cuckold Andrey Vinelander. After Greg Erminin tells Van of his marriage, that conversation continues:

> "I last saw you thirteen years ago, riding a black pony – no, a black Silentium. *Bozhe moy!*"
> "Yes – *Bozhe moy*. You can well say that. Those lovely, lovely agonies in lovely Ardis! Oh, I was *absolyutno bezumno* (madly) in love with your cousin!"
> "You mean Miss Veen? I did not know it. How long – "
> "Neither did she. I was terribly – "
> "How long are you staying – " (454)

In that split second of jealousy ("I did not know it. How long – ") when Van thinks Greg may have been one of Ada's lovers, his own words repeat Pushkin's lines, as if his hurt was the pain of a husband, his momentary jealousy the anguish of one who would hope to trust the faithfulness of his beloved. In Pt.1 Ch.2, Demon's fiery jealousy of Baron d'Onsky – a metamorphosis of the Baron d'O. (Onegin) in the play in which Marina has been Tatiana – is, too, like that of a deceived husband, as though he were the Prince N. to d'Onsky's Onegin and to Marina's weak-willed Tatiana. Of course it is natural that Demon and Van should be so bitterly hurt by the unfaithfulness of their mistresses, but this should only make them more aware of the anguish their own later adulteries will cause others. Instead both refuse to consider the pain they dole out to others.

As he leaves Greg, Van catches sight of Cordula de Prey, now Cordula Tobak, and easily seduces her. After "cornuting" Ivan Tobak, Van tells Cordula:

> "We shall do it again some day. Tomorrow I have to be in London and on the third my favorite liner, *Admiral Tobakoff,* will take me to Manhattan. *Au revoir.* Tell him to look out for low lintels. Antlers can be very sensitive when new. Greg Erminin tells me that Lucette is at the Alphonse Four?"
> "That's right. And where's the other?"
> "I think we'll part here." (457–48)

It will prove significant not only that these "antlers" recall the ones Van wishes at the beginning of Part 3 he had given Andrey Vinelander five years before the actual adultery, but also that Lucette is mentioned here in conjunction with Tobak's antlers as she had been, via the cable, in conjunction with Vinelander's.

Andrey Vinelander and Ivan Tobak, the two men with whose wives (Ada and Cordula) Van commits adultery in Part 3, are yoked closely together. When Demon comes in upon Van at his Manhattan apartment, left him by Cordula after her marriage, Van says:

> "I beg you, sir... go down, and I'll join you in the bar as soon as I'm dressed. I'm in a delicate situation."
> "Come, come," retorted Demon, dropping and replacing his monocle. "Cordula won't mind."
> "It's another, much more impressionable girl" – (yet another awful fumble!). "Damn Cordula! Cordula is now Mrs. Tobak."
> "Oh, of course!" cried Demon. "How stupid of me! I remember Ada's fiancé telling me – he and young Tobak worked for a while in the same Phoenix bank. Of *course.* Splendid broad-shouldered, blue-eyed, blond chap. Backbay Tobakovich!" (436)

But the freakish and therefore decisive link between the two husbands is the fact that both are descendants of explorers. Andrey Vinelander is described as "an Arizonian cattle-breeder whose fabulous ancestor discovered our country" (588), or as Van also puts it, "Vingolfer, no, Vinelander – first Russki to taste the labruska grape" (417). To Lucette Van explains in 1892 that "Cordula is now Mrs. Ivan G. Tobak.... His ancestor...was the famous or *fameux* Russian admiral...after whom the Tobago Islands, or the Tobakoff Islands, are named, I forget which" (382–83).[8]

When Cordula confirms for him that Lucette can be found at the Alphonse
Four Van tracks down his sister and tells her as he has Cordula that he is
sailing on the *Admiral Tobakoff* (named after Tobak's ancestor and owned by
his family). Lucette rings up Cordula and wangles the Tobak suite "in one
minute flat" (477). During the *Tobakoff* voyage towards America – which
itself retraces the routes of the imagined Russian admiral and of Vineland's
discoverer – Lucette is repeatedly associated with both "explorers," especially
as she sinks into death:

> She did not see her whole life flash before her as we all were afraid she might
> have done; ... but she did see a few odds and ends as she swam like a dilettante
> Tobakoff in a circle of brief panic and merciful torpor....she saw Van wiping
> his mouth before answering, and then, still withholding the answer, throwing
> his napkin on the table as they both got up: and she saw a girl with long black
> hair quickly bend in passing to clap her hands over a dackel in a half-torn
> wreath. (494)

Van writes that Lucette "swam like a dilettante Tobakoff" in memory of an
exchange with her earlier that day:

> "You're a divine diver...."
>   "But you swim faster," she complained, "...is it true that a sailor in Tobakoff's
> day was not taught to swim...?"
>   "A common sailor, perhaps," said Van. "When...Tobakoff himself got ship-
> wrecked...he swam around comfortably for hours...until a fishing boat rescued
> him...." (480)

Van's "She did not see her whole life flash before her...but she did see a few
odds and ends" and his "dackel in a half-torn wreath" echo Greg Erminin's
recent eagerness about Ada: "Did she marry Christopher Vinelander or his
brother?...Somebody told me she's a movie actress....Oh, that would be
terrible...to switch on the dorotelly, and suddenly see her. Like a drowning
man seeing his whole past, and the trees, and the flowers, and the wreathed
dachshund." (455) (In view of the "explorer of the Americas" theme, "Christopher" here – mentioned nowhere else – of course hints at Columbus.) The
vision that flashes through drowning Lucette's mind of Van rising from the
table before answering her refers back to the evening at the Ursus restaurant.
While Ada is off at the toilet, Lucette implores Van:

> "please, don't let me swill...champagne any more, not only because I will jump
> into Goodson River if I can't hope to have you..."

Here Van stood up again, as Ada, black fan in elegant motion, came back
followed by a thousand eyes.... (411)

The Goodson (Hudson) river alludes to yet another explorer of the Americas[9]
who ties Lucette, Andrey and Tobak together and arrays them against Van,
who as Mascodagama (Vasco da Gama explored in the opposite direction) asks
a girl who looks like Lucette for an adulterous assignation (*Ada* 185).

The most pointed connections of all are made as Lucette prepares for her
death:

> Having cradled the nacred receiver she changed into black slacks and a lemon
> shirt (planned for tomorrow morning); looked in vain for a bit of plain note-
> paper without caravelle or crest; ripped out the flyleaf of Herb's Journal, and
> tried to think up something amusing, harmless, and scintillating to say in a
> suicide note. (492)

The black and yellow clothes link Lucette with Aqua (who wore the same
colors on the day of her suicide) and with the repeated infidelities that ensured
Aqua's end. But on Van's last day at Ardis, Ada had also appeared – just after
Van had found out about her affairs – in black and yellow: Nabokov recalls
Ada's unfaithfulness, which caused Van such grief, in order to compare it
with the infidelities Van so easily expects women to engage in for him. The
"caravelle or crest" Lucette wants to avoid is the official insignia on the Tobak
and *Admiral Tobakoff* notepaper – "crest" here being also closely related to the
traditional emblem of the cuckold. When Van in parting suggests to Cordula
that she tell Tobak "to look out for low lintels. Antlers can be very sensitive
when new," Cordula calls him back: "'Wait. Here's a top secret address where
you can always' – (fumbling in her handbag) – 'reach me' – (finding a card
with her husband's crest and scribbling a postal cryptograph)" (458). But the
"caravelle or crest" also refers to Andrey Vinelander. In Van's concluding summary of the novel, he writes that its "principal part is staged in a dream-bright
America – for are not our childhood memories comparable to Vineland-born
caravelles..." (588). When Van and Ada are lunching by the side of Lake
Geneva, they notice

> Small grebes and big ones, with crests...They had, she said, wonderful nuptial
> rituals...
> "I asked you about Andrey's rituals."
> Ach, Andrey is so excited to see all those European birds! . . . that big *chomga*
> [grebe] there is *hohlushka* [crested], he says." (525)

By means of these connections, the passage above that records Lucette's preparations for death simultaneously associates the accumulated inconsiderateness of Van and Ada towards her with Demon's unending infidelities (Aqua's yellow and black), with Van's own experience of the pain unfaithfulness can cause (Ada's yellow and black), with the adulteries in which he so lightly engages Cordula and so passionately engages Ada (Tobak's and Andrey Vinelander's caravelles and crests).

Let us move now to the major focus on adultery, in Pt.3 Ch.8. After leading up to his first ecstatic reunion with Ada in his hotel room in Mont Roux, Van sums up "the duration of adultery" (521):

> That meeting, and the nine that followed, constituted the highest ridge of their twenty-one-year-old love: its complicated, dangerous, ineffably radiant coming of age. The somewhat Italianate style of the apartment, its elaborate wall lamps with ornaments of pale caramel glass, its white knobbles that produced indiscriminately light or maids, the slat-stayed, veiled, heavily curtained windows which made the morning as difficult to disrobe as a crinolined prude, the convex sliding doors of the huge white "Nuremberg Virgin"-like closet in the hallway of their suite, and even the tinted engraving by Randon... – in a word, the alberghian atmosphere of those new trysts added a novelistic touch (Aleksey and Anna may have asterisked here!) which Ada welcomed as a frame, as a form, something supporting and guarding life, otherwise unprovidenced on Desdemonia, where artists are the only gods. (521)

Even as Van describes the reunion as "ineffably radiant," Nabokov ensures that the details of this very paragraph denounce not only Van and Ada's present indifference to Andrey Vinelander but also their lack of thought for Lucette in the past.

The night before his first morning tryst with Ada at Mont Roux, Van meets the Vinelander party at the Bellevue Hotel. He renders the ensuing conversation as a parody of Chehovian style:

> ANDREY: *Adochka, dushka* (darling), *raskazhi zhe pro rancho, pro skot,* (tell about the ranch, about the cattle), *emu zhe lyubopitno* (it cannot fail to interest him).
>
> ADA: (*as if coming out of a trance*): *O chyom ti* (you were saying something)?
> ....
> IVAN (*to Andrey*): I know nothing about farming but thanks all the same.
> (*A pause*)
> IVAN (*not quite knowing what to add*):....(516–17)

But the scene the next morning has slid from Chehov to Tolstoy, to the Italianate phase of Anna and Vronsky's adultery: "the alberghian atmosphere of those new trysts added a novelistic touch (Aleksey and Anna may have asterisked here!).” In Pt. 2 Ch. 8 there is also an extended parody of Chehov – *Four Sisters* – and a switch to Tolstoy:

> But let us shift to the didactic metaphorism of Chehov's friend, Count Tolstoy.
>
> We all know those old wardrobes in old hotels in the Old World subalpine zone. At first one opens them with the utmost care, very slowly, in the vain hope of hushing the excruciating creak, the growing groan that the door emits midway. Before long one discovers, however, that if it is opened or closed with celerity, in one resolute sweep, the hellish hinge is taken by surprise, and triumphant silence achieved, Van and Ada, for all the exquisite and powerful bliss that engulfed and repleted them (and we do not mean here the rose sore of Eros alone), knew that certain memories had to be left closed, lest they wrench every nerve of the soul with their monstrous moan. But if the operation is performed quickly, if indelible evils are mentioned between two quick quips, there is a chance that the anesthetic of life itself may allay unforgettable agony in the process of swinging its door. (430–31)

Van is thinking here of the “indelible evils,” the “monstrous moan” of the pain of Ada's unfaithfulness. But the Chehov-Tolstoy shift and the “old wardrobes in old hotels in the Old World subalpine zone” point to the later passage set in an old, subalpine, Old World hotel where Van and Ada are depicted as Vronsky and Anna and have in their suite a “‘Nuremberg Virgin’-like closet.” Now the combination of “virgin” here and the earlier “Tolstoyan” image of shutting a closet call to mind one of Van and Ada's stratagems for keeping Lucette out of the way: “under the absurd pretext of a hide-and-seek game they locked up Lucette in a closet…and frantically made love, while the child knocked and called and kicked until the key fell out and the keyhole turned an angry green” (213).

By drawing a short thread from “Aleksey and Anna” to the “‘Nuremberg Virgin’-like closet” and a longer one from there to Tolstoy's “didactic metaphorism,” Nabokov has therefore managed to entangle Lucette in Van's summary of his adultery with Ada. But what is the “Nuremberg Virgin”? The “Iron Virgin or Iron Maiden” of Nuremberg

> was a terror-inspiring instrument of torture, and was made of strong wood, bound with iron bands. The front consisted of two doors which opened to allow the prisoner to be placed inside. The whole interior was fitted with long, sharp, iron spikes, so that when the doors were closed, these long sharp prongs forced their way into various portions of the victim's body. Two entered his eyes, the others pierced his back, his chest, and, in fact, impaled him alive in such a

manner that he lingered in the most agonising torture. When death relieved
the poor wretch from his agonies, perhaps after days, a trapdoor in the base was
pulled open and the body was allowed to fall into the water below.[10]

The image of Lucette as virgin and martyr, of the torment to which she was
subjected as Van and Ada pursue their own pleasure, has returned in its most
horrific form – and suggests already that if the two lovers ignore Andrey
Vinelander's feelings Nabokov certainly does not.

In an earlier chapter Nabokov has already associated Lucette with torture
and persecution. The scene is the dinner for which Demon has called at Ardis;
he and Ada are both savoring the asparagus:

> It almost awed one to see the pleasure with which she and Demon distorted
> their shiny-lipped mouths in exactly the same way to introduce orally from
> some heavenly height the voluptuous ally of the prim lily of the valley, holding
> the shaft with an identical bunching of the fingers, not unlike the reformed
> "sign of the cross" for protesting against which (a ridiculous little schism meas-
> uring an inch or so from thumb to index) so many Russians had been burnt
> by other Russians only two centuries earlier on the banks of the Great Lake
> of Slaves. (259)

The historical allusion is to the Great Schism in the seventeenth-century
Russian Orthodox church. One of the reforms that led to the schism was
the requirement proposed by Nikon, the Russian patriarch, in 1654–55, that
the benedictory sign of the cross be made with three fingers rather than two.
Persecution hounded the Old Believers who resisted this and other changes.
But the "sign of the cross" here is linked with Lucette's account of her sexual
initiation at Ada's hands: "She kissed my *krestik* while I kissed hers" (375).
Van feigns not to understand what Lucette means by "krestik" ("Come, come,
Lucette, it means 'little cross' in Russian, that's all, what else?" [378]) and
proceeds to taunt her:[11]

> "Oh, I know," cried Van (quivering with evil sarcasm, boiling with mysterious
> rage, taking it out on the redhaired scapegoatling, naive Lucette, whose only
> crime was to be suffused with the phantasmata of the other's innumerable lips).
> "Of course, I remember now. A foul taint in the singular can be a sacred mark
> in the plural. You are referring of course to the stigmata between the eyebrows
> of pure sickly young nuns whom priests had over-anointed there and elsewhere
> with cross-like strokes of the myrrherabol brush." (378)

The passage from the dinner scene in which Demon and Ada voluptuously devour asparagus stalks equates the supreme sensuality of father and daughter – but because Lucette's "krestik" becomes so entangled with signs of the cross, it also reflects the fact that Ada's sensuality is as ready as Demon's to disregard its potential for cruelty.

Lucette's kinship with martyrs and victims of persecution remains merely implicit in the asparagus image, but Aqua in the madness Demon precipitates becomes quite explicitly associated with visions of burning and torture: "Two or three centuries earlier she might have been just another consumable witch" (21); "Her disintegration went down a shaft of phases, every one more racking than the last; for the human brain can become the best torture house of all those it has invented, established and used in millions of years, in millions of lands, on millions of howling creatures." (22) Here Van uses all his verbal power to render the agony of the woman he thought of as mother until his fifteenth year. Yet Nabokov has also woven Andrey Vinelander – for whom Van shows nothing but poorly restrained contempt – into this same network of images. As Andrey, Dasha, Ada and Van sit down at the Bellevue, Andrey makes "a thready 'sign of the cross' over his un-unbuttonable abdomen" (513). The habitual gesture is perfectly in keeping with Andrey's Russianness and what Van deems to be his automatism,[12] but it also allies him with Lucette and the burnings of "so many Russians...by other Russians." And of course the "'Nuremberg Virgin'-like closet," associated via the Tolstoyan "didactic metaphor" with the anguish of unfaithfulness, adorns the very room where Van and Ada so gleefully cuckold poor Vinelander.

By being so scrupulously correlated with the "scapegoatling, naive Lucette" (378), who remains at the heart of all the novel's images of suffering, Andrey Vinelander is shown to matter, like so many other characters in the novel whom Van has dismissed as irrelevant to the triumphant love of "a unique super-imperial couple" (71). Van's lyric exaltation and the sheer joy of his and Ada's enduring love powerfully focus interest on the central characters alone. We cannot but be fascinated by the radiance and intensity of their passion, and it comes as a stern lesson (amid all the sheer pleasure of the book, of course) to realize what we have done in so thoroughly accepting Van and Ada's own enchanted sense of their loves and lives. When we see the delicate but profoundly just connections Nabokov has established between one character and another and one action and another and so are forced to reevaluate these characters and their actions we are compelled to recognize how easily our individual perspectives can make us discount the sufferings of others: we are driven to admit how much applies to us when Nabokov insists on acknowledging not only the grief people can inflict on one another but also the sad fact that even people of intelligence and sensitivity who are acutely familiar with their own pain may not be prepared to act as if the pain of others was real.

PART FOUR

ADA: THE METAPHYSICS
OF CONSCIOUSNESS

11. The Mysteries of Time

Nabokov's exploration of the metaphysics of consciousness in *Ada* ranges farther than Part 4 of the novel, Van's philosophical treatise, *The Texture of Time*. But before moving off into the unknown with Nabokov we should check that all is in order at base camp – and it is. Despite all its exuberant unconventionality Van's treatise is philosophically serious – even if it remains only a preliminary to the real daring of Nabokov's own imaginative speculations.

The Texture of Time

Van seeks to minimize if not altogether abolish the concept of the direction of time and describe instead time's texture, its feel within the present of individual consciousness. Paradoxically, Van attacks the idea of time as direction while giving his treatise the form of a journey. He is driving speedily and impatiently across Switzerland, eager to reach Ada, whom he has not seen since their adulterous two weeks together in Mont Roux in October 1905; it is now July 14, 1922, and Van is to meet her just after her husband's death, at the same hotel in Mont Roux. Van's thoughts on the texture of time develop as the journey progresses, comically interacting with his driving his car: "In the same sense of individual, perceptual time, I can put my Past in reverse gear...." (536)

He is steadily approaching a destination in space as time is steadily elapsing, yet his object is to sever space from time and to deny that motion is a significant part of time. But though Van's evolving thoughts are presented in terms of his journey, they are not the sequence-bound thoughts of a stream of consciousness but shaped impressions and gropings of the mind which have arrested, corrected, developed and refined themselves and their expression *against* the pressure of time. Both the thinking out and the initial writing of *The Texture of Time* have been done on his trip, but Van expects the reader to recognize that the whole treatise has been revised many times in the process of composition to give it its sense of immediacy and evolution. He trusts the reader will acknowledge that in the shaping of thought and its written expression the mind resists or ignores time, gives its own products a form and finality which owe nothing to the *sequence* of the reflections which gave rise to these finished thoughts.[1] While appearing to concede what his argument does not wish to concede, the importance of time's direction, Van's journey format shows lone thought arresting the moment, returning to an old idea, developing itself irrespective of the propulsion of time, even as it is able to recreate the floundering of thought within time.

Van's ideas are complicated by several features of his essay's organization and style. The combination of journey and cogitation creates an apparent lack of structure, in which one idea surfaces in his mind and then sinks as another appears, only to resurface later: there is no logical point-by-point development. The multiplication of the implied frames of reference adds to the challenge: the details of the journey (which, including Van's missing a turnoff and his making a wrong turn, can be traced out exactly on a Swiss road map); the swerving course of Van's thought, at times following the contours of the journey, at times in momentary parallel, sometimes darting aside, often altogether independent of anything but the pressure of image and idea; the lecture format half-implied in the essay's opening lines and intermittently throughout, as if the whole work were one of the public lectures on time Van describes in the middle of his argument: and, finally, not only the process of Van's own successive rewriting and rethinking, with its overlapping of many times other than the day of the journey itself, but also the reader's time: "I trust that my reader, who by now is frowning over these lines (but ignoring, at least, his breakfast), will agree with me" (540). Further complicating Van's concepts is the aggressively lush and tumbling metaphorism of the style, in part a parody of the fact "that Time is a fluid medium for the culture of metaphors" (537).

Despite all these complications of expression – a necessary consequence of Van's insistence on the difficulty of thinking about time within the changing moment – the essay's ideas are quite straightforward. (If we keep Part Two of this book in mind, we will see that they are also fundamentally Nabokov's own.) Van's concern with time is almost always with "individual, perceptual time" (536), with time in its relation to human consciousness. He has two chief aims: to show that neither Space nor "the Future" is part of Time, and to describe the feel of the Present and the Past, which *are* real components of Time.

First, the disregarding of Space. Van insists that Time and Space are utterly different – even though in describing the present, he notes that "The sharpest feeling of nowness, in visual terms, is the deliberate possession of a segment of Space collected by the eye. This is Time's only contact with Space." (551) Otherwise, Time and Space are completely distinct: "We reject without qualms the artificial concept of space-tainted, space-parasited time, the space-time of relativist literature" (541).[2] The measurement of time, the "miserable idea of measurement" (538), is to Van essentially spatial in nature and has little to do with the nature of change, the feel of the present, the reality of duration. Timing represents time "in terms of abstract boundaries of arbitrarily marked intervals – not in terms of the lived, concrete *intervals* of duration itself," as Charles Sherover writes in summarizing Bergson.[3]

Van attacks the "easy spatial analogies" (544) that disguise the sheer difference of space from time, that do not face the elusiveness of the notion of time and merely hand down confusion and centuries of accumulated laziness of thought. He assaults linear notions of time as motion in one irreversible direction. Time is not moving, and its irreversibility is merely the result of the limitations of human consciousness, which has no access to its own past except through memory working within the present: "The irreversibility of Time...is a very parochial affair: had our organs and orgitrons not been asymmetrical, our view of Time might have been amphitheatric and altogether grand." (538–39) Spatial analogies are wrong in implying that the present is moving, when it is only the locus of change, when it fills up the universe and has nowhere to move (Van dismisses the relativists' dismissal of cosmic simultaneity), and they are wrong too in implying that the future (whether the analogy is a person moving along a road or a point moving along a line) is as definite as the past, that it is merely not yet reached.[4] Van draws on his command of imagery to put to flight those who refuse to consider the meaning of the analogies they so readily adopt: "The idea that Time 'flows' as naturally as an apple thuds down on a garden table implies that it flows in and through something else and if we take that 'something' to be Space then we have only a metaphor flowing along a yardstick." (540–41)

Having severed Space from Time, Van can now consider Time itself. But for Van "Time is anything but the popular triptych: a no-longer existing Past, the durationless point of the Present, and a 'not-yet' that may never come. No." (559–60) He denies that the future is "an item of Time" (560); he argues that the present is not durationless but has a duration, and thus a reality, because consciousness retains "the still-fresh Past" (548); he maintains that the past is not "no-longer-existing," though it may be "intangible, and 'never-to-be-revisited'" (544); it is "a constant accumulation of images" (545) which, though we can no more visit than we can the future, "has at least the taste, the tinge, the tang of our individual being" (560).

The future, Van flatly declares, "is but a quack at the court of Chronos" (560): it is not a "not-yet," for its events "may never come." We cannot say that, because we did not know yesterday but do know *now* what would happen this morning, then "consequently the Future did exist yesterday and by inference does exist today. This...is execrable logic." (560) Anticipation, Van notes (550), is only an activity of the present, and just as he daringly presents in the form of a journey his dismissal of direction, motion and space as essentials of time, so he situates his dismissal of the future where the shadow of the anticipated reunion with Ada is cast over the essay's whole length.

Having dismissed space and the future, he can concentrate on describing the present and the past of which time really exists. First, the present – which is not durationless, for the mind's awareness of the immediate past gives it "duration and, therefore, reality" (560). Van attempts to determine the limits of the conscious present, and concludes that we have "three or four seconds of what can be felt as nowness" (549) if we include the mind's deliberate attention to time. It is rhythm that catches our attention to time, he feels – and here he finds true time, the real sense of becoming, the impalpable "grayish gauze" of time's texture. When one tries to apprehend time's essence by closely attending to the moment before consciousness, one sees it fade from consciousness even as one concentrates; *then* one is close to the nature of time even as one is driven to recognize that to investigate it means "struggling with the octopus of one's own brain" (557), with the very nature of human consciousness. When Van chooses to trace his thoughts along the course of a journey, he does so not because of the journey's forward direction, but to show himself concentrating on the "receding road," on time slipping away from his attention:

> To give myself time to time Time I must move my mind in the direction opposite to that in which I am moving, as one does when one is driving past a long row of poplars and wishes to isolate and stop one of them, thus making the green blur reveal and offer, yes, offer, its every leaf. (549)

Above all, he shows himself feeling the still-fresh past sliding away, feeling it by the rhythm that is time and not by the beats of the rhythm but by the "dim intervals between the dark beats" (548).

"Physiologically," then, the sense of the present "is a sense of continuous becoming, and if 'becoming' has a voice, the latter might be, not unnaturally, a steady vibration; but for Log's sake, let us not confuse Time with Tinnitus, and the seashell hum of duration with the throb of our blood." (559) Van continues: "Philosophically, on the other hand," the present "is but a memory in the making" (559), the process of storing new material to add to the past, which for Van is simply "a storage of Time" (560).

Van insists that the past is *not* "no-longer-existing" (559), though it is not directly accessible: "The Past is changeless, intangible, and 'never-to-be-revisited.'" (544) If the Past is unrevisitable, this is not because of its "passing away" but because of the limitations of consciousness. Van sees the Past "as an accumulation of sensa, not as the dissolution of Time implied by immemorial metaphors picturing transition." (544) It is not a passing away, but an accumulation: "what we are aware of as 'Present' is the constant building up of the Past, its smoothly and relentlessly rising level." (551) One's sense of succession is much weaker within that storage-house of the Past, Van emphasizes, than within the Present: "Our perception of the Past is not marked by the link of succession to as strong a degree as is the perception of the Present and of the instants immediately preceding its point of reality." (547) The rhythm of colored event and dim interval in the past forms a continuum in which succession is less important than the continuum's carpet-like texture:

> Reviewing those last steps of the immediate Past involves less physical time than was needed for the clock's mechanism to exhaust its strokes, and it is this mysterious "less" which is a special characteristic of the still-fresh Past into which the Present slipped during that instant inspection of shadow sounds. The "less" indicates that the Past is in no need of clocks and the succession of its events is not clock time, but something more in keeping with the authentic rhythm of Time, we have suggested earlier that the dim intervals between the dark beats have the *feel* of the texture of Time. The same, more vaguely, applies to the impression received from perceiving the gaps of unremembererd or "neutral" time between vivid events   Because of its situation among dead things, that dim continuum cannot be as sensually groped for, tasted, harkened to, as Veen's Hollow between rhythmic beats; but it shares with it one remarkable indicium: the immobility of perceptual Time. (547–49)

The Past for Van is "colored" and specific: it has "the taste, the tinge, the tang of our individual being" (560). It is "an accumulation of sensa"(544), and out of this accumulation, out of "the colored contents of the Past" (547) memory can choose what it likes, and in any order:

> The Past, then, is a constant accumulation of images. It can be easily contemplated and listened to, tested and tasted at random, so that is ceases to mean the orderly alternation of linked events that it does in the large theoretical sense. It is now a generous chaos out of which the genius of total recall, summoned on this summer morning in 1922, can pick anything he pleases:...a russet blackhatted beauty at a Parisian bar in 1901; a humid red rose among artificial ones in 1883;...a little girl, in 1884, licking the breakfast honey off the badly bitten nails of her spread fingers.... (545–46)

Direction no longer means anything in the past – and we shall see shortly how important it is that the past's colored reality can be recalled in any order so that one event can be placed beside another in a sudden illuminating collocation.

Morning

The best proof of Van's arguments about the future and the past and of his conclusion that texture is more significant than direction is to be found not in the ratiocination but in the narrative of his "novella in the form of a treatise in the Texture of Time" (562–63). When Van arrives in Mont Roux, he books the same hotel rooms as he and Ada had used when they were last together, during those adulterous trysts seventeen years earlier. He is out on the balcony, watching the sunset, when the phone rings: it is Ada, saying there's been trouble with the luggage, she's incredibly hungry, will he come down? She has "never – never, at least in adult life – spoken to him by phone" (555) and has done so only once in childhood, in 1886. The freshness, the "girlish glee" (555) of her voice seem to make a magical connection back to 1886 and their youthful past. But when Van comes down, the shock of change appals him: he is fifty-two, she is fifty and changed "in contour as well as in color" (556). Her rich black hair is "now dyed a brilliant bronze" (556), her figure is corseted and buxom. The suprise of age, the unfamiliarity, the lack of physical desire all engender awkwardness; their conversation remains unengaged. Suddenly, a chance remark they overhear sets things moving: "Young Van smiled back at young Ada. Oddly, that little exchange at the next table acted as a kind of delicious release." (557) But the relief does not last, the old intimacy does not return, and Ada says she cannot stay, she will have to "go back to Geneva directly after dinner to retrieve my things and maids....I promise to get in touch with you in a day or two, and then we'll go on a cruise to Greece with the Baynards." (558) Van returns to "their" room, alone, takes a sleeping pill and, while waiting for it to work, returns to *The Texture of Time* – the arguments in which now appear in much more orderly form, since he is working at a desk. He falls asleep, dreaming

> that he was speaking in the lecturing hall of a transatlantic liner and that a bum resembling the hitch-hiker from Hilden was asking sneeringly how did the lecturer explain that in our dreams we know we shall awake, is not that analogous to the certainty of death, and if so, the future –
>
> At daybreak he sat up with an abrupt moan, and trembling: if he did not act *now*, he would lose her forever! He decided to drive at once to the Manhattan in Geneva. (561)

He goes out towards the balcony, wondering if it might, "perhaps, be simpler – " (561) just to jump off – and then he sees, "One floor below, and somewhat adjacently...Ada engrossed in the view" (561). She looks up, "beaming, and... made the royal-grant gesture of lifting and offering him the mountains, the mist and the lake with three swans" (562). He runs down to the room where he conjectures she must be staying and finds her waiting for him:

> When, "a little later," Van, kneeling and clearing his throat, was kissing her dear cold hands, gratefully, gratefully, in full defiance of death, with bad fate routed and her dreamy afterglow bending over him, she asked:

"Did you really think I had gone'?"

"*Obmanshchitsa* (deceiver), *obmanshchitsa*," Van kept repeating with the fervor and gloat of blissful satiety.

"I told him to turn," she said, "somewhere near Morzhey ('morses' or 'walruses,' a Russian pun on 'Morges' – maybe a mermaid's message). And *you* slept, you could sleep!" (562)

Part 4 ends with Van telling Ada that his first draft is done, that he has tried

> to compose a kind of novella in the form of a treatise on the Texture of Time, an investigation of its veily substance, with illustrative metaphors gradually increasing, very gradually building up a logical love story, going from past to present, blossoming as a concrete story, and just as gradually reversing analogies and disintegrating again into bland abstraction. (562–63)

Van has said that the future is at every moment "an infinity of branching possibilities" (561). The unexpectedness of Van and Ada's failure to reestablish their relationship at Mont Roux, the horrible shock of their aging, and then the unforeseeable, miraculous reunion the next morning – a reunion that will last until they die – prove Van's point, that things could have turned out differently at any moment, that the relation of anticipation to what eventually happens is significant for the present but not for the future. Van's narrative has confirmed his views of the future, of the freedom of events in time.

What of the past? This is Nabokov's real territory – and he makes the whole of *Ada* erupt into order so that this marvelous morning on the balcony becomes even more of a celebration of pattern and the directionless design of time's gauzy fabric than it is a confirmation of the independence of unfolding events. We must now look back.

Ada's phone call to Van reminds him with singular vividness of their one previous exchange over the telephone, in 1886: "It was the timbre of their past, as if the past had put through that call, a miraculous connection ('Ardis, one eight eight six' – *comment? Non, non, pas huitante-huit – huitante-six*)" (555). That earlier phone call had been made between Malahar, on the Ladore River, and Ardis, when Van was arranging his only tryst with Ada in the four years between Ardis the First and Ardis the Second. They decide to meet at Forest Fork, just outside Ardis and the scene of their last previous embraces:

> The toilet on the landing was a black hole, with the traces of a fecal explosion, between a squatter's two giant soles. At 7 A.M. on July 25 he called Ardis Hall from the Malahar post office and got connected with Bout who was connected with Blanche and mistook Van's voice for the butler's.
> "Dammit, Pa," he said into his bedside dorophone. "I'm busy!"
> "I want Blanche, you idiot," growled Van.

> *"Oh, pardon,"* cried Bout, *"un moment, Monsieur."*
> A bottle was audibly uncorked (drinking hock at seven in the morning!) and Blanche took over, but scarcely had Van begun to deliver a carefully worded message to be transmitted to Ada, when Ada herself who had been on the *qui vive* all night answered from the nursery, where the clearest instrument in the house quivered and bubbled under a dead barometer.
> "Forest Fork in Forty-Five minutes. Sorry to spit."
> "Tower!" replied her sweet ringing voice....(179)

The grotesque (though accurate) description of the toilet is not gratuitous: it will be echoed by a similar description on the summer morning of 1922 when Van and Ada have another, much longer-lasting, reunion ahead of them: "Van welcomed the renewal of polished structures after a week of black fudge fouling the bowl slope so high that no amount of flushing could dislodge it" (561)

But before we return to that much later morning, let us look more closely at the morning of "Forest Fork the Second." The brief Forest Fork scene recalls, in some curiously exact ways, Van's first morning at Ardis in 1884. In Forest Fork the Second Van rings up Ardis and *interrupts* Bout, who is in bed with Blanche and thinks it is Bouteillan, his father, who has interrupted him. Van hears the sound of a bottle being uncorked and is surprised at Bout's "drinking hock at seven in the morning!"(179).[5] On his first morning at Ardis in 1884, Van, rising early, encounters Blanche. Though he is aroused by her pretty features, he is put off by "her strange tragic tone." Their little colloquy is *interrupted* by Bouteillan's arrival: "Now we have to separate, the sparrow has disappeared, I see, and Monsieur Bouteillan has entered the next room, and can perceive us clearly in that mirror above the sofa behind that silk screen" (49). It soon becomes apparent (when Van finds on the ground, later on what is probably the same morning, the tortoiseshell comb Blanche had had in her hair) that it is in fact Van who has almost interrupted Blanche and Bouteillan. And Bouteillan, like his son – who by that morning in 1886 had long replaced him as Blanche's lover – is also involved in early-morning "drinking": "The butler's hand in the mirror took down a decanter from nowhere and was withdrawn." (49)

That there is a special link betwee Van's first morning at Ardis and the phone conversation before Forest Fork the Second is confirmed on the way to Forest Fork the First (on the *last* morning of Ardis the First, and of course specifically recalled in Forest Fork the Second). Bouteillan attempts to warn Van that he must be careful in his affair with Ada: "Monsieur should be prudent" (157). Van feigns to take Bouteillan's warning as a reference to that first morning at Ardis when the butler came in upon Blanche and Van: "'If,' said Van, 'you're thinking of little Blanche, then you'd better quote Delille not to me, but to your son, who'll knock her up any day now.'"(157) On the morning of Forest Fork the Second it is indeed Bouteillan's son rather than Bouteillan himself who is making love to Blanche and who is providing an early "drink" and who is interrupted by Van.

But the first morning at Ardis the First in turn foreshadows the first morning of Ardis the Second. On the first morning of his earlier stay at Ardis, Van is seeking a way out of the chateau, whose obvious doors are bolted and chained. He is "still unaware that under the stairs an inconspicuous recess concealed an assortment of spare keys...and communicated through a tool-room with a secluded part of the garden" (48). As he looks for an obliging window, he comes upon Blanche. Stirred by the young maid's presence, he clasps her wrist and draws closer, "while looking over her head for a suitable couch to take shape in some part of this magical manor – where *any* place, as in *Casanova's* remembrances could be dream-changed into a sequestered seraglio nook" (49; italics added); as Blanche is talking, Bouteillan appears. On the first night of Ardis the Second, Van and Ada meet in the now-familiar old toolroom and are making love there when Blanche glides in with her key, "back from a rendezvous with old Sore, the Burgundian night watchman" (191), her latest lover. Van spends a "strenuous '*Casanovanic*' night with Ada" (198; italics added) on the bench in the toolroom. Early in the morning, they help themselves to a snack breakfast. While they are talking, Ada makes "what she called a warning frog face, because *Bouteillan had appeared* in the doorway" (195; italics added).

The first morning at Ardis the First also foreshadows Van's last morning ever at Ardis, when Blanche makes her dire disclosure. On that first morning at Ardis, Van chances upon Blanche because he does not know he can get out through the toolroom. He accosts her: "What was her name? Blanche – but Mlle Larivière called her 'Cendrillon' because her stockings got so easily laddered, see, and because she broke down and mislaid things, and confused flowers." (49) His arousal is evident: "His loose attire revealed his desire; this could not escape a girl's notice, even if color-blind." (49) He imagines the impending seduction scene, but is irked by Blanche's romanesque style: "*Monsieur* is a nobleman; I am a poor peat-digger's daughter...were I to fall in love – and I might, alas, if you possessed me *rien qu'une petite fois* – it would be, for me, only grief, and infernal fire, and despair, and even death, *Monsieur.*" (49) On Van's last morning at Ardis, he is awoken from his hammock by Blanche's coming through the creaking toolroom door. Blanche tries to look alluring, but is only a bedraggled and slatternly Cinderella ("no slippers"): "bare armed, in her petticoat, one stocking gartered, the other down to her ankle; no slippers" (292). Her invitation on this morning echoes antiphonally and in the same romanesque key the demurrer she made on Van's first morning at Ardis: "'*C'est ma dernière nuit au château,*' she said softly, and rephrased it in her quaint English, elegiac and stilted, as spoken only in obsolete novels, "'Tis my last

night with thee'." (292) While Van was aroused and not shy to manifest this
in 1884, he is now quite stirless as he enters the toolroom with Blanche and
remains unable "to work up the urge which she took for granted and whose
total absence he carefully concealed under his tartan cloak" (293). It is at this
point the disclosure breaks – Ada has been quite unfaithful – and Van knows
he must flee the enchantment of Ardis.

The morning meeting of Forest Fork, then, partially reenacts the first morning of Ardis the First, which in turn foreshadows the first morning and the last
of Ardis the Second. But Forest Fork itself foreshadows both the first and last
mornings at Ardis in 1888. The torrid hour at Forest Fork in 1886 anticipates
Van and Ada's active renewal of their affair in the first night and morning of
Ardis the Second merely by virtue of its being their only reunion at Ardis since
1884, their first lovemaking since that separation, their only lovemaking before
that long night at Ardis the Second. And when Ada declares to Van, just before
their first kiss at Ardis the Second, that she had and has "and shall always have
only one beau, only one beast" (190), she cannot help bringing to mind Forest
Fork, that "beastly, but beautiful, tryst" (180).

The ways in which the brief fervor of Forest Fork anticipates the *end* of
Ardis the Second – the picnic fight with Percy de Prey, the morning Van
rushes from Ardis in pursuit of his rivals, the duel next morning – are rather
more complicated. After ringing Ada to arrange the meeting at Forest Fork,
Van "rented a *motorcycle*..., and drove, bouncing...along a narrow *forest ride*"
(179; italics added). At the picnic on Ada's birthday in Ardis the Second, Greg
Erminin leaves his "splendid new black Silentium *motorcycle* in the *forest ride*"
(268; italics added). As we have already seen (pp. 164–165). Greg's new black
pony offered to Ada after the *first* Ardis picnic seemed to confirm that Van
had no rivals. In prefiguring Greg's "new black...motorcycle in the forest ride,"
Van's motorcycle then seems to anticipate that again when he meets Ada at
Ardis there will be no real rivals – and Greg's presence at the 1888 picnic is
certainly no threat at all.

But after Van makes love to Ada at Forest Fork the Second he realizes how
ill she is when she gets up feverish and totters and almost collapses, "mutter-
ing about gipsies stealing their jeeps" (180). Ada's half-delirious phrase has
verbally transformed Van's motorcycle and her own bike; but it also points
ahead to the second Ardis picnic, where unidentified strangers, perhaps
"Gipsy politicians"(268), inspect Greg's new motorcycle and then, as it glides
in, Percy de Prey's sleek convertible. The motorcycle Van brings to Forest
Fork the Second appears to foreshadow Greg's new black motorcycle in 1888,
a second avatar of his new black pony of 1884 – which in turn had been proof
of Van's having no real rivals then and was itself recalled in Van's black steed
of Forest Fork the First. But, in being transformed in Ada's delirium, it foreshadows also the car Percy, Ada's recent lover, brings to the 1888 picnic: it

foreshadows the real rival who will emerge during Ardis the Second, and in pursuit of whom Van will flee Ardis, two years to the day and almost to the hour after the reunion at Forest Fork.[6]

Forest Fork also foreshadows the morning after Van's departure from Ardis, the morning of his duel. Let us quote from the antecedents of the 1886 reunion:

> Van rented a room...Malahar...on Ladore River.... The toilet on the landing was a black hole. with the traces of a fecal explosion, between a squatter's two giant soles. At 7 A.M. on July 25 he called Ardis Hall...and got connected with Bout who...mistook Van's voice for the butler's.
>
> "Dammit, Pa," he said into his bedside dorophone, "I'm busy!" (179)

On the morning of the duel Bouteillan, the Ladore, the dorophone and the unpleasantly vivid fecal imagery recur:

> Van was roused by the night porter who put a cup of coffee...on his bedside table....He resembled somewhat Bouteillan as the latter had been ten years ago and as he had appeared in a dream, which Van now retrostructed as far as it would go: in it Demon's former valet explained to Van that the "dor" in the name of an adored river equaled the corruption of hydro in "dorophone."...
>
> He shaved...had a structurally perfect stool, took a quick bath....(309–10)

The brief meeting at Forest Fork in 1886, which at the time seems a triumph for Van and Ada, foreshadows the double doom that closes Ardis the Second, Van's furious departure and his near-fatal wound.

But when Van and Ada are reunited in Manhattan in 1892, the morning of their reunion redeems the doubled woe at the end of Ardis the Second. The recollection of the morning of the duel is quite straightforward: "he began ringing up Ardis Hall – vainly, vainly. He kept it up intermittently till daybreak, gave up, had a structurally perfect stool (its cruciform symmetry reminding him of the morning before his duel)." (389) The "structurally perfect" is a trap for the reviewers (such as Updike, "Van Loves Ada, Ada Loves Van," p. 68) and critics (such as Fowler, *Reading Nabokov*, p. 177) who might disapprove of Nabokov's recurrent fecal imagery without being able to see the structural perfection of which it forms part. The recollection of the last morning of Ardis itself is a little less obvious but no less precise. On that dire last morning, Van had seen Ada on her balcony, "signaling to him. She signaled telegraphically, with expansive linear gestures, indicating the cloudless sky (what a cloudless sky!), the jacaranda summit in bloom (blue! bloom!)" (295). This painful reminder of the joy he must leave, of their first early morning together – when Ada on her balcony was "stickily glistening"

(75) with the honey she was eating, when "her tower crumbled in the sweet silent sun" (76) as Van left the balcony – is recalled and reversed on the first morning at Manhattan, when Van waits for Ada "on the roof terrace (now embellished by shrubs of *blue* spiraea in invincible *bloom*)" (390: italics added)[7] and when after making love "our two lovers, now weak-legged and decently robed, sat down to a beautiful breakfast (Ardis' crisp bacon! Ardis' translucent honey!)" (393).

If the first morning of Van and Ada's Manhattan reunion specifically and exactly atones for the end of Ardis the Second, it also, on the other hand, forecasts the end of their Manhattan idyll. On Van and Ada's first morning at Manhattan breakfast is "brought up in the lift by Valerio, a ginger-haired elderly Roman" (393). On their last morning, Demon discovers his children are lovers when he arrives with the breakfast:

> Demon hastened to enter the lobby and catch the lift which a ginger-haired waiter has just entered, with breakfast for two on a wiggle-wheel table and the Manhattan *Times* among the shining, ever so slightly scratched, silver cupolas. Was his son still living up there, automatically asked Demon, placing a piece of nobler metal among the domes. *Si*, conceded the grinning imbecile, he had lived there with his lady [whom Demon assumes will be Cordula] all winter. (434)

That last morning at Manhattan, in *its* turn, is explicitly "redeemed" in the first morning of Van and Ada's next reunion, at Mont Roux in 1905. Van is in the throes of a vivid dream:

> yet he knew by the dimple of a faint smile that she was looking at his...raw scarlet. Somebody said, wheeling a table nearby: "It's one of the Vane sisters," and he awoke murmuring with professional appreciation the oneiric word-play combining his name and surname, and plucked out the wax plugs, and, in a marvelous act of rehabilitation and link-up, the breakfast table clanked from the corridor across the threshold of the adjacent room, and, already munching and honey-crumbed, Ada entered his bed-chamber. It was only a quarter to eight!
> "Smart girl!"said Van; "but first of all I must go to the *petit endroit* (W.C.)" (521)

That breakfast table recalls the "breakfast for two on a wiggle-wheel table" (434) which had accompanied Demon on the morning he separated his son and daughter for more than twelve years. The "*first of all* I must go to the *petit endroit*," we should note, also harks back to *the beginning* of Van and Ada's previous reunion, when Ada "stopped him, explaining that she must *first of all* take her morning bath (this, indeed, was a new Ada)" (392; italics added).[8]

The pattern of all these morning encounters is crowned by the reunion of Mont Roux in 1922 and that sudden shock of seeing Ada on her balcony in the morning light, in "her flimsy peignoir....Pensively, youngly, voluptuously, she was scratching her thigh at the rise of the right buttock: Ladore's pink signature on vellum at mosquito dusk." (562) This final reunion encompasses the promise and the threat of Forest Fork the Second, which it summons up directly by the "miraculous connection ('Ardis, one eight eight six'...)" (555) and by the toilet image ("black fudge fouling the bowl") which matches the earlier "fecal explosion." The 1922 reunion also overturns the poignant loss at the end of Ardis the Second: "standing on a third-floor balcony and signaling to him. She signaled telegraphically, with expansive linear gestures, indicating the cloudless blue sky (what a cloudless sky!), the jacaranda summit in bloom (blue! bloom!)" (295). In Mont Roux there is a paulownia "in sumptuous purple-blue bloom" (554); on the magic morning, "under the cloudless turquoise of the sky" (561), Ada on her balcony turns to Van, making "the royal grand gesture of lifting and offering him the mountains" (562).

The Manhattan morning which so richly redeems the end of Ardis the Second is itself now amply recalled. The fecal imagery, the rooftop terrace scene, the "blue spiraea in invincible bloom" all reappear in the fecal imagery, the balcony, the "purple-blue bloom" of Mont Roux. In 1892, moreover, Ada had chartered a plane to get to Manhattan and Van as quickly as possible; now, in 1922, before he sees Ada, Van wonders how he can catch her: "Should he rent a plane?" (561)

The morning of their reunion in Mont Roux in 1905 is also easily evoked, not only by the fact of the reunion's being again in Mont Roux and in the same hotel (a commemorative gesture on Van and Ada's part, of course), but also by the way that "marvelous act of rehabilitation and link-up" (521) in the 1905 reunion is recollected in the 1922 phone call's "resurrecting the past and linking it up with the present" (556).[9]

The balcony scene in Mont Roux is the key to the elaborate and exhilarating pattern running delicately through all the mornings that give shape to Van and Ada's lives: the first and last mornings of Ardis the First, their sole meeting near Ardis and their sole love-making ("Forest Fork the Second") in the four years of their earliest separation, the first and last mornings of Ardis the Second, the first and last mornings of their Manhattan sojourn, the first and last mornings of their first reunion in Mont Roux. No less part of the pattern are their first early morning together, "that blue morning on the balcony" (75) – the "honey" part of the "hammock and honey" chapter – and their first morning together as lovers, the day after the night of the Burning Barn, where the *baguenaudier* flowers and the *Jolana* butterflies let us know how Van and Ada spent their first few days of new happiness in 1922:

Blue butterflies nearly the size of Small Whites, and likewise of European origin, were flitting swiftly around the shrubs and settling on the drooping clusters of yellow flowers. In less complex circumstances, forty years hence, our lovers were to see again, with wonder and joy, the same insect and the same bladder-senna along a forest trail near Susten in the Valais. (128)[10]

We can see now how Van's philosophy fits into the much larger structure of Nabokov's own ideas. Van himself has chosen the unexpectedness, the utterly unforeseeable joy of Ada's return and his catching sight of her on the balcony below to cap his argument for the total openness of time, its infinitely branching possibilities, its endless surprise. When Nabokov supports Van's denial of the future, as his narrative does here, he is insisting – as we noted in Chapter 4 he does throughout hts work – on the independence of events in time. Van has also argued throughout the *Texture of Time* that the past is an accumulation of sensa, that its colored contents are not constrained by succession but are free to be selected and savored by memory. Nabokov too treats the past as a field for inexhaustible reinvestigation which memory can explore without being bound by succession, and as we noted in Chapter 4 he values the past above all as a repository of pattern discoverable in interlocking particulars. If Nabokov's love of independence lies behind that balcony scene over Lake Geneva, so too does his love of pattern. The "morning" pattern woven throughout *Ada's* narrative, crowned by Van's catching sight of Ada on the balcony at Mont Roux, discoverable when the most minute details of Van and Ada's past are suddenly seen together, convinces us more than any of Van's arguments could that time may be less important as direction than as an accumulation of sensa that can be freely arranged in memory.

If we had space to consider one of the early morning scenes on its own – the end of Pt.1 Ch.12 (74–76) would be a good example – we would see the breathtaking freshness and individuality and vitality of the single scene. The same qualities can be found in each of the morning scenes that form part of the grand pattern: in each there is a rare value in the independence of the moment, a sense of the freedom and the worth of each instant that can hardly be matched in literature. But in addition to this magic of local life we find, long afterwards, only after many readings, an astonishing pattern of interlacements.

Nabokov, surely, is asking us this: *if* within a closed system such as this novel, pattern can be discerned so long after we first encounter the imagined events, even when we are able to return endlessly and exactly to this fictive past, is it not possible that within a system – the whole world of time – that is *not* closed, where at least for mortal man there is no possibility of endless return, there is pattern of the same eerie complexity?

And is it not possible – though one shudders at the infinity of consciousness such design would require – that every life may be shaped with the care exhibited here, in a way too subtle to allow any mortal memory to see even the patterns of its own past, in a way that would still allow human lives their freedom and their responsibility and would leave time its unqualified openness? If in each of the scenes in his pattern, considered on its own, Nabokov has tenderly preserved the independence of time even as he designs a pattern too subtle to be perceived without many replayings of the fictive past, is it not possible that an infinite care could be allowing us total freedom while weaving its own designs through our free choices, so that even the most trifling or mundane details of our lives could take on unforeseeable significance?

Nabokov insists on the mystery of art, on art's appeal "to that secret depth of the human soul where the shadows of other worlds pass like the shadows of nameless and soundless ships" (NG 149). Nowhere is his own art more exact and more mysterious than in the independence and the patternedness of *Ada*'s scenes.

12. In Time and Beyond

A Mermaid's Message

In his first nights at Ardis, in summer 1884, Van is haunted by his sense of night and death in the black meaninglessness of space overhead. But on the special morning of the hammock and honey chapter, night and death are followed immediately by the "resurrection" (74) of the enchanted "honey" scene, "that blue morning on the balcony" when Van watches Ada at breakfast and we see for the first time how keenly she loves him. The unforgettable morning of the balcony scene in July 1922 bears a similar relation to the themes of night and death. The night before, Van falls asleep despondent, knowing his reunion with Ada has ended in failure:

> He dreamed that he was speaking in the lecturing hall of a transatlantic liner and that a bum resembling the hitch-hiker from Hilden was asking sneeringly how did the lecturer explain that in our dreams we know we shall awake, is not that analogous to the certainty of death and if so, the future –
>
> At daybreak he sat up with an abrupt moan, and trembling: if he did not act now, he would lose her forever! (561)

The dream garbles together Van's picking up a hitchhiker on his journey towards Mont Roux the previous day, his work on the treatise, which appears here in the form of the lectures on time he has given throughout his career, and his last moments with Lucette, in the movie theater of a transatlantic liner. The conjunction of Lucette, "the certainty of death," and waking from dreams is no accident.

When Van and Ada have made love later that morning, "in full defiance of death, with bad fate routed," Ada asks:

> "Did you really think I had gone?"
>
> ....
>
> "I told him to turn," she said, "somewhere near Morzhey ('morses' or 'walruses,' a Russian pun on 'Morges' – maybe a mermaid's message)...."
> (562)

Morges is a town about thirty-five kilometres along the road from Montreux (Nabokov's home while writing *Ada* and the obvious model for Mont Roux) to

Geneva (Ada's destination). But pronounced "Morzhey" as Ada pronounces it here, Morges resembles the Russian "morzhey" ("of walruses"). Van glosses it "'morses' or 'walruses.'" "Morse" is indeed an English word meaning "walrus," though it also brings to mind the Morse code: hence the "mermaid's message."[1]

But what does that "mermaid's message" mean? The night before, Van had resorted to his essay on time to hold his despair at bay. He takes a sleeping tablet,

> and, while waiting for it to relieve him of himself, a matter of forty minutes or so, sat down at a lady's bureau to his "lucubratiuncula."
>
> Does the ravage and outrage of age deplored by poets tell the naturalist of Time anything about Time's essence? Very little. Only a novelist's fancy could be caught by this small oval box, once containing Duvet de Ninon (a face powder, with a bird of paradise on the lid), which has been forgotten in a not-quite-closed drawer of the bureau's arc of triumph – not, however, triumph over Time. The blue-green-orange thing looked as if he were meant to be deceived into thinking it had been waiting there seventeen years for the bemused, smiling finder's dream-slow hand: a shabby trick of feigned restitution, a planted coincidence – and a bad blunder, since it had been Lucette, now a mermaid in the groves of Atlantis (and not Ada, now a stranger somewhere near Morges in a black limousine) who had favored that powder. (559)

The conjunction of Ada and Morges here in relation to *this* "mermaid" makes it certain that it is Lucette – dead, at the bottom of the Atlantic – who is the mermaid implied in the later "mermaid's message." Has the decision Ada makes to turn back to Mont Roux and to Van been inspired somehow by dead Lucette?

Such a suggestion seems to violate the ordinary rules of fiction – but similar transgressions occur more openly in "The Vane Sisters" and *Transparent Things* and *Invitation to a Beheading*. When Van and Ada conjecture "maybe a mermaid's message" they do so lightly, more as a tribute to the magnitude of the change in their lives than as a serious "attribution" of Ada's change of mind to Lucette. Nevertheless their offhand comment receives support that neither of them recognizes.

Van's disappointed observation that it should be Lucette, not Ada, whom the bird of paradise powder box brings to mind grossly understates the case. Not only was this Lucette's favorite makeup but she seems positively identified with the bird which serves as its trade mark. On the night of the Ursus restaurant outing Lucette in her dark furs, her very short evening gown of "lustrous...green" and with her eyes "made up in a 'surprised bird-of-paradise' style" (410) has been dressed by Nabokov to resemble exactly the Superb bird of paradise (*Lophorina superba*) in its state of display, when with brilliant green on a breast shield and above its eyes and a furry-looking black cape flared round its head, it seems extraordinarily like a woman in evening dress. Then the next morning, after the *débauche à trois*. Lucette flees, leaving a message scrawled in her green eyeshadow, to which Van alludes in his note of apology: "We are sorry you left so soon. We are even sorrier to have inveigled our Esmeralda and mermaid in a naughty prank.... We wished to admire and amuse you, BOP (bird of paradise)." (421) Here we find the same conjunction of "mermaid" and "bird of paradise" as in Van's lucubrations in Mont Roux.

Curiously, when Van addresses Lucette as "our Esmeralda and mermaid", he unwittingly recalls another similar conjunction. Lucette drowns after Ada's appearance as a gitanilla (gipsy) dancing girl in *Don Juan's Last Fling* suddenly breaks the spell Lucette had at last managed to cast over Van. *Letters from Terra*, Van's first book (published in 1891), oddly anticipates the night of his sister's death (in 1901), for the gitanilla dancer and Lucette's drowning are exactly prefigured in the novel's two leading ladies: Antilia Glems, whose queer name is an anagram of the *"gitanilla Esm*[eralda], *"* the gipsy dancing-girl from *Notre-Dame de Paris* with whom Lucette comes to be closely identified (see above, p. 138), and Theresa ("a micromermaid"). This suddenly suggests weird implications when we remember that the micromermaid in Van's novel sends messages to the hero from the putative planet Terra – which many in Antiterra in fact equate with a "Next World" (20).

If the "Esmeralda and mermaid" in Van's last letter to Lucette seems to pick up strange signals in *Letters from Terra*, the eeriness is compounded by Lucette's last letter to Van. She writes from Paris to his university address at Kingston, just in case he decides not to turn up on the *Tobakoff* and she has to go through with her suicide plan without even a final attempt at seducing him. He reads the letter, therefore, only after she is dead – and the letter itself ends with a poem which depicts an exchange between a ghost and a mortal:

> "I kept for years – it must be in my Ardis nursery – the anthology you once gave me; and the little poem you wanted me to learn by heart is still word-perfect in a safe place of my jumbled mind, with the packers trampling on my things, and upsetting crates, and voices calling: time to go, time to go. Find it in Brown and praise me again for my eight-year-old intelligence as you and happy Ada did that distant day, that day somewhere tinkling on its shelf like an empty little bottle. Now read on:

> > "Here, said the guide, was the field,
> > There, he said, was the wood
> > This is where Peter kneeled,

That's where the Princess stood.
No, the visitor said,
You are the ghost, old guide.
Oats and oaks may be dead,
But *she* is by my side." (146)

The poem, called "Peter and Margaret" (145), is Nabokov's own: "Peter" is Group Captain Peter Townsend, who might have married Princess Margaret had not royal pressures been applied (Townsend had been divorced in 1952, and since his ex-wife was still alive, his second marriage could not have been solemnized by the Church of England). Nabokov's own words explain the poem best: "it is a stylized glimpse of a mysterious person visiting the place, open to tourists,[2] where in legendary times ('legendary' in Antiterra terms) a certain Peter T. had his last interview with the Queen's sister. Although he accuses the old guide of being a 'ghost,' it is he, in the reversal of time, who is a ghostly tourist, the ghost of Peter T. himself...it should send a tingle down the spine of the reader."[3]

Let us recapitulate. Convinced that now they are middle-aged their old ardor cannot be revived and must be relegated conclusively to mere memory, Ada heads for Geneva airport. Near Morges she decides for some reason to turn back to Mont Roux, where she arrives too late in the night to disturb Van and anyway now feels too confident of their love to need to wake him at once. She takes a room beneath his, so that Van realizes she has returned and will remain his only when he spots her the next morning on the balcony below, in a way that sets the seal on the "morning" pattern in their lives. While Ada's taxi takes her to the airport Van returns to his essay on time in order to stifle his distress at the collapse of their reunion. At the very moment when Ada decides to return, the bird of paradise container catches Van's attention, suddenly reminding him of his sister: but not Ada, he muses, merely Lucette, whom he thinks of fleetingly as "a mermaid in the groves of Atlantis" only to dismiss the thought; fortified by his moroseness, he then inserts in his treatise a sneering refutation of the idea of retrieving time. Van's last note to Lucette was written in response to her message in bird of paradise eyeshadow; now a makeup box with the same design on its lid reminds him of Lucette in a way that for him seems only to confirm the irretrievability of the past. But the "paradise" and the image of her not as dead but a "mermaid" – quite alive, and moving in a different medium – hint strongly at her immortality and recall the messages sent by the "micromermaid" from "Terra" just when Ada rescinds her own rejection of the past and drives back to Mont Roux to make possible the restoration of her love for Van and at the same time the perfect culmination of the pattern of their past.

On the next morning itself there are recurrent indications of Lucette's almost being shadowily present or at least repeatedly implicated. She springs to mind first through "the lecturing hall of a transatlantic liner" in Van's dream – which recalls, of course, the fatal cinema hall on the *Tobakoff*. Then when Van wakes up, realizing that he must catch Ada immediately if he is not to lose her forever, he wonders should he ring up her hotel in Geneva before starting, or should he rent a plane?

> Or might it, perhaps, be simpler –
> The door-folds of his drawing-room balcony stood wide open. (561)

As the Darkbloom gloss at this point notes, Van is tempted to throw himself from the balcony – and thus to imitate the end Lucette chose in leaping down to her death. When Van steps out onto the balcony, and just an instant before he sees Ada, he wonders

> if he had ever satisfied the familiar whim by going platch – had he? had he? You could never know, really. One floor below, and somewhat adjacently, stood Ada engrossed in the view. (561)

The thought of crashing to his death and the strange speculation about a previous suicide-by-jumping eerily evoke Lucette's leap to her death, for an odd error remains in the passage describing her last moments: "Although Lucette had never died before – no, *dived* before, Violet – from such a height...." (493) Then, just when Van all but follows Lucette's example and gives up his life as hopeless, he catches sight of Ada – who seems to be there because of "a mermaid's message."

The whole sequence, from the dream in a setting reminiscent of the *Tobakoff*'s cinema through Van's starting up as he did from the cinema seat to the idea of jumping to one's death, recalls with peculiar force the role of *Don Juan's Last Fling* on Lucette's last night. At this point we should turn back for another viewing.

Insofar as the movie has a source it is Pushkin's version of the Don Juan legend. In Pushkin's *Kamenniy gost'* the ghost of Don Juan's victim finds vengeance by animating his sepulchral statue to become the "Stone Guest" that frightens Juan to death. In *Don Juan's Lost Fling* there is no ghost assuming physical form, yet there is a "Stone Cuckold's revenge" (490), which we can only construe therefore as some involvement of the dead "Cuckold" in the fates of the living, through some mortal agency. The revenge is not, as in Pushkin's play, the death of Don Juan, but instead Juan's impotence – after that "premature spasm" (489) drawn from him by Dolores – when after at last reaching Donna Anna's castle he is expected to make love to his hostess. This part of the movie's plot is made clear only in an unposted letter from Van to Ada. Van – who since the fatal *filmus interruptus* on the *Tobakoff* has seen *Don Juan's Last Fling* again and again – fondly recollects Ada's performance:

> the best moment is one of the last – when you follow barefoot the Don who walks down a marble gallery to his doom, to the scaffold of Donna Anna's black-curtained bed, around which you flutter, my Zegris butterfly, straightening a comically drooping candle, whispering delightful but futile instructions into the frowning lady's car, and then peering over that mauresque screen and suddenly dissolving in such natural laughter.... (500)

But if this is the Stone Cuckold's revenge, the plot of *Don Juan's Lost Fling* closely corresponds to much of the plot of *The Texture of Time*. Van rides toward Ada; just before the two are united, the phone call from Ada, a "miraculous connection" (555) that seems to be "resurrecting the past" (556), arouses his expectations far too high. Though of course the phone call has wrung no spasm from Van, his "senses certainly remained stirless" (557) when he comes down to find Ada so old and so changed: it is as if the Stone Cuckold has exacted his revenge.

This is not a flimsy and fanciful parallel but is woven right into the texture of *Don Juan's Lost Fling*. The leading female role in the film is that of "not too irresistible, obviously forty-year-old, Donna Anna" (488), a description appropriate to the events in *The Texture of Time* but not to the previously dominant sense of the film in which Lucette awaiting "a long night of love in her chaste and chilly chamber" is Donna Anna. In the film "the aging libertine" rides "to the remote castle where the difficult lady, widowed by his sword, has finally promised him a long night of love" (488). In Part 4 of *Ada* the fifty-two-year-old Van – nothing if not an aging libertine (his very name is "Casanovanic" and Don Giovannesque) – makes his way to Mont Roux, where he and Ada are meeting because at last Ada is a widow (Van of course has not killed Andrey Vinelander, though he has often imagined doing so). Note too that the "remote castle" to which Don Juan is travelling appears in Van's *Texture of Time*: "I delight sensually in Time.... I wish to do something about it; to indulge in a simulacrum of possession. I am aware that all who have tried to reach the charmed castle have got lost in obscurity or have bogged down in Space." (537)

Van's journey to Mont Roux and widowed Ada can be equated with Juan's journey to Donna Anna's castle, and Van's "stirless" response, after the excitement of the phone call, to a considerably aged Ada can be seen to match Juan's impotence, after his "premature spasm," with the "not too irresistible, obviously forty-year-old, Donna Anna." But how could Lucette be considered a "Stone Cuckold"?

Though she does not marry Van, Lucette at least proposes it (466), and when in the last chapter of the novel Van and Ada are working on a translation of John Shade's "Pale Fire" into Russian, Ada says:

> "Oh, Van, oh Van, we did not love her [Lucette] enough. *That's* whom you should have married, the one sitting…on the stone balustrade, and then everything would have been all right – I would have stayed with you both in Ardis Hall, and instead of that happiness, handed out gratis, instead of all that we *teased* her to death!" (586)

(Significantly, the passage in "Pale Fire" which Van and Ada have been translating and which prompts this outburst deals quite directly with the possibility of an afterlife.) But if Ada's regrets – the idea of Lucette's marrying Van, the stone balustrade – allow Lucette to be considered as the "Stone Cuckold," and if, like the Stone Cuckold in *Don Juan's Last Fling*, Lucette is a ghost who does not return physically yet influences the lives of mortals, her intervention in Van and Ada's lives has been an act not of revenge but of kindness. Dead Lucette has no part in the phone call that parallels the film's revenge, but her "mermaid's message" is an action manifesting the generosity that characterized her in life, a free gift of kindness that becomes the basis for the happiness of Van and Ada's lives and so of *Ada* itself.

When in *The Texture of Time* Van's hopes are raised far too high by the phone call's "miraculous connection" to the past, his premature arousal by a remembered image of Ada unmans him when he reaches the lobby and espies a fifty-year-old woman. That sequence itself should remind the good rereader of other patterns in Van's past. Returning from the picnic for Ada's birthday at Ardis in 1888, the twelve-year-old Lucette sits on Van's knee as twelve-year-old Ada had sat on his knee coming back from the corresponding picnic four years earlier. While Lucette nestles on his lap Van relives the previous ride and the act of reimagining the scene and the physical presence of Lucette bring him almost to orgasm. He restrains and diverts himself so as not to disturb Lucette (who has noticed something nevertheless) and because "after all no furtive friction could compete with what awaited him in Ada's bower" (281). In fact despite what seems to be a fairy-tale reenactment of the past, this scene only shows the extent of present change and future loss: the means Van adopts to distract himself is to scribble a note to Ada that she must not see Percy de Prey again (the picnic has made manifest the ominous tension between Percy and Van, who feels more uneasy than he dare admit to himself) while his projecting an image of Ada as he clutches Lucette and the orgasm that he decides to save for Ada herself of course mark Lucette's entanglement in their lives and foreshadow the night of her death. While he watches *Don Juan's Last Fling*, too, Van's senses all but brim over because of Lucette – until Ada appears on the screen and again another miraculous connection is established with the past as her posture and gestures crystallise in "a perfect compendium of her 1884 and 1888 and 1892 looks" all Van's memories of craning over her from behind.

On the picnic ride and on the *Tobakoff* the apparently stupendous retrievals of the past in fact incorporate signs of ineradicable change and imminent trauma. In Mont Roux the same teasing arousal by a sense of time recaptured seems to lead to the cruelest proof that time can mean only loss, decay, irretrievability, for Van and Ada must mutely resign themselves to the fact that their love cannot be resumed. Yet because of Ada's unforeseeable change of mind not only do their feelings surge back, but minutes after Van sights her on the balcony they make love and so jubilantly repudiate the "unmanning" effect of the phone call. Far from being an act of revenge, Lucette's intervention from the beyond offers Van and Ada a chance to establish a new serenity which will remain utterly steadfast and untroubled – unable to cause pain to a Lucette or an Andrey Vinelander or even a Demon, unthreatened by infidelity, marked by a considerateness unprecedented in the history of their amour.

And *this* time the retrieval of the past that the telephone call seemed to have promised so treacherously now climaxes in Van's rush of adoration when he glances down at Ada – a moment that by rounding off the pattern of their past mornings affirms an astonishingly complete triumph over time. It would appear that not only could Lucette sense that Van and Ada's love was far from irredeemable but also that having been granted the ability to reinvestigate the past endlessly and having discerned the "morning" pattern of which even Van and Ada are not aware, she has whispered to Ada to turn back to Mont Roux, she has wakened Van with the dream of the "lecturing hall of a transatlantic liner" and she has made him rush to his balcony with the momentary thought of suicide – only to look to Ada gesturing up at him. That sudden sight redeems Van's pain years ago when he saw his Ada gesture so ecstatically from her balcony as he was tearing himself away from Ardis the Second, knowing at last that she was unfaithful and that he had no choice but to put behind him all her charm. Now, in Mont Roux, the new ecstasy of this brilliant morning ushers in forty-five years of faithful and cloudless love.

Presumably Lucette now inhabits something like the "There, *tam, là-bas*" where "the gaze of men glows with inimitable understanding," as Nabokov imagines in *Invitation to a Beheading*:

> *there* the freaks that are tortured here walk unmolested; *there* time takes shape, according to one's pleasure, like a figured rug whose folds can be gathered in such a way that two designs will meet – and the rug is once again smoothed

out, and you live on, or else superimpose the next image on the last, endlessly, endlessly.... (*IB* 94)

Though Lucette cannot communicate directly with mortal lives she seems able to influence them gently so as to leave her own pattern in time. Like the transparent things who explain that "the most we can do when steering a favorite in the best direction, in circumstances not involving injury to others, is to act as a breath of wind and to apply the lightest, the most indirect pressure" (*TT* 92), she only stirs within Ada's mind the possibility of a change in plans. But because Ada does change her mind, the dawn that follows will crown all the regal mornings of Van and Ada's lives, and reveal – to herself at least – Lucette's own participation in the pattern of their lives.

Nabokov always envisages that mortal memory might be the forerunner of a consciousness to which the past might be directly accessible, open for the kind of endless reinvestigation which could lead to the discovery of the watermarks of time. Because as readers we can continue to re-examine the fictive past, Nabokov can offer us the shiver and thrill of discovering in the novel's events harmonies as unexpected as the "morning" pattern. In allowing such shockingly unforeseen pleasure and new insight into familiar events, Nabokov makes almost unbearably delightful the prospect of an immortality in which such discoveries would be rife.

If we have been offered this analogy, Lucette, it would appear, has been granted the thing itself. Lucette, always pushed to one side by Van and Ada and the reader, has come almost to dominate the novel. Her fate in life serves as a lens for focussing all the nastiness in Van and Ada and a film for making visible the infrared of evil that Van tries to bleach in the sunshine of his story. But although her death and its ramifications steep the book in an unexpectedly infernal hue, she herself after her death turns the story of Van and Ada into something more radiant than any reader could expect: in making possible the renewed and now flawless love of the aging Van and Ada, she also offers us intimations of a harmony even in this life somehow akin to a tenderness from beyond.

Outside Influence

The reunion of Van and Ada at the end of Part 4 endures throughout the rest of their lives, from 1922 until their deaths in 1967. Late in these years of shared old age Van begins to write *Ada*, an occupation he terms "the solace of what are, no doubt, my last ten years of existence" (576). He opens Part 5 jauntily, one page after that July morning at the end of Part 4, yet forty-five years later in time:

I, Van Veen, salute you, life, Ada Veen, Dr. Lagosse, Stepan Nootkin, Violet Knox, Ronald Oranger. Today is my ninety-seventh birthday, and I hear from my wonderful new Everyrest chair a spade scrape and footsteps creak in the snow-sparkling garden, and my old Russian valet, who is deafer than he thinks, pull out and push in nose-ringed drawers in the dressing room. This Part Five is not meant as an epilogue; it is the true introduction of my ninety-seven percent true, and three percent likely, *Ada or Ardor, a family chronicle.* (567)

Part 5 indeed forms the true introduction to *Ada*, for here we see the process of its composition and the conditions of tranquil love which make the whole chronicle possible. On the day of Van's ninety-seventh birthday the "master-copy" of *Ada*, a memoir on which the Veens have been working for ten years, is handed to Van – only to be revised and reread again and again by Van and Ada in their remaining months of existence.

Pt.5 Ch.4, the antepenultimate chapter, depicts in detail the origins and process of *Ada*'s composition. Ada spends her old age (her eighties and nineties) preparing French, Russian and English translations (from one language into the other two) "for the Oranger editions *en regard*" (577) – "Oranger" editions presumably because Ronald Oranger, Van's associate, secretary, protégé, literary adviser and "a born catalyzer" (578) has suggested the undertaking. One afternoon in 1957, as Van, Ada and Mr Oranger are discussing the problems of translation, Van realizes that his philosophical and psychological works

> were not epistemic tasks set to himself by a savant, but buoyant and bellicose exercises in literary style. He was asked why, then, did he not let himself go, why did he not choose a big playground for a match between Inspiration and Design; and with one thing leading to another it was resolved that he would write his memoirs – to be published posthumously. (578)

Van notes that despite "the unbelievable intellectual surge...that occcurred in the brain of this strange, friendless, rather repulsive nonagenarian" (577), it "took him six years to write the first draft and dictate it to Miss Knox, after which he revised the typescript, rewrote it entirely in long hand (1963–1965) and redictated the entire thing to indefatigable Violet, whose pretty fingers tapped out a final copy in 1967" (578). But the novel's antepenultimate chapter also reveals something more than this simple résumé: namely, that Lucette's influence still lives on.

While the chapter does not state explicitly that Ronald Oranger is the editor of *Ada*, it makes the deduction inevitable. The suggestion of the editor's identity in the book's prefatory note is confirmed here by his amusing delicacy and intrusiveness in regard to Violet Knox (Van's typist), which can be explained only as Oranger's pride in and fussy consideration for his wife (to whom in fact he only draws attention all the more gauchely):

> Violet Knox [now Mrs. Ronald Oranger. Ed.], born in 1940, came to live with us in 1957. She was (and still is – ten years later) an enchanting English blonde with doll eyes, a velvet carnation and a tweed-cupped little rump [......]; but such designs, alas, could no longer flesh my fancy. She has been responsible for typing out this memoir – the solace of what are, no doubt, my last ten years of existence. A good daughter, an even better sister, and half-sister, she had supported for ten years her mother's children from two marriages, besides laying aside [something]. I paid her [generously] per month, well realizing the need to ensure unembarrassed silence on the part of a puzzled and dutiful maiden. (576)

Oranger's editorial work is very limited: apart from the contributions in the passage just quoted, which are necessary to establish the identity of our "Ed.," he intrudes only fifteen times, or about once every forty pages. The one major flurry of editorial activity occurs in Pt.2 Ch.5, where Lucette (but not Ada) is present with Van. The redactor's remarks are elicited by Van's reconstructing the conversation between himself and Lucette with the help of the letter Lucette had sent him a year earlier:

> In the fall of 1891 she had sent him from California a rambling, indecent, crazy, almost savage declaration of love in a ten-page letter, which shall not be discussed in this memoir. [See, however, a little farther. Ed.] (366)

> "Van, it will make you smile" [thus in the MS. Ed.]
> "Van," said Lucette, "it will make you smile."... (371)

> "...because I was afraid of the cougars and snakes" [quite possibly this is not remembered speech but an extract from her letter or letters. Ed.], "whose cries and rattlings Ada imitated admirably, and, I think, designedly, in the desert's darkness under my first-floor window. Well [here, it would seem, taped speech is re-turned on], to make a short story sort of longish – " (374–75)

> [The epithetic tone strongly suggests that this speech has an epistolary source. Ed.] (378)

This burst of editorial intrusiveness should be contrasted with Pt.2 Ch.9, where it is obvious that Van is again drawing upon a letter (in this case, Ada's Dreams of Drama letter) for his dialogue, but where "Ed." makes no comments. The one other occasion when Oranger is fussily present is in Pt.2 Ch.8, immediately before the note Lucette writes to Van and Ada when she runs away from the debauch ("[sic! Ed.]" [420]) and immediately after Van's letter in reply ("[thus in the manuscript, for 'life.' Ed.]" [421]). The editor's presence, then, seems to coincide especially with messages between Lucette and Van.

Violet Knox's participation in the preparation of *Ada* is explained in Pt.5 Ch.4, where at the end of the chapter we see her limited competence: he "redictated the entire thing to indefatigable Violet, whose pretty fingers tapped out a final copy in 1967. E, p, i – why 'y', my dear?" (578) Van has to spell out the beginning of "epistemic," which he has used earlier in the page, and Violet Knox transcribes his correction. But if Violet's role is explained in Pt.5 Ch.4, it is first seen (and indeed this is the only other time her part in *Ada* is visible) at Lucette's death:

> Although Lucette had never died before – no, *dived* before, Violet – from such a height, in such a disorder of shadows and snaking reflections.... Owing to the tumultuous swell and her not being sure which way to peer through the spray and the darkness and her own tentaclinging hair – t,a,c,l – she could not make out the lights of the liner, an easily imagined many-eyed bulk mightily receding in heartless triumph. Now I've lost my next note.
>   Got it.
>   The sky was also heartless and dark, and her body, her head, and particularly those damned thirsty trousers, felt clogged with Oceanus Nox, n,o,x. (493–94)

Van has to spell out his wordplay ("tentaclinging") to Violet, but the poor secretary takes down the instruction too and then transcribes all Van says in his search for a note; and of course Van must spell out "Nox" so that Violet will not confuse it with her own surname or the verb "knocks."

This close association of Lucette and Violet becomes much closer still in Pt.5 Ch.4. Ada calls Violet "'*Fialochka*' and allowed herself the luxury of admiring 'little Violet''s cameo neck, pink nostrils, and fair pony-tail" (576). "Fialochka" is a diminutive of the Russian for "violet," "fialka," which links the Veens' typist with Lucette, who is described as she lies by the *Tobakoff's* pool as a "hardy girl used to bracing winds no less than to the detestable sun. Spring in Fialta and a torrid May on Minataor, the famous artificial island, had given a nectarine hue to her limbs." (477) "Spring in Fialta" is the title of one of Nabokov's stories (1936) (its main structural feature is the death of the heroine); "Fialta" is an invented place name that combines Yalta, the Crimean resort town, with "fialka," "violet."[4] Another play on Violet's name ("Violet knocks at the library door"[577]) also associates her with Lucette,[5] noted for her door-knocking ("the door had come alive: two small fists could be heard drumming upon it from the outside, in a rhythm both knew well"[190]; "and now their four eyes were looking again into the azure brook of Pinedale, and Lucette pushed the door open with a perfunctory knuckle knock" [392–93]). Violet is "A good daughter...and half-sister" (576), like Lucette, who tends to her dying mother and who is a half-sister to Van and Ada. Like Lucette, finally, Violet is also the object of Ada's lesbian attentions:

> Sometimes, at dinner, lingering over the liqueurs, my Ada would consider my typist...with a dreamy gaze, and then, quick-quick, peck at her flushed cheek. The situation might have been considerably more complicated had it arisen twenty years earlier. (576)

Not only is Lucette for some reason allied with Violet but she is also implied, even where she does not seem to be, throughout this chapter's account of *Ada*'s origin and composition. One representative paragraph must suffice. It appears to concern only Ada and Van's literary activities:

> Ada, who amused herself by translating (for the Oranger editions *en regard*) Griboyedov into French and English, Baudelaire into English and Russian, and John Shade into Russian and French, often read to Van, in a deep mediumesque voice, the published versions made by other workers in that field of semiconsciousness. The verse translations in English were especially liable to distend Van's face in a grotesque grin which made him look, when he was not wearing his dental plates, exactly like a Greek comedial mask. He could not tell who disgusted him more: the well-meaning mediocrity, whose attempts at fidelity were thwarted by lack of artistic insight as well as by hilarious errors of textual interpretation, or the professional poet who embellished with his own inventions the dead and helpless author (whiskers here, private parts there) – a method that nicely camouflaged the paraphrast's ignorance of the From language by having the bloomers of inept scholarship blend with the whims of flowery imitation. (577–78)

The two chief instances of the Ada-and-translation motif that occur earlier in the novel, Coppée's "leavesdropper" and the version of "Mémoire," both deeply implicate Lucette (one by the association of eavesdropping Lucette and the "leavesdropping" ardilla, the other, of course, by the *souci d'eau*). Griboedov, Baudelaire and Shade too are all associated chiefly with Lucette. The principal earlier allusion to Griboedov occurs in Pt.1 Ch.37, where on Mlle Larivière's advice Marina warns Van not to turn Lucette's head:

"Belle, with her usual flair for the right phrase, has cited to me the *cousinage-dangereux-voisinage adage* – I mean 'adage,' I always fluff that word – and complained *qu'on s'embrassait dans tous les coins.* Is that true?"

....

"I do not mean Ada, silly," said Marina with a slight snort.... "Mlle Larivière meant Lucette, of course. Van, those soft games must stop. Lucette is twelve, and naive, and I know it's all clean fun, yet (*odnako*) one can never behave too *delikatno* in regard to a budding little woman. *A propos de coins:* in Griboedov's *Gore ot uma*, 'How stupid to be so clever,' a play in verse...the hero reminds Sophie of their childhood games, and says:

> How oft we sat together in a corner
> And what harm might there be in that?" (232–33)

The most important of the Baudelaire allusions in *Ada* occurs when Baudelaire becomes entangled with "Charles" Chateaubriand, the discoverer of Chateaubriand's mosquito (which as we have seen marks the dangerous confusion of Ada and Lucette), and his "L'Invitation au voyage" fuses with Chateaubriand's "Romance à Hélène":

> *Mon enfant, ma soeur,*
> *Songe à l'épaisseur*
> *Du grand chêne à Tagne;*
> *Songe à la montagne.*
> *Songe à la douceur –*

– of scraping with one's claws...the spots visited by that...insect characterized by an insatiable...appetite for Ada's and Ardelia's, Lucette's and Lucile's...blood. (106)

The translating of John Shade's poem is even more insistently focussed on Lucette. Van and Ada are trying to render into Russian Shade's lines –

> ...We give advice
> To widower. He has been married twice:
> He meets his wives: both loved, both loving, both
> Jealous of one another...   (585–86)

– when Ada bursts out: "Oh, Van, oh Van, we did not love her" – Lucette – "enough. *That's* whom you should have married...and...instead of all that we *teased* her to death!" (586) Finally, the closing phrase of the paragraph above, "by having the bloomers of inept scholarship blend with the whims of flowery imitation" (578) refers back again to the "Mémoire" translation:

"As in the case of many flowers," Ada went on, with a mad scholar's quiet
smile, "the unfortunate French name of our plant, *souci d'eau*, has been traduced
or shall we say transfigured – "

"Flowers into bloomers," punned Van Veen. (63–64)

What is one to make of these oblique but insistent reminders of Lucette
in Pt.5 Ch.4 and the hints that she has some special relationship to Ronald
Oranger and Violet Knox? Miss Knox joins the Veen entourage in 1957. In
that year, as "Ada, Mr. Oranger (a born catalyzer), and Van were discussing
those matters one afternoon...it suddenly occurred to our old polemicist that
all his published works were not epistemic tasks set to himself by a savant,
but...exercises in literary style."(578) When Oranger then asks him why
he does not choose "a big playground for a match between Inspiration and
Design" he begins to edge with Ada and Oranger towards the resolution to
undertake his memoirs. Since then, he notes, there has persisted an "unbelievable intellectual surge." (577)

What seems to be suggested here is that Lucette, somehow acting through
the agency of Violet Knox and Ronald Oranger, has encouraged Van to write
Ada and has acted throughout as a source of inspiration: her aura seems to
produce in Van this prolonged intensity of mental excitement. Though the
suggestion is odd, it matches the bizarre compositional history of other
Nabokov works: *Transparent Things*, where the ghost of one or more of the
characters writes the novel; "Ultima Thule," where the narrator appears to
be inspired to write his story (in the form of a letter to his dead wife) by his
wife's acting through the agency of another character, whose sudden disturbing vision of humanly unbearable truth becomes the subject of the narrator's
"letter"; "The Vane Sisters," where the narrator is inspired to record his recent
past by the two dead girls about whom he writes – and who sign the story, in
its last paragraph, without the narrator's knowledge.

In *Ada* itself Nabokov signals quite clearly that this last case is particularly
appropriate to the Veens. The Vane sisters induce a dream in the narrator that
he feels is "somehow...full of" dead Cynthia Vane (*TD* 237). But when in the
story's final paragraph he declares that he could find less in the dream than he
expected, the very words in this paragraph form an acrostic that announces
to the reader but not to the narrator that dead Cynthia and dead Sybil have
mildly influenced the narrator's life the day before the dream, have induced
the dream itself, and have inspired the story. When on the morning of his *first*
reunion with Ada after Lucette's death Van dreams of his last day with Lucette
by the *Tobakoff* pool, the oneirically interchangeable Lucette and Ada and a
conflation of "Van" and "Veen" produce "one of the Vane sisters" (521). On
the morning of Van's *second* reunion – just after "a mermaid's message" has led

Ada to turn back to Van and Lucette has thus signed herself into the pattern of Van and Ada's lives – this earlier dream is recalled: for the last day on the *Tobakoff* again appears to Van in another dream, now of "the lecturing hall of a transatlantic liner" (561), a transfiguration of the cinema hall where Van sat with Lucette for the last time.

Pt.5 Ch.4's suggestions that Van's writing his last book might be partly the consequence of Lucette's messages from the beyond are confirmed by the force and precision of the twin themes of Lucette-and-letters and *Letters from Terra* that we have already begun to investigate.

The two themes are firmly welded together by means of allusions to *Hamlet*. Van writes *Letters from Terra* using the pseudonym "Voltemand," the name of a letter-carrying envoy in the play; when Lucette herself brings Ada's special letter to Van in Kingston in 1892, she not only acts Voltemand's part but finds Van in Voltemand Hall. Part of her conversation in the Kingston scene is reconstructed by Van from her first letter to him – written in 1891, the year *Letters from Terra* appeared (it was reviewed "by the First Clown" – Shakespeare's speech-prefix for the man we know as the gravedigger – "in *Elsinore*, a distinguished London weekly" [343]). As the end of the letter is assimilated into Van's version of the conversation, he answers Lucette's letter-cum-speech by quoting the end of Hamlet's letter to Ophelia ("Thine evermore, most dear lady, whilst this machine is to him," II.ii.123–24):

> "I hope I've thoroughly got you mixed up, Van, because *la plus laid fille au monde peut donner beacoup plus qu'elle n'a*, and now let us say adieu, yours ever."
> "Whilst the machine is to him," murmured Van.
> "Hamlet," said the assistant lecturer's brightest student. (379)

Nabokov also takes care to establish links between the circumstances of Van's writing *Letters from Terra* and of Lucette's death, although the two are ten years apart.

Van, who in his novel has quietly "borrowed what his greatest forerunners (Counterstone, for example) had imagined in the way of a manned capsule's propulsion" (339), revised the *Letters from Terra* typescript "during his voyage back to America on board the *Queen Guinevere*. And in Manhattan the galleys had to be reset twice." (342) Going back to America on the *Tobakoff*, "that not very grand ship so much shorter than *Queen Guinevere*"(461), Van attempts, the night before Lucette's death, "to read the proofs of an essay he was contributing to a festschrift on the occasion of Professor Counterstone's eightieth birthday" (474). In both cases, Counterstone, proofs, a transatlantic crossing. Or again: in Van's novel, after sending to Sig Leymanski a dozen of her "letters" from Terra, "Theresa flies over to him, and he, in his laboratory, has to place her on a slide under a powerful microscope" (340); on Lucette's last voyage, when Van comes out onto the *Tobakoff* deck, looking for Lucette, he spies "some other redhead...writing a letter at passionate speed and he thought that if he ever switched from ponderous factitude to light fiction he would have a jealous husband use binoculars to decipher from where he stood that outpour of illicit affection" (475–76). In both cases, Van's fiction, letters, an extramarital affair, and an optical instrument. Some insistent connection is being made between Van's writing *Letters from Terra* and the circumstances of Lucette's death.

The letter being written by a redhead on the *Tobakoff*'s sun deck which inspires Van with the thought of writing another novel with curious affinities with *Letters from Terra* is coupled with the most significant letter of all – written by redhead Lucette and first heard of by Van on the afternoon of her death as she lies on the sun deck with him: "I sent you a silly note to Kingston, just in case you didn't turn up" (478).

This crucial letter, Lucette's last, is the foundation stone of the novel, for the poem she quotes ("Peter and Margaret") is the one she learns while Van and Ada go off into the attic – in what now stands as the opening scene of the novel. This attic scene in the *first* chapter of the novel – which records also a cable from Marina which Dan receives while talking to a "cicerone" (5) – is very precisely recalled in the *last* chapter: the final typescript of Van's *Ada* is "produced on special Atticus paper" (587). That this phrase points to the "attic" scene is confirmed by the supporting connection, via Cicero's *Letters to Atticus*, with the cicerone present while Dan receives the first of the "letters" in *Ada*. The attic-and-letter association also seems to indicate that what matters most about the attic scene is not what Van and Ada think – that when they discover from the information in the attic that they are brother and sister, it only proves them even more justified in valuing the specialness of their love – but that Lucette has been excluded by Van's manipulating her innocence and affection until she went off to learn by heart the poem she quotes in her final letter.

While the attic scene that opens the novel takes place, Lucette learns a poem about a ghost communicating with a mortal. She recalls the poem in a letter Van reads only after her death. Both attic scene and letter are associated with the very paper on which Ada is finally typed. Lucette first mentions the letter to Van just after his seeing another redhead writing a letter spurs him to think of writing a novel with odd similarities to *Letters from Terra* – which has been quite insistently associated with other letters between Van and Lucette and which concerns the "messages" sent by a "micromermaid" from the almost otherworldly Terra. Surely all this can point to only one conclusion: dead Lucette is somehow still sending messages to Van, inspiring him to write his memoirs. Whose secret suggestion prompted Van to center his first chapter on Ardis's attic? Who sees the subtlest details of the past's pattern, and makes sure that Van records them? Van seems unable to answer these questions, but for us the answers seem quite definite – if only we keep on investigating the bizarre pattern of the novel's world.

Van seems to be aware of Lucette's presence no more than the narrator of "The Vane Sisters" can discern the role of Cynthia and Sybil Vane. But if Lucette has inspired Van to write *Ada*, her inspiration shows not only that she forgives Van and Ada for their part in her downfall and not only that she is beyond jealousy and wishes her brother and sister as much happiness as possible in mortal life (for these attitudes are manifest in her turning Ada back down the road to Van in 1922), but also that, in accordance with her deep kindness, she wishes others to share in the happiness of Van and Ada and to be warned of the need for the consideration whose absence contributed to her own suicide. In sending Van and Ada back to an investigation of their past, she generously gives them and their readers a foretaste of the delights of a life beyond time, where consciousness can survey and arrange the past in an endless blend of discovery and creative wonder. When he intimates Lucette's participation in *Ada* Nabokov surely fulfills more completely than he has anywhere else what he has defined as the aim of the greatest fiction, to afford "a sense of being somehow, somewhere, connected with other states of being where art (curiosity, tenderness, kindness, ecstasy) is the norm."

13. Conclusion

The Design of Time

If Lucette can see all the past she can act only in the present – through Ada's change of mind in 1922, or through the aura with which she surrounds Van in 1957–1967 – but she cannot know or have control over the future.

Yet there seems to be some force in the novel which *can* control events in advance and which Van, eager to unravel the mystery of Time, tries to apprehend. Observing some eerily curious coincidences in Scrabble games he has played, he feels "stung as a scientist by the curious affinity between certain aspects of Scrabble and those of the planchette" (225), and notes the results of a few games "in the hope – not quite unfulfilled – of 'catching sight of the lining of time' (which, as he was later to write, is the 'best informal definition of portents and prophecies')" (227). Van cites three Scrabble games, two of which contain immediately apparent coincidences while the third seems to be (on retrospection) mildly prophetic. But, curiously, Lucette's involvement – and particularly her "letters," whether Scrabble letters or postal ones – seem to lead to extremely complex coincidences behind those which Van sees, coincidences so highly patterned that they seem to confirm some careful foreplanning in the lives of the Veens.

Let us take one game:

> "*Je ne peux rien faire*," wailed Lucette, "*mais rien – with* my idiotic *Buchstaben*, REMNILK, LINKREM..."
>
> "Look," whispered Van, "*c'est tout simple*, shift those two syllables and you get a fortress in ancient Muscovy."
>
> "Oh, no," said Ada "Oh, no. That pretty word does not exist in Russian. A Frenchman invented it. There is no second syllable."
>
> "Ruth for a little child?" interposed Van.
>
> "Ruthless!" cried Ada.
>
> "Well," said Van, "you can always make a little cream, KREM or KREME – or even better – there's KREMLI, which means Yukon prisons. Go through her ORHIDEYa."[1]
>
> "Through her silly orchid," said Lucette.
>
> "And now," said Ada, "Adochka is going to do something even sillier." And taking advantage of a cheap letter recklessly sown sometime before in the seventh compartment of the uppermost fertile row, Ada, with a deep sigh of

pleasure, composed the adjective TORFYaNUYu which went through a brown square at F and through two red squares (37 x 9 = 333 points) and got a bonus of 50 (for placing all seven blocks at one stroke) which made 383 in all, the highest score ever obtained for one word by a Russian scrambler. (227)

Van does not state why he cites this game or what peculiar coincidence it involves. In fact, he records it because he feels it anticipates his impending discovery that Ada has been unfaithful, but leaves the prophecy unstated – in keeping with his strategy throughout Ardis the Second, where he riddles his narrative with sly, reproachful hints of Ada's infidelity while avoiding *explicit* references so that despite all the hints the discovery will be a surprise for the first-time reader too.

Each of the words in the Scrabble game anticipates one of the hints in Pt. 1 Ch.40 that the disclosure of Ada's infidelity is about to break – as indeed it does in the next chapter. The KREM (cream) foreshadows an embrocation for Van's knee (he hurt it while fighting Percy de Prey) which Ada promises to obtain when she goes on horseback to Ladore, but which she forgets, because she has been with Percy. The relationship between KREM and the "messy turpentine oil" (283) Ada promises to fetch while out riding is confirmed by the horsey associations of another Scrabble word, CITROILS – "CITROILS, which grooms use for rubbing fillies" (379) – which as we shall see blends with KREM.

The ORHIDEYa (orchid) foreshadows the fact that two days after Ada's failure to bring Van's embrocation Van finds only a single common orchid in his sister's bag when she returns from an ostensible botanical ramble. The real purpose of her outing had in fact been to farewell Percy de Prey as he embarked for the Crimea (287).

When Ada spells out TORFYaNUYu on the Scrabble board, Lucette objects that it is a place name, and therefore cannot be used. Ada concedes that Torfyanaya is Blanche's home village (more commonly Torfyanka or Tourbière), though in Russian which Lucette should not neglect for the sake of Blanche's Canadian "French – this quite ordinary adjective means 'peaty,' feminine gender, accusative case" (228). In terms of the foreshadowing of Van's discovery, it is Torfyanka Blanche who slips Van an ominous note – on the day Percy departs and Ada returns with that lone orchid – warning that he has been deceived. That TORFYaNUYu not only implies Blanche in a general way but also specifically anticipates her part in bringing the 1888 idyll to an end the text confirms by the peculiar repetition of the "French... adjective...accusative" in the last paragraph of Ardis the Second, as the coachman driving Van away from Ardis and Torfyanka warns him about touching Blanche, "*etu frantsuzskuyu devku....Étu:* this (that). *Frantsúzskuyu:* French (adj., accus.). *Dévku:* wench." (300)

It is curious that these three details of the last stage of Van's betrayal should be foreshadowed, but it is also *merely* curious: it might be only Van's bitterness at the discovery that makes him retrospectively construe the Scrabble words as anticipatory. What is really suggestive is that this game matches up with another game that Van has *not* noted as containing any special coincidences.

This other game Lucette mentions in her letter to Van: the game in which her Scrabble blocks happen to spell the Russian for "clitoris" and which now gives her occasion to pun "in an Ophelian frenzy on the feminine glans" (394). Van incorporates the letter into the conversation at Kingston and invents brilliant but rather thoughtless replies on the "clitoris" theme:

> " – I got stuck with six *Buchstaben* in the last round of a Flavita game....You examined and fingered my groove and quickly redistributed the haphazard sequence which made, say, LIKROT or ROTIKL and Ada flooded us both with her raven silks as she looked over our heads, and when you had completed the rearrangement, you and she came simultaneously, *si je puis le mettre comme ça* (Canady French), came falling on the black carpet in a paroxysm of incomprehensible merriment...and now let us say adieu, yours ever."
>
> "Whilst the machine is to him," murmured Van.
>
> "Hamlet," said the assistant lecturer's brightest student.
>
> "Okay, okay," replied her and his tormentor, "but you know, a medically minded *English* Scrabbler, having two more letters to cope with, could make, for example, STIRCOIL, a well-known sweat-gland stimulant, or CITROILS, which grooms use for rubbing fillies." (379)

This Scrabble game matches up with the KREM/TORFYaNUYu game in several very exact ways. In the "last round" (227) of the children's last game, Lucette says *"Je ne peux rien faire...*with my idiotic *Buchstaben"* (227); in the "last round" (379) of the game Lucette recalls she notes she was "stuck with six *Buchstaben"* (379). In one case, Lucette's letters are made to spell "cream" and in the other they spell "clitoris": as Lucette's puns ("You...fingered my groove," "came simultaneously") and Van's inventions make clear, there is a common theme of vaginal lubrication.[2] Van remarks of the final game that the difference between Lucette's paltry score and Ada's TORFYaNUYu was less important than other differences:

> The bloom streaking Ada's arm, the pale blue of the veins in its hollow, the charred-wood odor of her hair shining brownly next to the lampshade's parchment (a translucent lakescape with *Japanese dragons*), scored infinitely more points than those tensed fingers bunched on the pencil stub could ever add up in the past, present or future. (228; italics added)

At Kingston, Lucette and Van echo this as they compare memories of the library and its "stand with golden *dragons...*really a...stand *japanned* in red lacquer" (373; italics added). Lucette's resorting to "Canady French" (379) for one of her obscene puns recalls Ada's answer to Lucette's objection in the other game: "'Torfyanaya, or as Blanche says, *La Tourbière*, is, indeed, the pretty but rather damp village where our *cendrillon's* family lives. But, *mon petit*, in our mother's tongue...which my pet should not neglect for the sake of a *Canadian* brand of *French* – this quite ordinary adjective means 'peaty.'" (228; italics added)

Let us keep in mind these connections between the TORFYaNUYu game (with its evocation of Blanche's Torfyanaya or Torfyanka) and the KLITOR-STIRCOILS game (where Lucette puns "in an Ophelian frenzy" and Van responds by quoting *Hamlet*) as we watch Van on his way to Ardis for the first time:

> Sunflecks and lacy shadows skimmed over his legs and lent a green twinkle to the brass button deprived of its twin on the back of the coachman's coat. They passed through Torfyanka, a dreamy hamlet consisting of three or four log izbas, a milkpail repair shop and a smithy smothered in jasmine. The driver waved to an invisible friend and the sensitive runabout swerved slightly to match his gesture. They were now spinning along a dusty road between fields. The road dipped and humped again, and at every ascent the old clockwork taxi would slow up as if on the brink of sleep and reluctantly overcome its weakness.
>
> They bounced on the cobblestones of Gamlet, a half-Russian village, and the chauffeur waved again, this time to a boy in a cherry tree. Birches separated to let them pass across an old bridge. (34–35)

Even on a first reading, there is something suspicious and mildly unsettling about this passage: the repetition of "hamlet" and "Gamlet" cannot be accidental in Nabokov, surely, especially when coupled with the repeated gesture of the coachman. Coachman? No, chauffeur. Or rather, coachman, then neutral "driver," then chauffeur, for this is the famous first metamorphic voyage, and the hackney coach has become a clockwork taxi before turning into the horse on which Van arrives at Ardis. But if it is unlikely that we will note the metamorphic voyage on a first reading, we may already be made pleasantly uneasy (a common feeling when reading Nabokov) if we suspect a sort of time warp in the repetition of "hamlet" and "Gamlet" and the driver's wave.

If we know that "Gamlet" is the Russian for "Hamlet" (the character or play, not "hamlet," little village, which is "derevushka"), we become even more suspicious that "Gamlet, a half-Russian village" is a repetition in time rather than a neighbor in space of "Torfyanka, a dreamy hamlet" (which, the novel makes clear, is also a half-Russian village). The TORFYaNUYu associated with one of a curiously linked pair of Scrabble games and the *Hamlet* ambiance of the other also seem to confirm that Gamlet may be only a bizarre repetition of Torfyanka.

What makes significant the strange duplication of Torfyanka and the driver's wave as Van travels on through Gamlet is that it foreshadows the strange duplication in 1888 of the ride back to Ardis from the 1884 picnic. For during both the 1884 and 1888 rides the children's calèche passes through only one settlement, Gamlet:

> Poor Van shifted Ada's bottom to his right knee.... In the mournful dullness of unconsummated desire he watched a row of izbas straggle by as the *calèche* drove through Gamlet, a hamlet. (87)

> With the fading of that fugitive flame his mood now changed.... They were now about to enter Gamlet, the little Russian village.... (282)

On Van's first, metamorphic ride to Ardis, his carriage passes first through "Torfyanka, a dreamy *hamlet*" and then through "Gamlet, a half-Russian *village*" (35); on the first picnic ride back to Ardis, the carriage passes through "Gamlet, a *hamlet*" (87) and on the second through "Gamlet, the little Russian *village*" (282).

Van's first ride to Ardis seems, then, to foreshadow clearly the surprising repetition of the two picnic rides. That repetition was to Van the most glorious of the ways in which Ardis the Second seemed to reenact Ardis the First, but it was also the most precise anticipation – in the behind motif, in the confusion of the two girls, in Van's near-orgasm under Lucette as formerly under Ada, and in Van's arousing himself by a projected vision of Ada – of Lucette's fateful last night.

Foreshadowing seems to be doubling up upon foreshadowing, pattern upon pattern, as if events were being planned very carefully in advance. Nevertheless Ada must sit on Van's knee on the way back from the 1884 picnic and Lucette on Van's knee on their return from the 1888 picnic because of a delicate combination of chances each time. In 1884, the charabanc leaves with the hampers and footmen; Ada decides to ride back on the bicycle Van came on:

> Being unfamiliar with the itinerary of sun and shade in the clearing, he had left his bicycle to endure the blazing beams for at least three hours. Ada mounted it, uttered a yelp of pain [she has no underwear], almost fell off, googled, recovered – and the rear tire burst with a comic bang. (86)

There are only four places on the calèche for the five people left, so Ada must sit on Van's lap. Although at one stage of the *1888* picnic there are two spare cars and a motorbike, all the vehicles leave in rapid succession except one victoria. It has four places, enough for the coachman and Van, Ada and Lucette:

> Thus, a carefree-looking young trio, they moved towards the waiting victoria. Slapping his thighs in dismay, the coachman stood berating a tousled footboy who had appeared from under a bush. He had concealed himself there to enjoy in peace a tattered copy of *Tattersalia* with pictures of tremendous, fabulously elongated race horses, and had been left behind by the charabanc which had carried away the dirty dishes and the drowsy servants. (278)

They are now one place short, and little Lucette must hop up on her "cousin's" knee.

But despite the fact that it requires two quite unforeseeable combinations of accident to make the two picnic rides so startlingly similar, the pairing of the rides – and the ultimate, fatal Ada-Lucette confusion – seem already foreshadowed in the Torfyanka-Gamlet repetition on Van's first, metamorphic, trip to Ardis. And the peculiar linking of the TORFYaNUYu Scrabble game with another game swaddled in *Hamlet* allusions seems in turn to refer back, in an exceptionally oblique fashion, to this foreshadowing. Van appears to mention the TORFYaNUYu game in Pt.1 Ch.36 because he came to recognize that it eerily anticipated his finding out he had been betrayed; but he has no idea of the way the paired KREM/TORFYaNUYa and *CITROILS/Hamlet* games refer to the imminent doubling of the picnic rides and thus point to Lucette's entanglement in her sister's fate, a far more serious tragedy than his own being deceived by Ada. The narrator of "The Vane Sisters" declares, in the very lines in which the dead sisters sign their name to his story, that he can find no evidence of ghostly participation in his life; here, the very coincidences that seem uncanny to Van but that he still cannot declare to be more than unfathomably curious point to what *we*, being outside his world, can see as evident foreplanning and a tender concern for the lives being planned.

Van found no conclusive answers when trying to examine the possibility that the future might be somehow designed in advance – but he seems to be quite firm in denying that the "future" is part of ordinary human time. His clearest rejection of the idea of a humanly-discoverable future comes just before the end of *The Texture of Time*:

> Technological Sophists argue that by taking advantage of the Laws of Light, by using new telescopes revealing ordinary print at cosmic distances through

the eyes of our nostalgic agents on another planet, we can actually see our
own past (Goodson discovering the Goodson and that sort of thing) including
documentary evidence of our not knowing what lay in store for us (and our
knowing now), and that consequently the Future did exist yesterday and by
inference does exist today. This may be good physics but is execrable logic....
(560)

The "telescopes revealing ordinary print at cosmic distances" and the "Goodson discovering the Goodson" here rather unexpectedly recall Van's watching that redhead on the *Tobakoff* (named after another sailor whose name is
commemorated in a geographical feature, the "Tobago Islands, or Tobakoff
Islands" [385]) and his musing that "if he ever switched from ponderous
factitude to light fiction he would have a jealous husband use binoculars to
decipher from where he stood that outpour of illicit affection" (476): in both
cases, an explorer, and the idea of special lenses for reading ordinary text
at a distance. As we noted in the previous chapter, too, the suggestion of a
novel by Van centering on letters, adultery and an optical instrument points
in turn to Van's summary of *Letters from Terra*: after her interplanetary letters Theresa herself arrives and Sig Leymanski "has to place her on a slide
under a powerful microscope in order to make out the tiny, though otherwise
perfect, shape of his minikin sweetheart" (340). In fact Van's denunciation of
the future squares oddly with *Letters from Terra*, for Terra seems to share the
geography and much of the history of "our" Antiterra, but races about fifty
years ahead. Van's 1891 novel had depicted what to us is a strikingly modern
1890 (high rises and airplanes are common) peering towards what it took to
be a "contemporaneous," nineteen-fortyish Terra, a parodic version of our
world in about the 1930s and 1940s and thus despite the modernity of Van's
Manhattan of 1890, still a look into "the future" for Van and his readers.

   Letters from Terra seems to contradict Van's denial of the future in another
way – a way that has nothing to do with his conscious intentions. For the novel
weirdly foreshadows key events in the eerie history of communications between
Lucette and Van – and does this with such persistence that it seems to indicate
a foreplanning of Van and Lucette's lives that is as it were signed into Van's
book. *Letters from Terra*, published *early* in 1891, tells of a miniature woman
who sends maddening messages to a surrogate Van; *late* in 1891, little Lucette
sends Van her unexpected and "savage" declaration of love. As we have seen,
Theresa and Antilia Glems oddly anticipate Van's calling Lucette "our Esmeralda and mermaid" (421) in his last letter to her. The letters from Theresa, the
micromermaid from Terra, a sort of "Next World," appear too be be quite
precisely prophetic of the letter from Lucette Van receives only after her death
and of the strange messages Lucette seems to send from the beyond.

Van invents his grotesque analogy of interplanetary telescopes "revealing ordinary print at cosmic distances" in order to deride the notion of the future, but in making the analogy he accidentally recalls his own *Letters from Terra* – which uncannily hints at some foreplanning of what was then his "future" involvement with Lucette. But if this seems strange, there is stranger to come. For Van's lines refuting the future are written just when Lucette's "mermaid's message" reaches Ada near Morges and just when he notices the powder box; he starts to summarize his *Texture of Time* – and comes up with the telescope analogy (560). Right where Lucette is most actively intervening in the design of Van and Ada's lives, Van writes of the impossibility of there being any future which human consciousness could discern – and yet he writes this in a way that points to the foreplanning of his own and Lucette's life that seems encoded in his *Letters from Terra*. What do these relationships imply? One possible answer might be that Lucette is involved in a foreplanning that disproves Van's denial of the future. Another – the correct one, as we shall see – is that a contrast is being established between Lucette's involvement in continuing time here – her mermaid's message to Ada – and real foreplanning. Lucette's presence emphasizes that though she can make her mark in time, in the present, the "no future" rule applies to her too. She can see the past endlessly, and because of this has discerned the morning pattern in Van and Ada's lives and has tried to crown the pattern by inclining Ada to return to Mont Roux. But she has none of the power of whoever established the morning pattern (and even her own participating in it from beyond), or the pattern of Lucette and letters, or the strange doubling of Torfyanka and Gamlet, picnic ride and picnic ride, Dolores and Donna Anna, Ada and Lucette.

The last two of these patterns involve not only events too carefully arranged to be anything but planned in advance, but even a sort of tabulation of the patterns to allow retrospective checking – by means of Van's writing *Letters from Terra* and by means of the two Scrabble games that allude to the prefiguring of the two paired picnic rides. In both cases, letters and Lucette are prominent: quite directly in the *Letters from Terra*/letters to Van/messages from beyond pattern; and in the other case by means of Lucette's two references to her *"Buchstaben"* (German, "letters" of the alphabet), which provide the most exact connection between the two games, and by virtue of the fact that it is a letter from Lucette which records the KLITOR-CITROILS-*Hamlet* game that Van did not even consider as a case of curious coincidence.

Lucette clearly plays a very special role in all these strange patternings of time. But merely because we are outside the novel and its world, on a different level of being, we can see that she has not devised the patterns herself: rather, the force that created her and her world has seen that she and her "letters" form the focus of the designs of time. That the coincidences arising during the

Scrabble games are arranged in advance by a force unknowable to the characters within the work – even dead Lucette – is economically indicated by the
fact that the Scrabble set is given to the children by "an old friend of the family
(as Marina's former lovers were known), Baron Klim Avidov" (223), whose
name unscrambles as "Vladimir Nabokov." In a similar way the sources of the
mysterious foreplanning signed into *Letters from Terra* is indicated by another
play on "letters" when a reviewer discerns "the influence of Osberg…as well as
that of an…expounder of anagrammatic dreams, Ben Sirine" (344): "Osberg,"
as we have seen, is an anagram of "Borges" but within the world of the book
is the author of the novel about Dolores that we know as *Lolita;*[3] "Ben Sirine,"
as Mason notes (p. 165), puts into anagram form the fact that Nabokov has
"been *Sirin,*" the pseudonym he used for most of his Russian work.

Because we are in a position so unlike that of the novel's characters and
can see who has designed their lives we are invited to compare the chasm
between human consciousness and some possible foreplanning power with the
ontological breach between the characters of a story and their creator. Even
the patterns of Lucette's attentive involvement in continuing time after her
death are of a totally different order from those patterns which appear (upon
retrospection, of course) to have signaled in advance that they are foreplanned.
These latter imply some conscious control of "the future" and disclose a
boundless care on the part of the controller, a care genuine and profound even
when to a mortal eye the events of some of these patterns may seem merely
cruel. We can see that the foreplanning of Lucette's fate, the poignant exactness with which her maltreatment prefigures her death, has been undertaken
with a solicitude which aims to stir sympathy in all who watch over her and
which, of course, has nothing in common with the inconsiderateness with
which she is treated by the young Van and Ada.

Nabokov's role in *Ada* is that of a designing force whose very condition of
being cannot be known by mortal man or even perhaps by human consciousness transfigured beyond death. But some suggestive patterns may at least
dimly draw the attention of mortals to the possibility of such a controlling
fate – as some fatidic patterns indeed catch Van's attention. He notices some
uncanny relationships, some unfathomable coincidences, some mysterious
excess of design over chance, and hopes he is "catching sight of the lining
of time" (227). As he writes elsewhere, too, he feels that "some law of logic
should fix the number of coincidences, in a given domain, after which they
cease to be coincidences, and form, instead, the living organism of a new
truth" (361). The role that Lucette plays after her death, moreover, suggests
that though still unknown directly a foreplanning fate may be intuited through
the confident apprehension of its designs in an afterlife which by allowing
one to investigate to the full time's patterns would allow one also the thrill of
perceiving the infinite tenderness of these designs – a thrill perhaps as close
as one may come to the thrill of actual creation.

The World of the Novel

Nabokov's speculative sallies have opened up an enchanting universe, but his exploration remains within the confines of art, in the circumscribed world of his own work where he can arrange everything as he chooses. What of the real world in which we live, where we can know no such transcendent consolation as Lucette might have found, where pain, evil, death are immediate realities? They are realities for Nabokov too, and as the penultimate chapter of *Ada* makes clear, he is not chary of denouncing evil or deploring suffering.

Pt.5 Ch.5 of *Ada* describes the unauthorized film made in 1940 by the French director Victor Vitry from the book of *Letters from Terra* (1891). The phenomenally successful movie is a travesty of Van's completely unsuccessful and unnoticed novel. In that youthful work, Theresa had been a Roving Reporter on her planet before being beamed to Antiterra,

> thus giving Van the opportunity to describe the sibling planet's political aspect. This aspect gave him the least trouble, presenting as it did a mosaic of painstakingly collated notes from his own reports on the "transcendental delirium" of his patients. Its acoustics were poor, proper names often came out garbled, a chaotic calendar messed up the order of events but, on the whole, the colored dots did form a geomantic picture of sorts. (340)

Van relates that his book sprang from the "pleasurable urge to express through verbal imagery a compendium of certain inexplicably correlated vagaries observed by him in mental patients, on and off, since his first year at Chose" (338). The information Van has so diligently gleaned from his patients confirms that Terra is "presently" (at the time of Van's researches on his patients and his writing *Letters from Terra*) situated at about 1940 and that twentieth-century Terra is remarkably peaceful and thriving in comparison with the trouble nineteenth-century Antiterra has undergone since its "Great, and to some Intolerable, Revelation" (20) in those "evil days of 1859" (329).

Van explains, however, that the real purpose of his novel was not only to assemble his madmen's visions of Terra but also to suggest that this other world was not a place of perfect happiness: he tries to express in political terms his own doubts that human happiness can be unalloyed with grief. Nevertheless, despite his efforts, Van's record of Terranean politics in the twentieth century has to depend on the visions of his patients and so still conforms to the general notion of a serene Terra strikingly unlike turbulent nineteenth-century Antiterra.

Van's wish to indicate that life on Terra is not pure happiness is the result of his discovering the painfulness of what he had thought to be Ardis's perfect pleasure. At one of their finest moments at Ardis he and Ada had called each other "Spies from Terra" (264), but now he knows the torment Ada's infidelity has brought into the former purity of his joy. *Letters from Terra* reflects the bitterness of his new grief and the fact that in his jealousy and pride he can neither answer the imploring letters Ada sends nor forget her for a moment. All this becomes manifest in terms more direct and personal than those used in constructing the political dimensions of the novel when Van describes how he invented the characters who enact his story:

> In his struggle to keep the writer of the letters from Terra strictly separate from the image of Ada, he gilt and carmined Theresa until she became a paragon of banality. This Theresa maddened with her messages a scientist on our easily-maddened planet; his anagram-looking name, Sig Leymanski, had been partly derived by Van from that of Aqua's last doctor. When Leymanski's obsession turned into love, and one's sympathy got focused on his enchanting, melancholy, betrayed wife (née Antilia Glems), our author found himself confronted with the distressful task of now stamping out in Antilia, a born brunette, all traces of Ada, thus reducing yet another character to a dummy with bleached hair.
>
> After beaming to Sig a dozen communications from her planet, Theresa flies over to him, and he, in his laboratory, has to place her on a slide under a powerful microscope in order to make out the tiny, though otherwise perfect, shape of his minikin sweetheart, a graceful microorganism extending transparent appendages toward his huge humid eye. Alas, the testibulus (test tube – never to be confused with *testiculus*, orchid), with Theresa swimming inside like a micromermaid, is "'accidentally'" thrown away by Professor Leyman's (he had trimmed his name by that time) assistant, Flora, initially an ivory-pale, dark-haired funest beauty, whom the author transformed just in time into a third bromidic dummy with a dun bun.
>
> (Antilia later regained her husband, and Flora was weeded out. Ada's addendum.) (339–40)

But if the ordinary narrative level of *Letters from Terra* is evidence that his own pain has spurred Van to write the novel, there are other forces at work in its plot. Sig Leymanski is named in honour of Aqua's last doctor, "Herr Doktor Sig" (29); his trimmed surname, Leyman, recalls Van's punning at the beginning of Pt.1 Ch.3, the chapter in which he introduces both the notion of Terra and the story of Aqua's madness: "The details of the L disaster...are too well-known historically, and too obscene spiritually, to be treated at length in a book addressed to young laymen and lemans" (17). As these connections indicate, *Letters from Terra* is in part the result of Van's long fascination with his "mother"'s madness, brought on by the pain Aqua felt at Demon's unfaithfulness.

Theresa, the heroine of *Letters from Terra*, is both modeled on and a deliberate attempt not to evoke Ada. The identification of Ada with Theresa is confirmed when in the credits for *Don Juan's Last Fling* Ada is "obscurely and fleetingly billed as 'Theresa Zegris'" (492).[4] But when Theresa is said to be "like a micromermaid" she is at once connected with Lucette, "our Esmeralda and mermaid." The "*mini*kin" Theresa, a "micromermaid" and "microorganism" seen under a "microscope" (340) and in the movie as an actress "in miniature" (582), is also associated with Lucette's death in another way: when Van's New York palazzo is burnt down, he erects in its place "a most appetizing little memorial" (337), "his famous Lucinda [Lucette's official name] Villa, a *mini*ature museum just two stories high, with a still growing collection of *micro*photographed paintings" (336; italics added). The test tube "with Theresa swimming inside like a micromermaid" which is" 'accidentally' thrown away" (340), moreover, oddly anticipates both Lucette's throwing herself from the *Tobakoff* and the ironic title of *Don Juan's Last Fling*. Theresa, then, who "maddened with her messages a scientist on our easily maddened planet," incorporates not only Ada, who writes imploringly to Van, but also Lucette, who has sent Van an even more desperate letter declaring her hopeless love and who now sends much stranger messages from Terra the Fair.

Van writes that "When Leyman's obsession turned into love,…one's sympathy got focused on his enchanting, melancholy, betrayed wife (née Antilia Glems)" (340). Again, Van explicitly links Ada and Antilia: he has to stamp out "in Antilia, a born brunette, all traces of Ada." But in Antilia too Nabokov manages to implicate Lucette in ways that necessarily escape Van's detection and confound his artistic intention: the "betrayed wife" in his juvenile novel points to Lucette not only through the "*gitanilla Esm*eralda" anagram in her name but also because Antilia was an "imaginary archipelago west of Atlantis" (Webster's Second) – a name current just before the discovery of the New World.[5] Lucette is a mermaid "in the groves of Atlantis" (559) – and by her association with this imagined precursor of the Americas she is again ranked with the men Van has cuckolded, Ivan Tobak, descendant of Admiral Tobakoff, the invented discoverer of Tobago, and Andrey Vinelander, supposed descendant of the leader of the Vineland voyage.

If Van writes *Letters from Terra* to distract himself from the pain Ada's infidelity has caused him, then, Nabokov also devises this mirror-novel to reflect in Theresa and Antilia the pain caused by Van's inconsiderateness towards Lucette, towards the husbands of his adulterous partners, towards Ada herself. Behind Van's book is the lesson of the reality of another's pain. In a very different form and with a very different scope this same lesson lies behind the film version of *Letters from Terra*.

While Van's novel, written in 1890, looked towards a nineteen-fortyish Terra, Vitry's picture is *made* in 1940 – and its nineteen-fortyish Terra is definitely not equivalent to the Antiterra in which the film is released. Vitry's

Terra, unlike Van's, is marred by chaos, division, warfare, whereas Antiterra has now long been enjoying peace. Vitry's Terranean 1940, however, is still "contemporaneous" with the 1890 of its sister planet: Theresa still flies from Terra's 1940 to Antiterra's 1890. Now, though, this 1890 is no longer that of Van's surprisingly modern Manhattan but something curiously archaic and quaint:

> Vitry dated Theresa's visit to Antiterra as taking place in 1940, but 1940 by the Terranean calendar, and about 1890 by ours. The conceit allowed certain pleasing dips into the modes and manners of our past (did you remember that horses wore hats – yes, *hats* – when heat waves swept Manhattan?). (580)

It is not merely that Vitry has overturned Van's *Letters from Terra* but that the whole past appears to have been rewritten just by becoming no longer present. At the time, amazingly advanced; now, almost a dreamy masquerade. Van's conviction of the strangeness of the human sense of the "present" has been amusingly translated from personal to historical terms.

Another attractive irony is that though Vitry's film is an unconscionable travesty of Van's novel and perverts all the results of Van's arduous researches among the insane, it is far closer to a true picture of Terra – if we take that planet to be *our* earth – than Van's novel had been. Van had written that in eighteenth-century Terra's France, "a virtually bloodless revolution had dethroned the Capetians" (341). The "de-" and the "Capet-" subliminally hint at "decapitation"; in calling up the guillotine they belie the "virtually bloodless" revolution Van constructs. One factor contributing to the popularity of Vitry's film shows that somehow Vitry has a real sense of such details of Terranean history:

> A second attraction came from a little scene that canny Vitry had not cut out: in a flashback to a revolution in former France, an unfortunate extra, who played one of the under-executioners, got accidentally decapitated while pulling the comedian Steller, who played a reluctant king, into a guillotinable position. (581)

Perhaps an even stranger irony is that though Vitry does approximate actual earth history, the pseudo-newsreel style only makes earth's past seem singularly unreal and unconvincing in comparison with the fictional lives of Van and Ada that we have been following so closely:

> In an impressive historical survey of Terra rigged up by Vitry – certainly the greatest cinematic genius ever to direct a picture of such scope or use such a vast number of extras (some said more than a million, others, half a million men and as many mirrors) – kingdoms fell and dictatordoms rose, and republics half-sat,

half-lay in various attitudes of discomfort. The conception was controversial, the execution flawless. Look at all those tiny soldiers scuttling along very fast across the trench-scarred wilderness, with explosions of mud and things going pouf-pouf in silent French, now here, now there!

In 1905, Norway with a mighty heave and a long dorsal ripple unfastened herself from Sweden, her unwieldy co-giantess. while in a similar act of separation the French parliament, with parenthetical outbursts of *vive émotion*, voted a divorce between State and Church. Then, in 1911, Norwegian troops led by Amundsen reached the South Pole and simultaneously the Italians stormed into Turkey. In 1914 Germany invaded Belgium and the Americans tore up Panama. In 1918 they and the French defeated Germany. (580)

The predominance of French and Norwegian concerns is a comic reflection of the fact that Vitry is French and his wife Gedda, *Letters from Terra's* star, Norwegian. But the historical events listed are all accurate (with the exception of the "troops" of Amundsen) no matter how forgotten they may be or how unsure we are of dates and sequences.

At this point in our reading we feel these real events in our planet's history strangely distant in comparison with the immediacy of Van and Ada's lives. Jonathan Culler begins his excellent analysis of the poetics of the novel by stating, accurately, that "the basic convention which governs the novel…is our expectation that the novel will produce a world."[6] Nabokov parodies this fundamental convention of the genre by taking it literally, by making *his* novel produce its own world whose distinctness from Terra is emphasized an innumerable minor historical and geographical distortions – and then by making the reality of this invented world come to seem, after hundreds of pages of reading, more immediate and vivid than the abstractness even earth's recent past has in *Letters from Terra*.

But suddenly and terribly a paragraph that purports merely to describe the popularity of the *Letters from Terra* film pitches us into an abyss of uncertainty:

L.F.T. clubs sprouted. L.F.T. girlies minced with mini-menus out of roadside snackettes shaped like spaceships. From the tremendous correspondence that piled up on Van's desk during a few years of world fame, one gathered that thousands of more or less unbalanced people believed (so striking was the visual impact of the Vitry-Veen film) in the secret Government-concealed identity of Terra and Antiterra. Demonian reality dwindled to a casual illusion. Actually, we had passed through all that. Politicians, dubbed Old Felt and Uncle Joe in forgotten comics, had really existed. Tropical countries meant, not only wild Nature Reserves but famine, and death, and ignorance, and shamans, and agents from distant Atomsk. Our world *was*, in fact, mid-twentieth century.

Terra convalesced after enduring the rack and the stake, the bullies and beasts that Germany inevitably generates when fulfilling her dreams of glory. Russian peasants and poets had not been transported to Estotiland, and the Barren Grounds, ages ago – they were dying, at this very moment, in the slave camps of Tartary. Even the governor of France was not Charlie Chose, the suave nephew of Lord Goal, but a bad-tempered French general. (582)

The novel's world, hitherto accepted as Antiterra, as comically distant, proves to have been our own world, with its Roosevelt (Old Felt) and Stalin (Uncle Joe), its Nazi Germany and Soviet Russia, even its de Gaulle. This disturbing collapse of the book's world insists on the fact of evil and suffering in the world we know. In the novel's previous chapter, where he has indicated that Lucette seems to be inspiring Van to write *Ada* and, perhaps, to incorporate into these memoirs patterns from the past that she can now discern, Nabokov seems to have created not only a fictional world but a whole metaphysical universe. Now the right of the artist to create his own self-contained sphere is challenged: how can a writer devise his own separate and speculative world within his work when neither he nor his readers can be ignorant of the far from speculative realities of pain and cruelty in the world around them?

But Nabokov demonstrates that even in the midst of creating his own world and by the very exercise of his imaginative freedom he can analyze the brutality and decry the bloodshed of earth's actual past. According to Vitry's film of Terra, "In 1933 Athaulf Hindler (also known as Mittler – from 'to mittle,' mutilate) came to power in Germany" (581). Nabokov insists on Hitler's mediocrity (Mittler: German *mittler*, "mediocre") as well as his brutality (the English "mittle"); he points to the sad fact of the recurrence of violence in political history by linking Hitler with Hindenburg; he indicates the sordid trail of greed, ambition and the lust for conquest leading throughout man's past by yoking Adolf Hitler with Ataulf, King of the Goths, and Atahualpa, the last Inca, who lost his empire and his gold to Pizarro's weaponry. As Nabokov stressed in 1942, political power scants morality: "Morally, democracy is invincible. Physically, that side will win which has the better guns."[7]

Though such direct engagement with historical evils is unusual in Nabokov's novels, his works do not ignore the world we know. Even in the Antiterra of *Ada* the collapse of the novel's distinct world that seems to coincide with the success of *Letters from Terra* reveals that Nabokov confronts directly the problem of the relationship between the artist's quarantined world and the ordinary sphere of human conduct – but this too he does as part of his radical investigation of the role and possibilities of consciousness. Nabokov may disconcert the staid and the earthbound when he points out that the world that seems real and solid to us may be made of a fabric of flimsy truth, that it may be little compared with the deeper reality of other worlds and states of being whose unimaginability may be the best we can imagine. Yet if the position of consciousness in the universe remains always in question for Nabokov, the need for responsibility within the scope of the human and the known does not.

Precisely because human consciousness contains the imagination to call seriously into question its own ultimacy, it also positively insists upon responsibility. Consciousness allows each of us the extraordinary privilege of being able to imagine the feelings of others – in shared love, for instance – and with the privilege comes the challenge to take those feelings into consideration: "The forces of imagination...in the long run...are the forces of good" (*Eye* [10]). This becomes the basis of Nabokov's moral strategy as a novelist: he trips us into recognizing how we abuse our imaginative potential, he makes us fall into traps dug by our habits of self-concern and covered over by a dense matting of self-deceptions.

This means, in *Ada*, that he entices us to accept the limitations of Van's vision. He inveigles us into ignoring Van's hypocrisy, into condoning his certainty that the romantic intensity of his grief needs a vengeful outlet, and above all into disregarding Lucette except as a pest. We are encouraged first to make these mistakes and then gradually to become aware of our errors, to reread to the point where we can see what we should have been sensitive to at once, had we had taken enough thought for the feelings of others not represented in the mind – Van's – in which we have placed ourselves.

Lucette is at the centre of *Ada*'s "responsibility" theme, Nabokov's answer to the problem of reconciling the detachment of the world the artist creates and the pressures of our involvement in our own real world. Nabokov can decry large-scale evil and suffering, but it is individual responsibility that he considers the basis of morality, and it is a sense of individual responsibility that he aims to sharpen in the individual reader through the corrective effects of successive readings.

Yet these changes in reaction which make us attend to Lucette and so to the moral implications of her fate also allow us to distinguish her participation in Van and Ada's lives after her death and to perceive those patterns in the lives of the Veen children that she can now discern. In rereading we find that a scene at first striking for its free vitality comes to disclose, through re-examination after re-examination, the sort of patterns that might be discoverable in "real" life, if consciousness could timelessly reinvestigate the past, and that might reveal the participation of some force capable of designing the future. Such a force could lurk behind life itself, not only creating the world but permeating each molecule and each moment, leaving some of its patterns perhaps to be discerned even by human minds, perhaps offering to some state of being beyond the human the surprise of discovering its omnipresent control.

The continually deepening responses possible in *Ada* are essential not only to Nabokov's ethics but also to his whole metaphysics. At their final stages they offer a tentative promise of successive enrichments of reality and at the same time an insistence that the world of real, responsible life is the only one we know and the only one in which we act. Through Lucette Nabokov resolves the doubts he raises in us about the remoteness of his Antiterra from the real world of responsible life, for he shows that his fictional microcosm can be a means of testing and enlarging our own awareness of responsibility. But at the same time he also allows other worlds of wonderful possibility to surround the one we know, and he encourages us to look for these new worlds by looking deeper into the reality of this one, by seeking out the individuality and the eerie thrills of pattern he himself has found in both nature (in his beloved butterflies) and time (in that unrivalled memory).

Appendix: Spectral Hypotheses

> Thus, if I continue to harp
> on the subject, I do so for
> Sebastian Knight's sake.
>
> Nabokov, *The Real Life of Sebastian Knight*

The reader who has dipped into this book and knows William Woodin Rowe's *Nabokov's Spectral Dimension*[1] may suppose he and I are essentially in agreement. After all, we both note Nabokov's concern with an afterlife and both suggest that characters who die in the course of his stories may somehow come back into the action later, in ways that seem far from visible to the unwary reader. But it seems to me that not to make plain our disagreement would be a disservice to Nabokov. Rowe persistently trivializes his subject; were his findings true, Nabokov would be intellectually shallow and artistically cheap. Fortunately Rowe is quite wrong – wherever he does not merely muddy the self-evident.

Nothing in the world is easier than coming up with hypotheses. It is what we have been doing since we first thought there might be demons in the trees and gods in the skies. But any thinking that aspires towards truth must test each hypothesis for its internal consistency and to see whether it is in accord with and accounts for all the facts with which it purports to deal and whether or not there are alternative explanations. Naturally, if another hypothesis also appears to fit the case (and is incompatible with the first) then at least one of them must be wrong.

William Woodin Rowe seems unaware of such a process: he merely advances a hypothesis and assumes that by virtue of advancing it he has proved his point. His method in *Nabokov's Spectral Dimension* is exactly the same as in the section of *Nabokov's Deceptive World*[2] that Nabokov found so insulting.[3] In the earlier book, the hypothesis was "sex is everywhere," here it is "ghosts are everywhere." In neither work does Rowe feel it necessary to prove his case: he just points, and there's sex, in an innocent-looking word, or a ghost, in an innocent-looking cloud.

Let us take an example.

There is "a sudden onslaught of wind, and a black thunderhead" (*Lolita* 105) as Humbert is about to leave Ramsdale for Camp Q. Here is Rowe's response: "Given Charlotte's feelings at the time of her death, as well as Humbert's present intentions, the aggressive wind and looming thunderhead seem an appropriate suggestion of her hovering spirit." (*NSD* 67) This is Rowe's *main* evidence for Charlotte's spirit in *Lolita*; this flimsy conjecture he then wields as a license for interpreting other indications of weather at will.

Rowe follows this "method" consistently. A quite dubious piece of evidence is deemed to support an assertion; then he looks elsewhere, in the same novel or others, for similar effects, effects like sunsets or rain which one would think rather difficult for a novelist to avoid, and declares that these indicate ghostly presences, on the strength of the first supposed case. He then shores up the first case by anticipating others, saying this is what Nabokov "typically" or "generally" or "characteristically" does: a vicious circle of spurious confirmation.

Rowe does not stop to think that:

(1) Thunderstorms usually seem perfectly explicable phenomena, which novelists often include because weather exists and for atmospheric value. In other words there is a perfectly ordinary and simpler hypothesis that will explain Nabokov's choice.

(2) The feelings Rowe attributes to Charlotte's spirit should only become more intense as he proceeds to Camp Q and on to the Enchanted Hunters. On the basis of Rowe's "logic," there should be a cataclysmic thunderstorm accompanying Humbert and Lolita in Briceland. His hypothesis fails to fit in with the novel's obvious facts.

(3) Rowe's "explanation" would produce an impossible world. What if Miss Opposite's deceased boyfriend was particularly pleased, this same day, with her recollecting him fondly, and wanted the sun to shine just at this moment for her? This elementary consideration is by itself enough to rule out Rowe's hypothesis. And that is why his work seems so insulting to Nabokov: because he attributes to him ideas an intelligent child could reject.

(4) What makes this worse, as readers of Nabokov know, is that it directly contradicts Nabokov's explicit meditations. Time and again, in places like "Ultima Thule," "Signs and Symbols" and especially *Pale Fire* and *Ada*, Nabokov rejects possible forms of an afterlife or fatidic signaling for precisely the sort of reason sketched in (3).

Now the invention *and testing* of hypotheses is exactly Nabokov's method of thinking about the afterlife – which is why I can find it interesting, though by nature I tend to be of a rationalistic outlook and disinclined to believe in any unseen spiritual realms.

Nabokov asks what happens to human consciousness at death, and suggests two possible answers: it ends; it continues. (He sees *both* as possible throughout his work, from *Smert'* to *Look at the Harlequins!*) The second alternative is feasible as a mere hypothesis, but there seems to be good evidence against it in the fact that we do not know of this state or have contact with it. Nabokov considers examples of trying to find out about an afterlife (see *SM* 20, or "Ultima Thule") but has to rule them out: they tell us nothing. But if there is no communication with any form of consciousness beyond death, perhaps that is a consequence of limitations imposed on human consciousness (as he suggests in *The Gift*, "The Vane Sisters" and elsewhere) or on the postmortal consciousness too ("Ultima Thule," *Transparent Things*). In that case, Nabokov suggests, a consciousness beyond death – even one which participates in our world – might be perfectly possible. The hypothesis is not ruled out, but it remains a hypothesis.

William Gass proposes that a novelist's task should be not to render the world but to offer a philosophically coherent world. When Nabokov does include actual ghosts – as he does in *Transparent Things*, *Ada*, "The Vane Sisters," "Ultima Thule" and of course quite probably in much of his other fiction (though Rowe does nothing to advance these other possibilities) he uses the artist's license to render a philosophically coherent world, whether or not it is the actual world. He still insists everywhere that there seems to be no way that mankind can know if this is the actual state of things.

Nabokov can understand what a hypothesis is. Rowe seems not to – or at least he refuses to adjust an idea merely because all the evidence contradicts it. He declares for instance that the ghost of Tom, an Alsatian dog, intervenes in the action of *King, Queen, Knave*, his chief argument being that it is "typical" (p. 97) of a Nabokovian ghost to work through weather – and this on the basis of such pasteboard examples as the Charlotte Haze case. The evidence is this: "His faint influence upon the rain can be detected in its faint personification. As Martha, Franz and Dreyer all ride in the boat: 'The rain would stop one moment and the next start pouring again, as if practicing' (248). Influenced by Tom's spirit, the rain is 'practicing'...." With this assertion, slipped into a participial phrase, the case is supposed to be proved!

Against this, we should note:

(1) The fact that the rain is perfectly explicable, and the "as if practicing" a fine poetical touch just by itself. Rain does seem to hesitate, often, before coming down in earnest, but the idea of "practicing" adds a new charm to the observation.

(2) Not only is there no need for a further explanation, but there is also nothing to indicate that a possible further explanation need be in terms of Tom's spirit; but Tom has died, and Rowe has set up as a spook-spotter, and there is a lot of weather in Nabokov's novels. Rowe's only argument here, again, is that Nabokov often does this sort of thing – though each purported example when examined dissolves into a mere assertion "supported" by the other so-called instances. Rowe continually displays his indifference to context and to variation from work to work – just as he did in *Nabokov's Deceptive World*, when Nabokov criticized him for the "fatal flaw in his treatment of

recurrent words, such as 'garden' or 'water'": "not realizing that the sound of a bath being filled, say, in the world of *Laughter in the Dark* is as different from the limes rustling in the rain of *Speak, Memory* as the Garden of Delights in *Ada* is from the lawns in *Lolita*" (*SO* 305–306).

(3) Not only is there no need for a further explanation, and no evidence to support the further explanation Rowe goes on to offer, but the explanation he gives also seems quite antithetical to Nabokov's explicit beliefs. Nabokov was interested in animal life, but very much as a subject of human perception and scientific exploration, certainly not for the sort of animal consciousness that fascinated Lawrence, for instance, so much. Everything in Nabokov's work points to his viewing human consciousness as something radically different from anything else we know: the difference between an ape's memory and man's, remember, is the difference between an ampersand and the British Museum Library. Would somebody who can say this – and who always limits his hereafters to human consciousness, and even then wonders about the eligibility even of all humans ("Tyrants Destroyed," "A Busy Man," *Ada*) have the least interest in making an Alsatian inspire some perfectly ordinary rain?

Like all readers, Rowe recignizes that Nabokov employs deception as a strategy. But he then uses this as permission to attribute any level of counter-meaning he likes. In *Nabokov's Deceptive World* he was triggered off by Nabokov's genuine sexual word-play to extrapolate to other cases where sexual implication could be supposed. He quotes a passage describing Van kissing Ada's legs "from the A of arched instep to the V of velvet" (129). Self-evidently the "V of velvet" refers to Ada's pubic triangle. To conclude as Rowe does that therefore any passage where the letter "v" occurs contains possible allusions to the female pudenda seems close to idiocy. Rowe is not even fazed by the fact that the novel's aggressively male hero is Van Veen.

As in *Nabokov's Deceptive World*, so in *Nabokov's Spectral Dimension*: Rowe simply does not know where to stop. Again genuine evidence has set Rowe off on his grotesque extrapolations. In *Transparent Things* (1972) the narrator is obviously a ghost, and as Rowe noticed[4] after Nabokov pointed it out in an interview, the ghost is in fact the character R. In 1978 in her introduction to Nabokov's collected Russian poems Véra Nabokov identified "Nabokov's main theme" as "the beyond." In 1979 Rowe read my own doctoral dissertation, which covered all the ground covered in this book – a fact which incidentally invalidates Rowe's assertion that his detection of ghostly activity in Nabokov was "quite unprecedented" (*NSD* 9).

But it was "The Vane Sisters," another case in which Nabokov made explicit comments outside the story, that seemed to Rowe to provide a method and all the confirmation he needed. Here, weather and light effects are used by two characters who have died within the course of the story to guide the narrator, who however remains unaware of their influence – as Nabokov notes in the preface to *Nabokov's Quartet*. From here Rowe takes his cue for determining that weather, light or a character's inability to see ghosts are all proof of ghostly presence. He does not stop to think about the extraordinary precision of the "Vane Sisters" case which is absent from every instance he then finds for himself – just as the precision of "V of velvet" is absent from every voluptuous v he unveils. Although in "The Vane Sisters" weather and light and dead people occur together, Nabokov does not expect that to mean anything to the reader without the acrostic embedded in the story's last paragraph. That very exact pointer in turn swings into place only because Nabokov hints within the story at an acrostic in the last paragraph, and even that internal hint Nabokov has supported by an explicit clue outside the story every time it has been republished. Nabokov has rigorously controlled the reader's response: the hint within the text leads us to the acrostic, which spells out the ghostly involvement, which then can be checked against the specific events in the story, which in turn lead to well-defined metaphysical implications. If there is a code inserted within one of his works, this example suggests, Nabokov will supply the means to crack it; he will not leave everything to the suggestibility of the reader. When Rowe brings the crystalline logic of "The Vane Sisters" forward in support of his general thesis, it only shows the weakness of his position: Nabokov proves he does not expect or want readers to *guess* at ghosts.

Nabokov had been denouncing symbolism for forty years when Rowe published his first book largely devoted to the unmasking of sexual symbols in Nabokov's work. Fictional symbolism arose in the first place as compensation for the diffusion of meaning that results from the novel's attempt to render the visible world in detail: *symbolic* detail could serve at once as description and idea. Nabokov, who has always thought carefully about the nature of literary meaning, recognizes that despite what it seems to offer symbolism denies the independent reality of things and soon subjects every descriptive element to the possibility of more or less arbitrary decoding. Rejecting such a strategy for its inaccuracy and its misleading philosophical consequences, he has long sought new ways of adding meaning exactly to meaning without congesting, as Joyce does, the experience of reading. He has discovered a whole range of ways for the implied to be teased out because the supplied requires further explanation.

Nothing could be further from this method of activating specific implication than Rowe's assumption that since Nabokov can be deceptive a reader may *always* flounder around for an extra meaning. A scene in *Ada* will show what I mean. Shortly after Van arrives at Ardis for the first time he follows Ada up the shattal tree. When he signals to her she looks down and tumbles, taking Van with her. They collapse into a fork in the tree, Van with his head between pantyless and short-frocked Ada's legs. Rowe cites the beginning of the scene:

Van, in a blue gym suit, having worked his way up to a fork just under his agile playmate..., betokened mute communication by taking her ankle between finger and thumb as *she* would have a closed butterfly. (*Ada* 94, *NDW* 112–3)

Since Ada is a lepidopterist and since lepidopterists do take closed butterflies between finger and thumb – there is even a famous photograph of Nabokov in just such a pose – this seems merely a vivid sketching of gesture. But Rowe sees more:

"Butterfly," in Nabokov's works, can often be seen to symbolize the female private parts. Above, one has only to read the word *as* as *when* (or especially as *since*) to effect the transformation, which is carefully screened, but not at all encumbered, by the italics of *"she."* (*NDW* 113)

Rowe does not explain *why* we should change the words a writer has settled on after long deliberation. But in any case he seems too excited by the possibility of having a vagina in the sentence to think what happens if we do take his suggestion. If we substitute *when* for *as*, we might momentarily construe the meaning to be that Van took Ada by the ankle between finger and thumb when she would have a closed vagina. The subordinate verb however now has a conditional and recurrent value, while the action of the main clause happens only on one occasion. So in fact with the proposed transformation the sentence becomes the impossible: he took her ankle (once), when(ever) she would have a closed vagina. Except that in "would have" the verb "taken" is understood: he took her ankle (once), when(ever) she would have taken a closed vagina. Hmm. Shall we try *since*? He took her ankle since she would have taken a closed vagina. Sigh.

In this scene Van and Ada though each in love with the other are still far from being lovers and have had no sexual contact of any kind, so that when they tumble and Van's mouth accidentally presses against Ada's naked crotch, it seems as if gravity itself were conspiring to promote their relationship. So far as I understand it, Rowe suggests that there is some playful implication that Van signals to Ada by pinching her ankle, only because her vagina is closed; if it were open, he would signal by pinching her there. Even if this worked grammatically, which it doesn't, Rowe's suggestion of such a signaling at this stage of Van and Ada's relationship simply destroys the whole point of the scene: that the kiss on Ada's crotch is an undreamt-of advance on their previous intimacy.

Rowe's evidence for Nabokov's supposedly implying pudenda in "butterfly" is merely that he "often" uses the word in this way. To document the "often" he then enthusiastically trots out half a dozen lepidopteral images – not one of which asks to be read sexually. In the same manner in *Nabokov's Spectral Dimension* Rowe will declare that Nabokov "typically" describes weather or light when he wants to imply ghosts – and in the new book he also finds that butterflies are now generally not pudenda but (surprise, surprise) the spirits of those who have been associated with lepidoptera while alive.

Curiously, despite the fact that Rowe lingers on the shattal tree scene to discern "pants" when the children are "panting" and "crotches" in the "branches" of the tree, he ignores Ada's retrospective comment as she and Van narrate the incident: "At a time when the chastest of chances allowed you to snatch, as they say, a first shy kiss!" (95) The "snatch, as they say, a first shy kiss" seems to allude to a stock expression – but the actual idiom is "steal a kiss." Why then that "as they say" just after "snatch"? Because, of course, there is one colloquial use of "snatch": vagina.

Note how utterly different this pun is from Rowe's "butterfly" or "panting" or "branches." Here the "as they say" stands out as the signpost of some lexical twist; it amusingly feigns to refer to an innocent and actually nonexistent idiom; in fact it discloses the vulgar sense of "snatch" and its brilliantly apt conjunction, in this context, with "steal a kiss." *That* is how Nabokovian implication works: a pointer signals that something needs to be explained, and even if as here the pointer marks a false trail, that itself becomes part of the pleasure of the discovery; then the explanation is found – and confirms itself by enriching its context so exactly. For a frisson from "butterfly", on the other hand, Rowe offers explanations where none are required, misconstrues, produces no evidence save that Nabokov "generally" (according to Rowe) does such things, contradicts explicit meanings, and ignores the integrity of the scene – all this for an implication that even if it were there would be jejune.

The shattal tree incident suggests that besides being groundless Rowe's "discoveries" detract as much from their context as Nabokov's genuine implications add. What was true of the sexual symbolism of *Nabokov's Deceptive World* proves true again of the ghosts of *Nabokov's Spectral Dimension*. In fact every flaw in Rowe's approach that I have just catalogued in the "butterfly" case recurs throughout the later book.

Let us see how he deals with *Ada*.

Like Lucette's spirit, Aqua's appears via birds. Aqua dies in 1883, and Van visits Ardis in 1884. The first morning, he is "violently aroused by a clamorous caroling" of birds (47). Van gets up and meets Blanche, a young chambermaid. She is wearing an aquamarine on one hand and looking at a sparrow. Van is strongly attracted to Blanche. This attraction is promoted by Aqua's spirit (note the "aquamarine" on Blanche's hand) in an attempt to divert Van from Ada. (*NSD* 53).

In "The Vane Sisters", the "icicles by Cynthia" catch the narrator's attention so that he follows them along a whole row of house-eaves and finds himself in an unusual part of town – where he chances on a former acquaintance, D., who tells him of Cynthia's death. Despite the ghosts, that seems like a very comprehensible sequence: the icicles lead the narrator astray. But in Rowe's example from *Ada*, the fact that Blanche watches a sparrow supposedly incorporating Aqua's spirit somehow sparks Van's lust. How? Or if Aqua operates directly on Van's mind, why does she need to manifest herself as a sparrow?

The main "proof" that Aqua is present in the sparrow consists of the flat declaration that "Like Lucette's spirit, Aqua's appears via birds." When Van comes to Mont Roux to be reunited with Ada, "some 'grebes' appear, and he suddenly thinks of deceased Lucette (509)" (*NSD* 51). It is true that before Lucette dies Van has a dream of a peacock that somersaults "like a diving grebe," and in retrospect we can see that his anticipates Lucette diving to her death. But a grebe serving as a simile within a dream dreamt while Lucette still lives hardly constitutes proof that any later appearances of grebes (and there are several – as there are ducks, coots, gulls and so on) must be Lucette's spirit. In Rowe's "some 'grebes' appear, he suddenly thinks of deceased Lucette," he conveniently omits awkward evidence:

> The grebes were there for the winter but the coots had not yet returned.
> Ardis, Manhattan, Mont Roux, our little rousse is dead. (509)

If Rowe knew *Ada* well, he would know that Lucette had interrupted Van and Ada's first reunion at Ardis (in 1888) and their second reunion in Manhattan (in 1892). Van thinks of "Ardis, Manhattan, Mont Roux" as a sequence because another reunion with Ada is about to take place. That in itself makes it natural for Van to reflect that *this* time there will be no Lucette bursting through the door. But the name of Mont Roux and the russet vegetation of the hill behind the town ("Mount Russet…lived up to its name and autumnal reputation" [509]) also bring the *rousse* Lucette to mind. Why then do we need to assume that Lucette acts through the grebes (which happen to abound in Montreux at that season anyway) to make Van recall his sister? He has an excellent memory, and felt a deep tenderness for Lucette. Cannot he recollect her without its being prompted supernaturally?

Let us return to Aqua as the sparrow. Rowe identified Aqua here, remember, chiefly on the grounds that Lucette's spirit appears via birds. Weighty proof indeed! To Rowe the case seems to confirm itself because he can figure out a motive for Ada's ghost: Van's attraction towards Blanche is "promoted by Aqua's spirit (note the 'aquamarine' on Blanche's hand) in an attempt to divert Van from Ada".

It seems odd that Aqua should sense she needed to employ the sparrow as some sort of obscure aphrodisiac. If she were watching over Van she would know him to be already a lusty, even cocksure, lad. Why should a ghost need to intervene for him to be stirred by the attractive and hardly demure Blanche? And the fact that she is a servant makes her ready prey indeed to someone like Van, for as Aqua's spirit would know, Van adores and imitates his father, who has had affair after affair with servant girls. (On a later visit to Ardis Demon himself thinks of seducing Blanche: perhaps this too is motivated by Aqua?)

The absurdity of supposing Van aroused through the incredible device of a ghost-infested sparrow becomes clear when we recollect that Van had "glimpsed (and promised himself to investigate)" Blanche "on the preceding evening" (48) – in other words eight or ten hours before the sparrow caught Blanche's eye. Since the fact is noted in the very sentence preceding the description of Blanche watching the sparrow, Rowe seems deliberately to have suppressed evidence that he knows must disprove his point.

Aqua was destroyed by Demon's infidelities, including those with servant girls. Why should she encourage Van to take his father's hurtful line of sexual conduct? The "aquamarine" Blanche wears is much more likely to point not to Aqua's ghost in a sparrow but to the fact that Van's casual assumption he can avail himself of Blanche imitates his father's sexual style – which has injured both Aqua and Marina. It is no accident that when Van spots Blanche he describes her in exactly the terms he has heard Demon apply to pretty servants: "She wore what his father termed with a semi-assumed leer 'soubret black and frissonet frill.'" (48)

Rowe concludes his paragraph:

> Van now makes advances, which Blanche sadly repulses, adding: "Now we have to separate, the sparrow has disappeared. I see...." Unless one realizes that Aqua's spirit has been acting through this sparrow, it may seem somewhat strange that Blanche associates the sparrow's departure with the need to separate from Van. As we can see, Aqua's spirit has not been successful, and the affair with Ada soon begins. (*NSD* 531)

Again Rowe suppresses pertinent information. What Blanche in fact says is: "Now we have to separate, the sparrow has disappeared, I see, and Monsieur Bouteillan has entered the next room, and can perceive us clearly in that mirror above the sofa behind that silk screen." (49) Since Bouteillan is Blanche's current lover, it is hardly surprising that she does not want him to see her talking to the handsome young baron, while the reference to the sparrow, an impromptu observation that intrudes beautifully into the sentence Blanche had prepared in farewell, is the poetry of the unplanned – to which Rowe seems quite immune.

(In general Rowe demonstrates an uncanny insensitivity to the pleasures of the poetic, the enchantment of the "as if." Nabokov wrote in an unpublished letter of 1924 that shooting stars are the angels throwing away cigarettes when archangels go past. If Rowe had known this, perhaps he could have searched out the stars and cigarettes in Nabokov's books and found enough occurrences to which some ghost could be affixed to declare that these are "typically" Nabokovian tokens.)

Rowe has certain habitual devices which take the place of argument. One standard ploy is this: he modestly offers a mere possibility ("the appearance of grebes, plus Van's sudden recollection of Lucette, *suggest* that her spirit is present"), then reintroduces it as proven fact that will substantiate the next supposition ("Like Lucette's spirit, Aqua's appears via birds"). Rowe builds on the sparrow, as that was built on the grebes of Mont Roux. At the end of Ardis the Second,

> Blanche now writes Van a note about Ada's unfaithfulness and offers herself to him.... He almost makes love to her, and she tells him of Ada's affair with Rack. Then, as he leaves: "thrushes were singing so richly, with such sonorous force, such fluty fioriture that one could not endure the agony of consciousness." (294) (*NSD* 53)

Birdsong at dawn on a wooded manor hardly seems surprising, but Rowe implies that here it betokens Aqua's ghostly presence. Soon the implication returns as proven fact: "Blanche, influenced by Aqua's spirit," Rowe declares, "tells Van of Ada's unfaithfulness." (55) In the context of this scene and of the book as a whole, though, the thrushes' song tortures Van because it sums up all his joys at Ardis, which now he knows are over. At the same time the "fluty fioriture" bitterly recalls Rack, whom Blanche has described as squiring Ada "through the tall grass, a flute in his hand." (293) To have his ghost Rowe with his usual blithe inattentiveness destroys this marvellously ironic and poignant sentence and scene.

In the brief summary Rowe makes before quoting that sentence he botches elementary details. Not Blanche but her sister Madelon writes Van that note. Van does not almost make love with Blanche and in fact has to conceal that he remains totally unaroused. But these things are merely slipshod. Rowe becomes positively irresponsible when he completely ignores the explicit and amusing story behind Blanche's disclosure to Van. Rowe says Aqua's ghost inspires Blanche to tell Van that Ada has had an affair with Rack: Nabokov says otherwise. Blanche had intended to speak about Percy de Prey, but when Van seizes the initiative – "When and how had it started?" (293) – she begins her account from Ada's first infidelity, with Rack. Stricken Van breaks away before she can even mention Percy, but when Blanche next sees him she babbles out all she had had to tell. Blanche also makes it clear that she planned to enlighten Van about Ada's infidelity not because of Aqua the thrush but at the prompting of Madelon, whom Percy had sampled and set aside to pursue Ada:

> Only the other day from behind that row of thick firs...she and her sister Madelon, with a bottle of wine between them, watched Monsieur le Comte courting the young lady on the moss, crushing her like a grunting bear as he had also crushed – many times! – Madelon who said she, Blanche, should warn him, Van, because he was a wee bit jealous but she also said – for she had a good heart – better put it off until "Malbrook" *s'en va t'en guerre*, otherwise they would fight: he had been shooting a pistol at a scarecrow all morning and that's why she waited so long, and it was in Madelon's hand, not in hers. (299)

As this passage shows the disclosure of Ada's unfaithfulness has been planned for days before those thrushes, supposedly Aqua, burst into song and so supposedly prompt Blanche to explain the note Rowe thinks *she* wrote.

When Nabokov provides a character with perfectly good motives for performing an action, why should Rowe then declare the character inspired to it by a ghost Rowe alone sees in a butterfly or a raindrop or a bird? How does it help if as is always the case the motives of the ghost that he detects are feebler and murkier and far less likely than those of the live character? Why reduce Nabokov's vigorous interplay of lively men and women to a puppet show conducted by improbable sprites?

In a much later scene Van and Lucette and Ada lie in bed in an incestuous trio directed by Ada. Our eyes take in the picture by moving "up the younger Miss Veen's pried-open legs. A dewdrop on russet moss eventually finds a stylistic response in the aquamarine tear of her flaming cheekbone" (419). After noting the aquamarine, Rowe comments: "Since this scene helps to drive Lucette to suicide, one can imagine the presence of Aqua's anxious spirit, still seeking to disrupt the affair and to save Lucette" (*NSD* 54). One can imagine anything, and Rowe evidently does, but why should anyone else plump for his fantasy? Is it not much more likely that the aquamarine here emphasizes a tragic entanglement of two sisters and a brother that echoes the entanglement of Aqua and Marina with Demon? That complicated threesome, which leads to Aqua's suicide eighteen years before Lucette's, is recalled by Marina in opulent tones that precisely anticipate the later *débauche à trois*:

> Marina...used to affirm in bed that Demon's senses must have been influenced by a queer sort of incestuous pleasure...when he fondled, and savored, and delicately parted and defiled...flesh...that was both that of his wife and that of his mistress, the blended and brightened charms of twin peris, an Aquamarina both single and double, a mirage in an emirate, a geminate gem, an orgy of epithelial alliterations. (19)

Here as often Rowe ignores the more direct connection because for the duration of this book his code is only a spook-spotting one – and because he knows *Ada* too sketchily to be aware of more plausible and meaningful relationships.

Rowe works through speed, proceeding on the assumption that the reader will not pause to weigh his arguments any more than he himself has and routinely offering ghosts as an explanation for scenes that do not need explaining, only because he has now become convinced that ghosts rather than sex provide the key to Nabokov. In the process, he reduces splendid scenes to a helpless mishmash of fatuous motives.

I persist in believing Nabokov had other methods in mind.

Like Rowe, I know that Nabokov has a great interest in the afterlife and in some stories has planned a spectral role. Two instances are quite unequivocal: "The Vane Sisters," about whose two possible candidates for ghosthood Nabokov was explicit enough for even Rowe to be correct, and *Transparent Things*, which Rowe mutilates. But these do not allow us to see ghosts everywhere any more than an imagined double entendre on "eye" should allow us to see the "i"s in "Illinois" as illicit indicia of the vagina (see *NDW* 96). If a specific passage or a general pattern make sense *only* when we hypothesize that Nabokov has implied a ghost is present, then let us accept such an implication – but only after all other explanations have been exhausted.

At the risk of a little repetition, let us look back to the aspects of *Ada* discussed in Chapters 12 and 13 and consider them from two points of view: What needs explaining? What explanations suffice?

Lucette twice uses the word "*Buchstaben*" in connection with Flavita (Scrabble) games, two different games four years and 150 pages (227, 379) apart. This seems a relationship that needs explaining (even if the explanation is that it is pure chance), whereas the recurrence of some common word obviously would not. Similarly Van chooses the pseudonym "Voltemand" when publishing his *Letters from Terra*, and a year later moves across the Atlantic to live in a Voltemand Hall. Again, each choice is unusual, and the two together are much more likely to need explanation than a pseudonym "Brown" and a later Brown Hall.

For those puzzled by the striking connection of, say, the two "*Buchstaben*," I would suggest a number of hypotheses to explain the fact:

(1) It is accidental. But this seems unlikely given that Nabokov was writing in English, does not know German well, and uses German words infrequently. When we add to this the similarity of context – the last rounds of two Flavita games, the fact that it is Lucette who uses "*Buchstaben*" in both cases (the word certainly appears nowhere else in *Ada*) – these coincidences multiply the odds against its being chance to millions to one.

(2) Unconscious repetition: the memory of using "*Buchstaben*" with Lucette

in one instance triggers Nabokov's choice, without his realizing it, a second time.

(3) Deliberate, but without further significance: an example of Nabokov's love of pattern. Entirely plausible – and my own explanation on first discovering the *"Buchstaben"* in these two very similar settings.

(4) Deliberate, and with a significance that Nabokov has designed.

This is where matters become complicated. Why *should* Lucette's choice of the German word for "letters" (of the alphabet) be of any consequence? No necessary reason at all, of course.

But there are other facts in the novel which forced me to abandon explanation (3), facts which seem related to the *"Buchstaben"* and which seem cumulatively to make it more and more likely that they are part of a pattern whose deliberateness points towards some significance.

For instance:

(1) Lucette writes a *letter* to Van, just before her death, which he read just after she dies; this letter includes a poem which deals with the subject of a ghost talking to a mortal.

(2) In Van's last *letter* to Lucette, he calls her a "mermaid" and "bird of paradise" (421). Later he thinks of Lucette, drowned in the Atlantic, as the user of a face powder with a "bird of paradise on the lid" (559): "it had been Lucette, now a mermaid in the groves of Atlantis (and not Ada, now a stranger somewhere near Morges in a black limousine), who had favored that powder" (559). As we saw in Chapter 12, this coincides with what the novel suggests, with Nabokov-Darkbloom's support, may be a message from dead Lucette influencing Ada to turn back from Morges towards Mont Roux and Van.

(3) Van writes a book called *Letters from Terra* which is about "letters" (339) or "messages" (340) sent from Terra, from a girl called Theresa, a "micromermaid" (340); and Terra, within the universe of the novel, is a perhaps mythical planet often associated with the "Next World" (20). Van publishes *Letters from Terra* over the pseudonym "Voltemand," the name of a very minor character in *Hamlet* who acts as a letter-carrier. Van is living at a Voltemand Hall when Lucette comes to him, bringing a letter from Ada. As narrator Van reconstructs his conversation with Lucette in this scene by incorporating into the dialogue fragments from a *letter* she had previously written him, a letter in which she uses the German *"Buchstaben,"* "letter," and which as part of the "dialogue" dissolves into very explicit allusions to Hamlet's *letter* to Ophelia (379).

These are only parts of the pattern, but already it seems exceptionally insistent, especially in the way it involves Lucette and the idea of messages from an afterlife. I have set out the hypotheses I have drawn from this and other elements of the novel in Chapters 12 and 13. They may be wrong, but at least they try to explain peculiar facts about *Ada* that need explaining, and the identification of Lucette's ghost seems to have metaphysical implications of value in themselves and in harmony with the rest of the novel.

For Nabokov the possibility of consciousness beyond the human is something that even after the most searching thought he can express only indirectly – "not text, but texture" – through profoundly original artistic strategies. As a man, a scientist, an artist and a scholar, he knows that through effort and the slow accumulation of information the human mind can come to understand things previously inexplicable. The world is deceptive all right, but because there is always more truth to be learned, not because everything is only caprice. At the same time Nabokov seems sure that the mortal mind cannot know the ultimate nature of life and death. We may one day solve the riddle of the hereafter but only after we have ourselves passed through death.

Human consciousness Nabokov views as something trapped in a present connected only by memory to an inaccessible and apparently fading past. Beyond the human, he suspects, the next stage would surely be a time where the past was endlessly present. Especially in his later work Nabokov tries to lure the curious reader towards a sort of timelessness in relation to a novel's world. Details and implications hide, awaiting discovery, continually enticing us to reread and reread until we can identify every quirk and recall every echo, until every moment of a novel's unfolding past becomes equally accessible to our present. Only then, when we approach a timeless apprehension of the book, does Nabokov let us learn the full pattern of its world and the secrets of its beyond. His epistemology and metaphysics and artistic strategy are one.

To understand nature's design Nabokov would peer into his microscope and count out with patient delight the scales of a butterfly wing. That is what he wants of us: to explore and enjoy his worlds with this kind of precision, word by word. If we are ready to do that, he will reward unstintingly our unstinting curiosity.

Unlike Nabokov, William Woodin Rowe has no sense that things worth knowing might be subtle and complex and take effort to understand. In *Nabokov's Deceptive World* his focus was words, his formula sex – and the results greeted with general derision. In *Nabokov's Spectral Dimension* his focus is on fictional events and his formula ghosts, but now though the conclusions are no less risible they are harder to explode. When Rowe declares that "butterfly" means the female genitalia, the very text he quotes undermines him. When he announces that Aqua's spirit urges Blanche to inform Van of Ada's infidelity, we can see if we look at his argument alone that there is no evidence, but we have to remember what Rowe actually suppresses – that Madelon has already persuaded Blanche to tell Van all – before we can appreciate the enormity of his imposture.

Nabokov's interest in wordplay and in the emotional complexities of sexual love spurred Rowe on in his earlier book to the absurdity of finding sexual symbols everywhere, despite Nabokov's vociferous contempt for sexual or any other symbolism. Now Nabokov's imaginative inquiries into consciousness beyond the human have encouraged Rowe in his new book to find phantasms everywhere, despite Nabokov's express scorn for the chicanery of spiritualism and the triteness of conventional spookery. After a lifetime's art in shaping words sensitively and at times playfully enough to render all the contradictions of human passion, Nabokov howled in exasperation and outrage when Rowe tried to reduce all this to nonsense. He would have cried out with an even sharper sense of insult if he could have seen Rowe apply the same witless and destructive techniques to a subject even closer to his heart.

Still, I am very grateful to Rowe for finding one valid clue in *Ada* that I missed although he fails to realize how it exposes by contrast the randomness of his other assertions. The morning Van's adulterous tryst begins with Ada at Mont Roux he dreams, in direct reminiscence of his last day with Lucette, of sunbathing with a woman at his side: he wakes, after a dream fusion of Lucette and Ada, with the words "It's one of the Vane sisters" (521) fresh in his mind. Rowe points out (*NSD* 51) that the dream's "*talc* of a tropical beach full of sun-baskers" (520: italics added) echoes Van's spelling out for his typist a word he coins to describe drowning Lucette's "tentaclinging hair – t, a, c, l –" (494).

Not being aware of the Lucette-and-letters theme, Rowe could do little with this welcome discovery. Now that the theme *has* been established, we can appreciate that the scrambling or Scrabbling of the letters "t, a, c, l"–"talc"–strongly reinforces the interpretation of the theme in terms of spectral influence, both by explicitly associating it with the Nabokov story where acrostic letters emphatically announce ghostly inspiration, and by integrating Violet Knox (apparently Lucette's unwitting intermediary) into the pattern. The positioning of the one other recorded occasion when Van spells out a word to Violet now becomes particularly striking, especially when we remember that Violet joined the Veens in 1957:

> As Ada, Mr. Oranger (a born catalyzer), and Van were discussing those matters one afternoon in 1957…it suddenly occurred to our old polemicist that all his published works…were not epistemic tasks set to himself by a savant, but buoyant and bellicose exercises in literary style. He was asked why, then, he did not let himself go…and with one thing leading to another it was resolved that he would write his memoirs…
>
> He was a very slow writer. It took him six years to write the first draft and dictate it to Miss Knox, after which he revised the typescript, rewrote it entirely in long hand (1963–65) and redictated the entire thing to indefatigable Violet, whose pretty fingers tapped out a final copy in 1967. E, p, i – why "*y*," my dear? (578)

There the chapter ends.

From what we see of Van's career, "epistemic" refers especially to Van's research in one particular aspect of epistemology: that possible knowledge, among those at or beyond the border of sanity, of "Terra," a state of existence not quite ours. (It was as a relief from and an outlet for this work that he wrote his novel *Letters from Terra*.) Although Van thinks he has abandoned his philosophical inquiry in order to set down his memoirs, the memoirs appear to have been inspired by dead Lucette – and thus have answered his inquiry, though without his knowing. When he declares his renunciation of his lifelong "epistemic" task, that very word's letters are fumbled by the woman who seems to be – without her or Van's in the least suspecting – Lucette's unconscious letter-carrier (Violet types the book out on the special Atticus paper named after Cicero's *Letters to Atticus*, that also alludes to that first scene of the novel which takes place in the Ardis attic during the time that Lucette learns the poem about a ghost talking to a mortal which she quotes in a letter Van receives from her after her death: and for other pointed Violet-Lucette links, see pp. 213–16.) The letters Van must spell out to Violet stand right at the end of the account of *Ada's* composition; their puzzling presence seems to be Lucette's way of signing herself into the story, signing the "letters" she sends from beyond, at the very moment Van abandons his investigation of our ability to learn of the beyond.

Van renounces direct philosophizing, and is rewarded by an answer (albeit unknown to him) to his philosophical quest. The reward – when Lucette inspires his "unbelievable...creative explosion" (577) – is Nabokov's sign that Van has made the right choice. Nabokov is passionately concerned with philosophical questions, but he thinks that art at full stretch may get closer to plucking truth than philosophy can. Whereas the relentless pursuit of rectilinear logic eventually leads us, on this small planet, around in circles, a work of genuinely inspired art may draw on all that is best in human thought and at the same time be penetrated "by the beyond's fresh breath." (*SO* 227)

Or we can look at the matter another way. The declaration Van (or anyone) makes from within this world that the beyond remains philosophically unknowable could prove (for those able to look from the without) to be the very confirmation that where they are *is* a beyond. (Otherwise it would be humanly graspable, it simply would not remain *beyond*.) That conclusion, surely, lies at the heart of Nabokov's thinking,

Both Nabokov's tactics here and his meaning echo and amplify the ending of "The Vane Sisters." Nabokov takes care to set out his problem – the talc – t, a, c, l echo, or the whole Lucette-and-letters theme – and makes one smaller solution trigger off a larger: he makes the solutions as exact as chess problems, and philosophically and artistically worth our while. Nothing could resemble this characteristic precision and pointedness in his strategy less than the mere allegation that Aqua acts more or less through this sparrow or those thrushes – because, after all, the birds are there, and Aqua is dead, so her spirit might be around too.

PART FIVE

ADA: EPILOGUE
AND INTRODUCTION

14. *Ada* through the Attic[1]

Ada, Nabokov's longest and most ambitious novel, sets us down in his strangest and most contradictory world, his most colorful and comic, his most lyrical and discordant, his most unsettling and profound. Line by line, page by page, chapter by chapter he piles one bizarre choice upon another. He sets the action on a planet, Antiterra, whose geography appears identical to ours but whose history follows its own strange forks. He bestows on Van and Ada fabulous wealth, high birth, supreme intelligence, athletic vigor, tireless sexual energy, and an ardent love affair that lasts well into their nineties. So enraptured are they by the story of their own love, and so eloquent in evoking its charm, that we cannot help sharing in their delight. Yet Nabokov makes them not only brother and sister but almost male and female variants of a single design, so that their passion and their pride begin to reek of self-love and self-advertisement. And after holding up the first two summers of their affair for lingering, rhapsodic inspection, he lets the next eighty years of their lives plummet away, jerking from day to decade with ever-increasing speed and an ever-dwindling sense of control.

But then genius always opts for strange choices. Beethoven makes the last movement of his last symphony swell with song; Monet paints the same façade five times from the same point of view; Shakespeare forces a mad king, a fool, and a bedlamite beggar out into the windswept night – and we would not wish any of those moves unmade. *Ada* will one day seem as natural, as justified, as impossible to do without. Its quirks testify not, as some critics have thought, to idle caprice or a failure of distance and design but to Nabokov's desire to express more than he ever has before: "My purpose is not to be facetiously flashy or grotesquely obscure but to express what I feel and think with the utmost truthfulness and perception."[2] Never in more perfect command of his material, he fractures his world and reassembles it not simply for the fun of it all – though that is real enough – but in order to reexamine it more thoroughly than ever before.

II

Lecturing to his students at Cornell and Harvard, Nabokov always stressed that great writers are above all great enchanters. In *Ada* he offers enchantment itself in the story of Van and Ada's extraordinary affair, which dominates the novel from start to finish. Against all the odds, their rapturous first love for each other, in their early teens, proves also to be serene last love, as they reflect in old, old age on the summer, so remote, so near, when they first fell in love. Here Nabokov fuses two of his brightest themes – first love and the might of memory – with the theme of faithful married love, which he normally treats only by reticence (Fyodor and Zina, himself and Véra, John and Sybil Shade), by ironic or tragic negation (the Dreyers, the Luzhins, the Kretschmars, the Humberts, the Pnins) or through the pain of loss (Chorb, Sineusov, Krug). As brother and sister, Van and Ada cannot marry, but they spend their last forty-five years happily together. Their good-luck story wards off even the threat of lonely bereavement that might stretch its shadow over their sunset love, for they die together in their nineties: as if *into* the manuscript record of their past that they continue to revise until the last, as if into the timeless romance of their love.

Ada's special texture adds to its strange allure. A psychologist and a philosopher, Van Veen in 1922 writes *The Texture of Time*, one of his major works, and reprints it in toto as Part 4 of *Ada. Ada* itself, which he writes and revises between 1957 and 1967, is in a sense an expansion of the ideas of his earlier treatise. Van – with Nabokov behind him – deliberately sets up multiple rhythms of time and multiple relationships to time to turn *Ada* into an extraordinary study of that most elusive of concepts: but time as pure passion, not a cerebral abstraction.

In *The Texture of Time* Van severs space from time and rejects time as direction even as he is driving headlong across Switzerland toward Ada. In *Ada*, in similar fashion, he appears to concede the idea of time's direction only to turn around and challenge it. Part 1 of the book, more than half its length, covers two summers Van spends at Ardis manor with Ada: their first summer together, in 1884, and a second, four years later, in 1888. "Ardis the First," his 1884 sojourn, begins with the fourteen-year-old Van's initial distaste for his "cousin" rapidly turning to love and to agonies of impossible yearning: after all, Ada is only twelve, she is his cousin, he dare not even show his interest in her for fear that she might recoil in disgust or raise the alarm. Then starts the headlong slide towards the consummation of their love – a swift, undeviating advance that would itself seem to confirm what Van the philosopher dismisses as "the direction of Time, the ardis of Time, one-way Time." But what really stirs our own sense of excited anticipation as we read is that we already know that their love is a fact. Each early phase in their coming together has become a milestone that we are allowed to see immediately they will fondly recall: "When I kiss you *here*, he said to her years later, I always remember that blue morning on the balcony...." And what makes the Ardis scenes so enchanting is not the speed of their love, not the "ardis of Time," but that their time seems so expansive, so timeless, stretching out like any child's unending summer, and with detail after detail still immediate and intact eighty years later.

Van returns to Ardis in 1888, having seen Ada over the last four years on only two occasions, for an hour apiece. Dreading that time will have changed everything, he arrives "unexpected, unbidden, unneeded; with a diamond necklace coiled loose in his pocket. As he approached from a side lawn, he saw a scene out of some new life being rehearsed for an unknown picture, without him, not for him." He sees Ada in the distance in a new long dress "with no sleeves, no ornaments, no memories," and watches Percy de Prey kiss her hand and then hold it while he speaks to her and then kiss it again. Van walks off in icy fury and tears the necklace he has brought for Ada "into thirty, forty glittering hailstones, some of which fell at her feet as she burst into the room" to tell him that he is wrong, that nothing has changed, that she loves only him. At this point Ardis the Second becomes a glorious retrieval of the past, a metaphysical triumph over time, never more magical than in the picnic for Ada's birthday that seems to replay detail after detail from the picnic on her birthday four years earlier. And then the miracle crashes to the ground: Van discovers Ada has been unfaithful not only with robust Percy de Prey but with the family's plaintive and pathetic music teacher, Philip Rack. In a rage, he storms from Ardis in pursuit of his foes.

When Part 1 introduces young Van and Ada falling in love we also see behind them or through them the old Van and Ada collaborating fondly on the story of their past, still passionately in love decades later. The sunflecked happiness of the Ardis sections, the gentle drift of time through those two summer idylls, the bright unity of season and setting, the magical retrieval of time, and the glimpse of old Van and Ada still in love establish powerful expectations for the rest of the book. They are rudely dashed. Part 2, only half as long as Part 1, is more than half over before the lovers meet again, four years later, when Ada at last overcomes Van's jealous resentment. The intervening chapters have seemed jagged and disturbingly disjunct, and when Van and Ada meet, it is not at Ardis. Ardis, indeed, will never recur.

Part 3 in turn is only half as long as Part 2, and we reach the eighth and last chapter of this Part before Van and Ada meet once more, twelve years later, for a short series of snatched adulterous trysts. Part 4 is not even half the length of Part 3, and now a whole seventeen years later in time. When Van and Ada see each other in fifty-year-old bodies, they are so shocked at each other's appearance and at their awkward unfamiliarity with each other that they abandon their attempt at reunion. Only on the last page of Part 4 – and the few remaining pages between right thumb and fingers warn that Part 5 cannot be much more than half of Part 4 – do Van and Ada at last stop the catastrophic slide of time, the rapid radioactive decay of their elemental passion.

Just before Part 4 closes, Van and Ada seem to have wasted their lives and their love. What can Part 5 retrieve, a meager sixteenth of Part 1? But Part 5 begins triumphantly: "I, Van Veen, salute you, life, Ada Veen, Dr Lagosse, Stepan Nootkin, Violet Knox, Ronald Oranger. Today is my ninety-seventh birthday...." And the triumph continues: by the time he writes that, Van has spent forty-two years of cloudless love with Ada, the last ten reworking the story of their enchanted beginnings at Ardis.

Time's arrow had seemed to be hurtling away with greater and greater speed through an ever colder and more ragged sky. But no matter how strong the force of expectation, it cannot determine the shape of the future: against all likelihood, Van and Ada's course changes utterly in 1922, and from that point on they live together in harmony for as long as almost any happily-married couple. Ultimately, time for Van and Ada has proved to be not an ineluctable arrow but a rhythm of passionate union and bitter separation and the continual accumulation of a fondly-shared past.

Ever since writing *The Tragedy of Mr Morn* in 1924, Nabokov had been searching for a way to express his sense of a human life evolving in time. Not until *Ada* did he find how to show all he wanted: life not as one-way motion, not as the dramatic action and reaction of forces narrowing relentlessly to some inescapable climax, but as something much freer, with surprising jolts and changes of direction that nevertheless in retrospect fall into a unique pattern that characterize one person's individual fate. And at the same time, *Ada* records rhythms that are common to us all: the seemingly endless expanse of childhood time, the accelerating collapse of the years, the steadily swelling stores of memory.

III

When Nabokov identified a great novel by its power to enchant, he meant by that its appeal to the alert imagination of the reader. If *Ada* as a whole has its fairy-tale spell, its parts often show that Nabokov's gift for individual scenes has never been more magical.

Take one typical scene. Twelve-year-old Ada, as Van explains, has her private philosophy of happiness: "An individual's life consisted of certain classified things: 'real things' which were unfrequent and priceless, simply 'things' which formed the routine stuff of life; and 'ghost things,' also called 'fogs,' such as fever, toothache, dreadful disappointments, and death. Three or more things occurring at the same time formed a 'tower.'...'Real towers'...were the joys of life." Shortly after his arrival at Ardis, before he and Ada dare voice their feelings, Van leaves the hammock in which he has slept out in the summer night and joins Ada on the balcony where she is having breakfast in the early-morning blue.

Her plump, stickily glistening lips smiled.

(When I kiss you *here*, he said to her years later, I always remember that blue morning on the balcony when you were eating a *tartine au miel*; so much better in French.)

The classical beauty of clover honey, smooth, pale, translucent, freely flowing from the spoon and soaking my love's bread and butter in liquid brass. The crumb steeped in nectar.

"Real thing?" he asked.

"Tower," she answered.

And the wasp.

The wasp was investigating her plate. Its body was throbbing.

"We shall try to eat one later," she observed, "but it must be *gorged* to taste good. Of course, it can't sting your tongue. No animal will touch a person's tongue. When a lion has finished a traveler, bones and all, he *always* leaves the man's tongue lying like that in the desert" (making a negligent gesture).

"I doubt it."

"It's a well-known mystery."

Her hair was well brushed that day and sheened darkly in contrast with the lusterless pallor of her neck and arms. She wore the striped tee shirt which in his lone fantasies he especially liked to peel off her twisting torso. The oil-cloth was divided into blue and white squares. A smear of honey stained what remained of the butter in its cool crock.

"All right. And the third Real Thing?"

She considered him. A fiery droplet in the wick of her mouth considered him. A three-colored velvet violet, of which she had done an aquarelle on the eve, considered him from its fluted crystal. She said nothing. She licked her spread fingers, still looking at him.

Van, getting no answer, left the balcony. Softly her tower crumbled in the sweet silent sun.

At this stage of the novel, Van has passed beyond the stage of wondering "Was she really pretty, at twelve? Did he want – would he ever want to caress her, to really caress her?" He has been initiated into her private "philosophy." He spends his nights haunted by his longing for Ada, and on this particular morning wakes up resolute: "He was fourteen and a half; he was burning and bold; he would have her fiercely some day!" But when he sees her his desire has to remain as mute as here.

The scene is shot through with the tension between anticipation of an impossible dream and fond recollection after the dream has come true. Almost before the scene starts, Van recalls passionately recollecting it to Ada years later; within the scene, he silently anticipates ("my love's bread and butter") a happiness he still has no knowledge will ever come to pass. The crumb steeped in nectar, the throbbing wasp, the oilcloth, the honey-smeared butter define in an instant the space within which silent expectation stirs. Around the little that happens we feel the pressure of what doesn't happen – Ada doesn't tell Van that his presence makes the moment "priceless," that he is her third "Real Thing" – and what we anticipate *will* happen, that Van will find out that Ada, far from being too young for love, already adores and desires him. Young Van doesn't know this; young Ada can't simply tell him; but we and the older Van and Ada all know it – and we all look forward to the moment when young Van and Ada can frankly declare their love and recall to each other this moment and the feelings they dared not voice.

IV

Alongside the enchantment of much of *Ada* there also seems much that some readers find anything but enchanting. Three aspects of the novel particularly rankle: its sheer difficulty, or rather the sense it continually imparts that one may have missed this or that local obscurity, recondite allusion, half-buried joke; its lack of form, its centripetal sallies, its eruptive heterogeneity; and the attitude towards Van and Ada that the book seems to invite. John Updike, one of Nabokov's most enthusiastic readers, begins his review of *Ada* by declaring that "when a book fails to agree with a reader, it is either because the author has failed to realize his intentions or because his intentions are disagreeable," and then proceeds to quote *Ada*'s first speech in the first full scene of the novel, at the end of the first chapter.[3] Let us look at that scene.

After a tangled summary of marital relationships that parodies the family forebears paraded across the portico of many a nineteenth-century novel – Aqua Durmanov has married her cousin Demon Veen, her twin sister Marina has married her, Aqua's and Demon's cousin Dan Veen – Part 1 Chapter 1 discloses two naked and unnamed children rummaging in the attic at Ardis Hall. They have come across evidence of their parents' past: a wedding photograph in a newspaper, a reel of home movie, and a herbarium belonging to Marina. The leaves and flowers labelled in the middle of the herbarium, dated between September 1869 and March 1870, seem to act out "a regular little melodrama." To us, the sample entries are colorful but hardly much of a story:

> Golden [ginkgo] leaf: fallen out of book "The Truth about Terra" which Aqua gave me before going back to her Home. 14.XII.69.
> Artificial edelweiss brought by my new nurse with a note from Aqua saying it came from a "*mizernoe* and bizarre" Christmas Tree at the Home. 25.XII.69.
> Petal of orchid, one of 99 orchids, if you please, mailed to me yesterday, Special Delivery, *c'est bien le cas de le dire*, from Villa Armina, Alpes Maritimes. Have laid aside ten for Aqua to be taken to her at her Home. Ex en Valais,

Switzerland. "Snowing in Fate's crystal ball," as he used to say. (Date erased.)
   Gentiane de Koch, rare, brought by *lapochka* [darling] Lapiner from his "mute gentiarium" 5.I.1870.
   [blue-ink blot shaped accidentally like a flower, or improved felt-pen deletion] *Compliquaria compliquata* var. *aquamarina*. Ex, 15.I.70.

From this meager evidence the children make a host of fantastically elaborate deductions much more mystifying than the herbarium itself:

> "I deduce," said the boy, "three main facts: that not yet married Marina and her married sister hibernated in my *lieu de naissance*; that Marina had her own Dr. Krolik, *pour ainsi dire*; and that the orchids came from Demon who preferred to stay by the sea, his dark-blue great-grandmother."
>
> "I can add," said the girl, "that the petal belongs to the common Butterfly Orchis; that my mother was even crazier than her sister; and that the paper flower so cavalierly dismissed is a perfectly recognizable reproduction of an early-spring sanicle that I saw in profusion in hills in coastal California last February. Dr. Krolik, our local naturalist, to whom you, Van, have referred, as Jane Austen might have phrased it, for the sake of rapid narrative information (you recall Brown, don't you, Smith?), has determined the example I brought back from Sacramento to Ardis as the Bear-Foot, B,E,A,R, my love, not my foot or yours, or the Stabian flower girl's—an allusion, which your father, who, according to Blanche, is also mine, would understand like this" (American finger-snap). "You will be grateful," she continued, embracing him, "for my not mentioning its scientfic name. Incidentally the other foot – the *Pied de Lion* from that poor little Christmas larch, is by the same hand – possibly belonging to a very sick Chinese boy who came all the way from Barkley College."
>
> "Good for you, Pompeianella (whom *you* saw scattering her flowers in one of Uncle Dan's picture books, but whom *I* admired last summer in a Naples museum). Now don't you think we should resume our shorts and shirts and go down, and bury or burn this album at once, girl. Right?"
>
> "Right," answered Ada. "Destroy and forget. But we still have an hour before tea."

All *we* can deduce from this is that Van and Ada at fourteen and twelve are immeasurably bright, self-conscious and self-satisfied. From *Ada's* first sentence, we have been made aware that there may be much that eludes us in the world of this book. Now the young hero and heroine stand before us, glorying in the fact that nothing escapes *them*, and even – for they seem almost aware of us looking over their shoulders – deliberately shutting us out of any chance of understanding their exchange. Has their maker miscalculated?

Nabokov always values the excitement of discovery, but as a scientist, a scholar and a writer, he also recognizes the *effort* that discovery requires. He stresses the world's resistance to the mind that tries to apprehend it, as well as the delights ahead for the mind that exercises the curiosity and imagination to overcome as much of that resistance as it can. Never have these two sides of his epistemology played such a role in his fiction as in *Ada*. At one point, as Van and Ada meet for a last passionate tryst at the end of their first summer together, the novel lapses into code and emerges again, leaving us with a momentary twinge of frustration but at the same time tantalizing us. Is this scene simply too hot to print, even more ardent than all the vividly erotic scenes we have already been permitted to witness at Ardis? But the passage continues with Ada handing Van the code for their correspondence during their time apart – their incestuous relationship must of course remain a secret – and providing us at least with *some* reason for that burst of code. Still no key to the code, however, and the scene closes with no explanation of the ciphered words. Only in the next chapter do we find the code itself, and if we scurry back to "making *klv zdB AoyvBno...*" we can now read it as "making *his way through the brush and crossing a brook to reach* Ada in a natural bower of aspens; *they embraced.*" The promised Forbidden Masterpiece proves entirely innocent, and that joke itself is more than reward enough for the tease. Again and again throughout *Ada* Nabokov adopts the same tactics: an obvious obscurity, reminding us that we have no instant access to knowledge, and then a retrospective clarification, for those prepared to take the new evidence and search back for the hidden reward.

That is the pattern of the three chapters that comprise *Ada*'s prologue. The convoluted story of Van and Ada's parents obscurely glimpsed in the attic scene begins to unfold with dizzy speed and dashing romanticism in Demon and Marina's affair in the next chapter. Then in Part 1 Chapter 3, Van summarizes Aqua's uncertainty that she is really his mother:

> At one time Aqua believed that a stillborn male infant half a year old, a surprised little fetus, a fish of rubber that she had produced in her bath, in a *lieu de naissance* plainly marked X in her dreams, after skiing at full pulver into a larch stump, had somehow been saved and brought to her at the Nusshaus, with her sister's compliments, wrapped up in blood-soaked cotton wool, but perfectly alive and healthy, to be registered as her son Ivan Veen. At other moments she felt convinced that the child was her sister's, born out of wedlock, during an exhausting, yet highly romantic blizzard, in a mountain refuge....

When Aqua escapes from her next madhouse and rushes to Demon's house she finds all her things still in place in her bedroom: proof to her poor shattered mind that Demon has been faithful to her all along. In fact, Marina "had conceived, *c'est bien le cas de le dire*, the brilliant idea of having Demon divorce mad Aqua and marry Marina who thought (happily and correctly) she was pregnant again" – but when she smugly divulges her intentions, Demon throws her out of the house.

Nabokov intends the paragraph from which these two passages come as the key to his impossibly, parodically impenetrable exposition. No attentive reader should fail to note that the *"lieu de naissance,"* the *"X"* and the *"c'est bien le cas de le dire"* have occurred together before. Why the repetition? With only twenty pages to flick back through, we ought to have curiosity enough to begin the search. Once we track the phrases down to the attic scene, we realize we now have enough information to comprehend what Van and Ada deduce.

Demon and his cousin Marina have conducted an intense but on-again off-again affair from the beginning of 1868. In March 1869, "in the ecstasy of reconciliation neither remembered to dupe procreation," but before they discover Marina to be pregnant with Van, they have argued and parted again, and by late April Demon – who swoops through life at a breakneck pace – marries Marina's twin sister Aqua "out of spite and pity." She too becomes pregnant, but when Demon abandons her to return to Marina, Aqua has her first breakdown, retreating to a mountain sanitorium at Ex in Switzerland. Under cover of looking after Aqua, Marina conceals her own pregnancy from the world by retreating to Ex. Van is born on January 1, 1870 (the day Demon, with typically extravagant panache, sends those ninety-nine orchids). Two weeks later Aqua, six months pregnant and less than sane, skis into the stump of the larch that provided her Home with its Christmas tree. Her unborn child is killed, but Marina takes advantage of her sister's mental muddle to substitute her two-week-old Van for the bloody fetus. Two years later Marina again becomes pregnant by Demon. When Demon refuses to divorce Aqua and dismisses Marina for even suggesting the idea, Marina belatedly accepts the proposal her dull cousin Dan had made the previous year. Van is therefore raised as Demon and Aqua's child and Ada as Dan and Marina's, but they are full brother and sister.[4]

V

In the midst of writing *Ada*, Nabokov noted that "in art, as in nature, a glaring disadvantage may turn out to be a subtle protective device."[5] Not only does the swift, zany melodrama of Van and Ada's parentage more than compensate for the stilted stasis of the attic scene, but there is also fierce pleasure to be won from the realization that we can now construe what had seemed the incomprehensible evidence in the herbarium. In showing us that we can solve even something that appeared so opaque, if only we trust him enough to exert the effort, Nabokov invites us not to read on stolidly, page after page, but to look around, to explore, to discover, and he guarantees in advance that he will make the rewards behind any future difficulties worth the effort.

That in itself is a great part of his point in *Ada*, and in its introduction in particular. For what he has created here is nothing less than a parody of the very idea of narrative exposition, of an author carefully unfolding just what the reader needs to know in order to follow the tale about to commence. Information does not come to us a piece at a time, neatly labeled and sorted. Rather, this teeming world assaults us with more than we can assimilate, and Nabokov therefore violates conventional exposition for the very reason that the convention violates life.

His point is a serious one, arising from a considered and consistent epistemology. But that does not preclude his having fun – for after all part of his very epistemology is his sense that life keeps playful surprises hidden for us to find. Like a good nineteenth-century novel, *Ada* in its attic scene presents us with all the family relationships we must master, only to proffer them in such profusion that the exposition seems to expose nothing – until the ensuing chapters allow us to discover what we need to know. But nothing could be less like a nineteenth-century novel, less like the worlds of meek Fanny Price, Amelia Sedley or Esther Summerson, than an exposition that exposes little Ada standing there naked in the first scene of the novel, before her naked brother and lover.

Nabokov pushes the parody further as he takes aim at two other stock story-telling devices older than Oedipus: a mysterious birth, and the recognition scene that uncovers this mystery. In tragedy, the hero is likely to have already married his mother or his sister when the grim disclosure comes. In comedy or romance, a humble shepherdess may be prevented from marrying her noble lover until she suddenly proves to be of noble origin. Or a more sophisticated kind of comedy may merely toy with tragedy's horrified reaction to incest, leaving the characters aghast – that Fanny should be the sister of Joseph Andrews, that Mrs Waters should be the mother of Tom Jones – even as we recognize from the book's overall comic tone that the relationship will somehow prove *not* to be taboo. We are doubly caught, by ironic amusement at the unnecessary lamentations of the stricken characters and by tantalized curiosity: how will a second recognition scene dispel the shadow of incest?

Nabokov can parody the tradition of the mysterious birth and the recognition scene in which incest is discovered much more radically than was possible for Fielding. In the best romantic manner the circumstances of *both* lovers' births have been hidden and are both discovered together. Since they have already become lovers before finding out they are brother and sister, Van and Ada ought to be destined for tragedy. Yet far from being a cataclysmic horror, or even the toyed-with shadow of that horror, the disclosure which would be a dramatic peak in a traditional tale passes almost unnoticed and is quietly dismissed. To Van and Ada it is no more than welcome additional proof of the specialness of their case and of the naturalness of their mental harmony. They will continue to be the passionate and lucky lovers at the center of the tale: not only is their relationship not shattered, but it will endure for more than eighty years to come. Just where Van and Ada flout the oldest of taboos, Nabokov himself upends all the rules of his craft by piling right on top of his exposition the recognition scene that should come only after long delay and steadily rising suspense, to hurtle us down towards a final dénouement. In an exposition that at first glance seems to refuse to tell us anything, Nabokov lets us in on much more of the plot than we had any right to expect. And just where the characters of a traditional tale would be overwhelmed with revulsion, Ada turns to naked Van and tells him there's still time for another round of lovemaking before tea.

VI

Nabokov's care in controlling the complexities of the attic scene and his mastery of structure as he parodies its expository role should help allay the first two of the common objections to *Ada*. What of the third, the attitude Nabokov expects us to take towards Van and Ada? Does he not have too little distance from his inordinately gifted protagonists?

There is much to enchant in the story of Van and Ada's passion, and in the final passage of the novel, Van's lyrical built-in blurb, he stresses *only* the enchantment. That attitude pervades the attic scene. As the celebrant of his past, Van in his role as narrator seeks to reveal the uniqueness of young Van and Ada: their brilliance, their uncommon and even uncanny affinity; the carefree quality of their incestuous love. The capacity of this fourteen-year-old boy and his twelve-year-old sister to deduce as much as they do from the very spare, very oblique evidence in the herbarium is awesome, and it is amusing and exactly right that two bright young "cousins" who not long ago were strangers and are still eager to command each other's admiration should engage in this contest of mutual one-upmanship.

Yet there is also something decidely distasteful about his arcane exchange. Since Ada is consciously trying to outdo her brother, it is perfectly plausible that her "I can add...that...; that...; and that..." should echo so exactly Van's "I deduce...that...; that...; and that...." To Van the narrator, the similarity of the children's remarks proves the singularity of their mental kinship. But to us the similarity can only seem an unattractive basis for the children's love. Van and Ada feel so attracted to each other precisely because they are so unnaturally alike: each has found a duplicate self to worship. Passionate love for someone else proves unpleasantly close to ardent self-love, as if Narcissus were to find that the adoring Echo and the reflection he yearns for are one.

Not only are Van and Ada eerily alike, but their exceptional giftedness also makes them unlike everybody else. That Van and Ada sense this difference and relish it and augment it is evident in every detail of the conversation. They are proud that they can deduce what others could not, proud of their ability to respond to and take even further each other's cryptic concision. They elaborate their sentences as if for an audience that is deliberately being shown it cannot comprehend, as if they wish to stress and savor their superiority to any imaginable listener. Their pride blazes like a ring of fire set to mark out the charmed circle of their understanding and to keep the rest of the world at bay.

Van and Ada's dialogue jars, and I think it is meant to jar. But why?

Nabokov wrote of his chess problems, but with an eye to his novels, that although he tried to conform "to classical rules, such as economy of force, unity, weeding out of loose ends, I was always ready to sacrifice purity of form to the exigencies of fantastic content, causing form to bulge and burst like a small furious devil."[6] *Ada*, the story of the two children of a man named Demon, is full of these furious little devils. Of course, the novel has its own special harmony of form, in the rhythm of Van and Ada's meetings and partings, the accelerating decline of the years, and their triumphant final reunion that allows them to bask in the radiant, lingering recollection of their first falling in love. As the attic scene suggests, too, *Ada* has other architectural lines of development kept under strict authorial control. But again and again Nabokov disrupts the novel's sense of balance by sudden outbursts of obscurity from the overexcited pen of Van Veen or the overexcited mouths of Van and his sister. In her first speech, twelve-year-old Ada, with her extraordinary vocabulary and syntax, her casual mastery of botanical taxonomy, literature, and Roman art, and her evident immodesty in displaying the range of her knowledge and the speed of her thought, typifies the novel's sudden, strange, bewildering eruptions of multiple allusion, multilingual punning, multilayered arcana.

At such moments, all three of the major problems in reading the novel fuse: opacity of sense, apparent imbalance of design, unease with character. Has Nabokov succumbed to the temptation simply to dazzle us with his own cleverness, and can he not see how unattractive that impulse would be? On the contrary, I suggest, far from showing off, Nabokov has never kept so much of his own design so well concealed.

Van and Ada submit passages like their exchange in the attic as proof of their own brilliance. Nabokov lets us read them instead as evidence of their self-satisfaction – and their dishonesty. As narrator, Van playfully calls himself and Ada in this scene "Nicky and Pimpernella" or "Pimpernel and Nicolette," in honor of a newspaper comic strip they unearth in the attic, "the now long defunct Goodnight Kids, Nicky and Pimpernella (sweet siblings who shared a narrow bed)." As a character within the scene, young Van responds to Ada's reference to the famous fresco of the flower girl from Stabia, near Pompeii, by calling her "Pompeianella," as if he has overheard the nicknames in old Van's narrative – or as if old Van, pen in hand, has polished and repolished the ostensibly impromptu brilliance of his young self and his sister. Insisting on absolute fidelity to memory, Nabokov himself kept dialogue out of his memoirs, knowing that no one can recall conversations accurately decades after the fact. Van on the other hand loads *his* memoirs with masses of extended, intricately elaborate dialogue supposedly recollected eighty years later. Or rather, as we should suspect, he reworks all that direct speech, during the ten years he spends writing the book, in order to exaggerate the flair of the young Veens. As Nabokov commented in an interview, Van Veen could have exerted a good deal more self-control over his memory than he chose to.[7]

Amidst all the enchantment, the romance, the color and comedy of *Ada*, the book's lapses into smartness of tone or its sudden squalls of exhibitionistic allusion can set the teeth on edge. But Nabokov knows what he is doing. Just as he shows that for the human mind the delights of discovery are inextricably related to the frustrations of opaque fact, just as he portrays glory and grief as inevitably intermingled even in what seems the fairy-tale world of Ardis and Antiterra, so he suggests that even minds with such effortless command and range as young Van and Ada seem to disclose in that attic scene can have their own severe limitations and their blindnesses. And while "vain Van Veen" and his no less competitive sister happily indulge in abstruse self-display, Nabokov behind them has prepared and quietly concealed still more surprises for those who care to look.

VII

The attic scene introduces us to Van and Ada as lovers not simply unperturbed by their discovery that they are not cousins but brother and sister, but positively smug at the evidence that their closeness excludes the outside world. But this first scene also marks the exclusion of their half-sister Lucette – and her tragic involvement in Van and Ada's affairs.

Lucette receives one throwaway line in the attic scene. After recording Ada's birth and making it clear she is Demon's child, although her mother is married to Dan, Van notes: "Another daughter, this time Dan's very own, followed on January 3, 1876." Later we learn how this little girl becomes enmeshed in Van and Ada's fate. As the older siblings make love at Ardis, they have to evade Lucette's natural curiosity. In the desperation of desire, they try all sorts of stratagems.

In one scene, perhaps the most fateful of all, Van manipulates Lucette's affections before stealing off with Ada to the attic. Mustering all his charm, he tells Lucette in a conspiratorial whisper that he will present her with his book of "the most beautiful and famous short poems in the English language," "one of my most treasured possessions," if she can go to her room and learn an eight-line poem by heart in an hour.

> "You and I" (whispering) "are going to prove to your nasty arrogant sister that stupid little Lucette can do anything. If" (lightly brushing her bobbed hair with his lips), "if, my sweet, you can recite it and confound Ada by not making one single slip – you must be careful about the 'here-there' and the 'this-that,' and every other detail – *if* you can do it then I shall give you this valuable book for keeps...."
> "Oh, Van, how lovely of you," said Lucette, slowly entering her room....
> Van hastened to join Ada in the attic.

Van is proud of his stratagem at the time, but he recalls this moment with a grim shiver seventeen years later when Lucette drowns herself out of thwarted love for him.

At the age of eight, Lucette falls in love with her big "cousin" visiting Ardis for the first time. She succumbs to his charm, she imitates her big sister's passion, and she falls victim to Van and Ada's playing upon her devotion. She is also initiated into sex far too early: she cannot help knowing Ada and Van are up to something in this or that corner of manor or park, and like any eight-year-old child she cannot resist stealthily satisfying her curiosity. At twelve, on Van's next visit to Ardis, she finds herself caressed by Van at Ada's instigation – ostensibly to confuse the child and make it impossible for her to complain of Van and Ada's own caresses, but also to distract Van while Ada tries to wind up her affairs with Philip Rack and Percy de Prey. Two years later, with Van still refusing to forgive Ada and with Ada as sexually insatiable as ever, fourteen-year-old Lucette is introduced by her sister to lesbian lovemaking. When Lucette is sixteen, Ada pulls her into bed with herself and Van and leads Van's fingers over with her own to fondle Lucette, stretched out "in a martyr's pudibund swoon" – until Van ejaculates and Lucette can make her escape.

At twenty-five, despite this whole series of too-early initiations, Lucette remains a virgin, emotionally frail, compulsively but helplessly in love with Van. Hearing that he has booked a passage on a transatlantic liner, she joins the ship, determined to seduce Van – who has accepted Demon's edict that he must not see Ada while their parents remain alive – or to commit suicide if she fails. Before leaving Paris, she writes a letter to Van's American address, just in case he fails to turn up on the crossing. In that letter, which Van receives

only after her death, she cites the whole poem she had proudly learnt at eight
– while Van and Ada were in the attic.

Unlike Van and Ada's cryptic exchanges, Nabokov's essential points are not
designed to shut others out. They simply require that we observe, remember, and connect. In order to decipher the melodrama in the herbarium for
ourselves, we had only to recall and return to the attic scene as soon as we
read about Aqua two chapters later. That was an easy clue, an enticement to
the kind of active participation that reading *Ada* demands. The next, more
unexpected discovery about the attic scene is a little more difficult – the scene
of Lucette being cajoled into learning the poem by heart occurs more than a
hundred pages after the attic scene, and three hundred pages before her death
– but Nabokov leaves it up to us to discover that what matters most about the
attic scene is the little girl shut right out. Van and Ada in that dusty room may
celebrate a passion that excludes the rest of the world, but they have already
ensnared someone else's fate with theirs.

VIII

At first it may seem absurd to suggest that Lucette's absence from the attic
scene is almost the very point of the novel's opening scene. But the more one
reads *Ada*, the more the little girl whom Van and Ada overlook and shove
aside as they blindly pursue their passion comes to stand at the very center
of the novel. There is no space here for the detailed evidence; interested
readers may consult Part Three of my *Nabokov's* Ada. Let me simply restate
some conclusions.

Van and Ada are brilliant, ardent, eloquent. They claim that they are special,
a law unto themselves, and that their passion exalts them above all normal
considerations. But we all seem special to ourselves, and Van and Ada, with
all their prodigious good fortune and their concomitant self-esteem, are at
one level simply this private sense writ large. They act as if they *are* Antiterra,
a world unto themselves.

Nabokov demurs. We cannot be worlds of our own. We would not be
human without our contact with others, and the joys Van and Ada celebrate
depend on being able to share so much of each other's feelings. With the
privilege open to human consciousness of being able to imagine another's
feelings comes the responsibility to avert another's pain.

Whether or not we choose to attend to the feelings of others whom our
behavior affects is of course up to us. Van and Ada at first treat Lucette as no
more than a fetching but ordinary and ultimately irrelevant little sister who
makes a nuisance of herself by getting in the way of their extraordinary passion.
But she cannot be simply set aside: as innumerable patterns running through
Ada clearly demonstrate, her fate is inextricably involved with theirs.

That is the real point of the novel's incest theme. Family life and family love reveal us at our most interdependent, our most vulnerable. Never are we more responsible than within the family for the ways our lives touch those immediately around us. *Ada*'s playful allusions to Chateaubriand appear to make light of the whole subject of incest,[8] but good readers will recall or discover that Chateaubriand's beloved sister Lucile is thought to have committed suicide, and will note that the first Chateaubriand allusion in the novel refers only to Lucette, and that every subsequent allusion also involves Lucette or prefigures her death.[9] Van and Ada may dismiss incest, but Nabokov does not. Though Van and Ada's mental toughness leaves *them* quite unscathed, the bewildering secret of their passion turns the much more normal Lucette into a hysterical, frail, sex-obsessed young woman, headed for disaster.

Nabokov chooses incest as a standard by which to assess all human responsibility. Van and Ada celebrate to the hilt the joys of their love. Behind them Nabokov insists that the price of all the pleasure we can have through our intimate interconnections with others is our responsibility to others to the degree that our fates are linked with theirs.

IX

Aboard the *Tobakoff* on the last night of her life, as she sits beside Van while they watch a pre-release movie, Lucette hopes that her looks and her passionate proximity have won Van over at last. From the shockingly unexpected moment when Ada appears on the cinema screen – like her mother, Marina, Ada has become an actress – Lucette senses Van start to slip out of her spell again. Almost immediately, three prim old maids walk out of the cinema in disgust at the role Ada plays, and the Robinson couple – "old bores of the family" – sidle up and plump down next to Lucette. Although she needs desperately to reapply pressure on Van, Lucette turns to the Robinsons "with her last, last, last free gift of staunch courtesy that was stronger than failure and death." Van seizes the opportunity to make his escape. Safe in his room, he masturbates twice to rid himself of the sexual excitement Lucette has aroused all day and to immunize himself against any renewal of the temptation: after all, he does not want to complicate his, Ada's and Lucette's lives any further. When Lucette at last succeeds in extricating herself from the Robinsons and calls him up from her cabin, he feigns to have another woman there. Admitting defeat in her last-ditch attempt to win Van's love, Lucette stuffs herself with sleeping pills and jumps overboard to her death.

Her simple politeness toward the Robinsons, her refusal to show anything less than kindness even to people she does not care for and in the face of her own overwhelming need, represents for Nabokov human conduct at its most heroic. Contrast that with the way Van and Ada, in the imperious throes of their passion, treat not near-strangers but their susceptible little sister: they manipulate her affections, they play on her fears, they lock her up, they deprive her of her innocence with no regard to the consequences.

By a whole array of oblique, concealed, but precisely calibrated inter-connections, Nabokov sets Lucette up as a silent standard by which to judge all of Van and Ada's conduct: Van's fierce jealousy and sexual hypocrisy, his viciousness in dealing with his rivals or foes, his casually exploitative attitude towards women, his casual dismissal of the men he cuckolds; Ada's sexual insatiability, her thoughtlessness, her deliberate and elaborate duplicity. Again and again he associates their shortcomings, from sneering scorn for others to out-and-out savagery, with the passionate self-centeredness that allows them to overlook Lucette until it is too late.

By means of Lucette, Nabokov makes *Ada* a radical exploration of the moral consequences of human consciousness. He lets Van and Ada revel in the infinity of their emotion for each other, and then shows the absurdity of their acting as if the privilege of such feeling could exist without their being interconnected with other lives and without their being responsible for each of those interconnections. Subjecting his hero and heroine to rigorous scrutiny, he sets out an exhaustive criticism of the romantic egotism that in certain lights and at certain moments they can make seem so seductive. And he shows that even the greatest gifts of consciousness offer insufficient protection against the blindness of the ego – unless, like Lucette politely greeting the Robinsons, we remain determined not to let the tumult of our own feelings cause even the slightest injury to innocent others.

But Nabokov does not point out the flaws in Van and Ada's conduct from the beginning. In telling their story, Van and Ada celebrate their love in scenes like that breakfast on the balcony whose charm few can resist. Nabokov lets this charm inveigle us into dismissing Lucette, until it is too late, as no more than an amusing impediment to Van and Ada's resplendent love. He grants them such romantic verve, he makes us so eager for their next radiant reunion, that we can easily overlook the way they behave towards others. When we discover how scrupulously Nabokov has assessed Van and Ada's every action by the standard of Lucette, it can come as a salutary shock to see how inattentive we have been, how easily we have succumbed to the partiality of Van's vision.

Yet *Ada* paints far too complex a picture of life to be a mere denunciation of Van and Ada from end to end. Much of their behavior may be repellent, and the book does not stint at exposing their flaws, but they are not moral monsters like Hermann or Axel Rex or Humbert Humbert. In their last forty-five years together they hurt nobody by their love. For sixty years Van has regretted his treatment of Lucette and now tries to incorporate that regret into *Ada*. He ends the novel with a euphoric blurb advertising the "pure joyousness and Arcadian innocence" of his idyll at Ardis. The blurb mocks itself: Van knows its buoyant blitheness reflects only his own first raptures at Ardis, not his later discovery that life always mixes radiance and remorse.

X

Now we must return once again to the scene in the attic. While Van and Ada make love there, Lucette learns by heart a short poem of Nabokov's invention. The poem depicts a dead person's ghost talking to a mortal, and we find its text only in a letter that Lucette sends Van before her last fatal voyage and that he reads only after her death. Lucette and letters – epistolary, alphabetical – form a strange pattern that extends throughout *Ada* and that reveals that Nabokov not only centers on Lucette *Ada*'s study of the moral responsibilities of consciousness, but that he also focusses upon her the novel's exploration of metaphysical possibilities beyond human consciousness.

Once again, I refer readers interested in the detailed evidence to *Nabokov's Ada*, in this case to Part Four (especially pp. 203–219, 248–253). Perhaps a few items in the pattern should be mentioned, to indicate its persistence and point. Estranged from Ada after her infidelities during their second summer at Ardis, Van publishes a novel, *Letters from Terra* – about communications from a planet many on Antiterra suppose a Next World – over the pseudonym "Voltemand," a letter-carrier in *Hamlet*. That year he receives a passionate love-letter from the fifteen-year-old Lucette, who, distraught by Ada's initiating her into lesbian love-play, puns "in an Ophelian frenzy on the feminine glans." Still full of the bitterness of jealousy, Van refuses even to receive the letters Ada sends him by special courier, until Lucette herself brings a letter from Ada to Van at Voltemand Hall, Kingston University. In the scene in which she delivers the letter – thus herself reenacting Voltemand's role – agitated Lucette hysterically recalls the letters for "clitoris" in an unforgettable game of Russian Scrabble she played with Van and Ada. Or, rather, she reminded Van of this in her first letter to him, which he now incorporates into her dialogue in the reconstructed scene, while he himself replies to her with the closing words of Hamlet's letter to Ophelia.

Before following Ophelia to a watery grave, Lucette mails to Van's Voltemand address her last-ever letter, which he reads only after her death, and which cites that poem about a ghost talking to a mortal. Four years later, before his first reunion with Ada since Lucette's death, Van dreams of Ada and Lucette fused as "one of the Vane sisters" – which psychologist Van can appreciate as an oneiric recombination of the letters of his first and last names, but which only we can recognize as an allusion to Nabokov's story where two dead sisters attempt to communicate with the unwitting narrator in an acrostic formed of the initial letters of the last paragraph in his story. Then, just before his next and final reunion with Ada, Van thinks of dead Lucette as a "bird of paradise" and "a mermaid in the groves of Atlantis" – phrases that echo not only the "bird of paradise" and "mermaid" he called her in his last letter to her, many years ago, but also the "micromermaid" he used to describe the heroine from Terra in his *Letters from Terra*.

The pattern reaches its climax at the turning point of the whole novel.

Despite their unabated love, Van and Ada appear to have squandered their adult years first in jealousy and bitterness, then in obedience to the edict issued by Demon – the one person other than Ada whom Van unequivocally respects – after he discovers his children cohabiting. To ensure they remain apart, Demon pressures Ada to marry Andrey Vinelander. In 1905, the year Demon dies, Van and Ada meet for a round of gleeful adultery in Mont Roux. Just when they are about to abscond together, Ada finds out that her husband is dying of tuberculosis. She cannot abandon him in such a condition – and then the poor fellow takes another seventeen years to die. After his death, fifty-year-old Ada and fifty-two-year-old Van agree to a reunion in Mont Roux.

Despite the lapse of almost two lonely decades, Van still hopes he can recapture his youthful past with Ada. When she reaches the hotel where the reunion is to take place, she calls up from the lobby to his room. Her young voice seems to vouch that they will be able to reconnect with their remote past, but when he descends, they find each other old and fat and almost strangers. A chance remark from a neighboring table momentarily promises to dispel the tension, but the awkwardness returns. The reunion is a failure. Issuing a flimsy pledge to see him soon, Ada declares she must dash for Geneva airport.

Despondent, Van ascends to his room, takes his nightly sleeping pill and – to keep his thoughts of Ada at bay until the pill takes effect – continues writing his *Texture of Time*. The next morning he wakes and thinks suddenly he *must* pursue Ada at once or lose her forever. Or should he simply leap from the balcony and down to his death? As he steps out on the balcony, he sees Ada standing on a balcony below:

> Pensively, youngly, voluptuously, she was scratching her thigh at the rise of the right buttock.... Would she look up? All her flowers turned to him, beaming, and she made the royal-grant gesture of lifting and offering him the mountains, the mist and the lake with three swans.
>
> He left the balcony and ran down a short spiral staircase to the fourth floor. In the pit of his stomach there sat the suspicion that it might not be room 410, as he conjectured, or even 414. What would happen if she had not understood, was not on the lookout? She had, she was.

When, "a little later," Van, kneeling and clearing his throat, was kissing her dear cold hands, gratefully, gratefully, in full defiance of death, with bad fate routed and her dreamy afterglow bending over him, she asked:

"Did you really think I had gone?"

"*Obmanshchitsa* (deceiver), *obmanshchitsa*," Van kept repeating with the fervor and gloat of blissful satiety.

"I told him to turn," she said, "somewhere near Morzhey ('morses' or 'walruses,' a Russian pun on 'Morges' – maybe a mermaid's message). And *you* slept, you could sleep!"

"I worked," he replied, "my first draft is done."

After it had seemed that one-way time would hurtle him inexorably, ever more rapidly, toward a desolate death, Van is now back with Ada for life. And he has finished his *Texture of Time* – the events of which have just borne out his argument better than he could ever have hoped. The future is utterly open: when he wrote his final arguments the night before, all his eager hopes for his reunion with Ada had been cruelly shattered; now, the next morning, against all expectation, she is back, and all their remoteness banished. Even better: Van's glimpse of Ada on the balcony below suddenly establishes a pattern running through all the key moments of their lives: that first glorious wasp-and-honey morning on the balcony at Ardis, and their last morning at Ardis in 1884; a single tryst, one morning near Ardis in 1886; their first and last mornings at Ardis in 1888; the first and last mornings of their Manhattan reunion in 1892–1893; and their first and last mornings at Mont Roux in 1905. Without that 1922 balcony scene to crown the pattern, it would never have been detected – and like so many other patterns in *Ada* it seems invisible even on a rereading, until unexpected and unmistakeably exact details[10] suddenly click together.[11] This present moment on the balcony at the end of *The Texture of Time* proves with a gasp of surprise Van's other point in his treatise – that it is the pattern of the past that matters more than anything else in time – and that for Van and Ada the triumphant pattern of their lives is the rhythm of their meetings and partings.

But what does it mean when Ada says: "I told him to turn...somewhere near Morzhey ('morses' or 'walruses,' a Russian pun on 'Morges'– maybe a mermaid's message)"? Morges is a real town more than halfway from Montreux to Geneva; "Morzhey" is Russian for "of walruses," and "morse," besides suggesting a Morse code message, is an English synonym for "walrus."[12] In the notes he appended to the Penguin edition of *Ada*, Nabokov glosses the "mermaid's message" as an "allusion to Lucette." Lucette of course has drowned twenty-one years earlier: Ada, it appears, jokingly suggests that her own change of mind, en route to Geneva airport, has been prompted by dead Lucette.

To us as readers who can detect all the paterns of Lucette and letters, Lucette and messages from the beyond, which converge on this pivotal point of the novel, that idea seems no mere joke, but a possibility Nabokov has woven throughout the novel.[13] He suggests that Lucette is on some kind of Terra – another world inaccessible from this Antiterra, with a different relation to time – and that Van, for all his lifelong attempts to probe the mysteries of that putative planet, has not been able to recognize even the message that makes all the difference to his and Ada's lives. Kindly Lucette induces Ada to return to Van, and she does so in such a way that their morning glimpse of each other will set the seal on the pattern of the magic mornings running through their lives, a pattern that can be seen only from her timeless point of vantage, or from ours, outside the novel's world and time.

XI

Van's lifelong effort as psychologist and philosopher to probe the mysteries of consciousness and time and Terra arise from his fascination with Aqua, the woman he thought of as mother until after her suicide in his fourteenth year. The novel traces the theme of Van's career as a minor-key parallel to the major-key theme of his love for Ada. Whenever he and Ada part, he returns to the sorry refuge of his work – a pattern that changes only when his career and his love fuse in the harmony of the novel's close, in *The Texture of Time* and the later works that he and Ada write together, ending with *Ada* itself.

Like the herbarium in the attic, *Ada*'s location on Antiterra and the planet's relation to our own had been a colorful but unexplained mystery in the novel's opening chapter. But like the herbarium, Antiterra and Terra become a good deal more comprehensible in the last of the three chapters that form the novel's prologue, as Van explains Aqua's madness and its relation to the widespread belief in the existence of Terra. The "L disaster" in the mid-nineteenth century, which somehow gave rise to the notion of Terra, is too well known to Van's Antiterran readers for him to retell the whole story. From what he does disclose, however, we can piece together that this global catastrophe somehow discredited electricity, even made it unmentionably obscene, at the same time as it spawned the idea of Terra. Terra – apparently our earth, as dimly envisaged by Antiterrans – matches Antiterra in terms of physical geography, but the history of the two planets has numerous mismatches,

> because a gap of up to a hundred years one way or another existed between the two earths; a gap marked by a bizarre confusion of directional signs at the crossroads of passing time with not *all* the no-longers of one world corresponding to the not-yets of the other. It was owing, among other things,

to this "scientifically ungraspable" concourse of divergences that minds *bien rangés* (not apt to unhobble hobgoblins), rejected Terra as a fad or fantom, and deranged minds (ready to plunge into any abyss) accepted it in support and token of their own irrationality.

Aqua, like other sick minds, "identified the notion of a Terra planet with that of another world and this 'Other World' got confused not only with the 'Next World' but with the Real World in us and beyond us." As her madness deepens, she reaches a stage where she imagines she can hear water talking, and feels tickled at the thought that "she, poor Aqua, had accidentally hit upon such a simple method of recording and transmitting speech, while technologists (the so-called Eggheads) all over the world were trying to make publicly utile and commercially rewarding the extremely elaborate and still very expensive, hydrodynamic telephones and other miserable gadgets that had gone...to the devil" with the banning of electricity.

In light of the later "mermaid's message" from drowned Lucette, in light of all the images throughout the novel that prefigure or picture her watery death, in light of her subliminal centrality to the whole novel, the terms of Aqua's madness suddenly look rather different. Nor is it any accident that the disaster which makes Antiterra so unlike our world and has "the singular effect of both causing and cursing the notion of 'Terra'" is known as "the L disaster," the first letter of Lucette's name,[14] or that the force that then becomes a surrogate for electricity, by some weird hydraulic principle, is water, the element in which Lucette drowns, the element which holds Antiterra together.

Before the herbarium scene, *Ada*'s first chapter introduces the four protagonists of the prologue:

> On April 23, 1869, in drizzly and warm, gauzy and green Kaluga, Aqua, aged twenty-five and afflicted with her usual vernal migraine, married Walter D. Veen, a Manhattan banker of ancient Anglo-Irish ancestry who had long conducted, and was soon to resume intermittently, a passionate affair with Marina. The latter, some time in 1871, married her first lover's first cousin, also Walter D. Veen, a quite as opulent, but much duller, chap.

Such blatant patterning – twins Aqua and Marina, and their husbands, two "Walters"[15] and so almost "water," or Aqua and Marina all over again – seem too preposterous to be anything but parody: a parody of all "family background," a parody of all character pairing and contrast.

Some readers are disturbed by patterns so obvious that they seem to be there for the pattern's sake alone, as if in mockery of all seriousness of intent. But those who persist can discover the point behind the pattern. Twins Aqua and Marina are tragically, inseparably commingled, as sisters Ada and Lucette will be a generation later, and the turbulent fates of the four elder Veens coalesce to sweep Aqua into a state of mind in which she first thinks she sees Terra, then thinks she hears water talking, then takes her own life. Her madness and death prefigure both Lucette's suicide, after *her* fatal entanglement with *her* sister, and the messages Lucette seems to send from her watery grave or from Terra the Fair.[16] Even the absurdly obtrusive quartet of aqueous names that stares us in the face right from the start of the novel, then, cannot be seen at full value until we understand Lucette's role as the representative of all those shoved aside by impatient passion and until we understand that her presence has shaped the whole world Van and Ada have seemed to claim for themselves.

In the same way Nabokov suggests throughout *Ada* that the pattern of our life may be right before our eyes but remain utterly meaningless so long as we stay trapped within human time. Through the special conditions of his art he invites us to retrace events until we end up in a new relation to the novel's time, until everything flashes with new meaning as we see more clearly than ever both the constraints of mortal life and the freedoms that might lie beyond.

Or are we not taking too seriously the absurd Aqua-Walter-Marina-Walter or the dorophones that gurgle and splutter their convulsive course through the novel? Isn't Nabokov simply having fun? May he not be saying that art is a game in a world that itself seems a game we cannot understand?

He has remarked however that only a single letter separates the comic from the cosmic.[17] In *Ada* he asks us whether there is not something playful behind life – not in the sense of something that reduces life to a meaningless game, but something that makes it all richer than we could ever have dreamed, richer even than this wondrous and well-stocked world.

XII

Ada works throughout by unexpected relationships beneath the apparent ones, just as Van and Ada turn out in that scene in the attic to be full brother and sister and not the cousins they seem. The whole novel in fact is among much else a study of the very idea of relationship. Before its first sentence, Nabokov sets out a family tree, as if to picture pure relationship in stark diagrammatic form. In the first paragraph of the novel's first chapter, he toys with the ideas of resemblance and difference, with the relations between part and whole, model and mimic, the individual literary work and its wider tradition, and provides the first glimpses of that constant play of similarity and dissimilarity, on large scale and small, between Antiterra and Terra. As the chapter draws to a close, up in Ardis's attic, he introduces not only incest – family relationships doubled back on themselves – but also that troubling similarity between Van and Ada.

As a lepidopterist interested in the distinctions and the connections between species, Nabokov had from an early age studied problems of resemblance and difference and relationship. He brooded on them at length in his lepidoptero-logical work in the 1940s: "The idea of 'species' is the idea of difference; the idea of 'genus' is the idea of similarity. What we do when trying to 'erect a genus'…is really the paradoxical attempt to demonstrate that certain objects that are dissimilar in one way are similar in another."[18] He returned to the problem again in his notes for the *Butterflies of Europe* project he worked on after he finished *Pale Fire* – where he has John Shade observe that "Resemblances are the shadows of differences"[19] – and before he began *Ada*.

Ada recreates in microcosm the way the mind apprehends its world through discovering more and more differences, more similarities, more relationships. In the most radical dismantling and recomposition of his world he has ever attempted, Nabokov constructs his Antiterra as if from scratch, compounding patterns of sound and word, color and contour, object and character, date and event, into networks whose very profusion mimics that of our own Terra and proves the greatest obstacle to disentangling their sense. But the sense is always there.

15. The Art and the Ardor of *Ada*[1]

"A garden in a concert hall and a picture gallery in the garden – that is one of my definitions of Proust's art," Nabokov used to tell his students.[2] *Ada*, Nabokov's longest novel, published at the height of his career, a summation of all his work and themes at the same time as it stands apart from the rest of his fiction, seems to invite a similar kind of definition: a picture gallery within a theater within a brothel decorated according to a Garden of Eden design.

Art and ardor have been Nabokovian themes from the first, from the glow of first love in his first novel, *Mary*, to the glory of last love in his last novel, *Look at the Harlequins!*, from an epigraph of Pushkin in his first novel to the artistic mise-en-abîme of his last.

In *Ada* he raises these themes to the $n+1$st power. Ada is Van's first love, he hers, and eighty years later they are still together, dying together into the pages of Van's memoir of his love for his Ada. And from the first glimpse of them naked in an attic – in a scene that begins "According to the Sunday supplement of a newspaper that had just begun to feature on its funnies page the now long defunct Goodnight Kids, Nicky and Pimpernella (sweet siblings who shared a narrow bed)"[3] – to the last glimpse of them dying together in bed, working on the master copy of *Ada* – "the master copy which the flat pale parents of the future Babes, in the brown-leaf Woods, a little book in the Ardis Hall nursery, could no longer prop up in the mysterious first picture: two people in one bed" – we see Van and Ada in terms of images of visual and verbal art.

Ada also focusses on a new theme, the theme of relationships, of resemblances and differences, identity and distinction, novelty and repetition. This may seem a curiously abstract subject for a novel, but Nabokov makes it colored, concrete and comic. Van and Ada are lovers, but also brother and sister, and apparent first cousins, second cousins and third cousins: the family tree at the beginning of the novel does not even begin to tell the truth about the complexities of this family's relationships. Van and Ada are also uncannily similar as well as pointedly contrasted, so that their relationship on occasions veers towards narcissism, on others towards fierce separation. They live on a planet, Antiterra, that at times seems identical with our Terra, at times its "sibling planet," at times as remote from Earth as "this world" is from the "next world." And their memoir begins by inverting the opening of *Anna Karenina*,

in a sentence on the very subject of resemblance and difference – "All happy
families are more or less dissimilar; all unhappy ones are more or less alike"
– that Van declares has "little if any relation to the story to be unfolded now":
an opening that raises the question of the relationship between the typical
and the unique, part and whole, translation and original, specimen (this novel)
and species (the novel as genre), life and art.

Far from making *Ada* flat and grey, the theme of relationship is perhaps
what makes this novel the most bizarrely textured and the most opulently
colored in Nabokov's entire oeuvre. In sentence after sentence, chapter after
chapter, Nabokov raises the question of the relationship of part to part by
his accumulation of fantastic, apparently capricious and centrifugal detail that
only much later proves to be under his complex control. A single sentence
not only introduces us to Marina Durmanov and Demon Veen but rushes us
into their breathless relationship:

> As an actress, she had none of the breath-taking quality that makes the skill of
> mimicry seem, at least while the show lasts, worth even more than the price
> of such footlights as insomnia, fancy, arrogant art; yet on that particular night,
> with soft snow falling beyond the plush and the paint, la Durmanska (who paid
> the great Scott, her impresario, seven thousand gold dollars a week for public-
> ity alone, plus a bonny bonus for every engagement) had been from the start
> of the trashy ephemeron (an American play based by some pretentious hack
> on a famous Russian romance) so dreamy, so lovely, so stirring, that Demon
> (not quite a gentleman in amorous matters) made a bet with his orchestra-seat
> neighbor, Prince N., bribed a series of green-room attendants, and then, in
> a cabinet reculé (as a French writer of an earlier century might have mysteri-
> ously called that little room in which the broken trumpet and poodle hoops
> of a forgotten clown, besides many dusty pots of colored grease, happened to
> be stored) proceeded to possess her between two scenes (Chapter Three and
> Four of the martyred novel).

I have written a book on *Ada*, and a chapter on it in *VNAY*, where I tried
to avoid repetition of the book by focussing on *Ada*'s first chapter as a microcosm of the whole. Let me see if I can avoid repetition again by focussing
on its second chapter, which starts with this wildly romantic scene between
Marina and Demon.

The whole of Part 1 Chapter 2 hurtles along at a reckless pace – Demon's
characteristic tempo – in a fast-forward version of what Nabokov, writing
of Lermontov, called "the traditional tale of romantic adventure (amorous
intrigue, jealousy, revenge, etc.)."[4]

The chapter falls into two parts. The first depicts the enchanted start of
Marina's and Demon's affair, as Demon swoops impetuously on his cousin and
makes her his mistress before the first Act and the sentence end. The scene

closes in pure glamor: snow-flakes have star-spangled Demon's top hat "when Marina in a black cloak slipped into [his] arms and swan-sleigh."

The second part shifts to the romance of jealousy and revenge. Demon's jealousy flares in mock-operatic mode. He finds out the identity of his probable rival; upon "being questioned in Demon's dungeon, Marina, laughing trillingly, wove a picturesque tissue of lies; then broke down, and confessed"; Demon chases after the Baron d'Onsky – across the Atlantic, in a petroloplane! – catches him in Nice, and wounds him with his sword in a swashbuckling duel.

Ada's first three chapters form a sort of expository prologue. Within this, Part 1 Chapter 2's role is to explain why not only Demon's wife Aqua but also her twin sister Marina should be pregnant to Demon late in 1869. After the duel Marina and Demon are reunited, and in their joy forget to "dupe procreation." But a few days later Demon denounces the mediocrity of Marina's gift as an actress, and the two angrily separate. Demon writes to her that he can never forget his image of her answering a certain long-distance phone call (more of this in a moment), that it would have haunted "whatever bliss might have attended our married life." Within four weeks of leaving Marina the perpetually headlong Demon has married Aqua "out of spite and pity."

The theater scene where Demon's affair with Marina begins is as full of art as of ardor. Nabokov toys with the relationship between art and life by allowing Pushkin's imaginary world to spill over into what within *Ada* we accept as the real world. Demon, while watching Marina play the part of *Eugene Onegin*'s Tatiana, makes a bet with his orchestra-seat neighbor – who is none other than Pushkin's character Prince N., Tatiana's husband – that he can seduce Marina/Tatiana. With great ease Demon passes beyond the curtain as if into Pushkin's world, and returns triumphant to the front of the house where there still sits (now "cuckolded") a character strayed from Pushkin. [5]

Nabokov uses the stage version of Pushkin's poem to focus on another kind of relationship between art and life: the effect on "real" characters of the romantic passion of a "make-believe" world. In the scene from *Eugene Onegin* that we watch with Demon, Tatiana writes passionately to Onegin (though she has met the young fop only once) under the influence of the novels she has read. Marina, portraying this girl inflamed by the romance of imagined worlds, is in turn set emotionally aquiver by the imagined world she evokes on stage, and Demon in turn finds himself aroused by her ardor.

The theme of the relationship of art to life spirals into another subject, the relationship of a work of art to its heritage. For this scene in the theater evokes two distinguished novelistic traditions. In one, a character – like Pushkin's Tatiana, Cervantes's Quixote, Austen's Catherine Morland, Flaubert's Emma Bovary, Joyce's Gerty MacDowell – lives under the spell of romantic conceptions derived from fictive worlds. And indeed Nabokov throughout *Ada* explores – especially in the way Van and Ada Veen repeat and add to myths of love, from Adam and Eve to Venus and Cupid – what René Girard labels "mimetic desire," the imitative nature of erotic love.[6]

The other novelistic tradition touched on here is the nineteenth-century set-piece of the theater scene. A perfect example occurs in *War and Peace*, where Natasha, at the opera, suddenly becomes infatuated with Anatoly Kuragin. At first, Natasha's incomprehension of the opera's artificiality is a damning Tolstoyan indictment of empty sophistication. Under her growing susceptibility to the contrived attention of Kuragin, however, she starts to enjoy the stage action and to see it as natural – a dire warning from Tolstoy that she has fallen for sham values and fake emotions.

Both traditions fuse in *Madame Bovary*. At the opera, where "elle se retrouvait dans les lectures de sa jeunesse, en plein Walter Scott" ("she found herself back again in the reading of her youth, in the midst of Walter Scott," II.xv), Emma is sighing and ready for passion even before Léon appears.

Nabokov upends these traditions. F. W. Bateson has pointed out that "the convention that the novel uses is different...from any other literary tradition: it is the *convention of doing without conventions*."[7] From *Ada*'s first sentence, Nabokov mocks the novel's habitual reluctance to admit that it is part of a novelistic tradition. He parodies the tradition of the character absorbed in a world of romance by doubling it: Marina aglow through playing the imagined Tatiana, who is herself aglow as she identifies with the extravagantly passionate heroines of sentimental romance. He parodies the theater tradition not simply by establishing a parallel between the amour in the audience and the passions represented on stage, but by having one cross with the other. Where Emma imagines loving Lagardy, Demon makes love to *la Durmanska*.

The second half of *Ada*'s second chapter shifts from the charms of falling in love to the pangs of jealousy. Demon first suspects Marina's infidelity in February 1869, when he rings her up long distance and she tells him she is "in Eve's state, hold the line, let me put on a *penyuar*." In a later letter to Marina he recalls this moment, speculating that "Instead, blocking my ear, you spoke, I suppose, to the man with whom you had spent the night." He is proved right. Some weeks after the phone call Demon discovers a previously unknown sketch of Eve, "a naked girl with a peach-like apple cupped in her half-raised hand sitting sideways on a convolvulus-garlanded support." He is delighted to be able to identify the sketch – which has for him "the additional appeal of recalling Marina when, rung out of a hotel bathroom by the phone, and perched on the arm of a chair, she muffled the receiver while asking her lover something" – as the work of Parmigianino. To verify his attribution of the drawing, Demon takes it to an art expert, Baron d'Onsky, who "had only to cast one glance at that raised shoulder and at certain vermiculated effects of delicate vegetation to confirm Demon's guess." The next day Demon finds out from a female friend of d'Onsky that he must have remarked to her on the similarity of the sketch to the naked Marina: when she says to Demon, "Curious how that appalling actress resembles 'Eve on the Clepsydrophone' in Parmigianino's famous picture," Demon retorts: "It is anything but famous." Since no one else could have seen the picture or known that it was by Parmigianino, it must have been d'Onsky himself who noticed the resemblance of the Eve to the undressed Marina. D'Onsky, Demon correctly concludes, must be his rival.

The "small pen-and-wash" that Demon has found is in fact a fusion of three Parmigianino works, the frescoes of Adam and of Eve in the vault of the church of Santa Maria della Steccata in Parma, and especially a small preparatory sketch, now in the Uffizi, for the figure of Adam. Adam's posture in the sketch corresponds exactly to the position Nabokov describes: someone sitting sideways on a support, with a peach-like apple cupped in his hand, and with a strikingly raised shoulder, a posture uncannily congruent with that of a person "perched on the arm of a chair," muffling the mouthpiece of a telephone and talking to someone else.[8]

Art and life cross over in Demon's jealousy, as in his first falling in love with Marina. But just as the theater scene also raises questions about the relationship between one work of art and another, or between one mode of art and others, so too does the Parmigianino painting. Because Nabokov here surprisingly picks up and plays with a suggestion from Proust.

Parmigianino, sketch of Adam for Santa Maria della Steccata, Parma (*Uffizi*)

Ada repeatedly and explicitly alludes to *A la Recherche du temps perdu.* Just before the second chapter begins, and Van introduces the story of Marina and Demon, there is a detailed discussion of Proust; later, when Van's jealousy of Ada first echoes Demon's jealousy of Marina, there is a long, pointedly Proustian diatribe on jealousy.

Here, behind the Parmigianino drawing that brings to mind Marina on the phone, stands a passage from "La Prisonnière." Marcel tries to ring Andrée, but the line is busy:

En attendant qu'elle eût achevé sa communication, je me demandais comment, puisque tant de peintres cherchent à renouveler les portraits féminins du XVIIIᵉ siècle où l'ingénieuse mise en scène est un prétexte aux expressions de l'attente, de la bouderie, de l'intérêt, de la rêverie, comment aucun de nos modernes Boucher...ne peignit, au lieu de "La Lettre", du "Clavecin" etc., cette scène qui pourrait s'appeler: "Devant le téléphone", et où naîtrait si spontanément sur les lèvres de l'écouteuse un sourire d'autant plus vrai qu'il sait n'être pas vu.[9]

While waiting for her to finish her call, I wondered why, since so many painters are seek to revive the feminine portraits of the XVIII century, in which the ingenious setting is a pretext for expressions of expectation, sulking, interest, reverie, why none of our modern Bouchers...had yet painted, instead of "The Letter" or "The Harpsichord" etc., this scene which could be called "On the Telephone," and in which there would come so spontaneously to the lips of the listener a smile all the more genuine because it knows it is not seen.

Nabokov gleefully appropriates Marcel's suggestion and executes his proposal, not by inventing a modern painting but by turning to an impeccably pre-telephonic old master.

But the link between one of the novel's women and an old master work is also an echo of Proust. Like Demon, Swann (alluded to explicitly later in *Ada*) is a connoisseur of the visual arts. Like Marina, Odette is an actress, and both are explicitly associated later by Marina's revulsion from the obscene and invented Cattleya Hawkmoth, a playful echo of the Cattleya orchid that becomes a symbol of passion and (as "*faire cattleya*") a code-word for lovemaking for Odette and Swann. (Indeed Nabokov drew a Cattleya orchid for the cover of the original Penguin paperback of *Ada*.) Just as Demon sees his Marina in terms of a Parmigianino sketch, so Swann sees his Odette in terms of a Botticelli fresco in the Sistine Chapel.

   Through the Demon-Marina-Parmigianino parallel to Swann-Odette-Botticelli, Nabokov acknowledges a significant debt: the love of Demon and Marina in Part 1 Chapter 2 foreshadows Van and Ada's love affair in Ardis the First and Ardis the Second in the main body of the novel, just as Swann and Odette's affair in "Un Amour de Swann" foreshadows Marcel's affair with Albertine. In Proust the lingering love and morbid jealousy of an affair in one generation recurs in the next: "mon amour pour Albertine avait répété, avec de grandes variations, l'amour de Swann pour Odette"[10] ("my love for Albertine had repeated, with great variations, Swann's love for Odette"). In *Ada*, the generations are actually parents and children, and the sharp division between the theater scene and the discovery of d'Onsky as an admirer of the Parmigianino's resemblance to Marina on the telephone in Part 1 Chapter 2 prefigures the marked distinction between the enchantment of falling in love in Ardis the First and the atmosphere of betrayal, suspicion, jealousy and fiery revenge in Ardis the Second. But whereas in Proust "Un Amour de Swann" occupies the length of an ordinary novel, in *Ada* the breakneck narrative of Demon's and Marina's affair takes only six pages.

There are more complications of allusion and structure in this one chapter of *Ada*,[11] but as is typical in this novel, the complicated artifice, far from interfering with the ardor, somehow augments its wild speed. But as is also typical of *Ada*, beneath the swift, coruscating surface lies a profusion of currents whose relationships are so entangled that the reader with the time to dive into them can easily feel swamped. But that, Nabokov seems to think, is just like life: the world swarms with pattern to a degree that we can hardly begin to appreciate, and for that very reason seems somehow intrinsically artistic.

Taking issue with Freud, Nabokov claimed that "sex is but the ancilla of art,"[12] that the artfulness of nature lies behind the allures and the wiles of sex, as it lies behind so much else. In a novel like *The Gift*, Nabokov quietly conceals the artfulness lurking behind the apparently aimless clutter of that novel's world. In *Ada*, he obtrudes art from the first, in the midst of the novel's ardor – in a parody of Pushkin, in a pastiche of Parmigianino – but only to conceal a much greater artfulness beyond.

16. *Ada*, or Amplitude[1]

Of all Nabokov's works, none divides readers more than *Ada*. Some consider it his richest fare, others his most indigestible. Just after its publication, Mary McCarthy's revulsion moved her to consider recanting her rapturous 1962 appraisal of *Pale Fire*.[2] On the other hand, I recall my thesis supervisor's trying to interest another academic friend in Nabokov, only to fail with novel after novel until *Ada* left him entranced.

Nabokov himself had no doubts. His father had once given him a copy of *Madame Bovary*, which he had inscribed "*livre génial – la perle de la littérature française*" ("a book of genius – the pearl of French literature"). In his own copy of *Ada*, Nabokov wrote on the flyleaf: "*genial'naia kniga – perl amerikanskoi literatury*" ("a book of genius – the pearl of American literature").[3] Though this may well be a joke, a playfully outrageous echo, an Antiterran paradox, there must also have been a grain of seriousness to provoke that "pearl" into being. After all, *Ada*'s long Part 1 opens with an echo of the opening of *Anna Karenin* and ends with an echo of the end of Part 1 of *Madame Bovary*, as if it were signaling its intention to vie with the greatest novels of the Russian and the French traditions. That, some readers would say, is precisely the problem. Like Van and Ada themselves, Nabokov has become too sure of himself.

Most of Nabokov's major novels stand apart from the others, *Invitation to a Beheading* by its irrealism, *The Gift* by its texture, *Lolita* by its subject, *Pale Fire* by its structure. *Ada* stands out in all these ways. *Invitation to a Beheading* may seem odd for Nabokov, yet fabulation runs through fiction from Apuleius to Zamiatin. But *Ada* combines the things that shore up realism – a plethora of dates (enough to annoy John Updike),[4] places and details – with anachronisms, anatopisms, and inventions (shattal trees, skybab squirrels, skimmers) that presuppose a minute knowledge of our real world but undermine it at every line. *The Gift*'s slow unfurling, its combination of mental mobility within physical stasis, marks it out from all Nabokov's other fiction, but not as much as *Ada*'s manic shifts in space and time, subject, reference and tone, within one centrifugal sentence after another. In the afterword to *Lolita*, Nabokov compared the unacceptability of its subject to American publishers with that of two other themes, "a Negro-White marriage which is a complete and glorious success resulting in lots of children and grandchildren; and the total atheist who lives a happy and useful life, and dies in his sleep at the age of 106." (314) In *Ada* he found something to match: an incestuous love affair (and between two hugely and happily wealthy aristocrats) that lasts from childhood to old age, becoming a marriage in all but name, with the couple dying together peacefully in their late 90s. *Pale Fire* strikes immediately by its novelty of form, by the crazy fissure between Shade's poem and Kinbote's so-called commentary. *Ada* by contrast seems at first to play with the tradition of the novel by ironic imitation, but as each part shrinks to half the length of its predecessor, as the time between each part expands into decades, as the focus of each part judders further from Ada herself, *Ada* seems no longer to be playing with the form of the novel but to be unable to reassert it, to be plummeting out of control.

But it is not these aspects of its originality that provoke distaste. I suspect there are two main reasons.

The first is that *Ada* obtrudes its own difficulty and yet confronts us with its playfulness, even flippancy. In many ways *Ada* is more demanding than *Ulysses*, and lets us know it:

> "All happy families are more or less dissimilar; all unhappy ones are more or less alike," says a great Russian writer in the beginning of a famous novel (*Anna Arkadievitch Karenina*, transfigured into English by R. G. Stonelower, Mount Tabor Ltd., 1880). That pronouncement has little if any relation to the story to be unfolded now, a family chronicle, the first part of which is, perhaps, closer to another Tolstoy work, *Detstvo i Otrochestvo* (*Childhood and Fatherland*, Pontius Press, 1858).
>
> Van's maternal grandmother Daria ("Dolly") Durmanov was the daughter of Prince Peter Zemski, Governor of Bras d'Or, an American province in the Northeast of our variegated country, who had married, in 1824, Mary O'Reilly, an Irish woman of fashion. Dolly, an only child, born in Bras, married in 1840, at the tender and wayward age of fifteen, General Ivan Durmanov, Commander of Yukon Fortress and peaceful country gentleman, with lands in the Severn Tories (Severnïya Territorii), that tesselated protectorate still lovingly called "Russian" Estoty, which commingles, granoblastically and organically, with "Russian" Canady.... (3)

Why the distortion of *Anna Karenin*'s opening in the first line? Why the distortion of Tolstoy's title? What lurks in the strange name of the invented translator "Stonelower"? Why has the press been called "Mount Tabor Ltd."? Why quote from *Anna Karenin* at all if it has "little if any relation to the story to be unfolded now"? What is that unfamiliar Tolstoy work, *Detstvo i Otrochestvo* (*Childhood and Fatherland*), and why has it been published by the suspiciously-named "Pontius Press"? Why are there Russians in North America? Why is Peter Zemski "Governor of Bras d'Or," wherever that is? Where are the "Severn Tories", and does the name really translate "Severnïya Territorii," and what does "tesselated" mean, and why does it commingle "granoblastically," whatever that means, with "'Russian' Canady," wherever that is?[5]

Now that is a lot of questions for the first twenty lines of a novel, closer to the enigmas of *Finnegans Wake* than the solid, impeccably rendered world of *Ulysses*. But *Finnegans Wake* takes on the whole of history, the whole of language, and the murkiness of the human mind in sleep. It is imbued with Joyce's characteristic rigor and extremism of method, and, anyway, it invites a few devotees, not a widespread audience. But *Ada* seems in many ways a grand old-fashioned novel, a straightforward, if kinky, love story, a series of colorful and even racy adventures. It appeals to a much larger readership than *Finnegans Wake* (it even became a number two bestseller in France), and then it rebuffs the audience with its difficulty *and* its levity, its apparent offhandedness. A book may earn the right to be difficult if it takes itself seriously, but not, surely, if it undermines itself at every step?

The second reason *Ada* might deter readers is that Van and Ada are brilliant, conceited, delighted to stress their difference from others around them and their uncanny similarity to each other. But they invite us to admire them and identify with them even as they remind us we could never be as brilliant as they. Can we believe in their brilliance? Do we not resent their arrogant superiority? Does Nabokov not realize how repellent he has made characters who seem both to see with his eyes and to see themselves as enchanting?

Yet there is a great deal of real enchantment in Van and Ada's story. A sense of wonder, of the unprecedented novelty and liberation of love, saturates the Ardis the First chapters of the novel: as Robert Alter comments, "the expression in *Ada* of a lover's consummated delight in life and beauty is an achievement that has few equals in the history of the novel."[6]

One of Nabokov's great gifts throughout his work has been to invent new structures for new stories. While he admired the technical innovations of *Ulysses*, he rejected the Homeric parallels because they did not arise out of the story of Stephen and Bloom.[7] *Pale Fire*'s daring new structure, on the other hand, flows with perfect naturalness from the situation of a demented *littérateur* who appropriates for his own use a poem he vainly hoped would commemorate the past he imagines. In *Ada* too, story and structure animate each other. Because Van and Ada experience the magic of first love together, and against all the odds share the glow and comfort of last love, they can compose together the story of their common – and uncommon – past. That shapes our response to their story. Because we can glimpse them together in old age happily recalling the first flush of passion, we are both eager to see their young love triumph and so confident that they will share their adult life that their long separations disappoint us almost as sharply as they do Van himself.

First love and last love meant a great deal to Nabokov. His love for Valentina Shulgina gave rise to poem after poem in his youth, to his first novel, *Mary*, to his autobiographical story "First Love," and, fifty years after the fact, to much of the magic of the "Ardis" section of *Ada*. His married love for Véra Nabokov inspired "The Return of Chorb," the story of Fyodor and Zina in *The Gift*, the harmony of the Shades in *Pale Fire*, and now the serenity of the Veens in old age.

In fact *Ada* as a whole reads like Nabokov's wish-fulfilment fantasy. For Van and Ada, the breathtaking shock of first love and the calm confidence of last love can be one and the same. They also have extraordinary intelligence, imagination, memory, sexual energy, physical prowess, material wealth, cultural capital, social status, even sheer longevity. The three languages Nabokov loved, Russian, French and English, are spoken cosily together in a North America that blends European traditions, aristocratic privilege, magical summers on lush nineteenth-century family estates, with a modern freedom of sexual mores and easy democratic equality, as if America need no longer be only an émigré's haven, but can become a complete return to the Europe of Nabokov's childhood. Has he invented the enchantments Antiterra offers the Veens as vicarious treats for VN?

Ada and Van themselves exult in all their advantages and invite us to share their delight in themselves. But good readers balk at this. Has Nabokov simply created in his heroes little Nabokovs whose unattractive sides he cannot see? Joyce Carol Oates writes that Nabokov "assigns worth – which may seem to us quite exaggerated, even ludicrous, as in *Ada* – to a few selected human beings."[8] John Updike wonders "But is it intentional that... the hero is such a brute?"[9]

The perplexity of the critics drove Nabokov to reply. Far from seeing and spoiling Van and Ada as surrogate Nabokovs, he declared that he loathed Van Veen and that he was outraged that a reviewer could suppose there was any trace of Véra Nabokov in "bitchy and lewd" Ada (*SO* 120, 146). Countering objections to *Ada*'s apparent combination of complexity and caprice, he remarked: "...the main favor I ask of the serious critic is sufficient perceptiveness to understand that whatever term or trope I use, my purpose is not to be facetiously flashy or grotesquely obscure but to express what I feel and think with the utmost truthfulness and perception." (*SO* 179)

How does the evidence of the text stand up to Nabokov's claims and disclaimers outside it? At the beginning of Part 1 Chapter 10, Van reports, entranced,

eleven-year-old Ada's precocious mealtime conversations. His interest in
Ada has already been roused but still remains confined to a mutual acknowl-
edgement of intellectual kinship, and, on Van's part, eager and (as he thinks)
vain longing. Van and Ada conspire together to keep Marina, their mother
(ostensibly only Van's aunt) from dominating the conversation with her boring
reminiscences of her days as an actress:

> Van: "That yellow thingum" (pointing at a floweret prettily depicted on an
> Eckercrown plate) " – is it a buttercup?"
>
> Ada: "No. That yellow flower is the common Marsh Marigold, *Caltha
> palustris*. In this country, peasants miscall it 'Cowslip,' though of course the
> true Cowslip, *Primula veris*, is a different plant altogether."
>
> "I see," said Van.
>
> "Yes, indeed," began Marina, "when I was playing Ophelia, the fact that I
> had once collected flowers – "
>
> "Helped, no doubt," said Ada. "Now the Russian word for marsh marigold
> is *Kuroslep* (which muzhiks in Tartary misapply, poor slaves, to the buttercup)
> or else *Kaluzhnitsa*, as used quite properly in Kaluga, U.S.A."
>
> "Ah," said Van.
>
> "As in the case of many flowers," Ada went on, with a mad scholar's quiet
> smile, "the unfortunate French name of our plant, *souci d'eau*, has been traduced
> or shall we say transfigured – "
>
> "Flowers into bloomers," punned Van Veen.
>
> "*Je vous en prie, mes enfants!*" put in Marina, who had been following the
> conversation with difficulty and now, through a secondary misunderstanding,
> thought the reference was to the undergarment.
>
> "By chance, this very morning," said Ada, not deigning to enlighten her
> mother, "our learned governess, who was also yours, Van, and who – "
>
> (First time she pronounced it – at that botanical lesson!)
>
> " – is pretty hard on English-speaking transmongrelizers – monkeys called
> 'ursine howlers' – though I suspect her reasons are more chauvinistic than
> artistic and moral – drew my attention – my wavering attention – to some really
> gorgeous bloomers, as you call them, Van, in a Mr. Fowlie's *soi-disant* literal
> version – called 'sensitive' in a recent Elsian rave – sensitive! – of *Mémoire*, a
> poem by Rimbaud (which she fortunately – and farsightedly – made me learn
> by heart, though I suspect she prefers Musset and Coppée)" –
>
> "*...les robes vertes et déteintes des fillettes...*" quoted Van triumphantly.
>
> "Egg-zactly" (mimicking Dan). "Well, Larivière allows me to read him only
> in the Feuilletin anthology, the same you have apparently, but I shall obtain his
> *oeuvres complètes* very soon, oh very soon, much sooner than anybody thinks.
> Incidentally, she will come down after tucking in Lucette, our darling copper-
> head who by now should be in her green nightgown – "

"*Angel moy*," pleaded Marina, "I'm sure Van cannot be interested in Lucette's nightdress!"

" – the nuance of willows, and counting the little sheep on her *ciel de lit* which Fowlie turns into 'the *sky's bed*' instead of 'bed ceiler.' But, to go back to our poor flower. The forged *louis d'or* in that collection of fouled French is the transformation of *souci d'eau* (our marsh marigold) into the asinine 'care of the water' – although he had at his disposal dozens of synonyms, such as mollyblob, marybud, maybubble, and many other nicknames assocated with fertility feasts, whatever those are." (63–65)

Van knows nothing about taxonomy, and feeds a question to Ada to give her a chance to show off. Which she does, reducing him to a helpless "I see," a comically numbed "Ah." Marina tries to turn the conversation her way, but her sentence is crisply completed and her way curtly occluded by her daughter, and we agree we would rather not hear out the old bore. As Ada switches from the marsh marigold's name to its mistranslation from the French, Van perks up. Here he can relax, here he can play the game (and in fact he later shows himself a much better translator from the French than Ada), here he can throw in a pun of his own, while Marina shows herself even more helplessly out of her depth than ever. A sudden aside from Van in excited retrospect ("'who was also yours, Van, and who – ' (First time she pronounced it – at that botanical lesson!)") intensifies our anticipation, only for it to be buried in the torrent of Ada's talk.

This would be one of the thirty or so most difficult passages in *Ada*. Ada inundates us with masses of recondite information, all perfectly accurate, and she certainly enjoys her ability to dazzle Van and to talk over her mother's head. As readers, we could respond with irritation that Ada is obviously so much brighter than we were at eleven. Or we could respond to her mental powers with as much pleasure and amused awe as we did to stories of Pippi Longstocking's or Popeye's special physical powers. Because there is certainly an element of the fabulous here that mingles oddly – to my taste rather piquantly – with the pedantry.

And even the pedantry is fun. Ada's speech is simply so colorful ("*Kuroslep* (which muzhiks in Tartary misapply, poor slaves, to the buttercup)"), so mobile, so opinionated, so cocky, that it should amuse those who don't fear that someone else's magical brilliance is a put-down of their own prosaic powers (I wonder if people who react this way can read Sherlock Holmes?) or that they should know everything Ada happens to know.

Nabokov of course does not expect readers to know all Ada knows. That is the very point of the scene's humor and its drama. He manages to create scenes like this throughout *Ada*, where we may not know every (or even any) reference, but where the sheer flashing speed and bright detail easily compensate for the obscurity, and where we nevertheless readily understand the human drama, as we can enjoy here the interplay between Marina, Van and Ada: Marina's doomed attempts to control and direct, Van's avid amazement and his eagerness to show he can keep up with Ada whenever her topic allows him a chance, Ada's vivid delight in herself and her easy condescension to American peasants, Tartar muzhiks, her mother, her French governess, the translator Mr. Fowlie, the critic Elsie du Nord, her supposed father, in fact to everybody but Van.

But if Nabokov does not expect us to know everything here, he makes it possible for us to find out, and he makes it worth the effort. He criticized Joyce for the obscurity of the local referents in *Ulysses*, and he avoids them himself. He refers not to arcane ephemera or *Thom's Dublin Directory* but to a compact masterpiece of European literature, Rimbaud's "Mémoire," and by this and allusions elsewhere in the novel prompts us to read or reread it.

If we do, we will understand the weird looping aside Ada makes after Van's triumphant quotation from "Mémoire" (*"les robes vertes et déteintes des fillettes"*, "the green faded dresses of girls"). Politer to Van than to her mother, Ada acknowledges his interruption, which at least is pertinent, but maintains her own momentum on the subject of Mlle Larivière. As she continues, she recalls Van's line, and the green that her younger sister, red-headed Lucette, always wears, and responds belatedly with an impeccably controlled aside on "Lucette, our darling copperhead who by now should be in her green nightgown" that ends as she had planned, regardless of Marina's interruption, with an echo of the next phrase in Rimbaud's poem, "the nuance of willows."[10] Tracing Rimbaud's text allows us to savor another literary masterpiece in its own right, and to appreciate better details in *Ada* such as, here, the psychology behind rapid speech, and the comedy of Ada's impatient brilliance.

Nabokov also names the translator of Rimbaud's poem, whom he wishes to take to task for what are in fact quite astonishing blunders, if we take the trouble to check. As Ada points out, the worst "bloomer" of all in Wallace Fowlie's translation is his rendering the phrase *souci d'eau* not as "marsh marigold" but word by word as "care of the water," and so robbing the poem of a flower.[11]

We can check in dictionaries that the marsh marigold may be called "cowslip" in the US, or *kuroslep* or *kaluzhnitsa* in Russian, or *souci d'eau* in French. And we can also find that "mayblob" or "marybud" are names for, respectively, marsh marigold and marigold. Why then does Nabokov have Ada list "mollyblob, marybud, maybubble" as alternatives Fowlie could have used to translate *souci d'eau*?

This time the answer cannot be searched for. But anyone who knows *Ulysses* has the clue, and its precision confirms its correctness, as solutions to Nabokovian problems so often do. The suggestion of popping in "maybubble" combines with "mollyblob" to point unmistakably to Molly Bloom's famous musing on the blob of a ruptured hymen: "and they always want to see a stain on the bed to know youre a virgin for them…theyre such fools too you could be a widow or divorced 40 times over a daub of red ink would do or blackberry juice no thats too purply."[12]

For those who haven't read *Ulysses*, another route is possible – and again, this provision of multiple pathways to discovery is a standard Nabokovian tactic, a safeguard, a confirmation, and a reflection of the manysidedness of fact in the real world. The *"d'or… transformation… marigold… asinine"* at the beginning of the same sentence subliminally evokes the title of the Latin novel, the *Metamorphoses* or *The Golden Ass*. In Apuleius's famous tale, Lucius turns into an ass, and can be restored to himself by eating a rose. A flower in Fowlie's translation would turn the asinine transformation back to the original; or, in the terms of the Joyce allusion, Fowlie has "deflowered" Rimbaud's poem.

Now even Ada, for all her brilliance, cannot be aware of these allusions, speaking as she is spontaneously and at speed. Why then does Nabokov go to such trouble to align the loss of Rimbaud's *souci d'eau* with this stress on deflowering?

The answer lies in Ada's aside on Lucette. As Annapaola Cancogni comments, "in so far as Lucette habitually wears green, the [Rimbaud] line and the girl remain associated throughout the novel, and the poem."[13] And not only that. The tragedy of Lucette's fate is that she commits suicide after she fails to convince Van to deflower her. Entangled in the romance of Van and Ada, she becomes obsessed with Van, partly in immediate response to his charms, partly in imitation of her big sister, partly because their frenzied lovemaking awakens her too early to sex, partly because Van and Ada find it convenient to play on Lucette's adoration of Van, partly because the sex-mad Ada stokes her physical fires in other ways – and in short because Van and Ada are simply too obsessed with themselves to pay any attention to Lucette in her own right until she is dead and irrecoverable.

Lucette's whole emotional development has been skewed by her being sexually "initiated" far too young. The tragic irony of her fate is that she loses her innocence at too early an age but remains a virgin and cannot get Van to take the virginity she so desperately offers. She commits suicide by drowning; because she is not deflowered, she becomes in a ghoulish sense "the care of the water."[14]

Lucette's death is the central tragedy of the novel, and something Ada and especially Van belatedly try to accept responsibility for; but until her death, she is overlooked or dismissed – not only by Van and Ada, but also by us as readers – as only a troublesome impediment to Van and Ada's ardor.

But Nabokov never overlooks her. He has called her "my favorite child."[15] He makes this little girl slighted by Van and Ada central to the novel,[16] and he makes her entanglement in Van and Ada's fate stand for all human responsibility for those we are close to. No matter how much Van and Ada may celebrate their self-sufficiency, their triumphant apartness from others, they cannot escape their interdependence. They cannot enjoy the benefits of their intimate connections with each other – the magic of love that they celebrate so eloquently – without paying the moral price of responsibility exacted for the very possibility of human interconnectedness.[17]

In order to see that Lucette is central to *Ada*, despite Van and Ada's focus on their own story, it is not necessary to discover the barbs Nabokov has grafted onto the *souci d'eau*/Joyce/Apuleius allusions in Ada's botanical talk. Nabokov establishes Lucette's key role in many other ways: through other, simpler allusions (such as to Rimbaud's "Mémoire," itself, whose brookside setting, as we will see, interacts with a key brookside scene in *Ada* that foreshadows Lucette's death); through other patterns within *Ada*, such as the Chateaubriand-incest pattern, which if examined closely can be seen to focus on Lucette;[18] even, for good enough readers, by simply watching how Van and Ada and Lucette behave, and refusing to be swayed by Van and Ada's rhetorical ardor as storytellers.

When we discover the more arcane networks of meaning that bypass Van and Ada's control and privilege Lucette (and, by association with her, others whom Van and Ada mistreat),[19] we can see that Nabokov is far from standing uncritically behind Van and Ada's pride in their exceptional abilities. In fact one of his key points in the novel is that despite their gifts (and because of them), Van and Ada become dangerously self-centered and thoughtless towards others, just as Ada behaves heartlessly in that dinnertime conversation towards her mother. Having assessed Marina as boring, Ada simply humiliates her. Lucette, by contrast, on her last night alive, despite having managed to stir Van's desire, stops at this crucial juncture of her life to offer "her last, last, last free gift of staunch courtesy" towards "old bores of the family" (490, 475) – and by allowing time for Van to dispel the sexual pressure she has applied, she inadvertently seals her own doom.

Obsessed with their own brilliance, Van and Ada relegate Lucette to the periphery. But Nabokov never does. *Ada* opens with a mangled echo of the opening of *Anna Karenin*. Despite his disclaimer, Van quotes the Tolstoy mistranslation to imply that we are about to read the story of a unique happy family. But Anna Karenin takes her own life, and Lucette, as she lurches to her death, thinks in a jumbled stream of consciousness that recalls Anna's stream of consciousness on the way to her death. Still within the novel's opening lines, Nabokov points to the same implication another way: the mistranslation theme sounded so insistently here looks forward to the climax of the theme, the *souci d'eau* passage and its striking anticipation of Lucette's death. Van's implication that we are broaching the story of a happy family needs to be radically qualified.

Ada's last sentence begins with similar blitheness: "Not the least adorn-ment of the chronicle is the delicacy of pictorial detail: a latticed gallery; a painted ceiling; a pretty plaything stranded among the forget-me-nots of a brook." (589) Over the course of the novel, three things have in fact ended up stranded in that brook: a watch, hardly a plaything in a novel so preoccupied with Time; a condom, an awkward necessity in a novel also preoccupied with sex; and Lucette's rubber doll, which Ada has "had the bad taste" to perforate with a vaginal slit. Lucette fills the doll with water by the brook's edge, and squeezes it out again in fascination. Before long, the doll gets swept away, Van sheds his pants to retrieve it, and intemperate Ada, stirred by the sight, pretends she is a dragon, has Van tie Lucette up "so that Van might save her just in time. For some reason, Lucette balked at the notion but physical strength prevailed. Van and Ada left the angry captive firmly attached to a willow trunk, and, 'prancing' to feign swift escape and pursuit, disappeared for a few precious minutes in the dark grove of the conifers." Eight-year-old Lucette unties herself and for the first time spies on them as they make love, before returning and tying herself up again as best she can (143). Some time later, the doll does get washed away again, a grim memento of Lucette's first initiation and of her ultimate fate at the bottom of the sea. And for the reader of "Mémoire," the whole brookside scene, and especially the doll, and the willow under which Lucette is tied, will recall the "*jouet*" (plaything) and the "*saules*" ("willows") of Rimbaud's last stanza, and so will bring to mind Ada's dinnertime talk, and will all the more readily evoke, at *Ada's* close, the complex ironies of Lucette's fate.

Ada brings together all that has mattered most to Nabokov: the countries and languages and literatures he loves; first love and last love and family love; memory and time; art and science, art and life; the riches of consciousness, the loss of these riches in death, the possibility of a world beyond loss. And proof of its proximity, if not to the literal details of his personal past, at least to the things he treasured, can be seen in the fact that one of *Ada's* central motifs, Chateaubriand's line "*Du château qui baignait la Dore,*" was Nabokov's suggestion for the French title of his own autobiography.[20]

But this does not make *Ada* indulgent wish-fulfilment. In fact, if anything, the novel is Nabokov's most rigorous testing of himself, his most ruthless exorcism of his own weaknesses. He has always valued his originality, been conscious of his genius and proud of his difference from others, enjoyed a high and rich culture, been exclusive in his affections and protective towards those closest to him. In Van and Ada he first intensifies these qualities and allows them their full scope in his characters' command over their own means of expression, then criticizes them by means of their overt behavior and, to counter their own self-delighted rhetoric, by means of covert networks of internal and external allusion.[21]

Not that this makes *Ada* personal therapy. Nabokov admired Emerson, and would have agreed with the dictum he offers in "Self-Reliance": "to believe that what is true for you in your private heart is true for all men, – that is genius." All of us value our sense of difference from other people, the unique perspective of our own consciousness, the few who are closest to us. By inveigling us as readers to adopt Van and Ada's position,[22] to ignore the Lucette who stands outside their interests, he tests us as he has himself.

Far from making *Ada* a ready mix of memory and desire, Nabokov designed the novel as his most radical dismantling and reassembling of his world. He even creates for the novel its own world, Antiterra, with a complex, teasing relation to ours, and makes his hero a philosopher. Let us consider *Ada* in terms of philosophy's traditional divisions.

First, logic. As a lepidopterist intrigued by problems of taxonomy, Nabokov had long been concerned with notions of relationship, of identity, resemblance and difference.[23] In *Ada* the interest in relationship begins before the first sentence, in the chart of relationships set out in the family tree, and expands in the first chapter, with its investigations into the familial relationship between Van and Ada, and the eerie hints, in their first speeches, of their uncanny resemblance ("'I deduce,' said the boy, 'three main facts: that... that...and that....' 'I can add,' said the girl, 'that...that...and that...'" [8]). Even the first lines of the novel focus on ideas of resemblance and difference, in a text that curiously resembles and differs from Tolstoy's, and is said to have "little if any relation to the story to be unfolded now, a family chronicle."

One key reason for *Ada*'s subverting the notion of a nineteenth-century family chronicle and assigning such prominence to incest may become apparent if we listen to Wittgenstein's famous reflections on the complexities of relationship: "we see a complicated network of similarities overlapping and criss-crossing; sometimes overall similarities, sometimes similarities of detail.... I can think of no better expression to characterize these similarities than 'family resemblances'; for the various resemblances between members of a family: build, features, colour of eyes, gait, temperament, etc. etc. overlap and criss-cross in the same way."[24]

Antiterra raises the problem of relationship in another way. In hundreds of details it resembles and yet minutely differs from our earth, which may or may not be the same as the Terra some Antiterrans believe in as "another world," a "Next World." (20) Van notes: "There were those who maintained that the discrepancies and 'false overlapping' between the two worlds were too numerous, and too deeply woven into the skein of successive events, not to taint with trite fancy the theory of essential sameness; and there were those who retorted that the dissimilarities only confirmed the live organic reality pertaining to the other world; that a perfect likeness would rather suggest a specular, and hence speculatory, phenomenon" (18–19). Others come to believe in "the secret Government-concealed identity of Terra and Antiterra" (582).

Nabokov's investigation of the nature of relationship shows up in *Ada's* characterization (the strange similarities between Van and Ada, the confusions and overlappings of Lucette and Ada, the Veen children's complex inheritances from their parents and grandparents), its setting (Antiterra), its events (the more or less eerie repetitions of Ardis the First and Ardis the Second, or of picture-hatted women in bars, or of love-making "from behind"),[25] its allusions (their play on the relationship between original and copy, in translation, in adaptation, in parody; their strange blurrings of the relationship between art and life) and its language (the wildly centrifugal sentences that turn out at other levels to lead back to the book's center). *Ada* swarms far more densely than any other Nabokov novel with patterns of every kind. A seemingly simple exchange between Greg Erminin and Ada –

"I guess it's your father under that oak, isn't it?"
"No, it's an elm," said Ada. (92)

– though immediately amusing, also forms part of five different recurring patterns whose ramifying relationships prove as difficult to trace as Nabokov the lepidopterist found nature's own patterns.[26]

Second, epistemology. For Nabokov the logical and the epistemological overlap. Identity and relationship are never fixed and final; more can always be discovered, a new individuating detail, a hitherto unsuspected connection. Nabokov's sense of the difficulty and delights of his discoveries as a scientist are reflected in *Ada*, more than in any other of his novels, by the varying ways he imparts and withholds and disguises information, by his overloading us, distracting us, requiring us to link one seemingly offhand scrap of fact with another.[27] Once again, *Ada's* opening chapter, with its extraordinary upending of the conventions of exposition that appears to conceal rather than disclose the necessary information, but ends up by revealing far more than any other expository scene, reflects from the first Nabokov's attention to the frustrations and frissons of apprehending our world.[28] And at another level the mystery that for Antiterrans surrounds Terra – and our equal inability to determine whether Terra is in fact our planet, or whether Antiterra itself is not earth as distorted in the prism of Van's mind – serves at a more comic and cosmic level to remind us "that man being within nature, there cannot be any independent explanation of what we do and of the world in which we do it."[29]

Third, ethics. In considering Lucette's centrality to *Ada*, we have already seen how Nabokov turns Van's and Ada's responsibility towards Lucette's entanglement in their fates into an index of all human interconnectedness. In Van and Ada he shows the moral myopia possible even in people blessed with a capacity for tenderness and sensitivity, as he compares their treatment of Lucette with their infidelities to each other, their adulteries, their hypocrisies, their exploitations, their cruelties. I have dealt with this topic at length, at too great length perhaps, in Part 3 of *Nabokov's* Ada. Not that I overstated there the seriousness of Nabokov's moral concern in *Ada*, but in focussing on it so intently I may have obscured the novel's other tones and themes. In my eagerness to apportion responsibility, I also underemphasized what escaped a moral reckoning, the inextricability of the situation that had evolved, the sheer potential tragedy in things, by the time Lucette's death was imminent. Even when Van tries to act with a kind of wavering restraint (too late, of course), that only precipitates Lucette's final doom.

I must also confess I cannot confidently determine the degree to which Nabokov wishes to indicate that Van is deliberately trying to atone for Lucette's death in writing *Ada*. Van's case is quite different from Humbert's. Humbert happily nurtured for years his intent to kill Lolita's abductor, and when the murder fails to purge his bitterness, sets about writing Lolita to continue his campaign against Quilty and his own self-defense. He writes his memoir at speed, and is therefore presumably not meant to be seen as the conscious controller of many of *Lolita*'s concealed patterns. But Van reworks *Ada* for ten years, and does sincerely regret Lucette's death, and to some extent the behavior that led to it. Does the stream of consciousness he invents for Lucette in the scene of her death, a deliberate echo of *Anna Karenin*, link up *for him* with the opening quotation of Tolstoy's novel, in a belated attempt to reassert Lucette's importance at the very outset of the novel? Is the "plaything" in the last sentence, with its echo of "Mémoire," a last act of contrition?

Fourth, metaphysics. As a philosopher, Van tackles the subject of the link between space and time, and the nature and texture of time. As a memoirist, with Nabokov's help, he creates three powerfully counterpointed rhythms of time throughout the whole book. First, a thetic rhythm: a kind of transcending of time in Van's early love for Ada, their endless replaying, even within Ardis the First, of their new young love, their anticipating their future recollection ("My sister, do you still recall / The blue Ladore and Ardis Hall?" [138]), and their replaying in Ardis the Second the happiness of their first summer together. Second, an antithetic rhythm: the disintegration of that sense of timelessness, the assertion of time's decay, later in Ardis the Second, as Ada's infidelity becomes more and more inescapable, despite her denials, and in the rest of the novel, as the Parts shrink and the gaps in time between them lengthen horribly, as if Van and Ada's love has some alarmingly short half-life, as if the arrow of immortal love at Ardis has become the arrow (Greek *ardis*, "point of an arrow" [225]) of Time. And then, third, the synthetic rhythm:

the triumphant reversal of Time's direction, as Van and Ada in middle age reestablish their love together, and, as their bodies decay toward death, retell together the story of their love, in a way that permeates the account of their first summer together and gives it even there a sense of another kind of triumph over Time.

When Van is separated from Ada, however – and that is most of his life – he has to obtund the pain of her absence by immersing himself in his work. As a psychologist and philosopher, he studies the madmen who believe in the existence of Terra, which to some seems like a kind of Next World. As a writer of "physics fiction" (339), too (his *Letters from Terra*, which draws on his psychological researches), he feels he has to know what, according to Nabokov, professional physicists are reluctant to discuss: what lies on "the outside of the inside" (*SM* 301) – exactly, in other words, what we know as "meta-physics." But of course even madness or the possibility of another world hardly permits us to see from beyond the world of human consciousness. Yet Nabokov has woven within the novel a network of hints that, in ways Van cannot see, the dead Lucette seems to have influenced Van and Ada's lives – especially at the crucial moment when their last reunion appeared to have failed – and to be sending them now "letters from Terra," signals from a region beyond mortal time, signals which may even have inspired Van to write *Ada*, but which for all his attempts to "catch sight of the lining of time" (227) remain beyond his ken.[30]

Fifth, aesthetics. From the start, from its echo of *Anna Karenin*, *Ada* draws on prior art. With its parodic homage to the tradition of the novel, with Van and Ada's obsessive omnidirectional allusiveness and their adopting lines from Marvell, Chateaubriand and Rimbaud as personal refrains, *Ada* could serve as a one-text course in intertextuality. Works-within-the-work reflect the novel's outer story and often works-without-the-work in a succession of mises-en-abîme (Marina's travesty of *Eugene Onegin* in her performance in *Eugene and Lara*; Mlle Larivière's unintentionally comic *Les Enfants Maudits*, which echoes both Chateaubriand's *Mémoires* and his *René* and, despite her unobservant nature, the evolving story of Van and Ada; Van's doomed attempt to keep thoughts of Ada at bay in *Letters from Terra*; the complex tragic farce of Ada's film *Don Juan's Last Fling*, with its absurd echoes of *Don Quixote* and Pushkin's Don Juan mini-drama, *The Stone Guest*). Scenes freeze or frieze into tableaux from more or less famous works of art (a Parmigianino drawing,[31] a Toulouse-Lautrec poster,[32] a Bosch painting,[33] or various opulent hybrids). *Ada* explores the relation between one art and another (painting, literature, architecture, drama, film), between art and science (Ada's watercolors of invented orchids, Lucette's discoveries of Old Master butterflies), between artistic creativity and amatory energy (*passim*), between art and sport (Van's role as Mascodagama makes him a sort of *acrobate maudit* whose rapture "derived from overcoming gravity was akin to that of artistic revelation.... Van on the stage was performing organically what his figures of speech were to perform later in life – acrobatic wonders that had never been expected from them and which frightened children" [185]), between art and games (Ada's sun-and-shade games, Russian Scrabble, Van's sleight-of-hand at cards), between art and life. The gap between Terra and Antiterra may after all be read at one level as a book-length metaphor for the autonomy of the world of a book, for the perhaps uncrossable boundary between art and life, for the special Time of the world of art, for the riddle of whether art reflects or distorts or explains life by standing so far apart from it or by matching it so well.

Ada is Nabokov's *summa*. But although analyzing it according to the traditional divisions of philosophy provides some measure of the book's comprehen-sive–ness, it is not the kind of dissection the novel itself immediately invites. In *Ada* everything intertwines, and on Nabokov's own terms. The novel offers a succession of parodies of paradise, an examination of the human desire for perfect happiness that must face up to the innate imperfections of a life shadowed by loss. *Ada*'s trouble-free Antiterra collapses back into our trou-blesome twentieth-century Terra; Van and Ada's Ardis is a parody paradise, they themselves a new Adam and Eve; their flawed paradise is itself parodied in Eric Veen's Villa Venuses, where a dream of sexual sublimity and opulent exclusiveness ends in rank corruption, or in the "sacred secret and creed" con-structed by "romantically inclined handmaids" (409). Or *Ada* celebrates and criticises the *roman*, "romance," romanticism: the fairy-tale roots of the novel as a genre, and its tangled foliage of fact; its distance from and dependence on myths of love, like those of Venus, which the Veens embody and dismantle; the transcendent impulse behind romantic love and romantic literature, and the matching dangers of romantic egotism. Or it could be seen as a study of the ironies of originality, a novel that asserts its own originality the moment its first line copies another, and then evokes the breathless, unprecedented newness of falling in love – in a world already dense with allusion and echo, a decadent endgame Eden.[34] Or...

17. *Ada*'s Allure[1]

No one would have predicted two-thirds of the way through the twentieth century that the literature of our ironic age would produce the most idyllic and romantic of novels. No one, that is, except Vladimir Nabokov, who in 1966 had already started writing it.

Ada, conceived in glimpses and patches between 1959 and 1965 and composed between February 1966 and October 1968, at the height of his fame, would become Nabokov's longest, richest, most ambitious novel. In the corpus of his English fiction it takes pride of place with *Lolita*, the most perverse of love stories, written in the early 1950s, and *Pale Fire*, that flawless counterpoise of poetic realism and prose romance, written at the start of the 1960s.

Part 1 of *Ada* opens by scrambling the first sentence of *Anna Karenina*, which Nabokov by then thought the greatest of novels, and closes by reworking the last sentence of Part 1 of *Madame Bovary*, which he had *once* thought the greatest. *Ada* belongs in the company of the books it invokes.

Among other things, *Ada* is the closest the second half of the twentieth century has come to matching *Ulysses*. Both novels announce their originality from the outset, both prove inexhaustible, but they could hardly be more different. As it shifts Homer's hero from the mythical to the modern, from far-flung and fabulous seas to a painstakingly mapped Dublin, and from ten years of wandering to a single day, 16 June 1904, Joyce's masterpiece deliberately debunks. Where Ulysses acts the gentleman when he encounters princess Nausicaa on Phaeacia's shores, Leopold Bloom masturbates over Gerty MacDowell as he faces her on Sandymount Strand; where Penelope remains the archetype of the faithful wife during her husband's twenty-year absence, Molly Bloom makes vivid love to a dapper cad while *her* Ulysses wanders Dublin's streets for a single day.

Ada sets out to re-enchant. As Edmund White remarks, "Nabokov is the most passionate novelist of the twentieth century"[2] – and nowhere more so than in *Ada*. Its span covers a hundred years, 1868 to 1967, in a slightly unsteady world, Antiterra, that seems ours but not ours, identical to our Terra in topography but askew here and there in history, so that in its North America, French and Russian are almost as widespread as English, and so that *Ada* itself appears at once a historical romance, a novel of contemporary life, and slightly futuristic science fiction. Van's and Ada's love begins early in their book and their lives, rushes to its rapturous and repeated consummation, and endures through over eighty years of fond recapitulation, ending in the writing of *Ada* itself, as hero and heroine, after putting the last touches to the story of their love, die into each other's arms and the book itself. Its central setting, Ardis Park, is a parody of paradise, a garden of earthly delights; its two main characters, Van and Ada Veen, are "the children of Venus," while Van is also a modern Don Giovanni. As Robert Alter observes, "the expression in *Ada* of a lover's consummated delight in life and beauty is an achievement that has few equals in the history of the novel."[3]

Like *Ulysses*, *Lolita* had to be published first in Paris rather than in the English-speaking world, and from there slowly stirred up a scandal. *Ada* by contrast commanded instant attention on its publication in May 1969: a cover story in *Time* magazine, serialization in *Playboy*, a rhapsodic front-page review in the *New York Times*.[4] Yet that explosive start almost brought it to a halt, as subsequent reviewers reacted by rating *Ada* the most overpraised book of the decade.

Although one of the most comic of texts, *Ulysses* declares its high seriousness from the first: this is not just another novel; you will have to concentrate, you will have to slow down, but it will last you a lifetime. *Ada* on the other hand seems barely to take itself seriously. While at times it can erupt in flashes of colorful arcana, *Ada* is mostly light, swift, unstable, as playful and parodic as it is passionate, intensely focused on Van and Ada and yet wildly heterogeneous in its matter and manner, drawing on detailed but often slyly distorted history and geography, literature and art, philosophy and science. Always a love story, *Ada* also becomes by ticklish turns myth, fairy tale, utopian idyll, family chronicle, personal memoir, historical romance, realistic novel, science-fiction fantasy, erotic catalogue, natural history notes, psychology lecture, philosophical sketch, architectural scherzo, picture gallery and filmic folly.

Ada's combination of superheated passion and slippery surprise led readers and writers like John Updike and Joyce Carol Oates to disenchantment about what they felt to be its artistic and moral indulgence. To many, *Ada* seemed a succession of flashy local effects with too little human depth and too little awareness of Van and Ada's faults.

But Nabokov deliberately makes the novel a tightrope between enchantment and disenchantment. A celebration of romance, *Ada* also offers a sharp critique of the romantic. Van and Ada may be indulgent both in their lives and in their retelling, and Nabokov *seems* to invite us to adopt their position as uncritically as they themselves appear to do. Yet for all the dashing brilliance of his hero and heroine, he never loses his critical distance, and eventually makes us realize we ought not to have lost ours.

Van and Ada present their love as a triumph, and indeed it is. But entrancing though their story can be, it can also repel. We seem to be promised paradise, yet after the idyll of Ardis, where we remain for the first half of the novel, *Ada* seems to collapse into gaping emptiness and loss of direction, as romance yields to anguished betrayal, bitter loss, painful separation, sordid substitutions, only to surprise us, when all seems too late, with a restoration that explains at last the sustained note of celebration and the very shape of the story.

Van and Ada sweep us up so powerfully into the glow and glory of their passion that we can overlook their narcissistic self-regard, their arrogant exclusiveness, their thoughtless immoderation, even their cruelty to each other and to others, until, six-sevenths of the way through the novel, we see the cost of their inattention to others in the suicide of their half-sister, Lucette, whom they have heedlessly entangled in their lives and love.

For Nabokov, Lucette stands as close to the center of *Ada* as the two lovers who manage to make us dismiss her at first as just a comical side-show, an endearing nuisance, an absurd obstacle to their irresistible ardor. In forty years of writing fiction he had found new ways to conceal meanings that rereading can slowly reveal to us behind the backs of his most alert and eloquent narrators. As we reread *Ada*, we can discover that every gleam of what may have seemed catchy but capricious color has its considered place, and that astonishingly often that place will somehow commemorate the vulnerable, ordinary, kind Lucette whom Van and Ada ignore in their preoccupation with their own extraordinariness.

When Stephen Dedalus's thoughts dominate, or when a parodic style overlays the action, *Ulysses* can be taxing. But even Bloom's darting thoughts make for effortful reading. Here, Bloom has just lunched in Davy Byrne's "moral pub":

> His downcast eyes followed the silent veining of the oaken slab. Beauty: it curves: curves are beauty. Shapely goddesses, Venus, Juno: curves the world admires. Can see them library museum standing in the round hall, naked goddesses. Aids to digestion. They don't care what man looks. All to see. Never speaking. I mean to say to fellows like Flynn. Suppose she did Pygmalion and Galatea what would she say first? Mortal! Put you in your proper place. Quaffing nectar at mess with gods golden dishes, all ambrosial. Not like a tanner lunch we have, boiled mutton, carrots and turnips, bottle of Allsop. Nectar imagine it drinking electricity: gods' food. Lovely forms of women sculpted Junonian. Immortal lovely. And we stuffing food in one hole and out behind: food, chyle, blood, dung, earth, food: have to feed it like stoking an engine. They have no. Never looked. I'll look today. Keeper won't see. Bend down let something drop. See if she.

Bloom's saccadic and full but jumbled mind, his fixation on bodily processes, his easily encompassing the sublime and the ridiculous, as in his nosiness about whether the statues of the Greek goddesses in the National Library have rectal orifices – we can recognize all these on an attentive first reading, but it is a demanding kind of response to sustain for 700 or so pages.

Ada by comparison is a heady breeze. In the second chapter, the always impetuous Demon Veen has been so captivated by the stage impact of his cousin, the actress Marina Durmanov, that he sweeps backstage after one of her early exits "to possess her between two scenes" in a theatrical travesty of Pushkin's *Eugene Onegin*. The scene is the earliest in the novel, Manhattan, January 5, 1868. After he returns to his orchestra seat, Demon's

> heart missed a beat and never regretted the lovely loss, as she ran, flushed and flustered, in a pink dress into the orchard, earning a claque third of the sitting ovation that greeted the instant dispersal of the imbecile but colorful transfigurants from Lyaska – or Iveria. Her meeting with Baron d'O., who strolled out of a side alley, all spurs and green tails, somehow eluded Demon's consciousness, so struck was he by the wonder of that brief abyss of absolute reality between two bogus fulgurations of fabricated life. Without waiting for the end of the scene, he hurried out of the theater into the crisp crystal night, the snowflakes star-spangling his top hat as he returned to his house in the next block to arrange a magnificent supper. By the time he went to fetch his new mistress in his jingling sleigh, the last-act ballet of Caucasian generals and metamorphosed Cinderellas had come to a sudden close, and Baron d'O., now in black tails and white gloves, was kneeling in the middle of an empty stage, holding the glass slipper that his fickle lady had left him when eluding his belated advances. The claqueurs were getting tired and looking at their watches when Marina in a black cloak slipped into Demon's arms and swan-sleigh.
>
> They reveled, and traveled, and they quarreled, and flew back to each other again. By the following winter he began to suspect she was being unfaithful to him, but could not determine his rival.

The scene is typical *Ada*: the dashing romanticism, which Demon will pass on to Van and Ada, his children by Marina; the speed of the action, both in the theater scene and in the transition to a year later and suspicions of infidelity; the shimmer of improbability, at least in terms of our world (a wealthy young female aristocrat as a professional actress in the 1860s, succumbing *so* quickly, even to such a poised and precipitate rake as Demon), that nevertheless combines with details and sensations so vivid they compel our imaginations to respond.

As so often in *Ada*, romance coexists with much else, passionate rapture with dislocation (this feels more like St. Petersburg than Manhattan), parody (the theatricality of the stage seems suddenly to have seeped into Demon's life), and even comedy and disdain (here, Demon's or Van's contempt for the theatrical performance and the perverse stage adaptations of literary texts: the "claque third of the sitting ovation," "imbecile but colorful transfigurants," the "bogus fulgurations of fabricated life," "the last-act ballet of Caucasian generals and metamorphosed Cinderellas"). Samuel Johnson commented that in metaphysical poetry "the most heterogeneous ideas are yoked by violence together." Here, the miracle is that heterogeneous elements effortlessly fuse and that the risible absurdity of false theatricality offsets and underwrites Demon's euphoric sense of authenticity.

Unlike the passage from *Ulysses*, we can read this at speed, yet there are little dabs of surprise, tiny flecks of local color that we *could* stop and scrutinize, but are more likely to register at first simply as passing flashes of the exotic. "Lyaska – or Iveria" are places we neither know nor can locate in any atlas. In his notes under the anagrammatic alias of Vivian Darkbloom, Nabokov points out that the "colorful transfigurants" who in the previous paragraph were introduced as a ballet company from "Belokonsk, Western Estoty," have come from "the Russian twin of 'Whitehorse' (city in N.W. Canada)" (he could have added that Estotiland is an old European name for North America). "Lyaska" in this context sounds suspiciously like Alaska, and indeed the Russian for "Alaska" is *Alyaska*; the name here reflects the fact that Alaska remained a Russian possession until 1867.

The dash in " – or Iveria" is a dismissive jab. If we trawl for the placename we will find that "Iberia" can refer not only to the peninsula consisting of Spain and Portugal, but also to an ancient country in Transcaucasia (the eastern part of present-day Georgia); the dancers here first appear in the interpolated intermezzo ballet dressed in "the garb of Georgian tribesmen," a grotesquerie that, like so much in this farcical play, twists together several garblings of Russian literary classics.[5]

In reminding us that Alaska was Russian a century ago, or that there were two quite distinct Iberias, Nabokov adopts a strategy characteristic of *Ada*. Joyce was obsessive about the precision of his picture of Dublin, even instructing a friend to drop from the area railings at 7 Eccles Street, the real house at which the fictional Bloom lives, to ensure that Bloom could have reached the basement door this way after he has locked himself out. Nabokov on the other hand repeatedly introduces into *Ada's* Antiterra slight puckers in earth's history and geography, its flora and fauna, its literature and art. He gently pricks our curiosity rather than slows down our comprehension, so we can enjoy these often amusing flickers of roadside color, but where Joyce drew on local knowledge of Dublin, Nabokov invites us, if we wish, to discover – in publicly available sources, a dictionary, an encyclopaedia, an atlas – what lies behind details he may or may not have distorted.

Where Joyce sticks to the truth of particulars, Nabokov has a respect for their endless surprise, and for the curiosity that notices and explores them, but also an awareness that the details could easily be otherwise (Russia might easily have secured a larger foothold in North America, the French presence

in Quebec and Acadia and Louisiana could well have expanded). That awareness saturates *Ada* and allows it to affirm the unlikelihood and enchantment
of the particulars among which we live.

Just as "Lyaska – or Iveria" can first light up a fleeting smile but later may
lead us down history's forgotten sidestreets, so the absurdities of the theatrical
performance in which Marina nevertheless seems "so dreamy, so lovely, so stir-
ring" amuse us immediately but may prompt us eventually to recall or explore
Pushkin's *Eugene Onegin*, the first masterpiece of modern Russian literature,
and to see the hilarious betrayals of Pushkin's story – some reflecting the hor-
rors inflicted on it in Chaikovsky's opera – in this botched adaptation. Where
Joyce mixes Homer and Shakespeare with now-arcane ephemera or obscure
local detail, Nabokov's allusions send us on a semi-guided tour through some
of the major galleries of Western literature and art: Shakespeare, Cervantes, Marvell, Chateaubriand, Austen, Pushkin, Dickens, Flaubert, Tolstoy,
Rimbaud, Chekhov, Joyce, Proust; Pompeian murals, Boschean nightmares,
Florentine frescoes, Breughelesque romps, Caravaggian chiaroscuros, Rembrandt portraits, Boucher putti, Toulouse-Lautrecesque posters.

Details like "Lyaska – or Iveria" or "the last-act ballet of Caucasian generals and metamorphosed Cinderellas" do not hamper our enjoyment of the
swift scenic flow, but like much in *Ada* they create a world as elusive as it is
entrancing. Nabokov wants to reawaken us to the surprise of the particular.
We often blandly accept our world, but he reminds is that when we attend
to its details they may prove both improbable and inscrutable. To some, that
can seem disconcerting or frustrating, but Nabokov asks us to see it instead
as an invitation to wonder and discovery.

Unlike the passage from *Ulysses*, grounded in dense Dublin detail, the
theater scene in *Ada* seems to spring to life out of nothing before it is rapidly
spirited away: Joycean solidity gives way to Nabokovian insouciance, "this-is-
how-it-is" to "it-could-easily-be-otherwise." Yet despite Nabokov's conjuring
up and dismissing the scene so rapidly, it turns out to play its complex part
in the story. In pure plot terms, it helps prepare for the romantic complications that explain why Van and Ada are full brother and sister, the offspring
of Demon and Marina, even though they have been reared as cousins, as the
apparent children of Demon and Aqua and of Dan and Marina respectively.
Structurally, Demon and Marina's torrid affair serves as a precursor to the
rampant romance of Van and Ada, and even to Van's slowly mounting suspicions of Ada's infidelity and his sudden discovery of his rival. In psychological
terms, the complete collapse of the relationship between Demon and Marina,
the distance between their present detachment and the intense past they once
shared, stands as a contrast to the persistent centrality of Van and Ada's past
to their evolving present, whether they currently happen to be ecstatically
reunited or bitterly apart.

For all its lightness, the theater scene also connects with many other parts of the novel. One of the recurrent themes of *Ada* and all Nabokov's work is the rich and wry relationship of life and art. Like other writers – Cervantes, Austen, Pushkin, Flaubert, Tolstoy, Proust, Joyce – Nabokov explores the connection between romance in fiction and in real life (indeed, he has Marina in the role of Tatiana in the letter scene in Pushkin's *Eugene Onegin* – a prime example of the young girl whose head is turned by fictional romance – trigger Demon's desire). He echoes and parodically intensifies the nineteenth-century novelistic set-piece of an affair that begins at the theatre – although not usually with an aristocrat as actress or as instant conquest!

A theme Nabokov particularly explores in *Ada* is the relationship between novelty and familiarity, between original and imitation. Van and Ada, like most people falling in love, feel it unprecedented, yet must also recignize that it has happened before, and that they might not feel love quite the way they do, did they not know from all they have read what an impact it can have. These two highly self-conscious children see themselves as Adam and Eve, exploring a new paradise of emotion, yet in sensing that very analogy they know they follow an endless chain of precursors. Here Demon and Marina, in the shock of their new love, imitate Pushkin's Tatiana and the effects of her romantic reading, and anticipate the magic of Van and Ada's falling in love a generation later. Even in that, the structural pattern of the love in one generation as a preplay of the next, they imitate both raw life and the refinements of prior art (in Proust, whom Nabokov invokes here in numerous ways, Swann's love for Odette prefigures Marcel's love for Albertine a generation later).

Most crucially, though, the theater scene anticipates the night of Lucette's suicide. Lucette, hopelessly and desperately in love with Van, in partial imitation of her big sister Ada, was initiated too early into sex by the older pair, yet in her mid-twenties remains a virgin and deeply disturbed. She secretly books a transatlantic passage on a liner Van intends to take, in a last-ditch hope of seducing him over several days of enforced proximity. Her plan seems to be working, he *is* roused by her presence, until they sit down to watch a pre-release movie, *Don Juan's Last Fling*. Suddenly the atmosphere is shattered when the image of Ada, herself now an actress, appears on screen. Van breaks away, returns to his room, and masturbates to vent the sexual tension Lucette had stoked.

As so often in *Ada*, Nabokov connects one scene with another, despite all the differences here between Demon and Marina at the theater and Van and Lucette at the cinema (film rather than play, mid-Atlantic summer rather than Manhattan winter, masturbation rather than consummation): in both scenes an actress stepping into the performance, a travesty of a major classic, overthrows the feelings of the man watching her, who breaks from his seat before the show is over and rushes to sexual release.

Lucette cannot escape from the shipboard cinema when Van does, because "old bores of the family" sidle over to her and plump themselves down beside her, and she turns to them "with her last, last, last free gift of staunch courtesy that was stronger than failure and death." When the movie finishes, she phones Van in his cabin, but he says he is not alone – she knows that a predatory bleached blonde, a Titianesque Titaness, has been making eyes and mouths at Van – and, knowing her last desperate drive to win him has been derailed, she fills herself with pills and jumps overboard to her death.

Because situation, setting, cast, time and atmosphere are all so different, Nabokov ensures it will takes us time to detect the connections he has established between the dashing romance of the 1868 theater scene and the tragedy of the 1901 cinema scene. But the whole of the prologue to *Ada* (the story of Demon's relationship with Marina and her twin Aqua) more openly prefigures the main body of the novel (the story of Van's relationship with Ada and her sister Lucette): two sisters in two generations become pitifully entangled in their sisters' love for their rakish "cousins" and turn in despair to suicide.

Nabokov of course lets us see Lucette's suicide itself on a first reading, and so invites us to reconsider Van and Ada's relationship with Lucette, their indifference to her as a person while they pursue their passion. Perhaps on a first reading we may also notice the similarity between the fatal entanglements of Aqua and of Lucette in their sisters' love. But only gradually does Nabokov allow us to discover the full depth of his critique of the blindess of romantic passion in Demon and Van. Only gradually do we see the numerous ways in which he marks Van's moral shortcomings as echoes of Demon's more flamboyant ones, or as a contrast to Lucette's capacity to think of others – even those she does not care for – at a moment of her own inner turmoil. Only gradually do most of us come to realize how easily we have been swept away by Van and Ada's impetuous ardor.

The scene of Demon and Marina at the theater at first seems sheer romance, a passing enchantment, a delightful but disposible caprice. But like everything in *Ada*, it proves to have repercussions throughout the novel, as part of an intricate plot, an elaborate structure, a cast of vividly individual but tautly intertwined characters, and a dense network of themes, patterns and implications. *Ada* may seem flighty beside the solid earthbound realism of *Ulysses*, but that allows it to reach its own special altitudes.

After the "scrupulous meanness" of his early style, Joyce began to celebrate the abundance in words and his world in *Ulysses* and *Finnegans Wake*. As if in reaction, his one-time secretary, Samuel Beckett, developed his terminal minimalism, lowering the light on human life to a last slow solitary solipsistic fade-out – and somehow making it relentlessly comic. As if in a reaction to the reaction (Nabokov began reading Beckett only in the 1960s), *Ada* showers every kind of riches on the Veens: early love, endlessly repeated, and lasting a long lifetime, and an inexhaustible reserve of mental, physical, sexual, social, linguistic, cultural and fiscal capital.

When Updike complains about the lack of recognisable human experience in *Ada*, he probably has the over-endowment of Van and Ada particularly in mind. Literature has steadily moved from gods, demigods and heroes towards the ordinary man and woman. Where Homer's Achilles was a demigod and his Ulysses a hero and a favorite of Athena, Joyce invents Bloom as an every-man, endearing but fallible, curious but often confused. But there is nothing ordinary about Van and Ada.

Some readers seem to suspect that when Nabokov has Van and Ada cel-ebrate their superlative selves, he is either parading his own sense of singular-ity or indulging in wish-fulfilment. A better interpretation would see them as a larger-than-life-size image for the extraordinary wealth we can accumulate in the course of our experience, and as a way of critically examining its cost. Even for such exceptionally fortunate creatures as Van and Ada, cruelty shad-ows their sensitivity, and pain, loss, bitterness, and remorse complicate their happiness.

In a lifetime of 97 and 95 years, and a love lasting into its ninth decade, Van and Ada amass a vast treasury of memory, but in *Ada*'s last chapter they look at looming death: even before the pain and the "featureless pseudo-future, blank and black," "There is, first, the wrench of relinquishing forever all one's memories – that's a commonplace, but what courage man must have had to go through that commonplace again and again and not give up the rigmarole of accumulating again and again the riches of consciousness that will be snatched away!"

Or perhaps Updike had Antiterra in mind. Venus, still in the 1960s a mys-terious twin of Earth, veiled by the brightly reflective cloud cover that makes a handmirror its symbol, seems in one sense a good candidate for *Ada*'s Anti-terra, the "sibling planet" that oddly reflects our Terra. In a note he wrote at 19, Nabokov imagined looking up at the evening star, his favorite, and "apply-ing to it simile after simile, finding nothing on his evening walk more beautiful – not the fountains, nor the red roses black in the moonlight, nor the hills in the distance. Suddenly it speaks: 'Foolish man! What are you excited about! I'm a world too, not like the one on which you live, but noisy and dark like yours. There is sorrow and coarseness here too – and if you want to know at this very moment one of my inhabitants – a poet like you – looks on the star that you call "Earth" and whispers to it: "O pure, O beautiful.""[6] In Antiterra's strangeness, as in Van and Ada's extraordinary endowments, Nabokov insists on the mixed nature of all experience that is anything like human. Despite Van's attempt in his envoy to *Ada* to present a synopsis that is all sunshine, Nabokov keeps a firm focus on the blend of shine and shadow in Van and Ada's lives, the overlap of heaven and hell in any imaginable world.

Let us linger on one scene that Van presents as among the sunniest of all. *Ada*'s action begins when Demon and Marina fall in love in the city and the snow, but most of the novel's first half commemorates another romance, a generation later, in the country and the summer sun.

Van revisits Ardis Park in 1888, four years after his first radiant summer there with Ada. Every year on Ada's birthday, July 21, the family rides out by coach and charabanc for a picnic in a pineglade. In 1884, a series of confusions meant that more people than places were left in the last vehicle to return, and fourteen-year-old Van had twelve-year-old Ada assigned to sit on his lap at a time when their passion for each other was already intense but still undeclared: "It was the children's first bodily contact and both were embarrassed.... With his entire being, the boiling and brimming lad relished her weight as he felt it responding to every bump of the road by softly parting in two and crushing beneath it the core of the longing which he knew he had to control lest a possible seep perplex her innocence."

On his return to Ardis in 1888, "unexpected, unbidden, unneeded," Van arrives in the midst of a garden party, and from an upstairs room sees Percy de Prey, a former schoolmate of his, kissing Ada's hand as he prepares to leave, and impermissibly holding it before kissing it again. Livid with jealousy, Van tears apart the diamond necklace he has bought Ada, just as she bursts into the room to assure him that she has "only one beau, only one beast, only one sorrow, only one joy." On the picnic for her sixteenth birthday, a drunken Percy de Prey turns up uninvited. Bristling with hostility, he and Van fight; Van easily downs de Prey, but as he walks away the burly bully falls on him from behind. Again agile Van quickly dispenses with him, but his nerves remain jarred. By the time the Veen children prepare to return to the manor, de Prey has left. A footboy surfaces too late from under a bush and has to sit on the box seat Lucette would have taken at the front of the victoria; this time it is twelve-year-old Lucette who has to sit on the lap of big cousin Van, while Ada sits beside them:

> The little footboy was reading and picking his nose – judging by the movements of his elbow. Lucette's compact bottom and cool thighs seemed to sink deeper and deeper in the quicksand of the dream-like, dream-rephrased, legend-distorted past. Ada, sitting next to him, turning her smaller pages quicker than the boy on the box, was, of course, enchanting, obsessive, eternal and lovelier, more somberly ardent than four summers ago – but it was that other picnic

which he now relived and it was Ada's soft haunches which he now held as if she were present in duplicate, in two different color prints.

Through strands of coppery silk he looked aslant at Ada, who puckered her lips at him in the semblance of a transmitted kiss (pardoning him at last for his part in that brawl!) and presently went back to her vellum-bound little volume, *Ombres et couleurs*, an 1820 edition of Chateaubriand's short stories with hand-painted vignettes and the flat mummy of a pressed anemone. The gouts and glooms of the woodland passed across her book, her face and Lucette's right arm, on which he could not help kissing a mosquito bite in pure tribute to the duplication. Poor Lucette stole a languorous look at him and looked away again – at the red neck of the coachman – of that other coachman who for several months had haunted her dreams.

We do not care to follow the thoughts troubling Ada, whose attention to her book was far shallower than might seem; we will not, nay, cannot follow them with any success, for thoughts are much more faintly remembered than shadows or colors, or the throbs of young lust, or a green snake in a dark paradise. Therefore we find ourselves more comfortably sitting within Van while his Ada sits within Lucette, and both sit within Van (and all three in me, adds Ada).

He remembered with a pang of pleasure the indulgent skirt Ada had been wear-ing then, so swoony-baloony as the Chose young things said, and he regretted (smiling) that Lucette had those chaste shorts on today, and Ada, husked-corn (laughing) trousers. In the fatal course of the most painful ailments, some-times (nodding gravely), sometimes there occur sweet mornings of perfect repose – and that not owing to some blessed pill or potion (indicating the bedside clutter) or at least without our knowing that the loving hand of despair slipped us the drug.

Van closed his eyes in order better to concentrate on the golden flood of swelling joy. Many, oh many, many years later he recollected with wonder (how could one have endured such rapture?) that moment of total happiness, the complete eclipse of the piercing and preying ache, the logic of intoxication, the circular argument to the effect that the most eccentric girl cannot help being faithful if she loves one as one loves her. He watched Ada's bracelet flash in rhythm with the swaying of the victoria and her full lips, parted slightly in profile, show in the sun the red pollen of a remnant of salve drying in the transversal thumbnail lines of their texture. He opened his eyes: the bracelet was indeed flashing but her lips had lost all trace of rouge, and the certainty that in another moment he would touch their hot pale pulp threatened to touch off a private crisis under the solemn load of another child. But the little proxy's neck, glistening with sweat, was pathetic, her trustful immobility, sobering, and after all no furtive friction could compete with what awaited him in Ada's bower.

Like the theater scene, like much of *Ada*, the passage has a sinuous, glittering flow that bears us effortlessly along. Van's usual third-person narration slides easily to first-person, to a "We" that Ada soon joins: "We do not care to follow the thoughts troubling Ada." He does not follow her thoughts, not because of the perfectly plausible generalization about memories that he advances, but because – as we discover on a rereading, if we cannot yet guess – she is all apprehension that Van will find out about her recent relationship with Percy de Prey and challenge him to a duel. Van as narrator does not yet want to disclose what Van as character, despite all his rankling unease, does not yet know.

The overlay of novelty and repetition, reminiscence and anticipation so striking in this scene is characteristic of *Ada* – and in fact of all our experience. Van recalls Ada on his knees four years before, the differences as well as the similarities: her loose skirt then, Lucette's tight shorts now, Ada's "husked-corn" trousers (at the start of the picnic, at the beginning of the chapter, Van and Ada slip off to make love on the brink of a brook, where Ada declares "husked" the most extraordinary word in the language, "because it stood for opposite things, covered and uncovered, tightly husked but easily husked, meaning they peel off quite easily, you don't have to tear off the waistband, you brute"). A sudden side-swerve ("In the fatal course of the most painful ailments...") discloses a glimpse of Van in what he calls his "dot-dot-dotage," thinking up an image for the momentary reprieve his 18-year-old self has won from his ultimately unallayable misgivings.

Van on the victoria closes his eyes to concentrate on the bliss of the recollection and the magical recapitulation, only for Van the narrator to glide ahead again to his recollecting this moment still later, a glide whose rhetoric ("Many, oh many, many years later...") augments rather than diminishes the bliss. On the picnic ride he experiences the "complete eclipse of the piercing and preying ache," the dismissal of his qualms about Percy de Prey, but since these qualms will soon prove well founded, his later self tries to think back into that surge of confidence, which, had it been justified, would have spared him years of bitterness.

As so often in *Ada* the passage basks in bliss yet seethes with tension as it overlays time upon time. In 1888 Van recollects the ecstasy of 1884 as he relives something like it, consciously willing himself back into the past, in a triumphant reversal of time, even as he registers the difference between then and now. But Van as narrator, eight decades later, recalls this 1888 triumph *and* the dire disclosure ahead that he keeps half-hidden from the first-time reader as it was hidden from his young self, the bitter discovery that as it were pointedly insists that time's direction can never be reversed.

Even before Percy de Prey's affair with Ada darkens the picture, Van's sense in 1888 that the repeated picnic ride is a kind of magical replay of the past, a triumph over time, already depends on his awareness of the complex tension between past and present. Part of the joy of the original 1884 experience had been the novelty of the thrill of enforced contact with Ada in a protracted present, and the sudden promise of future intimacy. *Now* in 1888 his intimacy with Ada seems an immemorial, ever-renewable fact, as in that brisk throb on the brink of the brook earlier in the afternoon. *Then* Ada at twelve had seemed innocent and unattainable; *now* Lucette, herself twelve, is even more innocent and untouchable. *Now* Ada is his; *then* he could not imagine an Ada so intimately familiar; but it is the very distance he must keep from Lucette, the very resistance to lapsing back into that earlier temptation to melt "in animal laxity," the very change from Ada to Lucette, that re-animates the thrill of the past.

But here once again comes a different kind of tension, a further complexity in the overlay of time. When in 1901 Van breaks away from Lucette in the cinema that fatal night on the *Tobakoff* and retreats to his cabin, he again projects "upon the screen of his paroxysm" not the Lucette he has been sitting with, but the Ada he has seen on the cinema screen, "a perfect compendium of her 1884 and 1888 and 1892 looks," just as here he sits beneath Lucette but projects onto his private screen the image of Ada in 1884. The overlapping and interlacing of images of Ada and Lucette on the picnic ride point forward to the tragic entanglement of the two Veen girls that reaches its climax on the night of Lucette's death. The moment of past bliss, the moment of the present bliss of recollection and apparent triumph over time, the moment of the dire discovery about Percy that three days later will refute this bliss, the moment of the future paroxysm that will seal Lucette's doom – all meet here as *Ada* explores how the present overlaps and builds on the past and yet leads to the multiple surprises of the future.

Nabokov does not register the pulse of the present with Joyce's split-second accuracy, but he examines our experience of time in many other ways. To mention just four: he offers in the odd dislocations of Antiterran history a comically vivid image for our sense of the strangeness and remoteness from our present of different strata of our personal pasts; he structures *Ada* as a whole to reflect the rhythm of a human lifetime, the endless expanse of childhood, the eternal summers that do not match the summers before, the accelerating collapse of the years, and yet the power of an aging memory to resist that rush and revive the past; he shapes his plot to explore the openness of time, the problematic relationship between the direction and the texture of time, between time as advance and time as accumulation; he envisages a lifetime as the amassing of the personal riches of consciousness we each must nevertheless lose in death, and yet intimates a timelessness behind or around us if we could only access it.

Van's second return ride from one of Ada's birthday picnics presents still other aspects of *Ada's* treatment of time. Never before has a novel made the accumulation of human experience over a lifetime seem so richly romantic, never, not even in Proust, has the shock of the present been so amplified by repetition, recollection, anticipation, regret, remorse, amusement and rapture. Never before has a novel suggested quite how inexhaustible a story a life can build up in time.

Appendix: "Mémoire,"

by Arthur Rimbaud

Mémoire

I

L'eau claire; comme le sel des larmes d'enfance,
L'assaut au soleil des blancheurs des corps de femme;
la soie, en foule et de lys pur, des oriflammes
sous les murs dont quelque pucelle eut la défense;

l'ébat des anges; – Non...le courant d'or en marche,
meut ses bras, noirs et lourds, et frais surtout, d'herbe. Elle
sombre, ayant le Ciel bleu pour ciel-de-lit, appelle
pour rideaux l'ombre de la colline et de l'arche.

II

Eh! l'humide carreau tend ses bouillons limpides!
L'eau meuble d'or pâle et sans fond les couches prêtes;
Les robes vertes et déteintes des fillettes
font les saules, d'où sautent les oiseaux sans brides.

Plus pure qu'un louis, jaune et chaude paupière
le souci d'eau – ta foi conjugale, ô l'Epouse!
– au midi prompt, de son terne miroir, jalouse
au ciel gris de chaleur la Sphère rose chère.

III

Madame se tient trop debout dans la prairie
prochaine où neigent les fils du travail: l'ombrelle
aux doigts; foulant l'ombelle; trop fière pour elle;
des enfants lisant dans la verdure fleurie

leur livre de maroquin rouge! Hélas, Lui, comme
mille anges blancs qui se séparent sur la route,
s'éloigne par delà la montagne! Elle, toute
froide, et noire, court! après le départ de l'homme!

Memory
Translated by Wallace Fowlie*

I

Clear water; like the salt of childhood tears;
The assault on the sun by the whiteness of women's bodies;
the silk of banners, in masses and of pure lilies,
under the walls a maid once defended.

The play of angels – No...the golden current on its way
moves its arms, black and heavy, and above all cool, with grass. She,
dark, having the blue sky as a canopy, calls up
for curtains the shadow of the hill and the arch.

II

Ah! the wet surface extends its clear broth!
The water fills the prepared beds with pale bottomless gold.
The green faded dresses of girls
make willows out of which hop unbridled birds.

Purer than a louis, a yellow and warm eyelid:
the marsh marigold – your conjugal faith, O Spouse –
At prompt noon from its dim mirror, vies
with the dear rose Sphere in the sky grey with heat.

III

Madame stands too straight in the field
nearby where the filaments from the (harvest) work snow down; the parasol
in her fingers; stepping on the white flower, too proud for her;
children reading in the flowering grass

their book of red morocco. Alas, he, like
a thousand white angels separating on the road,
goes off beyond the mountain! She, all
cold and dark, runs! after the departing man!

*The later translation, in Fowlie, *Rimbaud: Complete Works, Selected Letters* (Chicago: Univ. of Chicago Press, 1966), pp. 123-125.

IV

Regret des bras épais et jeunes d'herbe pure!
Or des lunes d'avril au cœur du saint lit! Joie
des chantiers riverains à l'abandon, en proie
aux soirs d'août qui faisaient germer ces pourritures!

Quelle pleure à présent sous les remparts! l'haleine
des peupliers d'en haut est pour la seule brise.
Puis, c'est la nappe, sans reflets, sans source, grise;
un vieux, dragueur, dans sa barque immobile, peine.

V

Jouet de cet œil d'eau morne, je n'y puis prendre,
ô canot immobile! oh! bras trop courts! ni l'une
ni l'autre fleur: ni la jaune qui m'importune,
là; ni la bleue, amie à l'eau couleur de cendre.

Ah! la poudre des saules qu'une aile secoue!
Les roses des roseaux dès longtemps dévorées!
Mon canot, toujours fixe; et sa chaîne tirée
Au fond de cet œil d'eau sans bords, – à quelle boue?

IV

Longings for the thick young arms of pure grass!
Gold of April moons in the heart of the holy bed; joy
of abandoned boatyards, a prey
to August nights which made rotting things germinate!

Let her weep now under the ramparts! the breath
of the poplars above is the only breeze.
After, there is the surface, without reflection, without springs, gray:
an old dredger, in his motionless boat, labors.

V

Toy of this sad eye of water, I cannot pluck,
O motionless boat! O arms too short, either this
Or the other flower: neither the yellow one which bothers me
There, nor the friendly blue one in the ash-colored water.

Ah! dust of the willows shaken by a wing!
The roses of the reeds devoured long ago!
My boat still stationary, and its chain caught
In the bottom of this rimless eye of water – in what mud?

Notes

Chapter 1

1. All references in Part One are to *Ada* unless otherwise indicated.
2. The patterning of sound and word in Nabokov's prose has been treated in Carl R. Proffer, *Keys to Lolita* (Bloomington: Indiana Univ. Press, 1968), William Woodin Rowe *Nabokov's Deceptive World* (New York: New York Univ. Press, 1971), Jessie Thomas Lokrantz, *The Underside of the Weave: Some Stylistic Devices Used by Vladimir Nabokov* (Uppsala: Acta Universitatis Upsaliensis, 1973), Jane Grayson, *Nabokov Translated: A Comparison of Nabokov's Russian and English Prose* (Oxford: Oxford Univ. Press, 1977), and Jurgen Bodenstein, "The Excitement of Verbal Adventure: A Study of Vladimir Nabokov's English Prose," 2 vols., Diss. Heidelberg, 1978.
3. The dynamics of the relationship between author and reader in Nabokov's work has been discussed in Proffer, *Keys to Lolita*, and in *The Annotated Lolita* ed. Alfred Appel, Jr. (New York: McGraw-Hill, 1970).
4. Nabokov in fact wrote "between the author and the world," but I have altered this in accord with the phrase he preferred in an interview ("I believe I said 'between the author and the reader,' not 'the world,' which would be a meaningless formula, since a creative artist makes his own world" [*SO* 183]), which does seem to coincide more closely with the logic of the original context.
5. The only reviewer to take note of this first journey was John Thompson, "Books," *Harper's* (September, 1969), p. 124: no reviewer noted the second. Among critics, only Herbert Grabes has discovered the double metamorphic journey, but he considers it merely "a game that the author is playing with his reader's attentiveness" (*Fictitious Biographies: Vladimir Nabokov's English Novels*, trans. Herbert Grabes and Pamela Gliniars [The Hague and Paris: Mouton, 1977], p. 84).
6. The sentence begins: "On a sunny September morning, with the trees still green, but the asters and fleabanes taking over in ditch and dalk" (156). Asters are fall-blooming herbs: both "asters" and "stellas" are chosen for their precision, not for empty artifice. There seems to be no specific allusion to Sidney's *Astrophel and Stella* (pub. 1591).
7. Not half as amusing as this bizarre – and surely unparalleled – connection: in between the "asters" and "stellas" of Pt.1 Ch.25 are "star spurs"; in *Lolita*, on p. 291. we find "aster-like," "star performer" and "stellar care," in the same order.
8. Cf. the character Julia Moore in *Transparent Things* and Hugh Person's dream of Giulia Romeo – Julie – Juliet – Mr. Romeo (80–81). Nabokov, of course, is renowned for his anagrams.
9. See Appendix 2 for the text and a translation of Rimbaud's poem.

10. Updike, "Van Loves Ada, Ada Loves Van," *New Yorker*, August 2, 1969, p.70: "But is it intentional that...the hero is such a brute?"; Oates, "A Personal View of Nabokov," *Saturday Review of the Arts*, 1:1 (January 6, 1973): 37: "He then assigns worth – which may seem to us quite exaggerated. even ludicrous, as in *Ada*, to a few selected human beings."

Chapter 2

1. "Mirror, Mirror," *New York Review of Books*, June 6, 1968; repr. in Gass, *Fiction and the Figures of Life* (New York: Vintage, 1972). p. 111.
2. From unpublished lecture notes for a Stanford summer course in creative writing, 1941. Quoted by permission of Mrs. Véra Nabokov.
3. "Une voie pour le roman futur" (1956), in *Pour un nouveau roman* (Paris: Minuit, 1963), p. 20.
4. Golden, "A Study of Games Played in *Ada*," Diss. Northwestern 1972, p. 2; Appel, *Annotated Lolita*, p. xxxii.
5. Assuming that the division between "Chapter Three and Four of the martyred novel" corresponds to the division between Act I Sc. ii (Pushkin's III.xvi–xxxv) and Act I Sc. iii (Pushkin's III.xxxviii–IV.xviii) of Chaikovsky's version of *Eugene Onegin* (1879) which is implied throughout this scene and is mentioned directly on pp. 158 and 511 of *Ada*.
6. Ed. René Pomeau (Paris: Garnier, 1960), p. 276.
7. From Nabokov's commentary to his translation of Pushkin's *Eugene Onegin* (1964; rev. ed. Princeton: Princeton Univ. Press, 1975), I: 18. Cf. also the introduction to the anonymous *Song of Igor's Campaign*, where Nabokov writes that "Among other elements of our author's technique the good reader will note his art of transition," *The Song of Igor's Campaign*, trans. Vladimir Nabokov (New York: Vintage, 1960), p. 10.
8. "The Creative Writer," *Bulletin of the New England Modern Languages Association*, N.S. 4:1 (January 1942), 23; now in Vladimir Nabokov, *Lectures on Literature*. ed. Fredson Bowers (New York: Harcourt Brace Jovanovich/Bruccoli Clark, 1980). p. 374.
9. In this he might seem rather like Faulkner. But Faulkner tends to manufacture discrepancy in the hope that contrived confusion and contradiction will amount to a sophisticated notion of the elusiveness of truth.

Chapter 3

1. In *Pale Fire*, in the same way, Nabokov provokes and rewards curiosity right at the beginning of the novel to ensure we are alerted to the special energy with which we should read and the very special surprises we can expect if we make the right effort. On the third page of his Foreword Kinbote writes: "(See my note to line 991)" (*PF* 15). This note sends us on to the note to lines 47–48 which in turn directs us to the note to line 691. The note to line 991 mentions a secret that appears to be the very key to the book; the note to line 691 lets us into the secret. Before returning to the Foreword we can feel, if we have been inquisitive

enough, that we know the plot's secret three hundred pages before we ought to – and we should have learnt never to let curiosity settle into inertia.

2. In Fowlie, *Rimbaud* (New York: New Directions, 1946), pp. 76–78.

3. This is a later (1966) translation by Fowlie which, it is only fair to say, is very accurate and much the best translation into English of this poem. In *Rimbaud: Complete Works and Selected Letters*, ed. Wallace Fowlie (Chicago: Univ. of Chicago Press, 1966), p. 123. See Appendix, pp. 317–21, for "Mémoire" and Fowlie's revised translation.

4. James Joyce, *Ulysses* (New York: Random House, 1961), p. 769. The *Ulysses* link is stressed when Ada first introduces the subject: "'the unfortunate French name of our plant, *souci d'eau*, has been traduced or shall we say transfigured – ' 'Flowers into bloomers,' punned Van Veen." (63–64) Leopold Bloom uses the pseudonym Henry Flower.

5. The relationships between Lucette and the *souci d'eau*, Lucette and the evaluation of Ardis, Lucette and the victims or potential victims of Van's canes and alpenstock are explained in detail in Part Three below.

6. *Reading Nabokov* (Ithaca, N. Y.: Cornell Univ. Press, 1974), p. 17.

7. "Pouchkine, ou le vrai et le vraisemblable," *Nouvelle Revue Française*, 48 (1937), 377.

Chapter 4

1. Nabokov, in George Feifer, "Vladimir Nabokov: an interview," *Saturday Review*, November 27, 1976, p. 22.

2. *Pnin* (Garden City, N.Y.: Doubleday, 1957), p. 20.

3. Cf. "Sartre's First Try" (1949): "One has no special quarrel with Roquentin when he decides that the world exists" (*SO* 230).

4. Nabokov maintains that the scientific accumulation of information is not going to lead to a full human understanding of reality: "the greater one's science, the deeper the sense of mystery. Moreover, I don't believe that any science today has pierced any mystery." (*SO* 44) An image in *Bend Sinister* proves the point very well: a human body is now "a trillion of mysteries" "even more mysterious to us than it had been to the very first thinkers in their pale olive groves" (168).

5. *Walking to Sleep* (New York: Harcourt Brace Jovanovich, 1969), pp. 33–35.

6. "Prof. Woodbridge in an Essay on Nature Postulates the Reality of the World," *New York Sun*, December 10, 1940, p. 15.

7. Vladimir Nabokov, "Faint Rose, or the Life of an Artist Who Lived in an Ivory Tower," *New York Sun*, January 21, 1941. p. 11.

8. *King, Queen, Knave*, trans. Dmitri Nabokov with Vladimir Nabokov (New York: McGraw-Hill, 1968), p. 106; in future citations, *KQK*. Of the five sentences in this quotation. the second, third and fifth were added in Nabokov's "translation" (1966–1967) of the original *Korol', Dama, Valet* (1927–1928). The first sentence, too, is largely new. The whole passage shows how consistent Nabokov's thought remained even as his capacity to express it developed.

9. *LATH* 252.

10. The denial of the future is not a common philosophical position. Indeed, I can think only of the British philosopher C.D. Broad, who argued that "the future

does not exist so long as it is future" (*Scientific Thought* [London: Routledge and Kegan Paul, 1923], p. 69), but later rather abandoned the idea. Nabokov's analysis of the concept of the future, however, seems sounder than the work of most philosophers.

11.   This assumption is made almost automatically by many philosophers. It invalidates, for instance, J.M.E. McTaggart's discussion of time, as seminal for twentieth-century philosophy as the work of Bergson: "Each position [in time] is Earlier than some, and Later than some, of the other positions. And each position is either Past, Present, or Future. The distinctions of the former class are permanent, while those of the latter are not. If M is ever earlier than N, it is always earlier. But an event, which is now present, was future and will be past." ("The Unreality of Time," *Mind*, N.S. 17 [1908], 458.) McTaggart distinguishes two series of relationships between "events," the "A series" (past, present, future, depending on the position of the observer) and the "B series" (earlier-later), and finds that they contradict each other and thus prove time unreal – a conclusion accepted rather unquestioningly by such renowned philosophers as W.V. Quine. In fact, the A series has events on the "past" side of any "present," and only *possibilities* on its "future" side. In the B series, similarly, a "later than" event is not an event but only a possibility at the earlier time: or if the series is restricted by a more rigorous definition to *events*, then it can only include present and past.

12.   In *Dedushka* (*The Grand-dad*) (*Rul'*, October 14, 1923, p. 5), the Passer-by recalls his being saved from the guillotine at the last minute (he was standing on the scaffold with shoulders already bared) by a cry of "Fire!" It is curious that Nabokov should echo this forty-nine years later. The play has recently appeared in English in *"The Man from the USSR" and Other Plays*, trans. Dmitri Nabokov (New York: Harcourt Brace Jovanovich/Bruccoli Clark, 1984), p. 297.

13.   From the unpublished notebook for the Stanford lectures, 1941. Quoted by permission of Mrs. Véra Nabokov.

14.   Lightning is specified as the cause of the fire in *Lolita: A Screenplay* (New York: McGraw-Hill, 1974). The information that follows comes from both *Lolita* and the *Screenplay*. The miscegenation is illicit (some parts are mutually exclusive: the Junk setter becomes the Jung collie) but triply justified: the burning of the McCoo house, Charlotte's accident and the "pest of a dog" are in both works; Nabokov came to regret omitting the McCoo house scenes from the novel for which they were written (*Screenplay* x): and certain emphases in the treatment of fate are added to the screenplay as compensation for the loss of Humbert's reflections on the theme – which only shows how essential Nabokov felt it to be to any treatment of the *Lolita* story – or to make explicit the motivation implicit in the novel.

15.   This quotation comes from Nabokov's foreword to the Russian version of his autobiography: "Its aim is to describe the past with the utmost exactness and to search out the significant outlines in it, namely: the development and repetition of the secret themes of an evident fate" (" ...razvitie i povtorenie taynyh tem v yavnoy sud'be") (*Drugie berega*, New York: Chekhov Publishing House, 1954), p. 7)

16.   Cf. two more remarkably similar expressions of exactly the same theme: "awed at the bungling of destiny" (Krug's wife after discovering a missed opportunity of meeting Krug earlier in life, BS 121): "I met the first of my three or four

successive wives in somewhat odd circumstances, the development of which resembled a clumsy conspiracy....Yet out of those very mistakes he [the "main plotter"] unwittingly wove a web, in which a set of reciprocal blunders on my part caused me to be involved and fulfill the destiny that was the only aim of the plot." (*LATH* 3)

17. By this time the fall motif is understood to be echoing the past, the deaths of Hugh's father and wife, and to be recalling Hugh's repeated humiliation by gravity and the obduracy of matter.

18. Not to be confused with statements like "the moment in which I am saying this is already gone."

19. In an interview with Willa Petchek, "Nabokov since *Lolita*," *Observer Magazine*, May 30, 1976, p. 17.

20 *Mary*, trans. Michael Glenny with Vladimir Nabokov (New York: McGraw-Hill, 1970), p. 62.

21. *Invitation to a Beheading*, trans. Dmitri Nabokov with Vladimir Nabokov (New York: Putnam's, 1959), pp. 93–94.

Chapter 5

1. Feifer interview, p. 22.

2. "Ultima Thule," in *RB* 169. The image of the circle of human thought recurs throughout Nabokov: see, for instance, *Despair*, trans. Vladimir Nabokov (New York: Putnam's, 1966), p. 73, and *BS* 155. In *Bend Sinister* the central character, Krug, is one of the foremost philosophers of his day; his name is Russian for "circle."

3. In the Russian original: "Lazeyki...prosvety v tonchayshey tkani mirovoy...i v vechnoe proydi ukradkoyu naskvoz'" ("Kak ya lyublyu tebya," *PP* 80).

4. From the play *Smert'* ("Death"), *Rul'*, May 20, 1923, p. 13. In the Russian original: "*EDMOND:*...smert' – *GONVIL* – byt' mozhet udivlenie, byt' mozhet – nichego."

5. Cf. "v goryachechnoy rubashke ploti" ("in the straightjacket of the flesh"), in "O, kak ty rvyosh'sya v put' krylatyy" ("Oh, how you strain to wing your way"), *Russkaya Mysl'* 6–8 (1923), 162.

6. "Professor Woodbridge...Postulates the Reality of the World," p. 15.

7. *Conclusive Evidence: A Memoir* (New York: Harper, 1951), p. 217. Unlike the other limitations on man, that of personality can be altered to some degree. Much of the moral force of Nabokov's novels comes from the fact that characters yield to their obsessions and thus let personality become a much greater restriction than it need be.

8. "Pouchkine, ou le vrai et le vraisemblable," pp. 376–77.

9. *Drugie berega*, p. 7.

10. In the Russian original: "i na chto nezemnaya zenitsa,/ esli venzelya net ni na chyom?" ("Oko," *PP* 100).

11. *Glory*, trans. Dmitri Nabokov with Vladimir Nabokov (New York: McGraw-Hill, 1971), pp. 11–12.

12. *Nabokov's Dozen* (Garden City, N.Y.: Doubleday, 1958), p. 67.

13. *Conclusive Evidence*, p. 217.
14. *The Defense*, trans. Michael Scammell with Vladimir Nabokov (New York: Putnam's, 1964). p. 8.
15. I think that Shade's imaginative imitation of a foreknowing fate is much more daring than merely the counterpoint of Canto Two, that he in fact invents Kinbote, writes the Commentary and fabulizes his own death at the hands of Gradus. Similar readings of *Pale Fire* have been put forward by Andrew Field, *Nabokov: His Life in Art* (Boston: Little, Brown, 1967). Ch. 10, and by Julia Bader, *Crystal Land* (Berkeley: Univ. of California Press, 1972). Ch. 3. There is considerably more evidence than they have brought forward, but the argument is much too complex to begin here.
16. In a similar case, Nabokov was annoyed that the powers of his "transparent things" were taken by reviewers to be metaphors of the novelist's powers: "that kind of generalization is not only a dismal commonplace but is specifically untrue. Unlike the mysterious observer or observers in *Transparent Things*, a novelist is, like all mortals, more fully at home on the surface of the present than in the ooze of the past." (*SO* 195)
17. Indeed, Nabokov regards this as the only sphere of existence in which we ought to feel sure of anything, and one of his principal objections to Freudian thought is that its stress on early formative influences leads to arguments of diminished responsibility: "the Freudian faith leads to dangerous ethical consequences" (*SO* 116), in that it can "give comfort to a killer by laying the blame on a too fond, too fiendish or too indifferent parent" (*Ada* 364).
18. Witness, for instance, his attacks on the anti-Semitism in Eliot's writing. The prime responsibility of an artist, Nabokov says, is to truth: "Truth is what matters, isn't it?" (to John G. Hayman, "After 'Lolita': A Conversation with Vladimir Nabokov – with Digressions," *Twentieth Century* (December 1959), p. 448). Moreover a particular moral or social purpose is likely to thwart the artist's search for imaginative truth, and it is certainly insufficient (*SO* 33) to ensure artistic value.
19. From the short story "Draka" ("The Flight"), *Rul'* September 26, 1925, p. 3, in the Russian original: "A mozhet bït' delo vovse ne v stradan'yah i radostyah chelovecheskih, a v igre teney i sveta na zhivom tele, v garmoniy melochey...."
20. Nabokov has quoted faithfully from *The Letters of Franklin K. Lane, Personal and Political*, ed. A.W. Lane and L.H. Wall (Boston: Houghton Mifflin, 1922), p. 464. The book is thrust on Kinbote by the owner of a motor court who moves (suspicious!) like Shade.
21. *The Eye*, trans. Dmitri Nabokov with Vladimir Nabokov (New York: Phaedra, 1965). p. [10].
22. See William Carroll's elegant analysis, "Nabokov's Signs and Symbols," in *A Book of Things About Vladimir Nabokov*, ed. Carl R. Proffer (Ann Arbor, Mich.: Ardis, 1974), pp. 203–17.
23. *The Waltz Invention*, trans. Dmitri Nabokov with Vladimir Nabokov (New York: Phaedra, 1966), p. [vi].
24. That Nabokov's conception of design is not merely something unwarrantedly extrapolated from his mode of activity as an author can be shown by examining his other "professional" interest, lepidoptery. I briefly discussed Nabokov's

scattered speculations on the role the designs of mimicry might have played in evolution – even, perhaps, in the evolution of consciousness – in my "Nabokov and *Ada*," Diss. Toronto 1979, pp. 182–86.

25. "Prof. Woodbridge...Postulates the Reality of the World," p. 15.
26. "The Lermontov Mirage," p. 34.

Chapter 7

1. To judge by reviewers, by the experience of friends and fellow readers, and by my own recollections.
2. See above, pp. 51–61.
3. The "solipsism" interpretation is stated most concisely and emphatically by Mason: "*Ada* is about incest, and, as incest is treated in the book, it is virtually synonymous with solipsism" (Mason 13). The "self-love" argument is championed by Matthew Hodgart: "But the incest theme has another and deeper meaning. In the last analysis...self-love is all." ("Happy Families," *New York Review of Books*, May 22, 1969, p. 3.)
4. Cf. *Lolita*, p. 285: "The moral sense in mortals is the duty / We have to pay on mortal sense of beauty."
5. These of course depend on the prominence of incest in Chateaubriand's best-known works: *René* (1802) teeters on the brink of an ardent brother-sister affair; in *Atala* (1801) Chateaubriand contrives to make Atala's father the virtual stepfather of Chactas so that their most passionate moments can be given a quasi-incestuous tinge; and the *Mémoires d'outre-tombe* (1849) hint at an unusually close relationship between Chateaubriand and his sister Lucile.
6. "'A terrifying thought had struck me,' said Chênedollé when he heard the news [of the death, on November 10, 1804, of Lucile Caud], 'I fear that she may have attempted her own life. Great God! Grant that it may not be so!' It seems likely, on the contrary, that it was so, for not a single church in Paris has any record of a religious funeral and only suicide can explain why Chateaubriand did not even return from Villeneuve, why Lucile left the Augustinian convent on the eve of her death, why she was buried in the common grave and why Mme. de Marigny, who had 'paid the last tributes of respect' to her younger sister, did not follow the bier." (André Maurois, *Chateaubriand: Poet, Statesman, Lover*, trans. Vera Fraser [New York: Harper, 1938], p. 137.)
7. Mason, p. 94, also points out the "busybody" in "Ardelia."
8. The title also glances at Jean Cocteau's *Les Enfants Terribles* (1929).

Chapter 8

1. Note that Nabokov has named *his* street (Jeunes Martyres) in honour of young martyresses.
2. I wish I could report that this was wholly my own discovery; in fact, Nabokov himself pointed it out: "Nabokov notes that the picture Van imagines is 'none other than a beautifully stylized and glorified version of the Toulouse crudity, namely a Barton and Guestier ("the finest wines of France") publicity photograph (which appeared frequently in the *New Yorker* in the late sixties). It is

meticulously described by Van (460–1) and should be looked up by all admirers of Lucette"' (Mason 163). Neither Mason nor anyone else seems to have followed this delightful clue. The advertisement appeared in the *New Yorker* at least as early as the issue of 23 March 1963 (inside front cover), which contains an excerpt from *The Gift.*

3.   Thus J. D. O'Hara, in "Shadows of a Shadow," *Texas Quarterly*, 9:1 (Spring 1966), 18–21, playfully tracks down the identity of Borges and Nabokov. In an interview with Nabokov conducted between Sept. 25 and 29, 1966, Alfred Appel, Jr., stresses similarities between the two writers ("An Interview with Vladimir Nabokov," *Wisconsin Studies in Contemporary Literature*, 8:2 [Spring 1967], 142; repr. in *Nabokov: The Man and His Work*, ed. L. S. Dembo [Madison, Wisc.: Univ. of Wisconsin Press, 1967], p. 34 and *SO* 80). Cf. also Patricia Merivale, "The Flaunting of Artifice in Vladimir Nabokov and Jorges Luis Borges," *Wisconsin Studies.* 8:2 (Spring 1967), 294–309; repr. in Dembo, pp. 209–24. Borges was guest of honor at the Nabokov Festival at Cornell, Spring 1983; see *The Achievements of Vladimir Nabokov*, ed. George Gibian and Stephen Parker (Ithaca: Cornell Center for International Studies, 1984).

4.   "Ophrys," *Encyclopaedia Britannica*, 15th ed. (Chicago: Encyclopaedia Britannica, 1974), VII, 550.

5.   See the following examples: "A Guide to Berlin," *Details of a Sunset* 98; *King, Queen, Knave*, 161; *Gift* 354; "Pouchkine, ou le vrai et le vraisemblable," p. 378; *SO* 14.

6.   The *"Chère-amie-fait-morata"* puns on the *Serromyia amorata* flies that copulate "with both ventral surfaces pressed together" (135).

Chapter 9

1.   See also below, pp.179–80. Mason, p. 134, discusses and seriously distorts the yellow and black motif.

2.   "Nabokov's Ardor," *Commentary*, 48:2 (Aug. 1969), 49.

3.   *"Ada* Described," *Triquarterly*, 17 (Winter 1970), 182; repr. in *Nabokov: Criticism, reminiscences, translations and tributes*, ed. Alfred Appel and Charles Newman (Evanston: Northwestern Univ. Press, 1970), p. 182.

4.   As R.M. Adams notes in "Passion among the Polyglots," *Hudson Review*, 22 (Winter 1969–70), 722.

Chapter 10

1.   The *grand Joyce* is that the style here recalls the artful clumsiness of Joyce's Ch. 16, set in the Cabman's shelter, a small coffeehouse under the overhead railway lines by Dublin's Custom House. The awkwardness of "Our damp trio...undid their raincoats," the limpness of "a nice corner table," the repetition that shows a lack of forethought ("but she did not, because she had cut her hair because of dreadful migraines, because...") all resemble the stylistic flaws in the "Eumaeus" chapter. The reason for Van's parody is that he suspects Ada of deceit; the "Eumaeus" chapter is riddled with lying and all kinds of deception, associated especially with sailors: note Ada's "heavy-seas hat." The Joyce-Proust pairing

Ada makes isn't *only* distraction: it also echoes a similar pairing in Pt. 1 Ch. 1 which points to the absurdity of *Demon's* hypocrisy – and so to the model for Van's own behavior here. See Boyd, "Nabokov and *Ada*," pp. 483–84.

2. This is emphasized by the fact of Tapper's flamboyant homosexuality – which simultaneously associates Tapper with Cordula as the target of Van's rage in Pt. 1 Ch.27.

3. See above, p. 148, for the ardilla-Ardelia link: and via Lucette's eavesdropping the "leavesdropper" in *Ada's* second key mistranslation (see *Ada* 127 and 247) becomes a parallel to the *souci d'eau*.

4. Red hair in *Ada* always points to Lucette: "Fragile, red-haired 'Rita'...bore an odd resemblance to Lucette" (185): the harlot in the picture hat at the bar in Kalugano who anticipates Lucette in her Toulouse-Lautrec pose; her father Dan, of course; even the autumnal vegetation of Mont Roux: "Mont Roux, our little rousse is dead" (509).

5. The allusion is noted by Gene Barabtarlo, "Pushkin Embedded," *Vladimir Nabokov Research Newsletter,* 8 (Spring 1982), 29–31.

6. "*Lolita* and related memories," in Appel and Newman, *Nabokov: Criticism, reminiscences, translations and tributes,* p. 251.

7. "The Strong Opinions of Vladimir Nabokov – as imparted to Nicholas Garnham," *The Listener,* October 10, 1968; repr. in *SO* 119.

8. The two men are linked not only by the famous sailors in their past and the geographical names (Vineland, Tobago, Tobakoff) with which they are associated, but also by the wine (the labruska grape) in Vinelander and the tobacco in Tobakoff (Tobakoff in fact has a duel with Jean Nicot [383]. after whom nicotine was named).

9. Later it is imagined that we might be able to "See our own past (Goodson discovering the Goodson and that sort of thing)" (560).

10. John Swain, *The Pleasures of the Torture Chamber* (London: Noel Douglas, 1931), pp. 139–40.

11. Though "krestik" is Russian for "little cross," the sense Lucette intends derives rather from a pun on "crest," as the word is used in the *Perfumed Garden: "Abou tertour* (the crested one)" (by which, Burton notes, "the author wanted to designate...the *clitoris"*). *The Perfumed Garden,* trans. Sir Richard Burton, ed. Alan Hull Watson (St. Albans, Herts.: Panther, 1963), p. 188. (This is the edition Nabokov used for *Ada:* see *Ada* 344.)

12. "An allusion to the preprandial rapid little sign of the cross that a Russian makes with bunched fingers over the breastbone at the very moment he sinks into the chair (which the footman behind him slips under him). The movement is mechanical, no heads are inclined, no grace is said: it is little more than a checked button." (*Eugene Onegin* II:531)

Chapter 11

1. Cf. this remark: "it reveals as little relation to essential Time, straight or round, as the fact of my writing from left to right does to the course of my thought" (539).

2. Nabokov (Van may be left out here) writes two pages later: "At this point. I suspect, I should say something about my attitude to 'Relativity.' It is not sympathetic.... One especially grotesque inference, drawn (I think by Engelwein) from Relativity

Theory – and destroying it, if drawn correctly – is that the galactonaut and his domestic animals, after touring the speed spas of Space. would return younger than if they had stayed at home all the time." (543) With typically uninformed and uninquiring captiousness, Douglas Fowler quotes this passage and remarks: "Unfortunately for Nabokov, he can no more dismiss the theory of relatively [*sic*] by calling Einstein 'Engelwein' than the Inquisition could preserve the Ptolemaic Universe by the burning of Bruno" (*Reading Nabokov*, p. 200). In fact although "Engelwein" does evoke Einstein the name is a "translation" into German of the surname of Paul Langevin, the French physicist who first concretized the multiple times of Einstein's theory in the space travel parable known as "the clock paradox" in a paper delivered to the Congress of Bologna in 1911. Nabokov is likely to have encountered Langevin first in the pages of Henri Bergson's examination of Einstein, *Durée et Simultanéité* (1922) (see 2nd ed., Paris: Felix Alcan, 1923, p. 109), for Bergson has been one of Nabokov's "top favorites"(*SO* 43) since the 1920s. Subsequent quotations from this work will be from the 1965 translation (see n. 3) which has an excellent introduction by the astrophysicist Herbert Dingle, who has been arguing since 1956 that the special theory of relativity is both unproven and self-contradictory (this introduction contains a useful bibliography of Dingle's articles on the subject to 1965). Nabokov's dismissals are notoriously confident, but the confidence in this case may be backed up by Dingle as well as by Bergson: his copy of J.T. Fraser's *The Voices of Time* (New York: Braziller, 1966) underlines some key points in Dingle's contribution.

3. *The Human Experience of Time* (New York: New York Univ. Press, 1975), p. 169. Cf. Bergson himself: "The instant is what would terminate a duration if the latter came to a halt. But it does not halt. Real time cannot therefore supply the instant; the latter is born of the mathematical point, that is to say, of space." (*Duration and Simultaneity*, trans. from the 4th ed. by Leon Jacobson [Indianapolis: Bobbs-Merrill, 1965], p. 53.)

4. Cf. Bergson. *Duration and Simultaneity*, p.62: "we have no way of limiting our spatial representation of elapsed time to the past."

5. In fact the sound was not that of a bottle being uncorked, but of Blanche detaching herself from the fellatio she had been engaged in: "drinking *hock*" plays on the obvious rhyme-word. No wonder Bout cries out "Dammit, Pa, I'm busy!"

6. Forest Fork the Second begins at 7.45am on July 25, 1886. Van departs from Ardis the Second sometime between 7 and 9am on July 25, 1888.

7. The "blue spiraea in invincible bloom" stands out particularly sharply as an echo of the earlier "blue! bloom!" because that earlier phrase is remarkable in itself as a distinct echo of *Ulysses*: "Blew. Blue bloom is on the" (*Ulysses* 256); "Bloom. Old Bloom. Blue Bloom is on the rye" (*Ulysses* 262). It is evident in *Lectures on Ulysses: A Facsimile of the Manuscript* (Bloomfield Hills, Michigan: Bruccoli Clark, 1980) but not in the edited version, *Lectures on Literature*, that these quotations come from Nabokov's favorite section in *Ulysses*.

8. The butterflies are of the sub-genus *Jolana*, after which Van and Ada name the villa Van calls into on that journey towards Ada in *The Texture of Time*; the year "our lovers...see again...the same bladder-senna" has earlier been specified as 1922 ("mused Van, in 1922, when he saw those *baguenaudier* flowers again" [125]). The curious might be amused to know that Nabokov caught two males and a female of *Jolana jolas* in a clearing on the northeast edge of the Forêt de Finges, south of the highway near Susten on 4 July 1963.

Chapter 12

1. The point is confirmed by Nabokov's Darkbloom note on "Morzhey…maybe a mermaid's message" (562): "allusion to Lucette" (Darkbloom 477). But the point has to be established in the text before authorial intention can be allowed to confirm it.
2. Presumably Clarence House, from where – just after her thwarted suitor had left – Princess Margaret on October 31, 1955 issued a statement that she did not intend to marry Peter Townsend.
3. Quoted in Mason, p. 185.
4. "Minataor, the famous artificial island," is Taormina (in Sicily) posing as the labyrinth of Dedalus, in which the Minotaur was concealed.
5. As first noted by Mason, p. 110, who also notices other Lucette-Violet connections but cannot interpret the relationship.

Chapter 13

1. "ORHIDEYA" in all the published editions is a misprint for "ORHIDEYa," since in "TORFYaNUYu" Nabokov has adopted the convention of an upper case and a lower case letter to represent a single Cyrillic character that requires more than one character in transliteration, as does the "Я" (ya) that ends "ORHIDEYa."
2. For the sexual innuendo here, see D. Barton Johnson, "The Scrabble Game in *Ada* or Taking Nabokov Clitorally," *Journal of Modern Literature*, 9: 2 (May 1982), 291–303.
3. See above, p. 132.
4. Ada has chosen the "Zegris" as well as the "Theresa" in honor of Van's novel, which was published "under the imprint of two bogus houses, 'Abencerage' in Manhattan, and 'Zegris' in London" (342). Both names, as Nabokov notes, are those of families of Granada Moors whose "feud inspired Chateaubriand" (Darkbloom 472) in *Les Aventures du dernier Abencérage*. Van is commemorating his and Ada's theme song, "Ma soeur, te souvient-il encore / Du château que baignait la Dore" (138), which forms part of Chateaubriand's tale: Nabokov is implicating Lucette. See above, pp. 125–28.
5. The term Antilles "dates traditionally from a period before the discovery of the new world, when it was called *Antilia* and referred to semi-mythical lands somewhere west of Europe across the Atlantic." (D[onald] R[ay] D[yer]. "Antilles," *Encyclopaedia Britannica*, 1962).
6. *Structuralist Poetics* (London: Routledge and Kegan Paul, 1975), p. 189.
7. Report of a panel discussion, "What Faith Means to a Resisting People," *The Wellesley Magazine* (Wellesley, Mass.), April 1942, p. 212.

Appendix: Spectral Hypotheses1

1. Ann Arbor: Ardis, 1981. Henceforth *NSD* in citations.

2. New York: New York Univ. Press, 1971. Henceforth *NDW* in citations.
3. See his review "Rowe's Symbols," *New York Review of Books*, 7 October 1971, p. 8; repr. in *SO* 304–07.
4. See W.W. Rowe, *Nabokov and Others* (Ann Arbor: Ardis, 1979), Chapter 13, as well as *NSD*.
5. Except for the forthcoming grebes, Rowe brings forward no evidence of his own to support his assertion that Lucette's spirit repeatedly "acts through" "images of birds" associated with her (*NSD* 50). Instead he seems to have couched this paragraph to imply that my dissertation either suggests this notion or at least that I would support it. Neither is true. Because of the absolute precision and the singular emphases of the joint bird of paradise/mermaid references these do seem to me to lead to certain spectral conclusions but not to suggest that Lucette acts through some bird of paradise (where?) or any other bird.

Chapter 14

1. Published in *VNAY* (1991), Chapter 22. Reprinted by permission of Princeton University Press.
2. *SO* 179.
3. "Van Loves Ada, Ada Loves Van."
4. Nabokov's meticulous planning ensures that they are also putative first cousins, second cousins, and third cousins.
5. *KQK* viii.
6. *SM* 290.
7. *SO* 121.
8. Which perfumes, of course, Chateaubriand's *Atala* and *René* and his *Mémoires d'outre-tombe*. See Ch.7 n.5.
9. See above, pp. 125–28.
10. Like two "structurally perfect stools" Van has on two of these mornings – another feature of the novel Updike objected to, because he could not discern the concealed structural perfection of which they form a part.
11. See above, pp. 192–200.
12. See also Ch.12 n.1.
13. See Ch. 12.
14. Van at one point addresses her simply as "poor L." – in a *letter*, therefore, in which her name has only one *letter*.
15. The "Ds" stand for Demian (known as Demon) and Daniel (Dan), respectively.
16. For the chief links between Lucette and Aqua, see above, pp. 145-52 and Brian Boyd, "Annotations to *Ada* 3: Part 1, Chapter 3 (continued)," *The Nabokovian*, 33 (Fall 1994), 67–69.
17. *NG* 142.
18. *Nabokov's Butterflies: Unpublished and Uncollected Writings*, ed. Brian Boyd and Robert Michael Pyle (Boston: Beacon and London: Penguin, 2000), 335–56.
19. *PF* 265..

Chapter 15

1.   Published as "L'Art et l'ardeur d'*Ada*" in *Europe*, March 1995, 106–114.
2.   From an unpublished note in the Vladimir Nabokov Archive, Berg Collection, New York Public Library; cited in *VNAY* 177.
3.   The French audience for which this chapter was originally written would have recognized this as a highly misleading distortion, not of a somewhat suspect old children's comic strip, but of the perfectly innocent, quite contemporary and very popular television puppet series for children, "Bonne Nuit Les Petits" ("Goodnight, Children"), created by Claude Laydu for ORFT in December 1962. By 1963 the characters in the 5-to-7-minute episodes were renamed Nicolas (about three, a dark-haired, two-foot high puppet), Pimprenelle (about four, blonde, same height) and Nounours (Nursus, a big brown bear with a big heart, who like the Marchand de Sable or Sandman stood about four feet tall). Nicolas and Pimprenelle were indeed close siblings, very much alike in voice, vocabulary and moods. Always wearing nightdress—like the children who watched the 7.30 p.m. program, they were scrubbed after their evening bath and ready for bed—they would be visited by Nounours who came down by rope ladder from the steerable cloud he shared with his friend the Marchand de Sable. After being asked "Vous avez été sages?" ("Have you been good?"), the sweet siblings would play with their visitor then head off to sleep in the narrow wooden bed they shared. As Nounours intoned a husky but gentle "Bonne nuit les petits," the bedclothes would heave gently in time with the children's sleepy respiration.
4.   Mikhail Lermontov, *A Hero of Our Time*, trans. Dmitri Nabokov with Vladimir Nabokov, ed. with introduction Vladimir Nabokov, Garden City, New York, 1958, p. x.
5.   As noted in Proffer 254.
6.   René Girard, *Deceit, Desire and the Novel* (Baltimore: Johns Hopkins University Press, 1965) and *A Theater of Envy: William Shakespeare*, New York: Oxford University Press, 1991).
7.   "The Novel's Original Sin," in *Directions in Literary Criticism*, ed. Stanley Weintraub and Philip Young (University Park, Pa: Pennsylvania State University Press, 1973), 112-20, p. 115.
8.   Nabokov could have seen the Uffizi sketch of Adam and the Steccata frescoes of Adam and Eve together in Sydney J. Freedberg, *Parmigianino: His Works in Painting* (Cambridge, Mass.: Harvard Univ. Press, 1950), figures 108c, 100 and 101 respectively.
9.   *A la Recherche du temps perdu*, ed. Pierre Clarac and André Ferré, Paris, 1954, III, 99–100.
10. *A la Recherche*, III, 1015.
11. From that first garbling of the opening sentence of *Anna Karenina*, Ada attacks mistranslations and misadaptations of works of art, in part no doubt because of the furore in the mid-1960s generated by Nabokov's literal translation of *Eugene Onegin* and because of his disappointment with Stanley Kubrick's film adaptation of *Lolita*, but largely as a stage in the novel's exploration of the relationship between model and mimic, between one medium and another, between one work and another. Here in Part 1 Chapter 2, the work in question is once again *Eugene Onegin*. Nabokov takes aim here at particular howlers in rival translations

of Pushkin's great verse novel, and in passing attacks Robert Lowell's mistranslations of Osip Mandelstam (being published in the late 1960s), but his prime target is Chaikovsky's opera, which literate Russians know to be a travesty of Pushkin.

12. *Lolita* 261.

Chapter 16

1.   Published as *"Ada"* in *Garland Companion to Vladimir Nabokov*, ed. Vladimir Alexandrov (New York: Garland, 1995). Reprinted with permission of Garland Publishing Company.
2.   "Exiles, Expatriates and Internal Émigrés," *The Listener*, 25 November 1971, pp. 705–708.
3.   Note that Nabokov does not call *Ada* the pearl of English literature: he does not think he could take on Joyce, let alone Shakespeare.
4.   "Van Loves Ada...," p. 68.
5.   See Brian Boyd, "Annotations to *Ada*, 1: Part 1 Chapter 1," *The Nabokovian*, 30 (Spring 1993):9–48, pp. 14–22 for answers to these questions.
6.   "*Ada* or the Perils of Paradise," in *Vladimir Nabokov: A Tribute*, ed. Peter Quennell (London: Weidenfeld and Nicolson, 1979), p. 112.
7.   *Lectures on Literature*, ed. Fredson Bowers (New York: Bruccoli Clark/Harcourt Brace Jovanovich, 1980), pp. 287–88.
8.   Oates, "A Personal View," p. 37.
9.   Updike, "Van Loves Ada ...," p. 70.
10. The next line in Rimbaud after *"les robes vertes et déteintes des fillettes"* begins *"font les saules"* ("make willows").
11. See Ch. 3 nn. 2–3.
12. *Ulysses*, ed. Hans Walter Gabler (Harmondsworth: Penguin, 1986), p. 633 (18: 1125).
13. *The Mirage in the Mirror: Nabokov's Ada and its French Pre-Texts* (New York: Garland, 1985), p. 218.
14. See above, pp. 34–40, 102–03.
15. Interview with Bernard Pivot, "Apostrophes," May 30, 1975, from typescript, Vladimir Nabokov Archives, Henry W. and Albert A. Berg Collection, New York Public Library.
16. As I note in the Preface to the Second Edition, credit for first seeing the centrality of Lucette should go to Bobbie Ann Mason. Unfortunately Mason's terms for affirming Lucette at the expense of Van and Ada (Lucette's "natural" red coloring and green clothing, versus Ada's "unnatural" looks, dark hair and pale pigmentation) do not carry the moral charge she implies, and require the kind of symbolic reading of colors that Nabokov consistently objected to. Mason would have done better to trace the networks of implication that Nabokov linked to Van and Ada's behavior. She also overstates Van's callousness as narrator towards Lucette.
17. See above, Part 3.
18. See above, pp. 125–28.
19. See Chs. 9 and 10 above, "Lucette and Others."
20. Unpublished VN letter to Doussia Ergaz, October 30, 1951, Vladimir Nabokov

Archive. Interestingly, *Ada* was hailed in its French version as "le plus beau livre de souvenirs depuis Proust et Chateaubriand" ("the finest book of memoirs [!] since Proust and Chateaubriand"). (*L'Exprès*, June 9–15, 1975)

21. Nabokov revised *Speak, Memory* between November 1965 and January 1966, between the first flash of the story of Van and Ada (November 1965) and the discovery in February 1966 of the way of integrating that story with his "Texture of Time" and "Letters from Terra" projects, on which he had been working intermittently since 1959. *Speak, Memory* therefore fed into the romance of Van and Ada in important ways; and Nabokov's strategy of undermining his elegiac nostalgists may have been influenced by his unease that he came across as rather too precious and self-satisfied in *Speak, Memory*: "I told everything about myself in *Speak, Memory*, and it was not a very pleasant portrait. I appear as a precious person in that book. All that chess and those butterflies," cited in Andrew Field, *Nabokov: His Life in Part* (New York: Viking, 1977), p. 8.

22. By the late 1960s, especially after the 1967 republication of *Speak, Memory* for a wide audience, Nabokov could make special use of readers' knowledge of his past, his pursuits and his opinions to invite us to commit the mistake of identifying Van and Ada with himself and ourselves with Van and Ada.

23. See *Nabokov's Butterflies*, esp. pp. 216–32, 300–11, 335–45, 353–56.

24. *Philosophical Investigations*, trans. G.E.M. Anscombe (Oxford: Blackwell, 1962), p. 32e.

25. See above, pp. 129–44.

26. Brian Boyd, "Nabokov and *Ada*," unpub. diss., University of Toronto, 1979, pp. 80–84.

27. Cf. pp. 40–63 above for the epistemological implications of *Ada*'s style.

28. Cf. pp. 262–71 above.

29. "Prof. Woodbridge in an Essay on Natures Postulates the Reality of the World" [review of J.E. Woodbridge, *An Essay on Nature*], *New York Sun*, 10 December 1940, p. 15. Nabokov here summarizes with approval Woodbridge's "major assumption."

30. See Part 4 above.

31. See above, pp. 284-87, and Brian Boyd, "Annotations to *Ada*, 2: Part 1 Chapter 2," *The Nabokovian*, 31 (Fall 1993):8–40, p. 26.

32. See pp. 129–31 above.

33. Mason, 1974, pp. 160–62; Brian Boyd, "Annotations to *Ada*, 15: Part 1 Chapter 15," *The Nabokovian*, 44 (Spring 2000):64–91, pp. 74–91.

34. *Ada* could in this sense be read as a book-length study of the "mimetic desire"— desire, especially romantic or sexual, as something provoked in imitation of desire in others—that René Girard finds pervasive in the novel (*Deceit, Desire and the Novel*, Baltimore: Johns Hopkins University Press, 1965) and other genres (*A Theater of Envy: William Shakespeare*, New York: Oxford University Press, 1991). Nabokov explores this in psychological terms (Van's imitation of the sexual conduct of his father and of his older schoolmates; Ada's of the romantic figures she has read about in the Ardis library; Lucette's of Van and Ada; Blanche's of the figures she has read about in *Les Amours du Docteur Mertvago*, of the other servants, of Van and Ada; Eric Veen's of his adolescent reading) and in terms of both the Venus and the Edenic myths he invokes, and in the tension between

the shock of love's initial novelty and the eventual recognition of love's ceaseless repetitions.

Chapter 17

1. Published as Afterword to *Ada* (Harmondsworth: Penguin, 2000). Reprinted by permission of Penguin.
2. "Nabokov: Beyond Parody," in *The Burning Library: Essays*, ed. David Bergman (New York: Knopf, 1994).
3. "*Ada*, or the Perils of Paradise," 112.
4. 4 May, 1969. Alfred Appel, Jr., its author, expanded the review into "*Ada* Described": see Ch. 9, n.3.
5. See Brian Boyd, "Annotations to *Ada*, 2," 21.
6. *VNRY* 152.

Index of Passages in *Ada*

General Index

326n8, 329n5
Prey, Cordula de, 24, 159–63,
    165–66, 174, 177–78, 330n2
Prey, Percy de, 26–27, 119, 120,
    149, 161–63, 168, 169–72,
    196–97, 208, 221, 246–47, 259,
    312–15
"Prof. Woodbridge in an Essay on
    Nature Postulates the Reality
    of the World" (Nabokov), 69,
    107, 324n6, 326n6, 328n25,
    336n29
Proffer, Carl, 12, 14, 37, 133,
    322n2, 322n3, 334n5
prologue (Pt. 1 Ch. 1–Pt. 1 Ch.3),
    262–65, 277–79, 283, 308, 310,
    as parody of exposition, 266
Proust, Marcel, 24, 33, 160, 161,
    169, 281, 285–87, 308, 309,
    316, 329–30n1, 336n20
Ptolemy, 330–31n2
Pushkin, Aleksandr, 37, 38, 132,
    133, 174–77, 206, 281, 283,
    287, 301, 306, 308, 309, 323n5,
    323n7, 334–35n11
Pyle, Robert Michael, 333n18

Quine, Willard Van, 325n11

Rabelais, François, 52
Rack, Philip, 26–27, 160–63, 168,
    169, 246, 259
reader, 26, 35, 46–47, 60–62, 241,
    304, discovery and, 20–21, 43,
    50–51, 60–62, 265–66; ethical
    challenge to, 27, 35, 57–60, 62,
    116–17, 122–23, 125, 145, 183,
    235–36, 273, 295, 298, 304–05,
    310; expectation and, 26;
    metaphysical reward for, 105,
    250 (*see also* Nabokov: "resis-
    tance" in, rewards for reader in,

self, limitations of)
The Real Life of Sebastian Knight
    (Nabokov), 62, 77, 85–86, 92,
    95, 99, 102
reality, 29–30, 32, 42–44, 68–69,
    107, 130, 229, 236, 324n3
recognition scene, parody of,
    266–67
relationship theme, 279, 281–82,
    298, 301–02, 309, 333n4
relativity, theory of, 71, 188, 189,
    330–331n2
Rembrandt Harmenszoon van Rijn,
    137, 139, 308
René (Chateaubriand), 127, 301,
    328n5, 333n8
"Return of Chorb, The"
    (Nabokov), 258, 291
revenge theme, 26–27, 48–49, 122,
    143, 149, 156, 161–63, 164–65,
    168–74, 287 (*see also* jealousy
    theme)
rhythm of time, 258–60, 300–01,
    315 (*see also: Ada*: structure:
    separation and reunion)
riches theme, 88, 257, 291, 311,
    315–16, and accumulated riches
    of consciousness and time, 189,
    190, 191, 200
riding crop theme, 26–27, 47–49,
    59, 162, 164–65, 166, 168, 173
Rimbaud, Arthur, 25–26, 53–59,
    122–24, 150, 151, 157, 214,
    215–16, 292, 294–95, 296,
    297, 301, 308, 335n10, text of
    "Mémoire," 318–21
Rivers, J.E., 9
Robbe-Grillet, Alain, 32
romance, 283, 302, 303; celebra-
    tion of, 22, 145, 146, 304, 306;
    critique of, 23, 26–28, 59, 145,
    146, 149, 153–55, 175, 235,

273, 302, 304, 310; influence
of, 283, 294, 309, 336–37n34
"Romance à Hélène"
(Chateaubriand), 127, 215
Romeo and Juliet (Shakespeare), 24,
160
Roosevelt, Franklin Delano, 233–34
Rousseau, Jean-Jacques, 37
Rowe, William Woodin, 112,
237–53
"Rowe's Symbols" (Nabokov),
333n3
Rowohlt (publisher), 9

Santa Maria della Steccata (church,
Parma), 285, 334n8
"Sartre's First Try" (Nabokov),
324n3
science, 324n4
Scott, Sir Walter, 284
"Self-Reliance" (Emerson), 298
Shade, John, 208, 214, 215
Shakespeare, William, 11, 24, 107,
120, 150, 217, 222, 223, 225,
249, 257, 274, 308, 335n3
Sherover, Charles, 189
Shulgina, Valentina, 291
Sidney, Sir Philip, 322n6
"Signs and Symbols" (Nabokov),
81, 96, 98–99, 104, 238, 327n22
Sirin, Vladimir, 92, 228 (*see also*
Nabokov, Vladimir)
Sistine Chapel (Vatican), 286
Smert' (*Death*) (Nabokov), 238,
326n4
Song of Igor's Campaign, The (anony-
mous, trans. Nabokov), 323n7
Speak, Memory, 11, 13, 21, 23, 67,
80, 81, 84–83, 85, 87, 88, 89,
93–94, 99, 239, 240, 269, 297,
301, 325n15, 336n21, 336n22
(*see also: Conclusive Evidence*;

Drugie berega)
spiral, 67, 85–86, 87; and circle of
thought, 67, 86, 87, 326n2; and
structure of *Ada*, 300–01
"Spring in Fialta" (Nabokov), 99,
213–14
Stabiae, 14, 31, 269
Stalin, Josef, 233–34
Stanford University, 323n2, 325n13
Sterne, Laurence, 23, 34, 52
Stone Guest, The (Pushkin), 132,
133, 135, 206, 301
Swift, Jonathan, 34
symbols, 29, 32, 39, 40, 69, 125,
241, 251, 335–36n16 (*see also*
Nabokov: "independence")

Texture of Time, The (Veen), 68, 71,
72, 73–74, 79, 81, 82, 83, 86,
167, 187–93, 199, 202–204,
205–06, 207, 208, 209, 210,
216–17, 225–26, 227, 249,
258, 259, 275–77, 331–32n8;
composition of, Nabokov's,
336n21
Thackeray, William Makepeace,
266
Therstappen, Marianne, 9
Thom's Dublin Directory, 294
Thompson, John, 322n5
Three Sisters (Chekhov), 30, 172 (*see
also: Four Sisters*)
"Thyme Flowering among Rocks"
(Wilbur), 68–69
time (*see: Ada*: anticipation and
recollection, design in time,
time as theme; Nabokov:
future, past, present, time;
rhythm of time; *Texture of Time*)
Titian (Tiziano Vecello), 310
"To a Nightingale" (Keats), 171
Tobak, Ivan, 177–78, 231, 330n8